# Schizophrenia
# The Bearded Lady Disease

# Volume I

Compiled By:

## J. Michael Mahoney

ISBN: 1-4107-0344-4 (e-book)
ISBN: 1-4107-0345-2 (Paperback)
ISBN: 1-4107-0346-0 (Hardcover)

Library of Congress Control Number: 2002096470


This book is printed on acid free paper.


Printed in the United States of America
Bloomington, IN

1stBooks – rev. 12/25/08

# Dedication

To the mentally ill of all ages

"Nothing before had ever made me thoroughly realize, though I had read various scientific books, that science consists in grouping facts so that general laws or conclusions may be drawn from them."
— Charles Darwin, *The Autobiography of Charles Darwin*

"It's just that we don't understand what's the matter... Why did we lose peace and love and health, one after the other? If we knew, if there was anybody to tell us, I believe we could try. I'd try so hard."
— F. Scott Fitzgerald, *One Trip Abroad*

"It is only ideas of such colossal proportions that a symbol for them cannot be created that are vague and intangible and brooding, incomprehensible and fearful, that produce madness.

The very fact that a thing — anything — can be fitted into a meaning built up of words small, black words that can be written with one hand and the stub of a pencil means that it is not big enough to be overwhelming. It is the vast, formless, unknown and unknowable things that we fear. Anything which can be brought to a common point — a focus within our understanding — can be dealt with."
— Lara Jefferson, *These Are My Sisters*

# About the Author

Upon graduation from college in 1952, J. Michael Mahoney worked briefly for the federal government before spending four years in the Air Force. Upon discharge, he began work as a journalist, first in Ohio and then Georgia, with a two-year hiatus as a foreign correspondent in Africa.

It was while working as a journalist in Georgia that the author developed his abiding interest in psychology, having been assigned to do some reporting in that field. Fortunate circumstances enabled him to take early retirement, and he has devoted his full attention since 1966 to doing research that has led to the publication of this book.

He now lives in Northern California and has three children and five grandchildren.

# About the Artist

Judith Walker, the cover artist, was born in Philadelphia and grew up in Iowa. She studied at Sarah Lawrence College graduating in the year 2000 with a Bachelor of Arts degree with a concentration in Fine Arts. She now lives in Paris and continues to paint.

# Child Hurbinek

Hurbinek was a nobody, a child of death, a child of Auschwitz. He looked about three years old, no one knew anything of him, he could not speak and he had no name; that curious name, Hurbinek, had been given to him by us, perhaps by one of the women who had interpreted with those syllables one of the inarticulate sounds that the baby let out now and again. He was paralysed from the waist down, with atrophied legs, thin as sticks; but his eyes, lost in his triangular and wasted face, flashed terribly alive, full of demand, assertion, of the will to break loose, to shatter the tomb of his dumbness. The speech he lacked, which no one had bothered to teach him, the need of speech charged his stare with explosive urgency: it was a stare both savage and human, even mature, a judgement, which none of us could support, so heavy was it with force and anguish....

During the night we listened carefully: ...from Hurbinek's corner there occasionally came a sound, a word. It was not, admittedly, always exactly the same word, but it was certainly an articulated word; or better, several slightly different articulated words, experimental variations on a theme, on a root, perhaps on a name.

Hurbinek, who was three years old and perhaps had been born in Auschwitz and had never seen a tree; Hurbinek, who had fought like a man, to the last breath, to gain his entry into the world of men, from which a bestial power had excluded him; Hurbinek, the nameless, whose tiny forearm - even his - bore the tattoo of Auschwitz; Hurbinek died in the first days of March 1945, free but not redeemed. Nothing remains of him: he bears witness through these words of mine.[34]

—[34]*Primo Levi, "The Reawakening," pp. 25-26.*

# A Note of Thanks

A huge debt of gratitude is owed to all the authors, writers and publishers from whose material the quotations in this book have been drawn, and without which the conclusions reached in it could never have been adequately supported or defended. Their combined contribution to this work has made it possible to further advance the science of mankind, and it is sincerely hoped that each will gain some sense of satisfaction, pride and accomplishment from that knowledge.

Finally, sole credit for getting this book published is owed to Professor Fawaz A. Gerges, holder of the Christian A. Johnson Chair in International Affairs and Middle Eastern Studies at Sarah Lawrence College in New York. After having read the manuscript, Professor Gerges declared that it should be published and that he, personally, would do everything in his power to accomplish that end. This he has now done, and the author/compiler is immensely grateful and forever indebted to him for his constant encouragement, wise advice and practical help during all the stages leading to its publication. Without the tremendous and selfless dedication Professor Gerges gave to this project, the manuscript upon which this book is based would still be languishing in obscurity.

— J. Michael Mahoney

All proceeds accruing to the author from sales of this book are being donated to the Child Hurbinek Memorial Scholarship at Princeton University, USA.

# Note to Reader

The compiler of this work has written a commentary (in italics) after each quotation therein. His purpose in doing so was either to clarify or else emphasize a certain point(s) mentioned in the particular quotation. Unfortunately these comments tend to be extremely repetitious in content since they invariably deal with the same subject, namely, the primary etiological role of bisexual conflict in the development of functional mental illness. The compiler apologizes for this repetition and hopes the reader will understand the reason for it. Certainly the commentaries add very little to the immense insight into mental illness which is provided to us all by the content of the quotations themselves.

One Final Note:

This manuscript was hewn from a massive collection of illegible, handwritten notebook pages into its present polished form by Monica Wethmar-Christiaansen who, by dint of her awesome computer skills and indefatigable efforts, managed to create substance out of chaos.

# Statement of Purpose

The reason I have compiled the 639 quotations in this study, all dealing with the subject of mental illness, with special emphasis on the condition termed "schizophrenia," is to prove the hypothesis that (as Dr. Edward J. Kempf so clearly stated in quotation 001 herein), ". . . in man every case of emotional neurosis or psychosis is the result of more or less conflict and confusion involving bisexual differentiation."

To my knowledge only two investigators have ever unequivocally taken this view, the other being Dr. Maurits Katan, who is quoted later in this work.

The scarcity of investigators who have reached this conclusion is most astounding, considering the enormous amount of evidence supporting it. Why has the scientific community been so stubborn in resisting this hypothesis? Why has this hypothesis been catalogued as just one of many inconclusive theories which attempts to explain madness? These are questions to which there may be no clear answers. It is my feeling, however, that one of the primary causes for this lack of conviction could be the fact that no one has ever gathered, under one cover, sufficient and compelling evidence to prove it. That, basically, is the purpose I had in mind in compiling the following material. I wanted to provide evidence which would be so overwhelming in its sheer volume and impact that even the most stubborn doubter would grudgingly have to admit to the truth of this hypothesis.

Madness has been the instigator of so much suffering and destruction in the world throughout the ages that it is vitally important to uncover its mechanisms, for without doing so we will never be able to eradicate it. I believe that, armed with the knowledge and insights contained within the following material, we will be able to accomplish that task.

– J. Michael Mahoney

# Table of Contents

E. J. Kempf Article may be found at the end of this book.

# A "Conversation" Between

# Prof. F. A. Gerges and J. M. Mahoney

## QUESTION 1

*Gerges: How do you explain the fact that other researchers have not examined the subject of the bearded lady?*

*Mahoney:* Frankly, it is amazing to me that schizophrenia has not been generally and decisively linked to the bearded lady syndrome, except in isolated cases. A handful of investigators, notably Dr. Edward J. Kempf (see quotation 001 herein) has certainly made note of this phenomenon in mental illness, but the writings of others on the subject have not been extensive enough to make an indelible impression on the general public, nor, for that matter, even on the psychiatric profession. Theories are a dime-a-dozen, so to speak, and one has to gather an overwhelming amount of evidence to convince people of a theory's correctness, which so far no one else has done in this particular case. Darwin's theory of evolution could have been stated quite simply in a few pages, yet, after developing his theory, he had to spend the remainder of his life documenting it extensively in such books as *On the Origin of Species* and *The Descent of Man.*

The bearded lady syndrome in mental illness has been observed by many, yet no one has really been able to distinguish the forest from the trees; that is, the general applicability of the theory to all cases of mental illness and not just the few being observed at any one moment.

My favorite quotation (from Otto Fenichel's *The Psychoanalytic Theory of Neurosis*) I think explains this investigative blindness: "And the hero who solves every riddle must have been wise not so much because of his intelligence, but because his emotional freedom, unhindered by repression, enabled him to recognize the hidden truth." Unfortunately, many investigators are still hindered by their own repressions, varying both in strength and depth. These repressions can be the result of both religious and personal problems which have never been satisfactorily resolved. The purpose of Freud's Psycho-Analysis is to resolve and dissipate these repressions, but how many people have been psycho-analyzed? If an investigator has issues with his own bearded-lady self, which he (or she) has never satisfactorily come to terms with, the ambivalence caused by this repression will make it much more difficult to recognize this conflict in others.

Charles Darwin, in his autobiography edited by his granddaughter, Nora Barlow, put it another way. He was explaining how easy it is to ignore phenomena, even though they are plainly visible, if you do not know what you are looking for. "On this tour," he wrote, "I had a striking instance how easy it is to overlook phenomena, however conspicuous, before they are observed by anyone. We spent many hours in Cwm Idwal, examining all the rocks with extreme care, as Sedgwick was anxious to find fossils in them; but neither of us saw a trace of the wonderful glacial phenomena all around us; we did not notice the plainly scored rocks, the perched boulders, the lateral and terminal moraines. Yet these phenomena are so conspicuous that, as I declared in a paper published many years afterwards in the Philosophical Magazine, a house burnt down by fire did not tell its story more plainly than did this valley. If it had been filled by a glacier, the phenomena would have been less distinct than they are now."

The same holds true for the bearded lady syndrome. Its phenomena are so obvious in every case of mental illness/schizophrenia, if one knows what to look for, that, as Darwin so strikingly put it, "a house burnt down by fire did not tell its story more plainly than did this valley."

Nowadays, of course, academic psychiatry is preaching a so-called bio-chemical theory of schizophrenia, namely, that the disease is caused by certain chemical imbalances in the brain and that the cure lies in somehow correcting these imbalances through drugs and other physiological treatments. The drugs in use today, however, are merely band-aids covering the basic pathogen, i.e., the severe bisexual conflict of the bearded lady syndrome. Drugs can be useful in certain cases to stabilize the patient to the extent that he or she can begin psychotherapy. If psychotherapy is not undertaken then the drugs truly remain nothing but band-aids, or chemical straight-jackets, and the bisexual conflict pathogen itself is never resolved, forcing the patient to remain on drugs for the remainder of his or her life. The vast majority of these drugs greatly diminish the sexual drive and of course this aids in eliminating much of the toxic effect of the undischarged homosexual libido, thereby substantially reducing the symptoms of the mental illness.

The only true cure for schizophrenia is long-term psychotherapy wherein the afflicted person can finally come to terms with his or her intense bisexual conflict and resolve it satisfactorily by either accepting one's homosexuality or else maturing into heterosexuality.

## QUESTION 2

*Gerges: What would be the major criticisms of your work by scholars who are opposed to Freudian methodology and how would you critically respond to them?*

*Mahoney:* Freud's most important contribution to this work lies in his interpretation of Daniel Paul Schreber's psychotic illness which he so brilliantly expounds in his case study based on Schreber's autobiographical account, entitled *Memoirs of My Nervous Illness.* It was in this case study of Schreber's illness that Freud first promulgated the theory of paranoia as being caused by repressed homosexual wishes and drives, "perhaps invariably."

This was a revolutionary interpretation of paranoia. Unfortunately, Freud did not believe that this revolutionary formulation carried over into an understanding of "that far more comprehensive disorder, dementia praecox," the original name of the illness we now speak of as "schizophrenia." In reality, however, paranoia and schizophrenia are one and the same "disease," and if repressed homosexual tendencies and desires are the cause of paranoia, which they are, then they must also play a similar, basic pathogenic role in schizophrenia.

It would be impossible to have a dialogue with other "scholars and experts" who have studied Schreber's *Memoirs of My Nervous Illness* and thereafter failed to reach the same conclusions as did Freud from their reading of the case. There must be a common basis of understanding in the development of any theoretical construct, and the so-called "Schreber case" provides that common basis for an understanding of *Schizophrenia: The Bearded Lady Disease*. In short, if one does not believe in Freud's formulation that repressed homosexuality is "perhaps invariably" the basic pathogen in "paranoia," then there can be no understanding of this work. Freud's simple but brilliant theory of paranoia developed in the Schreber case gives us the key to understanding all mental illness.

In truth, however, this work is not about Dr. Freud or Dr. Edward J. Kempf or anyone else. It is about the overwhelming amount of evidence presented in the 639 quotations contained herein, evidence which points unfailingly to the basic pathogenic role of bisexual conflict and confusion in the genesis of mental illness. As Charles Darwin wrote in his autobiography, "Nothing before had ever made me thoroughly realize, though I had read various scientific books, that science consists in grouping facts so that general laws or conclusions may be drawn from them." This book consists of a grouping of "facts," the 639 quotations, and from these facts a general law or conclusion has been drawn about the etiology of schizophrenia and of mental illness in general. This general law would be valid even without the input of Freud, for the thing speaks for itself – *res ipsa loquitur*. It stands or falls on its own, and whether "scholars and experts" agree or disagree with the theories of Sigmund Freud, or of any other investigator, is completely irrelevant to the truth and validity to be found in the 639 quotations in this book.

# QUESTION 3

*Gerges: What are the shortcomings and weaknesses of the current scholarship on mental illness? And how can you remedy those shortcomings?*

*Mahoney:* The profound wisdom contained in a statement made by the distinguished American documentary film producer, Mr. Ken Burns, I believe aptly answers this question. "The great arrogance of the present," he said, "is to forget the intelligence of the past." Nowhere does this truth have more validity than in the current approach to the investigation of mental illness. "The intelligence of the past" has been almost totally forgotten, or woefully ignored, and the entire emphasis on research today seems to be in the field of bio-chemistry. Mental illness, we are told by the present-day "experts", is caused by chemical imbalances in the brain, which, with the right drugs, can be cured or greatly relieved. Thus the immense wisdom of the past masters of psychology and psychiatry is ignored. Freud is said to have been well-meaning but completely misguided in his theories and assumptions. Harry Stack Sullivan, who probably knew more about schizophrenia as it pertains to males than anyone who ever lived, is hardly ever mentioned at all in the present-day literature, devoted as it is to the latest "discoveries" in the biochemical field. Edward J. Kempf, Theodore Lidz, Harold F. Searles, Lewis B. Hill, and Maurits Katan, all brilliant clinicians and theoreticians, are likewise largely ignored. And how many of the crop of current investigators have read Daniel Paul Schreber's *Memoirs of My Nervous Illness*? Or have read Freud's case history based upon it wherein he outlines for the first time his brilliant theory of paranoia, the name the Greeks used to include all the various symptoms of mental illness?

Severe bisexual conflict and confusion was discovered to be the cause of schizophrenia over fifty years ago by Dr. Edward J. Kempf and others, but since the truth contained in this theory was unpalatable, it was ignored and others put in its place. But there can only be one theoretical "truth" to solve a particular problem and, consequently, all other theories dealing with mental illness which have ignored this basic truth must, of necessity, be fatally flawed.

The sole purpose in compiling *Schizophrenia: The Bearded Lady Disease* was to bring so much evidence to bear upon the validity of Kempf's original formulation – that schizophrenia is invariably caused by severe bisexual conflict and confusion (not only schizophrenia, but all mental illness, schizophrenia being but its end-stage) – that it would be impossible to continue to ignore these findings which were originally made so long ago.

Recently I read a small item in the local newspaper which I will quote in full, as it pertains directly to the point I am trying to make here. "For two years, my sister with schizophrenia lived on the California streets with her 10-year-old son. The family could do nothing; it was her right to wander in delusion. Then, without warning, the untreated symptoms of her illness caused her to dress her son as a woman and herself in battle fatigues, ride 60 miles in a taxi and kill our 78-year-old-mother. (*San Francisco Chronicle*, March 26, 2001, p. A24, by "A reader from Long Beach")."

Besides the obvious point that the woman's 10-year-old son should have been protected by the authorities from his delusional mother, the bisexual conflict and confusion always present in mental illness is glaringly obvious in this case – the son having been changed into a female and the mother into a male in the mother's paranoid schizophrenic thinking.

Thus the "remedy" for the present "shortcomings" in the current investigations of mental illness is for everyone involved to go back to school, so-to-speak, and do their "homework" – that is, read, or reread the great psychiatrists and psychologists of the past who have basically already solved the problem of mental illness, if only someone would pay attention to what they said and wrote, and to study their theoretical and clinical output thoroughly and intensely and with an open mind, hopefully unhindered by their own repressions and scotomas. And, if I may modestly add, a good place for an investigator to begin this study would be to read the following work, consisting of 639 quotations all dealing with the problem of mental illness and its etiology in bisexual conflict and confusion, stemming from the early sex-role alienation in the child later to become schizophrenic, or mentally ill.

## QUESTION 4

*Gerges:* *In light of the existing shortcomings and weaknesses in the scholarship on mental illness, does your work fill some of the gaps? What is the importance of your research, and how original is it?*

*Mahoney:* My "scholarship" consists mainly in the gathering together of a huge volume of evidence pointing to the truth of a single hypothesis – namely, that schizophrenia and all mental illness is basically the result of bisexual conflict and confusion which begins at an early age with sex-role alienation in the child who is later to become mentally ill. This etiology is present in every one of the cases presented in this book and could be shown to be the same in all cases everywhere, regardless of time, place, age or gender of the afflicted person. Or again, in the words of that great American psycho-analyst, Dr. Edward J. Kempf: "More than thirty years of intensive investigation of these problems permits me to make the general statement that in man every case of emotional neurosis or psychosis is the result of more or less conflict and confusion involving bisexual differentiation." . . . "Dementing schizophrenia is essentially a regression to the cloacal level of hermaphrodism. I am quite sure that it would be easy to demonstrate these factors in any case and often within an hour of investigation."

The sole purpose of my own "scholarship" is to give added weight to Dr. Kempf's hypothesis, to the point that it should be impossible to argue with its truthfulness, like it or not.

I began the research which culminated in *Schizophrenia: The Bearded Lady Disease*, in 1966 and am still engaged in it. Actually, it is impossible to escape from it because once you become aware of such a powerful natural law and its impact upon the human condition, you apply that law and look for its effects upon everything and everyone around you and in everything you do – both intellectually and emotionally. A truth once discovered can no longer be hidden or ignored and it is the primary purpose of this book to make this universal truth as widely known as possible. This knowledge can help people better understand themselves and others and also recognize that because of a general ignorance of this powerful law of nature, terrible crimes have been perpetuated upon mankind by rulers and others who have been driven insane, or paranoid schizophrenic, by their severe bisexual conflict and confusion. This includes, unfortunately, the maniacal terrorists of today who are inflicting immense suffering and tragedy upon the world.

My research is original only in the sense that I have devoted an extraordinary amount of time gathering evidence to prove this one basic hypothesis. Dr. Edward J. Kempf also stated this same hypothesis, but did not spend his entire life gathering evidence to prove it, case by case, under one cover as is done here. I had come to my own conclusions independently before I had ever heard of Dr. Kempf, and was both amazed and stunned when I first came by chance upon his short paper entitled "Bisexual Factors in Curable Schizophrenia." Why, I wondered then, was this truth not by now an established fact? The only answer I could surmise was that theories are ubiquitous, and in order to have one generally accepted, it required the gathering of such an overwhelming amount of evidence as to its truthfulness that it could no longer be ignored, much as Charles Darwin had done with his theory of evolution. Darwin's theory is basically a simple and straightforward one, which could have been explained in a few pages, but he had to devote the remainder of his life to writing *On the Origin of Species* and *The Descent of Man* to consolidate and validate it. He did this by providing multitudinous examples of its accuracy.

This, in a very small way, is what I have tried to do with *Schizophrenia: The Bearded Lady Disease* – provide so much evidence of the truthfulness of the theory first promulgated by Dr.

Edward J. Kempf in his short paper, "Bisexual Factors in Curable Schizophrenia," that, as I said in my Statement of Purpose, even the most stubborn doubter would have a difficult time ignoring the evidence (though, of course, there are those who do and always will ignore or deny evidence which displeases them, no matter how compelling it might be, as Charles Darwin learned only too well).

In short, what I have tried to do is add more flesh to the bare bones of Dr. Kempf's theory as outlined in the paper mentioned above, so that the world will sit up and take proper notice of it, to the world's benefit rather than to its detriment, as is now the case due to a general ignorance of it.

## QUESTION 5

*Gerges: Does the evidence you provide go beyond the contributions of Sigmund Freud and Edward J. Kempf?*

*Mahoney:* It has always been my opinion that Freud went 99 percent of the way towards bringing us out of the dark ages of psychology and into the light of reason and truth, only to fail to take that last all-important step when he made the grievous error of considering paranoia to be a separate entity from schizophrenia proper. We now know, of course, that the repressed homosexual tendencies which Freud discovered are "perhaps invariably" the cause of paranoia, must, therefore, play the same primary etiological role in schizophrenia.

Why was Freud unable to see that paranoia and schizophrenia were basically one "disease" entity and not separate from each other? The only reason which makes sense to me stems from his turbulent relationship with Dr. Wilhelm Fliess of Berlin, who had been at one time Freud's closest confidant and the man who first acquainted him with the concept of man's innate bisexuality and its great importance in the etiology of the neuroses and psychoses. Freud and Fliess later became bitter enemies when Fliess accused Freud of stealing his concept of bisexuality and incorporating it into his writings without giving Fliess due credit for having introduced him to it originally. Thus, for Freud to have completed his brilliant theory of psycho-analysis by stating that bisexual conflict is at the core of all psychogenetic, or functional, mental illness would have been to admit that his entire life's work basically added up to what his former great friend and later bitter enemy, Wilhelm Fliess, had told him so many years before. This I believe Freud could never do, whether consciously or unconsciously, and this is what I think caused him to veer off the track in his otherwise brilliant analysis of paranoia in the Schreber case, with the consequent derailment of his entire theoretical work in the field of the neuroses and psychoses and his subsequent emphasis on the role which the so-called "death instinct" plays in their etiology, a theory which has never been well received by even the most fervent "Freudian" psycho-analysts.

In the case of Dr. Kempf, no one has ever surpassed his brilliant theoretical and clinical work in the field of mental illness. Besides Daniel Paul Schreber's analysis of his own psychosis in his *Memoirs of My Nervous Illness*, on which Freud based his seminal study of paranoia, no more important book in the field of psychology and psychiatry has ever been written than Dr. Kempf's *Psychopathology*, first published in 1920. For anyone interested in the field of mental illness, these two books, with special emphasis on Kempf's *Psychopathology*, are required reading.

Many cases from *Psychopathology* have been quoted in *Schizophrenia: The Bearded Lady Disease* and in fact this latter work is no more than a pallid extension of the former. No one has ever really "gone beyond" Dr. Kempf, and in fact the great majority of investigators in the field have never even caught up with him. This great work was out of print for many years but fortunately was finally put back into circulation several years ago.

Kempf tells the tale that he was so convinced of the correctness of his observations concerning the vital importance of bisexual factors in the etiology of the neuroses and psychoses that he undertook a trip to Vienna where he had an audience with Dr. Freud. According to Kempf, Freud was very polite, but noncommittal, basically telling Kempf to keep up the excellent work he was doing, but not otherwise validating his findings.

Thus only Dr. Edward J. Kempf has "gone beyond" Freud, and no one has "gone beyond" Dr. Kempf. The truth is the truth and it is very hard to embellish it once you have found it.

One other brilliant investigator should be mentioned here, along with Freud and Kempf, and that is Dr. Maurits Katan, who has uncovered the energy source which fuels the hallucinations, both audio and visual, which bedevil the psychotic person. According to Dr. Katan, this energy source is none other than the repressed homosexual excitement which, frustrated and diverted from its natural genital orgasmic path, expends itself by the process of conversion into the visual hallucinations and voices experienced by the psychotic. Nature, frustrated at one level, searches out and finds another. Thus is the repressed sexual excitement drained off, allowing the organism (person) to reach some kind of physiological stability until that excitement builds up once more, whereupon the same process is repeated, ad infinitum, or until psychotropic drugs neutralize the sexual excitement. Dr. Katan can, in this regard, be credited with having "gone beyond" Dr. Kempf, if only by explaining the mechanics of how the actual symptoms in the psychoses arise.

## QUESTION 6

*Gerges: Why have you chosen this methodology of using hundreds of direct quotations to prove your hypothesis rather than analyzing the materials making your case?*

*Mahoney:* I chose this methodology because I thought it would be the best way to present the overwhelming amount of evidence I had gathered over a thirty-five year period to prove the hypothesis, as first stated by Dr. Edward J. Kempf, that severe bisexual conflict and confusion lies at the etiological core of all functional mental illness, up to and including the most severe forms of schizophrenia. To attempt to put this overwhelming amount of material in regular book form seemed, in my opinion, to be like trying to put the proverbial camel through the eye of the needle. The material was just too vast to attempt that task. Dr. Kempf came close to accomplishing that feat in his book Psychopathology, as did Charles Darwin in his *On the Origin of Species* and *The Descent of Man*. In this case, I determined that the most effective way to present such an overwhelming amount of evidence would be to let that evidence speak for itself, with minimum commentary from me. The truth of the matter is that regardless of the quantity or quality of the proof of an hypothesis which is presented by a researcher, there will always be those who deny it. This has held true both in Dr. Kempf's case and also in Charles Darwin's. The great and irrefutable laws of nature discovered by them are still not accepted as fact by the majority of mankind. Many people specializing in the field of psychology and psychiatry have either never heard of Dr. Kempf or, if they have, they have ignored his findings, considering them outdated and not relevant in this era of heavy emphasis on mental illness as being a "disease of the brain" best treated by drugs and not by psychotherapy.

In short, today the mentally ill are considered not so much emotionally disturbed as suffering from a so-called chemical imbalance of the brain, and supposedly only the use of drugs can cure or alleviate this chemical imbalance. Just one reading of Dr. Kempf's *Psychopathology* would quickly cure any non-biased reader of this erroneous and harmful assumption, just as I hope any one reading of *Schizophrenia: The Bearded Lady Disease*, with its 639 quotations demonstrating the invariable pathological role of bisexual conflict and confusion in every case of mental illness, will do likewise.

That bisexual conflict and confusion is invariably the basic etiological factor in all mental illness is one of the great and as yet unacknowledged laws of nature, and if we continue to ignore this law we do so at our own peril. This law and the truth contained therein affects each of us in a direct and powerful manner, and through us the world at large. It has done so with disastrous consequences in the past and in the present, and will continue to do so in the future unless we gain a thorough understanding of its mechanisms and find the tools with which to neutralize its baleful effects.

## QUESTION 7

*Gerges: Why are publishers reluctant to publish your work? What explains their ambivalence? Does it have to do with your thesis or the nature of your work?*

*Mahoney:* *Schizophrenia: The Bearded Lady Disease* is obviously a work produced in a very unorthodox fashion. It is a collection of 639 quotations, each followed by editorial comment, the sum of which is meant to prove what today would be considered a very controversial thesis, namely, that the condition we call "schizophrenia" invariably is caused by severe bisexual conflict and confusion.

Thus, from a publisher's point of view, the content of this work is not only highly controversial, but is also constructed in a fashion perhaps unique in the annals of publishing. These factors, I believe, would explain a publisher's refusal to produce it. (As to a publisher's "ambivalence," one of the outstanding symptoms of schizophrenia is ambivalence itself, running the gamut from "normal" ambivalence to ambivalence of psychotic proportions.)

Finally, there is the natural human tendency to shy away from truths which cause discomfort or which counter general opinion and belief. Furthermore, this work is not one which reads easily. It requires diligence and concentration to study it. To read it carefully from cover to cover requires much time, thought and energy and, most important of all, an intense interest in the subject. All these factors would reduce the potential pool of readers, and any potential publisher would be well aware of these facts and forced to take them into consideration before making any publishing decisions.

Publishers publish books to make money. If a manuscript does not show any financial potential, it most likely will not be published by a commercial publisher. This leaves but one route for the person to travel who has produced a controversial manuscript which shows little earning potential, and that is to self-publish. It is encouraging to know that this route is still open to those who feel strongly that they have something to say, but have no other way to get their message out.

## QUESTION 8

*Gerges:* *What do you want the reader to get out of this manuscript?*

*Mahoney:* In the dedication to this manuscript, I quote the poignant plea expressed by F. Scott Fitzgerald, the American writer, wherein he seeks understanding of how his life and that of his wife, Zelda, could have started so well and ended so badly. "It's just that we don't understand what's the matter," he writes. "Why did we lose peace and love and health, one after the other? If we knew, if there was anybody to tell us, I believe we could try. I'd try so hard."

Enough information is contained in this manuscript to answer that heartfelt question. For both Scott and Zelda suffered from the bearded lady disease, schizophrenia. I have pointed this out in some quotations directly pertaining to both of them. They were each afflicted with severe bisexual conflict and resultant gender confusion, as is easily discernable from their life histories. Scott fought his schizophrenia by medicating himself with alcohol, while Zelda became overtly psychotic and had to be institutionalized. I would like to think that if Scott had been given the opportunity to read this manuscript, he would have understood it and thus found the answer to the question he posed above: "Why did we lose peace and love and health one after the other?"

There have been millions of Scotts and Zeldas who have lost peace and love and health, one after the other, for exactly the same reason Scott and Zelda did. "If we knew, if there was anybody to tell us," pleads Scott. The purpose of this manuscript is to tell Scott and everyone else suffering from mental illness why they are ill and the truths they must face before they can get well, no matter how unpalatable they may be.

The mentally ill are different from the rest of us so-called normal persons only to the degree that their bisexual conflict is more severe. For we are all afflicted with some degree of bisexual conflict due to our sexually unnatural upbringing – unnatural because we have not been allowed the full sexual freedom from infancy onwards which is enjoyed by all other species including our closest cousins, the primates. Because of the sexual restrictions imposed on us by society and culture, we have all been sexually crippled to a greater or lesser extent and, consequently, our innate bisexual tendencies, present in all mammals, have been unnaturally strengthened, leading to the bisexual conflict and confusion which are always to be found at the root of mental illness.

Finally, I would like to hope that anyone who took the time to read through this manuscript thoroughly would be able to feel a great sense of intellectual excitement and wonder at seeing unfold before their eyes one of the most powerful, immutable laws of nature, a law which has been generally ignored by mankind, greatly to its detriment. This law, of course, is the law which holds that whenever man has a conflict between his male and female sides, or his homosexual and heterosexual self, mental illness, to a greater or lesser extent depending upon the severity of the actual conflict, invariably and inevitably ensues. Once one is aware of this natural law, the scales fall from one's eyes when it comes to examining every case of mental illness, for this law is operative, as all general laws of nature must be, always, in each case, without exception. If there were exceptions then it could no longer be called a general law, but of course in this case there are none.

The workings of this law are at times more obvious than at others, but if one looks deeply enough and has gathered enough information on a case, it can always be seen at work. Paranoia is a good example of this conflict being less obvious than usual, with its delusions of persecution and grandiosity, etc., but Sigmund Freud brilliantly uncovered the workings of this general law in his famous case study of Daniel Paul Schreber, who was severely afflicted with paranoid schizophrenia.

With the insight and knowledge gained from this manuscript, the reader should never be able to look at the world in the same way again. A much better understanding of one's self and others should occur, to the benefit of all mankind. That is my hope.

# SCHIZOPHRENIA:

## The Bearded Lady Disease
## Volume I

001          More than thirty years of intensive investigation of these problems permits me to make the general statement that in man every case of emotional neurosis or psychosis is the result of more or less conflict and confusion involving bisexual differentiation. ... Dementing schizophrenia is essentially a regression to the cloacal level of hermaphrodism. I am quite sure that it would be easy to demonstrate these factors in any case and often within an hour of investigation. — "Bisexual Factors in Curable Schizophrenia*," Edward J. Kempf, M. D. (*Presented at the Annual Meeting of the American Psychiatric Association, May 18, 1948), <u>Journal of Abnormal and Social Psychology</u>. 1949 Jul Vol 44(3) 414-419 [According to the Rightslink records of the American Psychological Association, this article is now in the Public Domain.] [The complete E. J. Kempf article is the final item in the book.]

*Dr. Edward J. Kempf was a highly-respected and brilliant psychiatrist and psycho-analyst whose productive years encompassed well over half a century, ending with his death in 1971. Thus, when Dr. Kempf makes the claim that "in man every case of emotional neurosis or psychosis is the result of more or less conflict and confusion involving bisexual differentiation," the world should sit up and take notice. Unfortunately, not enough notice has been taken of his findings, for today investigators profess to be searching still for the "elusive" cause of functional mental illness, up to and including the dysfunction labeled "schizophrenia."*

*The purpose of this monograph of 639 quotations from various sources is to prove the validity of this theory of Dr.*

*Edward J. Kempf,* * *and to set at rest once and for all any questions about the etiology of mental illness.*

002     There is evidence of sexual upsurgence and an intense effort at control, repression and denial. There is also much sexual confusion, especially as regards his own sexual identity, which is very poorly established. The patient is extremely defensive, and his defenses for the most part follow an obsessive – compulsive pattern with a definite tendency toward paranoid ideation. — David and Lisa, Theodore Isaac Rubin, M. D., Ballantine Books, New York City, 1962, p. 141.

*In this case reported by Dr. Rubin, the patient is obviously suffering from severe bisexual conflict, uncertain whether he is male or female. He is in the throes of what is termed a "homosexual panic," caused by his ego's repression of his effeminate, same-sex, sexual cravings which are threatening to erupt from the unconscious into consciousness, which is the only pathway they can use to gain orgasmic satisfaction and consequent diminution of their drive. The "paranoid ideation" is the direct result of this bisexual conflict.*

---

*Dr. Edward J. Kempf was a Life fellow of the American Psychiatric Association and of the Association for Research in Nervous and Mental Disease; a member of the American Medical Association, the American Psychopathological Association, the American Association for the Advancement of Science, the New York Academy of Sciences, and the American Psychological Association. He was the author of over 30 papers and books, including his famous Psychopathology, published in 1920, and "The Origin and Evolution of Bisexual Differentiation," published in 1947.

Dr. Kempf graduated from medical school at Case Western Reserve University in Cleveland, Ohio, in 1910; interned at the state mental hospital in Cleveland from 1910-11 and at the state mental hospital in Indianapolis, Indiana, from 1911-13. He performed his residency at Phipps Psychiatric Clinic, Johns Hopkins University Hospital, Baltimore, Maryland, from 1913-14. From 1914 to 1920 he was a clinical psychiatrist at St. Elisabeth's Hospital in Washington, D.C.

003    Such fundamental doubts about their sex, though seldom expressly stated in the literature (Bleuler, 1951; Rosen, 1953) we have found an invariable feature of schizophrenia (Macalpine, 1954; Macalpine and Hunter, 1953, 1954a, 1954b, 1955. —Memoirs of My Nervous Illness, Daniel Paul Schreber, translated by Ida Macalpine and Richard A. Hunter, Wm. Dawson & Sons, Ltd., London, 1955, p. 407.

       *In this quotation, Doctors Macalpine and Hunter (a mother-son team) state an extremely important truth: in essence, that all schizophrenics are basically "bearded ladies" – persons who do not know at a deep unconscious level whether they are male or female. They have very strong homosexual feelings, always repressed, which conflict directly with their conscious heterosexual drives, resulting in a blockage of all sexual satisfaction. It is this situation of total sexual frustration which drives them "crazy," i.e., schizophrenic.*

004    The primary delusion of a change of sex may appear in patients in various guises, often as the only symptom: complaint of excessive hairiness in women, lack of hairiness in men, symptoms associated with "change of life" in women, even men. Following hysterectomy, complaints about voice being too high or too low, the breasts being too small or too flat, differences between the right and left halves of the body, etc. Examples could be multiplied *ad infinitum*. Not uncommonly female patients complain that they have a male mind in a female body, and male patients that they have a female mind and request their body be altered accordingly, by surgery or hormones. —Memoirs of My Nervous Illness, Daniel Paul Schreber, Ibid., p. 405.

*It is interesting that Macalpine and Hunter here point out that a great many female schizophrenic patients complain that they have a male mind in a female body and vice versa for male patients. Of course this is also a common complaint among homosexuals and people desiring transexual surgery. Basically, schizophrenia is <u>the negation of</u> homosexuality. The cure for schizophrenia lies in the patient coming to terms with his or her homosexuality, and either remaining at a <u>conscious</u> homosexual level or, through psychotherapy, maturing into heterosexuality.*

005   Perversions, alongside the manifestations of normal drives, are much more pronounced in schizophrenics than in neurotics. The homosexual components, especially, play an unsuspectedly large role. But we will not go into further details at this point. —<u>Dementia Praecox or the Group of Schizophrenias</u>, Eugen Bleuler, International Universities Press, New York, 1950, p. 411.

*Eugen Bleuler, the psychiatrist who first made use of the term "schizophrenia" in the monograph cited here, calls attention to the important role homosexuality plays in that condition. Unfortunately, when he said he would "not go into further details at this point" on the subject, he meant it, and even more unfortunately, he never took up the subject again in any depth. This glaring theoretical omission has had the effect of minimizing to a great degree the profound role homosexual, or bisexual conflict, does play in the etiology of schizophrenia.*

006   Other patients are in love with a ward – mate with complete disregard of sex, ugliness, or even repulsiveness. (Ibid., p. 52)

*Dr. Bleuler here calls our attention to instances of overt homosexuality among his hospitalized mental patients.*

007    His basic bisexuality had developed into a true manifest ambisexuality, male and female potentials being equally matched. He was as much both as he was neither. Thus he says 'that I have to imagine myself as man and woman in one person having intercourse with myself.' (S.282) and 'playing the woman's part in sexual embrace with myself' (S.285). These ideas culminated in fantasies of self-impregnation.

    In this fundamental doubt Schreber exhibits a common characteristic of schizophrenics. Usually, however, this balanced imbalance of sex has to be deduced from psychotic expression and is not freely accessible. The insight afforded by Schreber on this point gives to his memoirs their unique value. —Memoirs of My Nervous Illness, Daniel Paul Schreber, Ibid., p. 402.

*Here, for the first time in this monograph, we meet Daniel Paul Schreber, considered by many to be psychiatry's most famous patient. He was first brought to the public's attention when Dr. Sigmund Freud wrote a case history dealing with Schreber's psychosis, wherein Freud made the claim that Schreber's illness was caused by repressed homosexual longings. C.G. Jung had given Freud a copy of Schreber's autobiography, Memoirs of My Nervous Illness, and had based his case history on the material in this book.*

*Schreber's memoirs were first translated into English in 1955 by Doctors Macalpine and Hunter. In commenting on Schreber's illness, Macalpine and Hunter point out the obvious, namely that Schreber's female, or homosexual side, is so powerful it had overwhelmed his male, or heterosexual, side. His memoirs demonstrate this fact irrefutably. He is truly a "bearded lady."*

008    Clearly passive homosexual urges, whether conscious or unconscious, should be sharply distinguished from the confusion about their own sex invariably found in

schizophrenia. That in the primary fantasy of change of sex or belonging to the opposite sex, homosexuality is likely sooner or later to play a part secondarily, is undisputed. (Ibid., pp. 404-405)

> *Macalpine and Hunter attempt to separate homosexuality from "the confusion about their own sex invariably found in schizophrenia." Homosexuality plays a <u>primary</u>, not a secondary, role in schizophrenia, as Macalpine and Hunter would lead us to believe.*

009    Zilboorg (1941) says that 'Freud's views on schizophrenia, ... were based ... on ... the Schreber case ... Later clinical studies corroborated Freud's views that certain aspects of unconscious homosexuality are the determining factor in the development of schizophrenia.' Fenichel (1945) gives a long list of confirmatory publications. (Ibid., p. 11)

> *Homosexuality's vital role in the etiology of schizophrenia is confirmed by Fenichel's findings, as well as in the "long list of confirmatory publications." When we speak of "homosexuality" in this regard, we are always referring to unconscious, or repressed, homosexuality, never <u>conscious</u> homosexuality. Basically, it is the repression of strong homosexual cravings which drives people crazy, or "schizophrenic."*

010    It is instructive that Schreber was diagnosed in his first illness as suffering from severe hypochondriasis; his second illness commenced as an 'anxiety neurosis' with attacks of panic, then hypochondriacal delusions and suicidal depression; later catatonic excitement alternating with stupor. From then on he might well have been diagnosed variously as suffering from catatonic schizophrenia, paranoid schizophrenia, dementia paranoides, dementia praecox, monomania, chronic mania,

involutional melancholia, paranoia paraphrenia, obsessional neurosis, anxiety hysteria, tension state, transvestitism, psychopathy, etc. (Ibid., p. 15)

*This quotation confirms what Dr. Edward Kempf said in quotation 001, namely, that "in man every case of emotional neurosis or psychosis is the result of more or less conflict or confusion involving bisexual differentiation." Daniel Paul Schreber, during the course of his illness, suffered from every named psychiatric syndrome, thereby substantiating Dr. Kempf's hypothesis that not only is bisexual conflict the etiological basis of schizophrenia but of all other emotional disorders as well.*

011   For all students of psychiatry, Schreber, its most famous patient, offers unique insight into the mind of a schizophrenic, his thinking, language, behavior, delusions and hallucinations, and into the inner development, course and outcome of the illness ... Indeed the memoirs may be called the best text on psychiatry written for psychiatrists by a patient.
        Schreber's psychosis is minutely and expertly described, but its content is – as Dr. Weber explained to the court – fundamentally the same and has the same features as that of other mental patients. Schreber's name is legion. (Ibid., p. 25)

*Schreber's name is legion, in that every mentally ill man suffers from the same bisexual conflict as did Schreber. Furthermore, bisexual conflict forms the etiological basis of mental illness in all females as well.*

012   M. Bleuler (1953) in a personal communication stated that E. Bleuler would have agreed that 'schizophrenics are almost invariably, if not indeed invariably, in doubt about the sex to which they belong.' (Ibid., p. 25)

*Manfred Bleuler, son of Dr. Eugen Bleuler, here confirms the fact that his father had found sexual confusion to be a prominent, if not invariable factor, in the disease he had named "schizophrenia." Unfortunately, Dr. Bleuler had not emphasized this point sufficiently in his monumental textbook on the subject.*

013    In the pre-psychotic phase homosexual tendencies differ from those of the homosexual perversion. The unconscious wish of the pre-psychotic male to be a woman arises not as a defense against the positive oedipus complex but from the constitutional bisexuality of the individual – '... in its deepest nature schizophrenia arises from bisexual conflicts, and this bisexual conflict eventually leads to a state where the heterosexual factor is relinquished.' (Katan, 1954) ... Katan concludes that a part of the personality behaves as if the pre-psychotic phase was still in existence. The non-psychotic part of the personality ('the non-psychotic layer') does not remain constant in size but changes all the time. The extent of the non-psychotic layer is dependent upon the activity of the homosexual conflict. If the homosexual urge is not too powerful the remnants of the ego can function fairly adequately. However, when the homosexual drive increases in intensity, the relative strength of the ego will determine the outcome, i.e. whether or not the subsequent reaction will be in accordance with reality or whether a psychotic symptom will make its appearance. ... The delusion constitutes the psychotic mastery of the conflict (Katan, 1954). Katan interprets hallucinations from a dynamic – energic standpoint. He suggests that the energy of the homosexual urge is withdrawn in the psychotic phase, to avoid the danger arising from it, and used to form a hallucination. This releases the tension caused by the homosexual drive and prevents a complete break with reality. This suggests that 'the goal of maintaining contact with reality can be achieved only by abandoning it for a short while

through the formation of a psychotic symptom (the hallucination). It is like avoiding a major evil by accepting a minor one' (Katan, 1954). —<u>Chronic Schizophrenia</u>, Thomas Freeman, John L. Cameron, Andrew McGhie, preface by Anna Freud, International Universities Press, New York, NY, 1958, pp. 37-38.

*Dr. Maurits Katan agrees with Dr. Edward J. Kempf that "... in its deepest nature schizophrenia arises from bisexual conflicts" and adds that "this bisexual conflict eventually leads to a state where the heterosexual factor is relinquished."*

*Dr. Katan is the only investigator I am aware of who has unearthed the mechanism of delusion and hallucination formation in schizophrenia. He explains that the energy which fuels these symptoms arises from the homosexual libido which is blocked from normal orgasmic genital discharge by the repressive ego. This homosexual libido consequently "converts" itself into the energy force which fuels the delusions and hallucinations of the disease, thus achieving its energic discharge in a roundabout way, in the manner in which all conversion hysteria symptoms are formed.*

014      One of the most widely mentioned transference problems is that of dealing with homosexual impulses which may threaten the therapeutic relationship when working with paranoid schizophrenics. Techniques for dealing with disturbing homosexual elements of the transference have varied from the utilization of a female helper (Federn, 34, 35) to the direct energetic discouragement of such tendencies in the patient, forcing him to recognize the dangers in the fulfillment of his homosexual fantasies, and advising him to have heterosexual intercourse (Eidelberg, 28). It seemed advisable in the latter case to transfer the patient's sexual wishes at least in part to a female object in order to lessen the

tension aroused by his homosexual trends and hence make them more analyzable. Some authors have suggested that the prospect of recovery in such patients may actually be better when they are treated by women since discussion of the homosexual tendencies is less likely to provoke a panic-like state than when treated by men. —Psychotherapy With Schizophrenics, edited by Eugene B. Brody and Frederick C. Redlich, International Universities Press, Inc., New York, 1952, p. 54.

*Federn and Eidelberg here point out the enormous tension aroused by the homosexual conflict in schizophrenia, which causes difficulty in the therapeutic setting when therapist and patient are of the same sex. Of course this holds true for female patients as well as male.*

015    Federn (34, 35) especially advocated extreme caution in analyzing or interpreting transference manifestations for fear of losing the positive relationship. He emphasized that the experience of a good transference is the chief normal reality to the psychotic in treatment but felt also that optimum results could be obtained only if the psychotic had a helper who served as a sort of harbor for him when his transference to the psychotherapist became uncertain. In view of the psychotic's tendency to confuse his homo – and heterosexual feelings, Federn felt that this helper should be a woman. (Ibid., p. 48)

*Federn's comments apply equally to schizophrenic women, including the fact that it would be best if their "helpers" were men.*

016    In the Schreber case (1911) Freud demonstrated that unconscious homosexual tendencies were to be found underneath the delusions of persecution. In this paper he gave a detailed account of the mechanism of delusion formation. It

is unnecessary here to discuss the minutiae of this mechanism beyond saying that an essential feature is the projection of unconscious homosexual trends. —<u>Chronic Schizophrenia</u>, Freeman, Cameron, McGhie, preface by Anna Freud, International Universities Press, New York, 1958, p. 27.

*Freud used the Schreber case to demonstrate his theory that paranoia is invariably rooted in repressed homosexual longings. He was the first investigator to make this claim, and in so doing pointed the way to solving the problem of schizophrenia, although making the egregious error of believing that paranoia and schizophrenia were different disease entities, which of course they are not.*

017 Subsequent to the publication of the Schreber case (1911) other reports appeared, e.g., Ferenczi (1914) confirming Freud's theory that delusions of persecution were associated with repressed homosexual tendencies. (Ibid., p. 28)

*Since Freud published the Schreber case, the vast majority of investigators have confirmed his findings regarding the essential role played by repressed homosexuality in the etiology of delusions of persecution, as well as in every other manifestation of paranoid schizophrenia.*

018 Nunberg (1921) followed the development of delusions of persecution in a schizophrenic patient. Initially the patient transferred to him (Nunberg) the remnants of his homosexual libido and tried to maintain a relationship with him. As this failed, the patient, abandoning the boundaries of the self, merged himself with Nunberg. (Ibid., p. 30)

*Nunberg confirms the vital role played by homosexuality in schizophrenia.*

019     This led initially to the recognition of the connection between
        infantile sexual experiences and the content of later psychotic
        symptoms (Abraham, 1908). This was extended to the
        appreciation of unconscious homosexual conflicts in cases of
        paranoia and schizophrenia in general. (Ibid., p. 41)

        *Here the role of unconscious homosexuality in the*
        *etiology of paranoia is extended to "schizophrenia in general,"*
        *where it in fact plays the key role, paranoia being but one of*
        *the many and varied manifestations of the disease.*

020     For example, the female patients often queried their sex in the
        presence of a male therapist. In an earlier example one patient
        asked if she was a doctor. She continued: 'Trousers. Each man
        and woman has trousers on.' Another patient would frequently
        stand in front of the fire holding a poker in front of her
        genitals. When asked about this she said she was 'a man
        standing up.' (Ibid., p. 54)

        *The desire to be a man and have a penis has gone from*
        *unconscious wish to psychotic wish-fulfillment for the woman*
        *holding the poker in front of her genitals.*

021     One of the female patients (Emily), who frequently confused
        herself with the male therapists, would on these occasions
        begin to remove hair grips from her hair or take off her
        stockings, muttering angrily about women's clothing. This
        type of activity ceased at times when her speech and behavior
        indicated her identification with the nurse. (Ibid., p. 56)

        *This patient shows obvious signs of sexual confusion, at*
        *times identifying herself as male, at other times as female.*

022     As already mentioned, Andrew Gray experienced
        hallucinations of a voice which whispered obscenities in his

ear and urged him to masturbate and swear. At other times he experienced visual images, mentioned above, which were again sexual in nature. These experiences were often of a manifestly homosexual type. The genesis of this patient's hallucinations becomes evident when his past history is considered. From his early youth Andrew had participated in a number of incidents with older men involving fellatio and other homosexual stimulation. The beginning of his psychotic breakdown occurred when he was posted by the R.A.F. to a lonely station on the Orkneys where, it can be suggested, the intense pressure of a small closely knit all male culture proved too strong for his basic homosexual conflicts. The voices and visual images the patient now began to experience represented his own homosexual urges which were unacceptable to the ego, and so lost the ego cathexis necessary to identify them as originating within the psyche. The externalization of his own thought processes, concurrent with the break with objective reality, led to the further adjustment which reunited outer reality and the inner processes that had become the psychotic 'reality.' This adjustment took the form of an unknown individual who tormented him with 'a machine' that communicated to him the oral and visual obscenities so repugnant to his own ego. On occasions he would declare his suspicions that the operator of this 'F-ing machine' was an older man who had first persuaded him to indulge in fellatio. His description of the machine itself being like 'an old granny blethering away' has also significance as the patient was reared for the most part by his rather prim grandmother. The reality adjustive function of this delusion became evident when the patient was faced with interpretations which threatened its existence, when his reaction was to refuse further attendance at the groups. (Ibid., p. 67)

*Andrew Gray illustrates the clinical fact that homosexual feelings that were once conscious can, after repression by the ego, lead to classic schizophrenic symptomatology.*

023     Barbara, for example, denied the existence of two sexes and produced long abstract arguments to the effect that each person was bisexual. This further distortion of reality enabled her to be the mother of her phantasy children while still denying that they were the product of any sexual activity on her part. The fact that others declared that they could not see the children was answered by Barbara's assertion that they were so tiny as to be invisible to the casual observer. (Ibid., p. 68)

*Barbara, of course, is correct when she says that everyone is bisexual. Barbara's schizophrenia is the direct result of her bisexual conflict, as is true with all schizophrenics.*

024     Within a few days Mary again became depressed and developed the delusion that she had venereal disease and had infected the nurse in the treatment center to whom she was deeply attached. Her concern in this case was not for her own condition but for the nurse whom she believed she had infected. (Ibid., p. 70)

*For Mary to believe she had infected the nurse with venereal disease must mean that in her delusion Mary was a man and had been sexually intimate with her nurse. Mary's intense repressed homosexual love for this nurse is further shown by the fact that she was "deeply attached" to her and was more concerned about the nurse's condition than she was her own.*

025     On one occasion Andrew had been speaking of an experience involving fellatio which he had had in the Air Force. David, a

very demented patient, was behaving in a restless and disturbed manner, making sucking noises with his mouth. A therapist asked him if he were upset because of remembering some similar experience. David replied, 'That's a horrible thing to say to a man.' It is difficult to convey to the reader the startling incongruity of such a remark coming from a very disturbed man like David who had not previously produced one intelligible statement in several months of work. (Ibid., p. 90)

*It is very obvious that David's schizophrenia is the direct result of having repressed very powerful homosexual oral cravings.*

026     It will be recalled that in examples given earlier it was shown how the patients, through confusion of themselves with others, frequently were unsure of their sex. This phenomenon occurred particularly in relation to staff members. On one occasion, when the patient had been speaking in a confused and perplexed way on this subject, she said suddenly and quite clearly, 'There are no differences in sex. The difference is only individual. There was a time in the history of mankind when all people were the same and they have evolved differently – each one unique.' The confusion of identity remains clear despite the elaboration by the secondary process activity. (Ibid., p. 92)

*This is another example of the sexual identity confusion always to be found in schizophrenics.*

027     Federn (1953), speaking of this, states: 'While every neurotic patient easily transfers from his mother to the psycho-analyst, the psychotic does not do so to a male analyst. This demonstrates how the psychotic depends on reality more than does the neurotic, that is, when he is forced to transfer his

mother-relationship to a man, he confuses homo – and heterosexual feelings and becomes more perturbed.' (Ibid., p. 108)

*Every person who becomes functionally psychotic has been driven to this state by his or her confusion and conflict over homosexual versus heterosexual drives.*

028    Patient B, a married man of German descent, was 40 years of age at the time I became his therapist. He has been admitted to two psychiatric hospitals previously – once for a period of one and a half years, and the second time for a period of six months. His symptomatology during his stay at each of the two previous hospitals had been, as it was when I first saw him, typical of paranoid schizophrenia.

During the first interviews with me, he allowed silences of no more than a second or two. He kept up an almost incessant stream of conversation, consisting in a melange of references to books he had read, interspersed with comments reflecting self-misidentification, such as, 'Of course I'm Cortez … I died in 1920 as Tolstoy … . I was Esther Williams in [name of a motion picture]'… He apparently considered himself to be, from one moment to another, a limitless number of prominent persons, present and past, including Alexander the Great, Pericles, General Lee, Lincoln, Goethe, Senator Vandenberg, various movie actors and actresses, and so on, and made references to various supernatural powers which he possessed. —Collected Papers on Schizophrenia and Related Subjects, Harold F. Searles, M. D., International Universities Press, New York, 1965, p. 80.

*The bisexual conflict in Dr. Searles' Patient B is made obvious by his stating that he is both a man – Tolstoy, Cortez, etc. and a woman – Esther Williams and other "actresses." It would be difficult to find a more obvious example of sexual confusion in a schizophrenic.*

029      For example, on one or two occasions in my years-long work with a physically attractive and often very seductive paranoid schizophrenic woman, I have felt hard put to it to keep from going crazy when she was simultaneously (a) engaging me in some politico-philosophical debate (in which she was expressing herself with a virile kind of forceful businesslike vigor, while I, though not being given a chance to say much, felt quite strongly urged to argue some of these points with her, and did so); and (b) strolling about the room or posing herself on her bed in an extremely short-skirted dancing costume, in a sexually inflaming way. She made no verbal references to sex, except for charging me, early in the hour, with having 'lustful,' 'erotic' desires; from there on, all the verbal interaction was this debate about theology, philosophy, and international politics, and it seemed to me that the non-verbal interaction was blatantly sexual. (Ibid., p. 258)

*This paranoid schizophrenic woman acts out her bisexual conflict by being "simultaneously" a "virile" and "forceful" debator on "politico – philosophical" matters and an extremely provocative woman in a "sexually inflaming way."*

030      One of my earlier experiences with what I think of as oedipal love in the countertransference occurred in the course of the analysis, several years ago, of a woman in her middle twenties. Initially, she had manifested a poorly established sexual identity; her femininity was considerably repressed, with an overlay of much penis envy. But over the course of four years of an unusually successful analysis, she developed into a woman whom I found very likeable, warm and sexually attractive. I found myself having, particularly during about the

last year of our work, abundant desires to be married to her, and fantasies of being her husband. (Ibid., p. 289)

> *Every schizophrenic woman manifests the same psychodynamics as does this analysand of Dr. Searles, and each could similarly be transformed into a healthy, feminine woman by the right kind of psychotherapy with a dedicated psychotherapist.*

031  After an initial two-year period in which negative feelings seemed to predominate in the transference and the counter-transference, I began finding myself feeling surprisingly fond of him, and to be having not infrequent dreams of a fond and sexual nature about him. One morning, as I was putting on a carefully selected necktie, I realized that I was putting it on for him more than for any of the several other patients I was to see that day.

He referred to us now in the third and fourth years of our work, as being married, and at other times expressed deeply affective fantasies of our becoming married. When I took him out for a ride in my car for one of the sessions, I was amazed at the wholly delightful fantasy and feeling I had, namely that we were lovers on the threshold of marriage with a whole world of wonders opening up before us. I had visions of going upon innumerable rides with him, going to look at furniture together, and so on. When I drove home from work at the end of the day I was filled with a poignant realization of how utterly and tragically unrealizable were the desires of this man who had been hospitalized continually, now, for fourteen years. But I felt that, despite the tragic aspect of this, what we were going through was an essential, constructive part of what his recovery required; these needs of his would have to be experienced, I felt, in however unrealizable a form at first, so that they could become reformulated, in the course of our work, into channels which would lead to greater possibilities for gratification. (Ibid., p. 295)

*What this quotation illustrates above all is the incredible power of the unconscious drive in the schizophrenic person. In this particular case the drive is so strong that it draws Dr. Searles into a homosexual counter-transference with his patient. In the transference this patient identifies himself as a female in love with a male, and in the counter-transference Dr. Searles perceives the patient in this role. As he explains, this transference and counter-transference between himself and the patient is a necessary part of the healing process for the schizophrenic, who is thereby provided the opportunity to come to grips with his feminine, homosexual cravings within the therapeutic setting.*

032　My whole paper is written, purely for the sake of simplicity of presentation, on the assumption that the child's Oedipus complex is normally a 'simple' one, whereas actually we know that it is really a 'complete' one, as Freud pointed out in 1923 in the first edition of <u>The Ego and the Id</u>. He mentioned here that '... one gets an impression that the simple oedipus complex is by no means its commonest form, but rather represents a simplification or schematization which, to be sure, is often enough justified for practical purposes. Closer study usually discloses the more complete Oedipus complex, which is twofold, positive and negative, and is due to the bisexuality originally present in children; that it to say, a boy has not merely an ambivalent attitude towards his father and an affectionate object-choice towards his mother, but at the same time he also behaves like a girl and displays an affectionate feminine attitude to his father and a corresponding jealousy and hostility towards his mother' ... . (Ibid., p. 297)

*Dr. Searles does an excellent job in explaining the theory of the positive and negative oedipus complexes as first elucidated by Sigmund Freud. What he does not tell us, however, is that the <u>negative</u> oedipus complex is the one which lays the foundation for future schizophrenic manifestations in both the sexes. For when the negative oedipus complex becomes too powerful, due to faulty parental attitudes, it sets up the severe bisexual conflict which is always the etiological root of schizophrenia.*

*Again, by <u>negative</u> oedipus complex is meant the situation where the boy develops a feminine, affectionate, passive attitude towards the father, along with a jealous, hostile attitude towards the mother, and the girl develops a masculine, aggressive, libidinal attitude towards the mother and a hostile, competitive attitude towards the father.*

033   Particularly does the child bear the brunt of the mother's various massive dissociations, and from our own experience in therapy, we know how alone and anxious it makes us feel to be aware of powerful emotions in the other person of which he himself is unaware. It took me several years to realize that, for example, the rape which schizophrenic women fear is, above all, rape by the mother who unconsciously fantasies herself as possessing a penis – a fantasied penis, that is, which is dissociated in the mother herself. (Ibid., p. 322)

*Dr. Searles here makes the profound and totally accurate observation that schizophrenic women invariably have mothers who themselves are very deeply disturbed, at an unconscious level, about their own sexual identity, thereby providing sexually confused role models for their daughters.*

034   She has become, over the years, partly by dint of much hard work on the part of both of us, much better integrated. Life for her now involves more continuity, less anxiety, more genuine

happiness; and I feel vastly more comfortable in the hours with her. But we have lost much, too. Just how much, I tend to forget until I look back through my old notes concerning our work. The beer-hall bouncer I used to know is no more. The captured American pilot, held prisoner by the Germans but striding proudly several paces ahead of the despised prison-camp guard, is no more. The frightening lioness has gone from her den. The incarnation of paranoid hatred, spewing hostility at the whole world, has mellowed into someone unrecognizably different. (Ibid., p. 346)

*The powerful masculine strivings of this patient become obvious in her choice of self-fantasies as a beer-hall bouncer and a captured American pilot "striding proudly" in front of the prison guard.*

035     By the end of four years of work, when she was finally able to move to a ward for undisturbed patients (though still in a locked building), she had become appreciably freer in revealing fond feelings towards me, towards certain of the nurses and some of the other female patients, although not able as yet to divulge any fond memories about, or fond current interest in, her mother. A little less than one year later (at the end of four and three-quarters years of work) my patient, who throughout these years had been manifesting deep confusion as to her sexual identity – she had consistently referred to herself as 'a girl' but had misidentified other persons on innumerable occasions in terms of a projected male-female unconscious image of herself – referred to herself for the first time in all my experience with her as 'a woman.' Intense feelings of dependency, loneliness, and grief were now emerging from her in the hours as she began expressing fond memories of transitory acquaintances with various girls and women in the past both at school and in hospitals. Although still maintaining her letter-writing to the tenaciously-clung-to

Dr. Jones, she was now addressing these letters in such a fashion as to make it clear that they were directed as much to me as to him. In a fit of pique at feeling snubbed by Dr. Jones, she expostulated, 'Why, I'd rather be married to a woman!'

By now (just one month short of five years) we had become so consciously, but as yet very shyly, fond of one another that we could not look at each other during the session without our faces revealing this fondness. I recall that I fantasied now, and continued to fantasy for many months thereafter on innumerable occasions during our highly productive hours together, that I was giving suck to her from my breast. This was a highly pleasurable experience free from either anxiety or guilt.

She came to express glowingly libidinized memories of various girl friends, expressive of feelings of adoration and sexual desire which were at least as intense as those she had long expressed earlier in our work, with regard to various father figures. These included long-repressed feelings of intense interest in the female breast. (Ibid., p. 369)

*This patient's bisexual conflict is vividly described by her therapist. It is so powerful, in fact, that in the counter-transference it causes the therapist to assume the role of a mother suckling her infant daughter. Furthermore, that simple declaration, "Why, I'd rather be married to a woman! ", sums up the unconscious mental content of every schizophrenic female, combining as it does extreme confusion of sexual identity with strong homosexual strivings.*

036        In conclusion, I want to note that the schizophrenic patient responds with great regularity to the therapist's maternal warmth as being a sure indication that the latter is a homosexual or a lesbian. The younger therapist needs to become quite clear that this is, in actuality, a formidable resistance in the patient against the very kind of loving

mother-infant relatedness which offers the patient his only avenue of salvation from his illness. I do not mean that the therapist should depreciate the degree of anxiety, referable to the deep ambivalence of the patient's early relationship with his mother, which is contained within this resistance. I mean that the therapists's deep-seated doubts as to his own sexual identity – and what person is totally free of such doubts? – should not make him lose sight of the fact that the patient's contempt (or revulsion, or what not) is basically a resistance against going ahead and picking up the threads of the loving infant-mother relatedness which were long ago severed. (Ibid., p. 379)

*Schizophrenics will always project upon those in close contact with them their own bisexual confusion, as Dr. Searles makes very clear in this quotation.*

037       In my experience, the child defends himself against mutual ambivalence of such degree in the relationship with the mother by the perpetuation, into chronological adulthood of a symbiotic relatedness with her and by the retention – inherent in this same process – of fantasied infantile omnipotence. With, later on, the maturation of the anatomical and physiological sexual apparatus, a sexual differentiation comes to be required at a psychological level, too, the acceptance of oneself as <u>either</u> male <u>or</u> female, which runs counter to the infantile fantasy of being <u>both</u> – of being, in fact, the whole perceived world. (Ibid., p. 433)

*The concept of "infantile omnipotence" plays a key role in the understanding of schizophrenia and lesser emotional disorders.*
*The most important psychological task anyone ever has to face is that of choosing which sex they are going to belong to, both consciously and unconsciously. The schizophrenic, as*

*well as the neurotic, has never made this choice at the unconscious level. Unconsciously, he or she is still both – that is, both a he and a she – an androgynous being, enjoying the best of both worlds. However, this androgynous freedom in the unconscious world wreaks havoc in the conscious world by creating the severe bisexual conflict which leads to schizophrenia.*

*Emotional maturity lies in making the irrevocable decision, both consciously and unconsciously, to accept unreservedly the sex which Nature has assigned one, relinquishing forever the "infantile omnipotence" of childhood, with its seductive androgynous freedom.*

038  Much later on, in adolescence or young adulthood, the boy's struggle to become a man is hampered by an introject of his mother's warded-off femininity or of her phallically destructive strivings; or the girl's struggle to become a woman is complicated by an introject of the phallic mother, or in some instances, of a father who, for some of the reasons I have already suggested, early usurped the symbiotic mother role. The weaker the ego, the more likely it is that the lust will be experienced as a function not of the self but of the introject – as something alienly lustful and, further contradictory of the person's own sexual identity, such that the boy may sense a lustful female within him, or the girl, a lustful male. (Ibid., p. 435)

*Every boy goes through a stage where he senses a "lustful female" within, just as every girl goes through a stage where she senses a "lustful male" within. This is a normal part of the person's growth process. However, if these "opposite" sexual feelings are not fully relinquished, they will lead either to overt homosexuality or, if repressed, to mental illness, represented in its most extreme form by schizophrenia.*

039     The great problem of the pre-schizophrenic person, of course,
        is that, in keeping with the perpetuation, at an unconscious
        level, of the undifferentiated mother-infant stage of ego-
        development, he has not achieved any deep-reaching sexual
        differentiation of himself and perceived others into *either* male
        or female. The struggle to achieve such differentiation is
        probably one of the internal causes of his conception of all
        possible human feelings and behavior traits as bearing, like all
        French nouns, some sexual labels. Such judgements have been
        fostered in his superego development by parents who were
        themselves insecure about their sexual identities, and who
        inculcated in the son the erroneous idea that, for example,
        gentleness and a love for artistic things are feminine qualities,
        or in the daughter the notion that assertiveness and practicality
        are masculine attributes. Such notions, when applied not only
        to these few human qualities but extended over the whole
        range of psychological experience, and when applied not to
        the moderate degree found in the background of the neurotic
        person but invested with all the weight of actual biological
        attributes, have much to do with the person's unconscious
        refusal to relinquish, in adolescence and young adulthood, his
        or her fantasied infantile omnipotence in exchange for a sexual
        identity of – in these just described terms – a 'man' or a
        'woman.' (Ibid., p. 437)

        *Dr. Searles here points out, among other things, that
        schizophrenics invariably have parents who themselves are
        insecure in their sexual identities. The children of these
        sexually insecure parents experience an even greater degree
        of sexual insecurity, at a level intense enough to lead to
        schizophrenic manifestations.*

040     Bleuler (1911), Rosen (1953), Macalpine and Hunter (1955),
        and others note that schizophrenic patients regularly show
        confusion as regards their sexual identity, and Katan asserts

that '... in its deepest nature, schizophrenia arises from a bisexual conflict, and this bisexual conflict eventually leads to a state where the heterosexual factor is relinquished' (Katan, 1954, p. 121). (Ibid., p. 429)

*Dr. Maurits Katan pierces to the heart of schizophrenia when he states that "...in its deepest nature, schizophrenia arises from a bisexual conflict, and this bisexual conflict eventually leads to a state where the heterosexual factor is relinquished." If the schizophrenic person would then shift to a homosexual modus vivendi, a cure would be effected. However, the repression of the bisexual conflict causes both the homosexual factor and the heterosexual factor to be relinquished, leading to total sexual frustration. It is this total frustration of all sexual drives, both heterosexual and homosexual, which results in the enormous increase of undischarged sexual tension leading to the so-called "schizophrenic break."*

041        Finally, there is the formidable threat to the therapist's sense of sexual identity, arising from the patient's projection upon him of confusion or lack of differentiation in this regard; and, particularly for the male therapist, from the patient's intense reactions to him as a mother in the transference. It takes some of these patients several years to become clear about their own and their therapist's sexual identity. (Ibid., p. 442)

*Again, we are reminded of the intense confusion of sexual identity in all schizophrenics.*

042        Thus, with striking frequency the schizophrenic patient reacts to the development of what is really new ego with the conviction that he or she is pregnant. (Ibid., p. 457)

>  *The key phrase here is the "conviction that he or she is
> pregnant." For a <u>male</u> to believe he is pregnant is the <u>ultimate</u>
> in sexual confusion.*

043      One patient came to experience herself as a 'baggage car';
another as 'Noah's ark.' Still another experienced herself as a
trojan horse filled with a hundred people; and a man portrayed
in a dream his own state of being filled with introjects: he
dreamt of a man with a belly so enormous that he could
scarcely move about.
         A woman met me as I walked towards her building, for
a therapeutic session with her, and in great agitation showed
me a page in a story she was trying to read, a page on which
the protagonist, 'I,' was describing a conversation involving
several participants. She said: 'Four men and a girl – which
one is 'I?' – There's William and George and Peter – maybe
Peter is 'I' ... Which one is 'I'?' And as we walked into the
building she said: 'You've got too many people here, Dr.
Searles ... I get overwhelmed by people.' (Ibid., p. 468)

>  *The patient who "experienced herself as a trojan horse
> filled with a hundred people" obviously is identifying as a
> male, for the trojan horse was filled not with a hundred
> "people," but specifically with a hundred <u>male</u> soldiers.
> Unconsciously this patient would like to be one hundred male
> warriors, with all their physical and mental attributes.*
>  *And the man who dreamt he had a huge stomach was
> clearly identifying himself as a pregnant female.*

044      Another patient required several years of therapy to
become free from her long held, though previously
unconscious, self-concept as a 'snow man in a glass' – one of
those little snow men in a glass globe, with artificial snow –
quite outside the realm of living human relatedness, and it was

with the keenest pleasure that she finally became aware that
'I'm alive, Dr. Searles.' (Ibid., p. 479)

*This patient thought of herself as a snow* <u>man</u> *in a
glass.*

045          The threat which his genital lust poses to the paranoid
schizophrenic   individual   can   be   understood   most
meaningfully, I believe, in connexion with the structural
phenomena   of   symbiosis,   non-differentiation,   and   de-
differentiation which I have already touched upon. His sexual
identity is poorly differentiated, and although other areas of
his personality are equally poorly demarcated, the culture is
particularly   punitive   in   regard   to   incomplete   sexual
differentiation. Moreover, his own unresolved infantile
omnipotence,   a   facet   of   the   unresolved   mother-infant
symbiosis, is directly threatened by the necessity for him to
accept a single sexual identity, as either male or female, and
relinquish the complementary one; he cannot be wholly a man
or she wholly a woman – without relinquishing that
tenaciously held fantasied omnipotence. Further, the advent of
genital lust at a time when his object-relations are at a level
predominantly of symbiosis with the mother – herself poorly
differentiated sexually, with a strongly, though unconsciously
phallic body image – means that the sexual drive will be
directed   either   towards   the   mother,   or   towards   mother-
surrogates,   with   connotations   of   both   incest   and
homosexuality for the child, whether boy or girl. Another
important ingredient, in the threat which lust poses for these
young   people,   is   traceable   to   their   greatly   thwarted
identificatory needs; the young woman's need to identify with
an   adequate   mother-figure   is   experienced   as   an   utterly
unacceptable 'lesbian tendency,' and the young man's need to
identify with an adequate father-figure is experienced as an
equally shameful 'homosexual tendency.' (Ibid., p. 483)

*Again, Dr. Searles emphasizes the importance of relinquishing the sense of "infantile omnipotence" to enable one to become either a male or a female, rather than an androgynous mixture, with its resultant sexual confusion and emotional turmoil.*

046    It became very clear (and she herself substantiated this) that she felt herself to be God, selecting various dead leaves and other things to be brought to life. (Ibid., p. 493)

*This patient thinks she is God, which is undoubtedly as masculine and as powerful as one can become, according to traditional religious thinking.*

047    When one becomes alert to the significance of this phase of the therapy with the schizophrenic person, one is struck by how frequently one hears therapists make, in supervisory sessions or in staff presentations, such comments as 'There's been a lot of anger this past week,' without specifying in <u>whom;</u> or, likewise, 'There's a manicky mood around – there's a lot of giggling'; or, 'There is a very strong dependency there,' without specifying *where.* The therapist may make repeated slips of the tongue concerning the sexual identity of the patient – a response not only to the deep-seated sexual confusion in the patient which has now come to light, but a function also of the therapist's lack of differentiation between his own sex and that of the patient. (Ibid., p. 535)

*Dr. Searles reemphasizes the fact that the deep-seated sexual confusion in the schizophrenic patient can cause similar repercussions in the therapist's own sense of sexual identity.*

048    For years he had transposed in his comments, and clearly often in his actual subjective experience also, the sexes of persons in

his current life and in his remembered past – referring to (or in conversation addressing) a woman as a man, and vice versa. He explained, now, like a parent explaining to a child, the meaning of hatred: 'To hate means to change a person's sex.' (Ibid., p. 571)

*This patient makes a very powerful and meaningful statement when he asserts that "To hate means to change a person's sex."*

*Every schizophrenic male is the product of a mother who unconsciously "hated" her son's sex, due to her intense penis envy and jealousy of the male sex in general. All mothers of schizophrenic sons suffer from severe cases of "penis envy," to use Freud's terminology. Because this envy and resultant anger towards men is repressed, it must find devious channels for expression, and one of its favorite targets is the defenseless male child. Any masculine attributes this child may display are subtly discouraged by the mother, and his feminine attributes are encouraged. This malignant non-maternal behavior has the effect of creating a serious bisexual conflict in the son, which, subsequent to puberty, leads either to neurosis, psychosis or overt homosexual behavior.*

*This same type of mother has a similar malignant effect upon her daughter. Because of her own intense, unconscious dislike of being a woman, she discourages feminine tendencies in her daughter and encourages masculine ones, with the result that her daughter experiences severe bisexual conflict at puberty, the precursor of schizophrenia.*

049       A fifth analytic student began receiving supervision from me concerning her work with a hospitalized, chronically paranoid, middle-aged woman who presented a formidable demeanor of almost incessant condemnation and reproach, interlarded with sudden eruptions of lustful interests, expressed with a shocking kind of vulgarity, towards the

student-analyst. It quickly became apparent to me that the latter reacted to the older woman as being an intimidating parent figure and that in supervision she seemed likewise, during the early months of our work, to feel intimidated by me as an authority figure. (Ibid., p. 599)

*The fact this patient is able to show "sudden eruptions of lustful interests" towards her young female analyst is in reality a very healthy sign, since it has been the <u>repression</u> of these powerful homosexual feelings which has made the patient ill. The road to recovery lies in bringing these once conscious (but later repressed) feelings back into consciousness, where they can be assimilated into the total personality by means of the therapeutic process of intellectual and emotional "working through."*

050       With a somewhat less deeply ill woman I was able to delineate, piecemeal but quite specifically, various of the affects which one of her former denial-symptoms had served to keep repressed. She described her never having seen any men during her trips from her suburban parental home into Philadelphia. It developed that this scotoma had at least the following determinants in various different areas of her unconscious: (a) her parents had ingrained in her the deep-seated conviction that it is immoral for a young woman to 'see men'; (b) she was so fully, though at a deeply denied level, absorbed in unworked-through feelings of loss of various girls and women she had known in the past, that men did not exist for her; (c) she was afraid, at another unconscious level, that if a man's face registered in her perception, she would lose control of her rage towards men and hit him on the jaw (for, as she felt it, robbing her of her feminine friends); and (d) the sight of a man's face would bring before her, also, the unresolved grief over the death of a young male cousin whom she had loved. (Ibid., p. 636)

*This patient illustrates a very interesting facet of the emotionally disturbed woman's psyche, namely, the anger and rage she feels against men for having usurped her place in the affections and interests of her "girlfriends." The woman who is homosexually inclined must suffer the pangs of unrequited love frequently. She sees one girl friend after another wooed and won by a male. This, of course, incites in her great rage, envy and hatred towards men. Every schizophrenic woman, at a deep unconscious level, feels the same emotions as does this patient of Dr. Searles.*

051        Actually, both her mother and Dr. X were remembered by her as being multiple figures, of varying sexual identities. (Ibid., p. 677)

*Again we are reminded of the immense sexual confusion to be found in all schizophrenics.*

052        Several years ago, for example, it dawned on me that the schizophrenic woman's fear of rape is not basically a fear lest she be raped by a man, but rather a fear lest she be raped by a phallic mother-figure – by one or another woman round about, to whom she reacts as possessing a very real and terrifying penis – the projection of the penis which, at an unconscious level, she herself possesses on the basis of identification with the mother who, during the child's upbringing, in various ways acted out her unconscious conviction that she, the mother, possessed such a penis. It is often striking, too, to sense the biological literalness with which the patient perceives the male therapist as having female breasts and a vagina. (Ibid., p. 724)

*It is the masculine mother who produces the schizophrenic child, regardless of its sex. The daughter identifies with this masculine mother, and becomes masculine herself, while the son is effeminized by her. Denial by the daughter of her masculine, homosexual strivings can lead to schizophrenia; denial by the son of his feminine, homosexual strivings can lead to the same result.*

053   It was only after several years of therapy, and after her husband had divorced her, that the therapeutic investigation had proceeded deeply enough to reveal the extent to which she had been projecting upon both him and me, as well as upon many other people round about, an unconscious castrated male image of herself. Significantly, as this image became resolved, she came to realize for the first time in all our work that she (who had continually been sexually misidentifying herself and other people) is a woman and that I am a man. (Ibid., p. 726)

*Every schizophrenic woman has "an unconscious castrated male image of herself," as Dr. Searles so aptly puts it, and she projects this image onto all her acquaintances, both male and female. She acquired this image from her mother, who is similarly afflicted with this unconscious psychological defect, but to a lesser extent; otherwise she, too, would be schizophrenic.*

054   A comparatively simple example comes from the marital-family situation of a paranoid woman with whom I worked for several years. Among herself, her husband and her teen-aged daughter, it was evidently generally agreed upon, though at an unconscious level in all three (until this came more into the open in the patient's 'delusional' material), that the husband occupied the role of wife and mother in the family, and that the daughter had succeeded in displacing the patient from the husband and father role. (Ibid., p. 730)

*This is an excellent example of the tremendous sexual confusion and role reversal invariably found in the families of schizophrenics.*

055     As nearly as I could determine, that person consisted in the
        mother whom she loved, and the hard-boiled person was the
        mother whom she hated. I had learned long ago that she
        referred to her mother, more often than not, as 'he.' (Ibid., p.
        360)

        *Again, we find the masculine mother of the
        schizophrenic daughter, here psychologically correctly
        identified by the daughter as a "he."*

056     One hebephrenic woman, unable as yet to conceptualize her
        subjective unfeelingness as such, recurrently saw an eerily
        unhuman 'plastic man' appear, terrifyingly, at her window;
        another, unaware of her murderous rage as such, experienced
        instead an hallucination of a line of exploding teeth marching
        unendingly up one wall of her room across the ceiling, and
        down the other side; and a hebephrenic man, whose self
        concept as a little girl was repressed and projected, saw in his
        clothes-closet an 8 – or 10-year-old girl, swimming in purple
        liquid, and pleading urgently for me to rescue her. (Ibid., p.
        475)

        *A schizophrenic man unconsciously identifies himself
        as a prepubertal girl. This is another striking example of the
        intense sexual confusion which forms the core of
        schizophrenia. The "eerily unhuman 'plastic man'," which
        appeared to the hebephrenic woman, was really her
        unconscious image of herself as a male figure.*

057     I am Mr. Papa and not Madame Mama; I am Madame Mama,
        and not Mr. Papa. [Schizophrenic patient, sex not stated,]
        <u>Dementia Praecox or the Group of Schizophrenias</u>, Eugen
        Bleuler. (Ibid., p. 195)

*The secret of schizophrenia is given to the world by this "insane" man or woman, it matters not which, for the total confusion of sexual identity demonstrated by these two statements could be applicable to either.*

058    He was eleven and went to a freak show. He saw a boy who was supposed to be turning into an elephant but that didn't bother him. Then he saw a man who put needles through his skin, and he didn't like that at all. At another platform he saw a dwarfed, hunch-backed man billed as 'the human frog,' and he felt terribly sorry for him. Then he came to Alan-Adele – half man, half woman. He looked, fascinated – one side bearded, the other side smooth-shaved; flat-chested and full-breasted; long hair, short hair. Then he made the error; he thought of himself. He became terrified and ran out of the show shaking and sweating. He still felt odd when he thought about it. But he couldn't talk about the memory to anybody ... not yet. <u>Lisa and David</u>, Theodore Isaac Rubin. (Ibid., p. 128)

*David has unlocked the secret of schizophrenia, thanks to his visit to the "bearded lady" in the freak show. In seeing himself in this figure, he can now come to grips with the severe bisexual conflict which forms the basis of his mental illness.*

059    Since then I have wholeheartedly inscribed the cultivation of femininity on my banner, and I will continue to do so as far as consideration of my environment allows, whatever other people who are ignorant of the supernatural reasons may think of me. I would like to meet the man who, faced with the choice of either becoming a demented human being in male habitus or a spirited woman, would not prefer the latter. Such and <u>only such</u> is the issue for me. —<u>Memoirs of My Nervous Illness</u>, Daniel Paul Schreber. (Ibid., p. 149)

*In this quotation Judge Schreber has unlocked the secret of mental illness in all males. To unlock it for all females he should have added: "And I would like to meet the woman who, faced with the choice of either becoming a demented human being in female habitus or a spirited man, would not prefer the latter."*

*What this "gifted paranoic," as Freud called him, is telling us is that to avoid the ravages of mental illness one must consciously accept his or her homosexual self.*

060       The month of November 1895 marks an important time in the history of my life and in particular in my own ideas of the possible shaping of my future. I remember the period distinctly; it coincided with a number of beautiful autumn days when there was a heavy morning mist on the Elbe. During that time the signs of a transformation into a woman became so marked on my body, that I could no longer ignore the imminent goal at which the whole development was aiming. In the immediately preceding nights my male sexual organ might actually have been retracted had I not resolutely set my will against it, still following the stirring of my sense of manly honor, so near completion was the miracle. Soul voluptuousness had become so strong that I myself received the impression of a female body, first on my arms and hands, later on my legs, bosom, buttocks, and other parts of my body. I will discuss details in the next chapter.

'Several days' observations of these events sufficed to change the direction of my will completely. Until then I still considered it possible that, should my life not have fallen victim to one of the innumerable menacing miracles before, it would eventually be necessary for me to end it by suicide; apart from suicide the only possibility appeared to be some other horrible end for me, of a kind unknown among human beings. But now I could see beyond doubt that the order of the world imperiously demanded my unmanning, whether I personally liked it or not, and that therefore it was <u>common</u> <u>sense</u> that nothing was left to me but reconcile myself to the thought of being transformed into a woman. (Ibid., p. 148)

*Schreber here rationalizes his intense homosexual wishes to be turned into a woman, stating that it is demanded of him by the "order of the world," whether he likes it or not. If at this point he had been able to accept the fact that he <u>himself</u> wished this transformation to occur he would no longer have been psychotic, for he would have been acknowledging the reality of his own wishes. He could have dispensed with the necessity of remaining psychotic to shield himself from his own "perverse" desires.*

061    These considerations therefore lend an added weight to the circumstance that we are in point of fact driven by experience to attribute to homosexual wishful phantasies an intimate (perhaps an invariable) relation to this particular form of disease. Distrusting my own experience on the subject, I have during the last few years joined with my friends C. G. Jung of Zurich and Sandor Ferenczi of Budapest in investigating upon this single point a number of cases of paranoid disorder which have come under observation. The patients whose histories provided the material for this enquiry included both men and women, and varied in race, occupation, and social standing. Yet we were astonished to find that in all of these cases a defense against a homosexual wish was clearly recognizable at the very centre of the conflict which underlay the disease, and that it was in an attempt to master an unconsciously reinforced current of homosexuality that they had all of them come to grief. [1] [[1]Further confirmation is afforded by Maeder's analysis of a paranoid patient J. B. (1910). The present paper, I regret to say, was completed before I had an opportunity of reading Maeder's work.] This was certainly not what we had expected. Paranoia is precisely a disorder in which a sexual aetiology is

by no means obvious; far from this, the strikingly prominent features in the causation of paranoia, especially among males, are social humiliations and slights. But if we go into the matter only a little more deeply, we shall be able to see that the really operative factor in these social injuries lies in the part played in them by the homosexual components of emotional life. — "Psycho-Analytic Notes on an Autobiographical Account of a Case of Paranoia (Dementia Paranoides) (1911)," Sigmund Freud, The Complete Psychological Works of Sigmund Freud, Vol. XII, The Hogarth Press and the Institute of Psycho-Analysis, London, 1958, p. 59.

*Freud's discovery that repressed homosexual impulses form the core of paranoia must rank as the greatest contribution anyone has ever made to the field of clinical psychology. The tragedy of Freud's life is that he did not realize that paranoia and schizophrenia are inseparable, and therefore have the same etiological base – repressed homosexual cravings. On page 77 of the above-cited work, he states: "Moreover, it is not at all likely that homosexual impulsions, which are so frequently – perhaps invariably – to be found in paranoia, play an equally important part in the aetiology of that far more comprehensive disorder, dementia praecox." (Eugen Bleuler, in his monumental study of the psychoses, first used the term "schizophrenia" in place of "dementia praecox.")*

*Freud's inability to see the connection between paranoia and schizophrenia resulted in his not being able to consummate his brilliant libido theory of the neuroses and psychoses. From complete ignorance concerning the cause of mental illness, he brought the world ninety-nine percent of the way to a full understanding of it, then failed to take that final step which would have completed his theory by recognizing that paranoia and schizophrenia are inextricably bound, that*

what forms the etiology of the one also forms the etiology of
the other.

062      It is clinically well known that schizophrenics are very
sensitive in the area which may loosely be called
'homosexual.' This sensitiveness, however, amounts
principally to fears and preoccupations with the thought that
someone else might think the patient homosexual or with
efforts to determine in self-defense which persons in the
environment may be homosexual. The patients make elaborate
efforts to avoid the implication of being homosexual. It is so
common for the fear of the patient who goes into panic to
include some homosexual content that these panics have even
come to be known as 'homosexual.' —Psychotherapeutic
Intervention in Schizophrenia, Lewis B. Hill, M. D., The
University of Chicago Press, Chicago, 1955, p. 61.

It can truly be said that schizophrenia is the negation of
homosexuality. A schizophrenic is a person who is strongly
homosexual, but would rather "die than admit it," so to speak.
Consequently, many do die, from suicide, alcoholism, drug
addiction and other self-destructive behavior, all of which are
but symptoms of schizophrenia.

063      Also, having arrived, these schizophrenic children appear,
none of them, to have been really the preferred children. At
least in their own opinion, some other sibling was preferred,
and many of these schizophrenic patients set about early in life
seriously squelching their own personalities in order to
produce an imitation of the envied sibling. It did not matter
whether this sibling was of the same or of the other sex. This
may be a factor in the high incidence of homosexual
preoccupation in schizophrenic patients or, to put it accurately,
in their uncertainty as to their sex. (Ibid., p. 114)

*If a girl envies her brother, she will identify with him as a male and either become neurotic, psychotic (schizophrenic) or homosexual. The same applies to the boy who envies his sister.*

064    The young lady, knowing that he knew she was not averse to or inexperienced in extramarital intercourse, was furious. She counterattacked in his most vulnerable spot. She knew that he had been preoccupied, while acutely ill, with homosexual fears and had only recently had self-confidence enough to enjoy dancing with a few women patients. So she went to them and told them he was a homosexual and an exhibitionist. They taunted him with this, and he promptly withdrew into a confused and semistuporous psychosis lasting some weeks. On learning of this eventual outcome of her talk, the young lady became agitated and then apathetic. She was ill for several weeks. (Ibid., p. 155)

*Ironically, the young lady mentioned here has as severe a problem with her own homosexual impulses as does the young man with his, but obviously has not yet come to grips with that fact.*

065    For example, there was a psychotic woman, one of whose delusions was that she was a young man who was in love with and going to marry a girl whose name was hers and whose appearance was her own. Failing in the accomplishment of this fantasy, she became mute, retarded, and unresponsive to anyone. She had been in this state for some months when I undertook to treat her. (Ibid., p. 159)

*The bi-sexual conflict in this woman's schizophrenia is obvious.*

066    In her first year, however, she fell in love with a classmate, a girl. This girl introduced her to some heavy 'spooning.' This word will date this patient for older readers. The patient felt guilty, ashamed, angry, and fascinated. At the height of her conflict her partner suddenly and contemptuously jilted her. Her story then became confused. She thinks that within a few days her mother took her home, where she was in bed, was spoon fed by the mother, and was untidy. She was ill for about six months. (Ibid., p. 165)

    *This girl's "schizophrenic break" was due to her severe conflict over her homosexual tendencies.*

067    During his professional career this young man went out with his colleagues and, because he did not want them to think him queer, occasionally had intercourse with a party girl. After a few years, the firm for which he worked decided to raise two of its employees to junior partnership. The patient was perhaps the brightest of the five candidates, but he was not chosen. He complained about this and was told that he did not have the personality for executive work. He could stay on as a worker doing technical detail. In the next few months he became aware that strange things went on in the office. One day six men came out of the boss's office carrying a coffin. The patient looked into it and saw the boss smoking a cigar. Several men, including those who had been promoted, began to sneer at him and to call him 'queer.' They drank together, and he saw one of them kiss another on the stairway in broad daylight. The coffin appeared again and again. The patient appealed to his sister, who recognized his condition. In his anxious tension and near-panic he made some effort to embrace her. She was not certain whether he was trying to seduce her or to kill her. On the way to the hospital the patient spent a night with his uncle, sleeping in the same bed with him. He slept very deeply, as if drugged. In the morning he

saw a spot of blood on the outside of the seat of his pajamas. It meant to him that his uncle had had anal relations with him. (Ibid., p. 168)

*This is a classic case of paranoid schizophrenia resulting from powerful, repressed homosexual drives. The patient's delusion that his uncle had engaged in anal intercourse with him was triggered by unconscious wishes that just such an event had occurred.*

068        Both the man and the girl boldly identified with what they feared, with what they had been previously struggling so hard to deny. The principle this implies is *identify with that which haunts you, not in order to fight it off, but to take it into yourself; for it must represent some rejected element in you.* The man identified with his feminine component; he does not become homosexual but heterosexually potent. As he dances wearing the hat and dress of a woman, and the girl the officer's hat and jacket, you would think you are seeing a film of a masquerade. But not at all: none of the villagers who are dancing smiles a bit; they are there to perform a significant ceremony for members of their community, and they partly share the trancelike quality in which the patients are caught up. The girl and the man were emboldened to 'invite' the daimonic by the support of their community.

           Particular emphasis should be placed, indeed, on the importance of the backing of the neighbors, friends, and fellow townsmen of the individual as he faces his 'demons.' It is hard to see how this man or girl would have been able to muster up the courage to encounter the daimonic if they had not had the participation and tacit encouragement of their group. The community gives a humanly trustworthy, interpersonal world in which one can struggle against the negative forces.

We note that both of these persons happen to be identifying with someone of the opposite sex. This reminds us of Jung's idea that the shadow side of the self which is denied represents the opposite sex, the <u>anima</u> in the case of men and, in the case of women, the <u>animus</u>. —<u>Love and Will</u>, Rollo May, Dell Publishing Co., Inc., [W. W. Norton & Company, Inc.], New York, 1969, p. 132.

*This is a fascinating example of how a so-called "primitive" culture is so much wiser than ours is about recognizing the vital role bisexual conflict plays in the etiology of madness.*

069    The classical example for this is Freud's patient who tried to take her clothes off with her right hand while making an effort to keep them on by grasping them with her left. She was identifying herself simultaneously with a man raping and a woman being attacked. —<u>The Psycho-Analytic Theory of Neurosis</u>, Otto Fenichel, M. D., W. W. Norton & Company, Inc., New York, 1945, p. 222.

*A clearer example of the etiological function of the "bearded lady" syndrome in mental illness would be hard to find than in this case of Sigmund Freud's.*

070    A patient with an extreme social fear of the erythrophobic type was afraid that everybody was laughing at him and saying that he was 'feminine.' He was not able to state exactly of what this femininity consisted. Anyhow, people were looking at him and making remarks that he was homosexual. The same patient used to look into the mirror and imagine being in love with himself, fantasying first that he was a handsome man and then that he was a beautiful woman. (Ibid., p. 430)

*This is another excellent example of the "Bearded Lady" syndrome in action, so to speak.*

071        The normal superego is, as a rule, an introjected object of the same sex. The marked increase of homosexual tension in schizophrenics causes a resexualization of the desexualized social and superego cathexes; this is true either because the homosexuality is reached as a mid-point between heterosexuality and narcissism on the regressive road of withdrawal of libido or because it is reached as a result of an attempt to recapture the objects in the process of restitution. (Ibid., p. 431)

*In schizophrenics, the "normal" superego is always an introjected object of the <u>opposite</u> sex. It is this unconscious identification with an opposite-sex figure which creates the "marked increase of homosexual tension" invariably to be found in the schizophrenic.*

072        Another example of helpful reformulation stems from the experience of one of our associates with a severely disturbed schizophrenic girl. This patient reported to the psychiatrist with whom she had been working over a long period of time: 'I moved up and down and up and down in my bed and was quite upset. I don't know why you told me that I had to wear spikes while doing this.' This patient had been recently moved from the most disturbed ward of the hospital to a less disturbed one. On this occasion she had made the resolution to stop manual masturbation. She was as mixed up about her own sex as most schizophrenics are. The psychiatrist, to whom the patient had previously given information about both these facts, reformulated the patient's statement for her as follows: 'So there was sexual excitement and relief from jumping up and down in your bed. And you were not sure whether or not one had to be a boy ["spikes"] in

order to jump around that way. And you <u>do</u> feel that you need the psychiatrist to tell you about it.' —<u>Principles of Intensive Psychotherapy</u>, Frieda Fromm-Reichmann, M. D., The University of Chicago Press, Chicago, 1950, p. 95.

*The key phrase here is: "She was as mixed up about her own sex as most schizophrenics are."*

073     After that, she understood what it meant to the patient to fill one of the cavities of his body to capacity, to enjoy the feel of it, and to be gleefully puzzled and intrigued. The patient tried to experience himself as a pregnant female. This interpretation proved to be correct. The patient accepted it avidly, as one would accept a great revelation, and commented instantly upon his envy of his wife, whose privilege it was to experience a third pregnancy. This birth-envy was subsequently discovered to be an important factor in the psychopathology of the patient. (Ibid., p. 93)

*Freud wrote extensively about the phenomenon of "penis envy" in women. In this quote we have an excellent example of the phenomenon of "vagina envy" in men. In both cases this opposite-sex envy plays a fundamental role in the development of mental illness.*

074     The third example is that of a patient who visualized his blue-eyed female psychoanalyst as bearded and brown-eyed. That is, the distorted picture of the psychiatrist coincided with the appearance of his dead father, who had been brown-eyed and had had whiskers. Concomitantly with the distortion of the psychiatrist's looks, he, of course, also misinterpreted the doctor's reactions and behavior as being similar to childhood experiences with his father. (Ibid., p. 103)

*This is another very obvious example of the extreme confusion of sexual identity to be found in schizophrenics.*

075     Except for seriously disordered patients who were markedly mixed up about their sex role, I have not found any confirmation of Freud's conception that women experience childbirth as equivalent to at last coming into possession of a penis of their own. (Ibid., p. 203)

*<u>All</u> "seriously disordered patients" are "markedly mixed up about their sex role."*

076     In this connection I remember a patient who married hastily two months prior to beginning treatment. Having heard, as she put it, that the psychoanalytic process might entail the discovery and discussion of a person's homosexual problems, she wanted to begin her treatment with the record of a satisfactory heterosexual adjustment. (Ibid., p. 207)

*This reminds one of Freud's dictum that a substantial portion of anyone's psycho-analysis should be spent discussing their homosexuality.*

077     As one's experience with Mr. Y broadened, it became apparent that his illness represented a struggle against homosexual impulses. In his own story he turned from the peddler, who had wreaths of flowers strung along a stick (probably a symbol of sex to the patient), to the strange girl. His choice of the girl was a flight from homosexual temptation to heterosexual activity. After this incident in which the perverse sexual temptation probably came close to consciousness, he reinforced his defenses by suddenly changing from an easy-going, passive individual whose greatest delight was to putter about the house, to an aggressive, drinking individual, who began to go to houses of

prostitution and to fight with his friends. Later, in the sanitarium where he was confined, it was observed that he became disturbed when any attempt was made to substitute men for women nurses in taking care of him. His constant insistence upon his potency was also a defense as was his consistent hatred of anyone whom he called a sissy. This was further corroborated by material brought out in dreams; he dreamed that he was being married, but much to his astonishment he was a woman instead of a man, and a man, a friend of his, holding a long stick, persisted in attempting to thrust it into him.

In this case, the various elements determining the vivid martyrdom-asceticism picture are clearly visible. The erotic element was explicit; it was of a confused nature involving heterosexual facades for the denial of homosexual urges. — Man Against Himself, Karl A. Menninger, Harcourt, Brace & World, Inc., New York, 1938, p. 97.

*This is a case where the repressed homosexual element in the etiology of the patient's schizophrenia is very clear.*

078     Ego support is implicit in the therapeutic objectives with a young paranoid patient which included supplying him with paternal affection without a homosexual tinge, giving factual sexual information, building up his selfregard and helping him make decisions about his own plans (Knight, 72). (Ibid., p. 52)

*What this young man needs most is what the therapist is supplying him with: "paternal affection without a homosexual tinge." The patient is of course very insecure in his masculinity due to his repressed homosexual strivings.*

079     One of the most widely mentioned transference problems is that of dealing with homosexual impulses which may threaten the therapeutic relationship when working with

paranoid schizophrenics. Techniques for dealing with disturbing homosexual elements of the transference have varied from the utilization of a female helper (Federn, 34, 35) to the direct energetic discouragement of such tendencies in the patient, forcing him to recognize the dangers in the fulfillment of his homosexual phantasies, and advising him to have heterosexual intercourse (Eidelberg, 28). It seemed advisable in the latter case to transfer the patient's sexual wishes at least in part to a female object in order to lessen the tension aroused by his homosexual trends and hence to make them more analyzable. Some authors have suggested the prospect of recovery in such patients may actually be better when they are treated by women since discussion of their homosexual tendencies is less likely to provoke a panic-like state than when treated by men. (Ibid., p. 54)

*Again we see the all-important role homosexual impulses play in schizophrenia.*

080   Indeed, we have noted, in a few instances, that the acceptance and examination of a dream has led to dissolution of paranoid features. For example, the recounting and acceptance of a dream with homosexual implications directed towards the therapist has removed the need to distort and circumvent to keep the patient and the therapist from becoming aware of impulses of which the patient is already partially conscious. (Ibid., p. 177)

*This case illustrates the fact that the cure for schizophrenia is for the patient to become aware of his unconscious, repressed homosexual desires, and to deal with them on a conscious level where they can be worked through both intellectually and emotionally, thus negating the need for psychotic defenses against them.*

081 Nedda, whose name already foreshadowed the disappointment of the parents in her sex, was thirty-eight years old when I first met her. She had been hospitalized since 1943, and had apparently settled into the hopeless mold of a posturing, oddly attired, emotionally inappropriate hebephrenic. (Ibid., p. 181)

> *It is noteworthy that many parents give their children, both male and female, androgynous names. This undoubtedly reflects the parents' unconscious uncertainty as to their own sexual identity, as well as dislike of the gender which nature has assigned their children.*

082 I remember a patient, a psychotic, who came to me after he had been treated by many other psychiatrists, and told me that once, while being treated by another psychiatrist, he had a dream in which he was cornered by his father and came in close contact with his penis. Then he said, 'Imagine, this psychoanalyst told me that it meant that I have homosexual wishes. I recognized at once that this man was insane himself and I left him.' (Ibid., p. 209)

> *This is a good example of the ability of the conscious mind to repress unpleasant truths and corroborates Freud's view that "in schizophrenia the victory lies with repression."*

083 The suffering which she experienced in this regard – suffering which various of her other symptoms made impossible to alleviate at all quickly – seemed fully as immediate and intense as though she were experiencing feelings of loss of parts of her body. In the early months of the therapy she often used to grab at my penis, my glasses, my wrist watch, and my belt, talking fragmentarily of her own desolation at not possessing these, and it was my distinct impression that the watch, the glasses, and other inanimate possessions caused her to feel as painful a lack in herself as did my penis. —The Non-

Human Environment (In Normal Development and in Schizophrenia), Harold F. Searles, M. D., International Universities Press, Inc., New York, 1960, p. 154.

*Dr. Searles misses the point here, by not realizing that his watch, glasses and belt represent his masculinity just as much as does his penis, for men wear different styles of glasses, watches and belts than do women.*

084        The patient was an ambulatory schizophrenic young man who was in psychotherapy with me in an outpatient clinic. His paranoid ideation was so formidable that he could barely maintain himself outside a hospital and he lived, of course, an extremely isolated existence. He initially sought psychotherapy partly because of his being tortured by obsessive thoughts of a homosexual nature. After a time, as he began to respond to psychotherapy, I noticed in one of the hours that there were now two indications that he was improving: he no longer referred to his feeling of loneliness as something constant, but rather as being, now, intermittent; and he mentioned that he was no longer having the 'perverted thoughts,' as he called them. But then, during the next hour, in emphasizing to me his loneliness, he said in a distinctly regretful tone, 'I don't even have the fears [that is, the 'perverted thoughts'] I used to have. Sometimes I compare which is worse [the 'perverted thoughts' which he used to have, or the loneliness which he now feels]. Before, I had so much to think about that I didn't have time to think about feeling lonely. Now I haven't anything to think about. It's all loneliness.' (Ibid., p. 168)

*This patient is on his way to recovery from schizophrenia now that he has begun dealing with his homosexual feelings, the repression of which had driven him into psychosis.*

085        The second patient, a twenty-six-year-old man who upon admission to Chestnut Lodge was suffering from acute catatonic schizophrenia, undertook psychotherapy with another of the therapists on the staff. This colleague, in a presentation of the patient's case before the staff, mentioned a number of points which indicated anxiety on this man's part lest he become non human. Prior to his hospitalization, the patient had been noted at times to walk stiffly, 'like an automaton.' He manifested, early in his stay in the hospital, a loss of ego boundaries, such that he sometimes felt at one not only with other persons (such as his wife, his hospital roommate, and so on) but also with non human objects. He referred to himself as 'it,' while crouching on the floor in a fetal position. (Ibid., p. 187)

*The key phrase in this quotation is that the patient had experienced a "loss of ego boundaries" to the point where he "felt at one" with his wife, and certain other people. If he "felt at one" with his wife, it means that unconsciously he identified himself as a female, which, since he was a male, would result in a severe bisexual conflict leading to schizophrenia. That, of course, is exactly what happened.*

086        The head nurse of the ward had the same general sort of impression of this patient, as functioning like an animal. In one of her notes, for example, many months after the patient's admission, when the animallike quality had become more of a friendly than a repelling sort, the nurse put the following amused report in her notes: 'Galloping over the pasture – er, I mean the ward. Being friendly and overactive ...' On another occasion the patient was described, in the nurses' notes, as having run out onto the porch, lifted her leg over a waste basket and urinated into it, like a dog. In my work with this woman, I found abundant evidence that she frequently felt herself to be an animal. (Ibid., p. 215)

*Dr. Searles misses a key point about this schizophrenic woman's conduct. It is true she felt herself to be an animal, but an animal of which sex? She obviously identified herself as a male because only <u>male</u> dogs lift their legs over objects and urinate on them. Female dogs squat down to urinate, as even the most casual observer of nature knows, and as this schizophrenic woman undoubtedly knew also.*

087     A deeply schizophrenic woman, twenty-nine years of age at the time when she began psychotherapy with me, for more than two years showed confusion as to whether she was male or female. This confusion she expressed indirectly, as in the exchange with me which is quoted below. Two words of prefatory explanation: the patient's first name was Nanette, the comments in brackets are mine.

'An âne is a donkey, isn't it?'

['In French, yes'] 'A âne is a donkey in French, yes. It's a game where you're blindfolded and you pin a tail on a donkey. That's my name: *â-n-e* (laughing). The 'a' has that – what do you call it, over it? – an inverted V.'

['Let's see what an inverted V brings up.'] 'My nose is sort of in the shape of a V. I had a pin that was V-shaped – well, I didn't have it. I didn't have any jewelry. It was Ruth's (Ruth: her younger sister) ... âne – I don't know whether it's masculine or feminine. It doesn't have to be either; it's l-apostrophe.'

Note her repeatedly associating *âne* – of which she says, 'I don't know whether it's masculine or feminine' – with herself.

This confusion about her own sexuality she repeatedly projected onto her environment. She once spoke of a 'statue of a woman in Rock Creek Park,' imitating with upraised arms the posture of the statue, and went on to say that she liked it very much because of it's 'masculine grace.' I replied in surprise, 'It's <u>masculine</u> grace?' She nodded and went on speaking. Also, she described on several occasions, during the first two years of the therapy, an incident when, prior to her hospitalization, she had visited, uninvited, the home of a young man with whom she was having an autistic love affair. Each time she spoke of this, it was evident that she was confused as to whether the person who met her at the door was male or female. She was not sure whether this was the young man himself, or his sister who lived there with him and their father. In one of her accounts of this, she at first said she knew the person was a girl, but she kept referring to the person as 'he,' saying at one point she 'was 60 percent sure' the person was a boy. She described, however, the person as having 'bright red lipstick and lots of powder, and blond hair swept up in back.' This person's name, the patient found upon inquiring, was Janet – very similar to the patient's own name, Nanette; and the patient herself had blond hair. The patient went on to say, giggling tensely, 'He looked like a fashionable sketch,' and then added, 'The other day Dr. _____ [a doctor at the lodge with whom she had, for a long time, an autistic love affair] looked like a fashionable sketch.' This last hinted at her confusion concerning the sex of Dr. _____, a confusion which similarly emerged on various other occasions. All this kind of material from her is suggestive that her confusion about the sexuality of figures in her environment is related to her confusion about her own sexuality.

It is well known that schizophrenic individuals are frequently confused as to their own maleness or femaleness. ... Some of the material suggestive of this point emerged in one hour when she was again describing her experiences of going to the young man's home. She said, 'When it came out of the bedroom it looked just like Fred [the name of the young man] – bright lipstick, a lot of some kind of powder base, and hair done up. It's eyes and nose and mouth were just like Fred's. It was very tall and broad,' she said with a gesture of revulsion. 'I've never seen anything so broad.'

... I shall not attempt to provide here any detailed material to show further how terrified this young woman was concerning the subjective threat of sexual activity. In the words of her administrator, she was 'crawling with terror' for several months after her admission to the disturbed ward, and in her hours with me she left no doubt that one of her greatest fears was of being raped. She used to plead for, and demand, reassurance that she would not be raped. The psychotherapy eventually brought to light her very strong homosexual desires to rape other persons, and desires on her own part to be raped. She had, as is perhaps by now obvious enough, intensely conflictual <u>desires</u> to be male plus a hatred of and aversion to, maleness.

In one hour with her I experienced what appears to have been a kind of participation in her own intensely anxiety-laden confusion as to her sexuality. She had come into the hour vividly lipsticked and face-powdered and with a very sexy coiffure, and was lying on the couch with her head propped up and her feet crossed – a posture which impressed me as masculine. I suddenly got a strong conviction that she was a man dressed up as a woman. I kept trying to dismiss the idea as patently absurd, because I knew that the nurses had helped her to change menstrual pads and had given her baths; so I knew it utterly irrational to think that under these circumstances she could have remained on a female ward for many months. But the idea persisted during the remainder of that session, and was accompanied by an eerie feeling which was most uncomfortable. Within the ensuing week, she produced sufficient verbal evidence (some of which I have given above) of her own confusion as to her sexual identity, so as to suggest to me that, as I mentioned in one of my notes during that week, ... my feeling about Nanette as a transvestite probably was not entirely 'imaginary,' i.e. self-produced – probably reflected Nanette's doubt as to her own sex, a doubt reflected in her posture, her mannerisms, and so forth.

My belief is that I had experienced here, a taste of the eerily uncomfortable feelings which presumably assailed the patient herself in connection with her uncertainty concerning her sexual identity, and that it was partly to relieve just such anxiety as this that her unconscious conception of herself as nonhuman arose. (Ibid., pp. 229-232)

*This particular quotation, perhaps more than any other, demonstrates the incredible sexual confusion to be found in schizophrenics.*

088  The first of these two patients, a woman of forty-two with a hysterical personality structure, had been on the verge of a paranoid psychosis when I began seeing her, after she had already undergone approximately six years of work with a series of three previous analysts. Over the course of the first two years of her work with me, the threat of psychosis gradually subsided. But she retained an abysmally low self-esteem; she showed an intense penis envy and, behind this, a basic despair as to her ability ever to become a woman among women.

The analysis with me was an unusually stormy one, as had been her work with each of the previous analysts. She expressed a tremendous amount of hostility toward me for about three years, and as she became gradually aware of the intensity of her hostility, this awareness seemed, for many months, only an additional burden to her low self-esteem; she despaired of ever becoming a person capable of receiving and giving love. (Ibid., p. 261)

*By coming to grips with her intense penis envy, this woman has been saved from paranoid psychosis.*

089  The second of these two patients, a twenty-nine year old woman chemist with a character disorder, showed at the

beginning of analysis an ingrained harsh and sarcastic approach to other persons; an intense penis envy founded upon despair of becoming, in her own eyes, a real woman; and a severe repression of her tender feelings in her interpersonal relationships in general.

Although married and the mother of three young daughters, she reacted to her own external genitalia with loathing, and was convinced that her menstrual flow was pathological. She was horrified on more than one occasion, during the early phase of the analysis, to find what she considered to be gruesomely abnormal bits of material in the menses.

In the fourteenth month of the analysis there occurred a dream which marked a significant forward step in her becoming free from all these symptoms:

'I had the persistent feeling that I was trying to be a man, or act like a man, and was getting very tired of it. Didn't think I could go on with it. Then I dreamed – I was thinking that – uh – suddenly I saw a rosebush, blooming with lovely red roses the color of blood.' (Ibid., p. 263)

*This is a striking example of how psycho-analysis can be of tremendous benefit in some cases. By coming to grips with her enormous dislike of being a female, this woman can salvage her unhappy emotional life by transforming it into something both productive and enjoyable.*

090    For instance, in one of his sessions with me he let me know that he was impatiently awaiting 'my mate – Jupiter or Juno or a pig or a sewer rat, whatever it is.'

... The patient told me of his fear, during that period, when he would awake at night and his mother would be standing over the bed. She became, as her symptoms rapidly progressed, a raving maniac, would talk about being Circe and turning men into swine, would threaten to kill the two sons, and repeatedly made onslaughts upon them with dangerous kitchen implements. The mother had to be placed in a state hospital, where she remained for what proved to be the last year of her life. She finally died while very deeply and very disturbedly psychotic. (Ibid., pp. 273, 275)

*This schizophrenic man is awaiting his mate, either "Jupiter or Juno or a pig or a sewer rat, whatever it is." If his mate can be either Jupiter or Juno, it means he is willing to have either a man or a woman as his mate. Thus his bisexual conflict is made patently clear. Furthermore, his schizophrenic mother's intense bisexual conflict and resultant murderous penis envy is glaringly evident.*

091        Interestingly, when she became able, very slowly, to relate herself a bit more closely to other patients, this sometimes took the form of her treating them as if they were dolls. For example, here is an excerpt from a nurse's report sheet, approximately twenty months later on in therapy than the one just quoted:
Ate sandwiches and drank juice constantly all evening. Went into Grace Randall's room. Played with Grace's body some and jumped from bed to dresser, etc. After 11:00 p.m., there was some noise in her room. I went back and watched. She was using Clara [her roommate] like a baby doll, moving her all over the bed and undressing her and playing some with her breasts. (Ibid., p. 279)

*This patient's homosexuality is obvious.*

092        During the eight months of therapy – much too short a time, of course, for psychotherapy to establish a solid recovery in so deeply and chronically schizophrenic a person – the patient did not develop a durable sense of individuality vis-a-

vis her mother, although she was making a real beginning in that direction when the treatment was interrupted.

The bit of material suggestive of 'phylogenetic regression' was reported to me by her mother. The mother, after a visit with her daughter during the seventh month of the psychotherapy, told me:

She got into the confused idea of who were relatives and who weren't and whether she was man, woman, or child ... she said we both had been buried deep in the earth and the worms had eaten us ... (Ibid., p. 260)

*This "deeply and chronically schizophrenic" woman did not know whether she was "man, woman, or child." Her bisexual conflict is very apparent.*

093          Upon one occasion when I went into the living room on the ward, for a psychotherapeutic hour with her, I found her engaged in a lively, and unmistakably friendly, conversation with another woman patient, sitting near her. The other woman quickly excused herself so that the patient could have the therapeutic session. A few moments later, while talking volubly as she generally did with me, my patient made, to my amazement, some verbal reference to the other woman – with whom she had been sharing an unmistakedly friendly togetherness so shortly before – as 'that thing.' Not only this verbal phrase, but also her tone in referring to the other woman, was as utterly impersonal as though the other patient were an inanimate object. This occurrence fit in with other evidence that she had to deny any feelings of fondness, however obvious these feelings might at times be to other persons. Another manifestation of this denial was her adamant refusal to sleep in a dormitory with several other women patients; she endured this sleeping arrangement for two or three nights, but thereafter could stand it no longer. The therapy revealed that she was not yet prepared to face the

welter of repressed conflictual feelings, among which intense fondness was a most prominent ingredient, toward other women. She dealt with this by perceiving the other women patients as being sub human, and for <u>that</u> reason she could not endure their proximity during the night. She asserted with chilling scorn, loudly enough for all these others to hear, 'I won't spend another night in that dormitory with those cattle.'

Then in an hour nine days later, she was evidently seeing me, convincedly, as being one of the Jews whom she held responsible for all the outrages which she experienced as happening to her currently; for instance, she was sure that during the previous night something had been stuck into her vagina in order to make a man of her.

... She had great cause, by reason of her past experience with seeing her two brothers to be favored, time and again, over herself, to feel especially envious towards men. . . .

It required literally years of intensive psychotherapy before she could begin to acknowledge any feeling of envy.

The over-all course of the psychotherapy provided much data which suggested that, as long as she was unable to become aware of her repressed envious desires to, for example, humble the glamorous jet pilots by turning them into lowly bugs, she had to project these repressed desires, and consequently lived in fear and trembling that she herself would be turned into one or another infrahuman form of life by supposedly external malevolent powers. (Ibid., pp. 284–285, 287-288)

*This woman suffers from severe penis envy, repressed homosexual desires and unconscious wishes to be a man, all of which are the basic determinants of her schizophrenia.*

094      She had begun the hour in a characteristic way, bellowing a lot of paranoid material about 'their' trying to

make a man out of her, and 'their' raping her; much of this raging was directed toward me, as had often happened. She went on, still in a not unusual vein, to rant that she knew she had again been made pregnant against her will (which, she had long been convinced, happened over and over again), because she could 'feel life' in her abdomen. She most vigorously disclaimed my suggestion that maybe in a way she wished very much that she were pregnant. (Ibid., p. 296)

*This patient's severe bisexual conflict is illustrated by the fact that while a part of her wants to be a man, the other part wants to be raped and be made pregnant, like a woman.*

095     He describes the extraordinary house constructed, in a play-therapy kind of experiment, by a schizophrenic young man who complained of having no feeling in the front of his body. This house had only a screen rather than a solid front; the solid part of the house was confined to a projection at the back, corresponding with the builder's experiencing his own feelings as being localized to his spine and rectum. Further, in the outline of the house-form could be recognized the posture – i.e. with protruding buttocks – of the young man. (Ibid., p. 318)

*This man is repressing very strong anal erotic feelings, which if made conscious would take the form of passive, pederastic desires, placing him in the category of an effeminate, anal-receptive homosexual. This reality is what he is resisting and what forms the basis of his schizophrenia.*

096     During the period of multiple therapy, in one session he gazed at the other therapist and myself and began talking, 'They take the upper halves of the bodies of two men and attach them to the lower halves of the bodies of two women . . .', convincing both the other therapist and myself,

independently, that this was how he was perceiving us – not as really human beings but as the strange kind of, as it were, manufactured combinations which he had described. This fit in with his own manner of walking, which was a grotesque, disharmonious combination of exaggeratedly feminine hip-swinging and mincing gait, plus a carriage of his arms, chest, and shoulders which caused one of my colleagues, seeing him for the first time emerging from my office, to take me aside and ask in astonishment, 'What was that?' I replied, in some amusement, 'What did it look like?' He replied, 'It looked like somebody trying to walk like a gorilla.' (Ibid., p. 361)

*This is a classic case of the "bearded lady" syndrome in schizophrenia. It could not be more apparent. In the circus the bearded lady is usually split down the middle, the left side one sex, the right side the other. In this case the patient had made the split across the middle, the top half male, the bottom half female. That is the picture the patient has of himself, half male, half female – both sides competing against each other and neither one able to gain ascendancy.*

097    For spirits when they please
       Can either sex assume, or both; so soft
       And uncompounded is their essence pure.
            – John Milton, Paradise Lost, Book One, Lines 423-
       425.

*Milton here perfectly describes the mind set of all children, who, in their androgynous freedom, "can either sex assume, or both; so soft/And uncompounded is their essence pure." Unfortunately, it is this androgynous freedom, a characteristic shared with all mammals, which in man is the essential ingredient leading later to severe bisexual conflict and schizophrenia.*

098     'In the north of Brazil,' she explained, 'they have this superstition, if you pass underneath a rainbow you change sex.'

— Elizabeth Bishop, the poet (as told to James Merrill).

*The fact of man's innate bisexual constitution is intuitively recognized by many cultures.*

099     G: There's a nurse on the ward that I'm very fond of, and I've always been very uncomfortable talking to her; and when I would talk to her and she would sit in my room and talk to me, I would notice that my penis was there. With the penis there, that makes it a healthier relationship. I can sit in my room with this nurse and know I'm not having homosexual feelings. I think she would be very appalled and disgusted and everything else if she thought I were having homosexual feelings for her. I am what I am. I'm somebody who sometimes likes women and sometimes doesn't; who sometimes likes men and sometimes doesn't; and who sometimes gets confused about who I am and what I am and sometimes gets scared about who I am and what I am. That's why sometimes I have a penis and sometimes I don't. Is that O.K. with you? What do you want? You tell me what I can give you that will please you, and I'll do that for you. —Splitting (A Case of Female Masculinity), Robert J. Stoller, M. D., Dell Publishing Co., Inc., New York, 1973, p. 25.

*Mrs. G illustrates the incredible lengths the conscious mind, or ego, will go to deny certain unpleasant realities, such as the fact that one has strong homosexual desires. To deny this obvious reality, Mrs. G has developed the psychotic delusion that she really does have a male penis hidden inside her vagina, thus proving to herself that she is not an ordinary homosexual woman. She would almost rather die than admit to that truth, and actually came close to doing just that during the course of her treatment with Dr. Stoller.*

100     G: Why worry about this one little thing? It's not hurting anybody. I'm not hurting anybody with it. And it's not hurting me. It's not a delusion. It's inside of me. This is something I've always known, and I've always felt; and it's there, and it's real, and it's mine; and you can't take it away from me, and neither can anybody else, so you might as well kiss my ass.
S: Does this penis ever show up in your daydreams?
G: How can it show up when it's really there? What are you talking about? You make it sound like it's a dream.
S: Have you ever had sexual daydreams in which you had a penis like a man?
G: No.
S: What's the matter?
G: Nothing.
S: Don't say 'nothing' to me.
G: You're just bugging me, that's all. I've told you all there is to know. [Shouting] I have this. I have it and I use it and I love it and I want it and I intend to keep it, and there's nothing you can do about it. It's mine. It makes me what I am.
     (Ibid., p. 15)

*Mrs. G fiercely defends her delusion rather than admitting she wishes she were a man so she could make love to women as a man would do, that is, with a penis. This is a case of Freudian "penis envy" carried to its ultimate psychotic resolution.*

101     In the Schreber case, Freud [14] described how the patient tried to deny his homosexual impulses by delusions and hallucinations. Something similar occurred with Mrs. G: she became psychotic, within moments, when other devices failed to protect her from her own accusation of being a

homosexual. Schreber's homosexuality was unacceptable to him also. Both Schreber and Mrs. G could consider sexual relations with a person of the same sex only if this were not 'homosexuality,' and both used transsexual delusion and hallucination to enable them to have such relations. (Ibid., p. 289)

*Here we see the direct connection between psychosis and repressed homosexuality. The psychosis serves to keep in check the conscious awareness of homosexual impulses, just as it also did in the Schreber case – and in all cases of functional psychosis.*

102    Moreover, she did not develop the complicated delusions we are used to seeing in schizophrenia, delusions that Schreber exemplifies. Instead, she would explode into a panic state, with confusion, terror, a buzzing, noisy hallucinosis (rather than clear-cut spoken language), poorly formed visual hallucinations such as blood pouring off the walls or black holes appearing in the streets, and an overpowering drive to kill herself. Except for the possibility that she might kill herself, the prognosis of her psychotic episodes was much better than in those of the typical schizophrenic reacting against her homosexuality.

When my relationship with Mrs. G had become strong enough, after several years of treatment, and when I understood her well enough, I began charging in upon the subject of homosexuality. For the first year or so, when I did this I could count on her becoming psychotic – sometimes right before my eyes, and sometimes after an hour or so, initially it would happen even if homosexuality was only implied, later, each time I stated unequivocally that she was homosexual. To what extent she gradually became 'used' to this subject because of growing insight, or because of growing familiarity with not being destroyed by the thought, I cannot say. It seems to have been a combination of both.[15] (Ibid., p. 290)

*One of the dangers in a psycho-analysis is that the analysand has the potential of becoming psychotic as a defense against dawning awareness of his or her homosexual tendencies.*

103   G: All the girls that I've had something to do with are going through my mind. They've all given me about the same thing – in different ways, I guess. You know, they give me warmth and peace and quiet. When I'm <u>with</u> a girl I don't think crazy – I don't think I think crazy, and it isn't necessary for me to be crazy. I don't need anything really, just that kind of nearness. I don't want to think that's a bad thing. I don't see how it can be bad.
S: I don't either. Will you ever have to go crazy because you love a woman?
G: I don't think so.
S: I think it's time that you be done with that, huh?
G: Yeah. Being crazy <u>after</u> being with a woman spoiled all the good things. You know when I ... like E, leaving her and vomiting all the way home. All the warmth and good feeling was just spoiled. It really isn't necessary to do that. I wonder why I thought it was necessary.
     (Ibid., p. 299)

*"Will you ever have to go crazy because you love a woman?" That simple question lays bare the core of all insanity in females, just as would the question "Will you ever have to go crazy because you love a man?" lays bare the core of all insanity in males. We have all heard the expression "I am crazy about him (her)," or "I am crazy in love with him (her)." That is where all "craziness" stems from, love. And when love is repressed or denied, because it is thought to be*

*perverted, unnatural, sinful, it can and does lead to "craziness," otherwise known as "schizophrenia."*

104    [16]There is an apocryphal story (told to me by Frederick G. Worden), of a ward set up for young, male, acute paranoid schizophrenics in which all the personnel were overt homosexuals: tender, overt homosexuality was encouraged among the patients and staff. The story is that the cure rate was high. (Ibid., p. 372)

*The cure for schizophrenics of any age, or either sex, no matter how acute their symptoms, is to cease repressing their powerful homosexual drives and to work through them both intellectually, emotionally and physically, either with the aid of fantasy or in actual homosexual experience. To be truly curative, both methods must lead to orgasmic discharge of the dammed-up homosexual excitation.*

105    On the other hand, the women we are now concerned with fully believe and openly state that they do have penises. This is bizarre. Yet, of the three patients of this kind I have seen, only one, Mrs. G, has had episodes of psychosis. The second has a borderline personality without such episodes, and the third is not even borderline. Psychotics of either sex frequently report either that parts of their bodies are changing sex or that they in their entirety, are changing sex or have done so. But Mrs. G always believed she had a penis, even when she was in remission. As we have seen, her description of her penis, which she felt as a physical object, was independent of her degree of contact with reality, presence or absence of hallucinations, confusion or clarity of thinking, or domination by primary – or secondary – process thinking. (Ibid., p. 390)

*Any woman who truly believes she has a penis is obviously psychotic. Dr. Stoller is wrong in saying that one* *such patient is only "borderline personality" and the other "not even borderline." A delusion is <u>always</u> a symptom of psychosis, and for any woman to sincerely believe she possesses a penis is irrefutable proof of the fact she is schizophrenic.*

106    A young man imagines that he is about to be married by the holiest father, even the Pope. He sees himself as being such an attractive young girl that no man can resist him. Having in this way warded off the incestuous possibilities with mother now perhaps mother will love him. Understanding this, I forbade the patient to marry anybody but me, but then continued, '*I want you to be my son.*' Almost a year later, when the patient's unconscious homosexuality came up in his analysis, he revealed this episode in the psychosis and remembered what a relief it was to him when, through me, he accepted himself for what he was, a male.

    Often female patients pull their hair out or cut their hair off as soon as they have an opportunity to do so. To these patients I denounce their act with fury, announcing that if they become a boy, I will hate them. As a man, I only love daughters. It is to be borne in mind that this does not complete the interpretation required for the girl who has snipped off her hair. I have to relate her act back to the mother in line with my understanding that if the patient is a boy, she will not be competing with her mother for her father, and then perhaps mother will love her.

    In both these instances I take a parental role and with considerable feeling deny that I want either the boy to be a girl or the girl to be a boy and instead that what they are is what I want. If they try to be anything different, I'll hate them, not love them. —<u>Direct Analysis (Selected Papers),</u> John N. Rosen, M. D., Grune & Stratton, New York, 1953, p. 15.

*This quotation is so straightforward it does not need much interpretation. Dr. Rosen clearly sees that bisexual conflict is at the root of his patients' problems, and he encourages them to accept themselves in their correct biological roles.*

107    He was told that there was no monster present, and reassurances were repeated. Thereupon, he burst into gales of laughter. 'She was a girl. She's a man now. The richest man in the world.'

The patient made the motor noise, and the physician shouted to him: *'You can't get away like that anymore. The plane doesn't work. It's broken.'* He replied: 'I love torture. No, I don't. Where is Uncle Ned?' The physician said: *'Here I am.'* 'You mean Ralph wants to fly a P-4. Let's go back. Quick. No. Ned, Ned. I'm not a woman. Where's Ned? He's gone.' The physician interrupted with: *'No, I'm here. I'm Uncle Ned.'* 'Where's Oscar? Can I kill him?' As this question was directed to the examiner, it was assumed that he recognized the latter as a person with authority and power, apparently the beginning of evidence of a positive transference. He continued, 'I don't want Rachel [his baby sister] in me.' At this point he made the motor noise which now seemed to be preponderantly a means of escape. When the material was of a threatening nature, he would use the motor noise to escape it. Here, apparently, he was struggling with the fantasy of being pregnant, an identification with his mother. This might be construed as a defense against passive homosexuality stimulated by the physician's assurance of love. (Ibid., p. 33)

*This young schizophrenic's bisexual conflict is very obvious. He fantasizes himself as being pregnant and then denies he is a woman. "I'm not a woman." His sexual confusion is further shown by his statement "She was a girl. She's a man now. The richest man in the world."*

108    As if in direct response to this request from the patient's unconscious, the man began: 'Do you mean about that woman? It was around 1926. We were on strike. One of the men took me home. These people were friendly with the trainman, who was a fag. We went to a masquerade fairy ball. I was introduced to a woman and we had a box. We looked down at the fairies dancing. I didn't dance with them. After this experience, my sickness got very much worse. Wherever I went in the street, people looked at me and said: 'That is a woman.' No matter where I went, even in other cities, it was the same thing. I never went even to another fairy ball.' Once at a doctor's office, he had a rectal examination for hemorrhoids. The rubber finger-cot broke, and he was seized with a pain that went from his rectum over his entire body. (Probably an orgasm.) At another time, while he was in 'some kind of a hospital,' he received an enema which resulted in the same kind of terrible pain. After this, he found that he couldn't see things. He thought that his eyes were out of focus. Again, he went to a hospital and they found that his vision was normal. (Ibid., p. 59)

    *This schizophrenic man clearly has very strong repressed homosexual cravings, centering around his passive anal eroticism.*

109    The patient's anger towards the physician mounted in subsequent visits. Each session was: 'Fuck yourself. Kiss my ass,' and so forth and so forth. He seemed constantly to refer to father taking mother from his bed. His fantasy-life was preoccupied with all kinds of thoughts of intercourse with his sister. During the next few days, he described himself as being hypnotized, and he was compelled to walk on his toes and shake from side to side. He was asked to demonstrate this walk for the physician. It was characteristic of theatrical demonstrations of a 'pansy.' He felt that crowds of people were

following him, jeering at him. *'The interpretation of this may be painful to you, but what it means is that you want to be a woman and you want to attract a man.'* 'I used to walk for years with my eyes almost shut. When I opened them again, the light actually hurt my eyes. I did it so that I should not see men.' *'Did men tempt you?'* 'I don't know.' *'What about the voice that told you to take men's pricks in your mouth?'* 'That came from me. I don't hear that anymore.' *'If your eyes were shut you couldn't see yourself either.'* 'I was ashamed. Tell him you want to suck his cock.' *'Who?'* 'You. A funny thing happened to me in 1928. The hair fell off my chest and never came back.' The physician examined the patient to verify this psychosomatic compliance. Although his body had more than the usual amount of hair – well distributed – his chest was smooth. (Ibid., p. 62)

*This patient reveals to us the etiology of the "voices," or auditory hallucinations, that plague schizophrenics, when he says, in answer to a question from Dr. Rosen about a particular voice which tells him to "take men's pricks" in his mouth, "That came from me. I don't hear that anymore." What the patient is admitting is he now realizes that the voice which told him to perform such an act is only a projection of his own wish to do exactly that. With this insight the patient is well on his way to recovery from his schizophrenia, for he has taken the first step in accepting reality – the reality of his own "perverse" homosexual cravings.*

110          Another example is the paranoid schizophrenic, whom I invited in the latter stages of his treatment to assist me in understanding the peculiar behavior of a catatonic patient. What was puzzling to me was the fact that when the catatonic patient was seated he showed hardly any anxiety. On arising, however, he presented a picture of increasing panic. He seemed to be searching for something. He gazed around the

room, looked in his pockets, pulled out his handkerchief, put it back again – all to the tune of increasing distress. I had made many interpretations to the effect that he thought he was castrated and was looking for his penis that had been sacrificed – and so on. None of these proved effective.

It took my paranoid patient to add the ingredient that solved the riddle. He told me:

'He is not worried that he has a penis or not while he is sitting down because when he is sitting down, he is a girl and that is the way girls do it. [Meaning urination]. When he stands up, he is doing it like a boy, but he is not sure that he is a boy and what he is searching for is the answer to this question.'

I felt that if this understanding were valid, my problem was to convince the patient that he was a man, that is, that he had a penis. I tackled it directly at the very next visit. When the patient stood up, I told him to put his hand on his penis and assisted him in this maneuver. As soon as he felt his penis, he was immediately reassured, and the diminution in anxiety was at once apparent. He ceased searching and followed me out of the waiting room with an evident lack of concern. This symptom did not recur. (Ibid., p. 74)

*The phrase "he is doing it like a boy, but he is not sure that he is a boy" sums up the psychological dilemma of all schizophrenic males. They act like males but they have such strong unconscious feminine identifications, usually with the mother, that their sense of masculinity is very precarious. Like the patient mentioned here, at the unconscious level they do not really know if they are male or female, homosexual or heterosexual.*

111     Another patient, a woman in her early forties referred to herself as 'the Holy Trinity.' Although this patient was raised in a very religious community where all forms of

sexuality were strictly forbidden to the 'good girls,' she exhibited herself to her brother and indulged in a good deal of homosexual play with a sister and niece. When she married, she was able to tolerate sexual relations with her husband only if she could imagine he was a negro. She gave birth to a daughter and was horrified to discover that she enjoyed handling the child's genitals. Her homosexual interest in her daughter provoked increasing anxiety and for many years she lived in fear that she would die of heart trouble or of some terrible disease. Doctors could find nothing wrong with her except an ulcer, which cleared up when she was put on a diet. She complained so much about her symptoms that her family finally took her to Mayo Clinic where her complaints were diagnosed as psychosomatic. Several months later she became psychotic.

When the ego can no longer properly defend itself, the unconscious homosexuality threatens to emerge. In the unconscious, homosexuality is the equivalent of castration because both conditions preclude the continuance of the stream of life. When this homosexual attitude takes over, it constitutes the threat of imminent biological death. At this point, in the case of the patient just mentioned, her *imaginations* gained the force of reality. She became the Holy Trinity, incorporating her masculinity, her femininity, and her child. She dealt with the instinctual drives that seemed to threaten her life, in a well-known paranoid manner, by saying that the tempting devil was responsible for all within herself that she felt to be evil. As the Holy Trinity, she was safe from the devil. (Ibid., p. 109)

*The denial and frustration of her strong homosexual nature has driven this woman insane, as is the case with all schizophrenic females.*

112          The schizophrenic wish to be reborn is nothing new. Girls often try to be reborn into boys. One of my patients said, 'Somebody sewed up my hole. I think the doctor did it when I had my baby and my pee comes out through a tube attached to my belly button.' This phenomenon is by no means limited to women patients. Men seek to become reborn as women, and, although I have had no such specific evidence as this in a male patient, I always find a homosexual fixation with the father figure as the object and the father's penis as the breast. (Ibid., p. 110)

          *Again we see an example of the severe bisexual confusion and conflict that rages in the mind of a schizophrenic patient.*

113          On the fifth day of therapy, I insisted for the first time that Joan stay in the treatment room with me. She stayed in the room but when I asked her to sit down on the couch, she gave no indication that she had heard me. She wandered about the room gaily examining my books and furniture. Then, spying a cigarette on the table, she picked it up. When I said, 'Drop the cigarette,' very firmly, she dropped it on the floor and made a dash for the door. I grabbed her, pulled her back in again, and forced her down on the couch. While I held her wrists, Joan squirmed, kicked, and wrestled violently. She kept up a continuous stream of productions which indicated she was fantasying enormous sexual experiences. The struggle lasted about half an hour, and I made no interpretations until she had quieted down from sheer exhaustion. Very often at the end of this type of struggle the patient seems closer to reality.

          P: See saw, Marjorie Daw. [Sings] Mother must get a new master.

          D: *Have you got one now?*

          P: Brother, you can say that again. Let him guess, he wants it. He threw it away, away, away. He threw it away,

away, away. A minute, a moment. Girl, he broke my bones. I gave it the candle. You put it out. But it's out. Out. Out. Briefnotes. Ooh, brief. Can this be brief? [Hums]

D: *Lie still and don't move.* [Patient lies on stomach and bounces up and down, groaning in the pillow.] <u>Stop it, Joan!</u>

P: They don't know when the lights are out. I don't know when anything can possibly be worth such a bunch of crap.

D: *Stay right where you are.*

P: I don't know where I am. I am a little son out of the cunt. A.K. A.K. Break it again. In and out, in and out. That's what we don't see. We don't see it. Look at her arm [Gasps] Help, help, help, help, help. Pee. Oh, wait brother, I have to pee. If not, on the floor. That's all obvious. Well, look how obvious that object is. Object. Who has to scratch it? Her cunt. Pee on the floor. On the floor. No, there is a dark well that doesn't come back. It doesn't come back. Nice little secretary, please. [Appeals to secretary in wheedling tone]

D: *She is only here to take notes.*

P: You must imagine. Oh – you don't know what you can imagine in the dark, when you are so sick in the dark.

D: *Are you going to lie still now or does the fight go on?*

P: Yes, of course, if you will let me go. It wasn't worth it, was it?

D: *No, it's better to lie down.*

P: Oh, rest. [Sighs] Where is that son? Where is that son?

D: *Put your head on the pillow.*

P: My head on the pillow.

D: *Come on. No more fucking. Lie down. Put your head down here. Pull your skirt down.*

(Ibid., p.110)

The age of the 'See-saw, Marjorie Daw' contains a whole world of discovery which includes the experience of early masturbation and the search for a more specific anatomic knowledge of the genitals.

'Oh, throw it away, away, away,' could be a castration wish. 'I gave it the candle,' is a description of a well-known masturbatory experience. The birth concept of the Marjorie Daw child results in what the patient soon talks about: i.e. 'A bunch of crap,' which is herself being born. And then she states, 'I don't know where I am. I am a little son out of the cunt.' 'I am a little son ...' clearly indicates that *her wish has gained the force of reality*, and she now thinks of herself as a boy. (Ibid., p. 114)

Her psychotic productions became less irrelevant and now related mainly to her lack of a penis and her confusion regarding her sex. She still spent a great deal of time acting out birth fantasies. I interpreted her symbolic remarks and acts and constantly affirmed her femininity by calling attention to all her attractive feminine qualities, even insisting that her female genitals were far more useful and desirable than a male's. On the twelfth day of treatment, she giggled and said, 'Gee, I think I am a lady, sir. That feels swell. Did we cut them deep in the groove?' I replied, *'Deep in the groove is your vagina. You have discovered that you are a woman.'*

The next day, when she was all dressed up, Joan asked me if I didn't think she looked nice. Since she was calling my attention to her feminine attractions, I felt it was important to make a direct analytic response which would emphasize the desirability of being a woman rather than a man. *'Imagine how sad it would be if you didn't have your beautiful vagina. Your vagina has great value. It produced your two children. That's something wonderful that could happen only inside of your wonderful body. How I wish I could make a baby inside of my body.'*

I could tell that Joan was impressed with my evaluation of her femininity, because from that moment on she ceased to give me the impression of clumsiness and heaviness. (Ibid., p. 115)

*It is of clinical interest that the patient ceases to give "the impression of clumsiness and heaviness" as she begins to accept her femaleness.*

114    P: Yes sir. So the eyes in the family is brown eyes. As I said I felt this uncertainty after the war, the more I felt the uncertainty, the more I told myself that it wasn't so. I kicked the uncertainty out. So we're in Boston and life remains pretty tough. It becomes more insecure all the time. So I meet a young lady, she has blue eyes, she has my mannerisms and my own expressions, at the same time, before or while I met her someone was plotting to me in my sleep.

   R: <u>Was that a dream</u>?

   P: Oh no, this was fact  ...  and she was saying the same things that were being said to me in my unconscious mind or some of the things anyway.

   (Ibid., p. 159)

   P: Yes, that's true, that's quite true, that's different. I know that. I know I'm in a turmoil, my emotions are gone, I said my mind isn't my own. My emotions are all gone anyway. Thinking like a woman, talking like a woman. [To make a homosexual interpretation at this time would be a serious error.]

   R: *You said this woman had your characteristics.*

   P: Some of them  ...  yeah.

   R: *Well that means you had some of her characteristics.*

   (Ibid., p. 161)

I hated my mother, but I felt sorry for her. So this time I thought I was subconsciously in love with the father and kept thinking about a father and the father's penis and something like that the way the Freudians put it. So subconsciously it was this love for the fatherly penis that when I met this blue-eyed vixen it enabled me to be completely by empathy, be myself in herself, her in me, she appeared sexual gratification, psychosexual gratification, by the father's penis, is that how you put it?

R: *Be damned if I know what you're talking about.*

P: You know damned well what I'm talking about.

R: *Sounds awfully crazy to me. But I don't know ... I suppose there are some men who are homosexuals, I don't think you are, are you?*

P: Not that I know of, I don't know, I don't think so ... could be, could be.

(Ibid., p. 162)


P: I have been afraid of being psychically empty here. I have been afraid of emptying my mind psychically and someone would knock me on the head and give me amnesia and there wouldn't be anything left at all.

R: Oblivion? That won't happen. I know too much about your kind of case. You won't find oblivion, that's not the way out ... . The only hope of your recovery is for you to gain a real understanding of this whole mess.

P: Help me get an understanding then.

R: I wish I were up here, I would.

P: Well, how do I get an understanding?

R: There are other doctors here, perfectly well qualified to help you.

P: How am I getting better just sitting in the ward walking back and forth, having everybody gesticulating, sticking a penis up my ass?

(Ibid., p. 172)

*Dr. Rosen is trying to dissuade this patient from accepting his powerful homosexual cravings, when in reality such acceptance is the patient's only hope of escape from his schizophrenia.*

115      The patient was a young man who had excelled in athletics, particularly basketball prior to the outbreak of his psychosis. In his illness he manifested strong fear of outwardly direct aggression, feminine phantasies and serious doubt about his masculinity. —<u>A Psychotherapy of Schizophrenia: Direct Analysis</u>, Albert E. Scheflen, M. D., Charles C. Thomas, Publishers, Springfield, Illinois, 1961, p. 97.

*When mothers, or other caretakers, discourage young males' natural aggressiveness, the feminine side of their psyches becomes overly stimulated, leading to future bisexual conflict with consequent emotional disturbance.*

116      One patient evidenced panic when he became increasingly aware of his strong dependency upon Rosen and revealed homosexual phantasies of the relationship. The patient insisted that he be allowed to go to Florida. The trip was permitted and he drove there with little money and a host of delusions. He called almost daily, describing strong paranoid trends but felt reassured after talking with Rosen. He returned two weeks later much improved. (Ibid., p. 118)

*The "paranoid trends" this patient was experiencing were the direct result of the repressed homosexuality which was just beginning to emerge into the patient's awareness through phantasies directed towards Dr. Rosen.*

117          For several weeks this young male patient had had a delusion that his hands looked like those of a woman. (Ibid., p. 153)

          *Again we see the "bearded lady" syndrome in schizophrenia.*

118          His predominant anxieties were his fear of losing himself and me, and his difficulty in differentiating between himself and me, between reality and phantasy, and also between inside and outside. He talked about his fear of losing and having lost his penis: 'Somebody has taken the fork away;' 'Silly woman.' He was preoccupied with being a woman, and he had a wish to be re-born a girl: [1] '*Prince* Ann.' By analyzing material like 'The Virgin Mary was killed,' or 'One half was eaten,' [2] and 'Bib (penis) was killed,' we began to realize that he attributed his dangerous, murderous feelings against his mother, and against women in general, to his male half and his penis. We also understood that his fantasies of being a woman were greatly reinforced by his desire to get rid of his aggression. When he began to understand this method of dealing with his aggression, his wish to be a woman lessened and he became more aggressive.  —Psychotic States (A Psycho-Analytical Approach), Herbert A. Rosenfeld, International Universities Press, New York, 1966, p. 78.

          *Here we see the connection between the denial of natural aggressiveness in males and the consequent stimulation of their femininity, which, when subsequently repressed, leads to emotional disturbance up to and including schizophrenia.*

119          During the next session the patient talked about her mother as a murderess from Russia who had killed many people. She herself was also a murderer. She said she was very clever and

I was stupid and empty-headed. She stressed again that her mother was a man. I said that she wanted to show me that she now was a man herself and had a penis. She responded very quickly 'Yes, I had one until I was twelve years old and then I had a haemorrhage. Harold shot me and pushed my teeth in.' She immediately asked me whether I was Harold. I said she believed that Harold had taken away her penis and made her ill and she felt now that I was Harold and had taken away her penis and her mind. I also interpreted that she was envious of me and my mind and that was the reason why she wanted to enter my head and wanted to take away my penis. In this session she shouted at me several times that I was mad and prevented me from talking. (Ibid., p. 163)

*When this patient "stressed again that her mother was a man," she was being psychologically very discerning, as the mothers of all schizophrenic women have strong masculine drives themselves, otherwise their daughters would not have become embroiled in severe bisexual conflict and sexual identity problems, which form the bedrock of schizophrenia.*

120              During the next session the patient was at first manically excited and danced around the room. She declared she wanted to marry me, examined my hand, saw my ring, became furious and shouted that she hated me and my wife. Then she became manic again and very superior and said she was now a doctor of medicine and a man. In her manic excitement she had reversed the situation, in an omnipotent way; however, the manic state did not last long. She quickly became aware of her dependence on me, was overwhelmed by fury, and attempted to destroy the furniture in the room. At the same time she shouted that she wanted to break up marriages. (Ibid., p. 164)

             . . . During the next day she at first did not want to look at me. She said, 'I don't love you, I myself am married and I love somebody else, I am Hitler and hate the Jews.' In one moment she said she wanted to break in my face; afterwards she tried to tear her own dress. Later on she said, 'Kill me and rape me; I do not want to live any more.'

. . . During the next few months many fantasies and situations were repeated in the transference. Sometimes she complained that I visited her during the night. These nightly hallucinations often had a sadistic and persecuting character. She sometimes expressed delusions of being split into a masculine and feminine self. She called her masculine part after the musical play 'Annie Get Your Gun.' Her omnipotent manic impulses and fantasies were often related to this masculine self as an expression of her independence and denial of needs. When she was in the feminine role she often said she was full of blood and spiders and attacked her abdomen in order to press all the bad things out. Sometimes she tried to cut off her breasts or to damage them. She said they were full of blood and I should suck the blood out of them. The bad things which she experienced inside herself were, among others, a stolen penis, blood, children and the breasts of her mother, which she felt she had stolen and spoilt in her fantasies. This made it impossible for her to identify with her good mother and to accept her own femininity. As I explained before, the patient was unable in the chronic mute state of the illness to bear a strong sexual transference to me and acted it out. In the acute state it became apparent why her sexual impulses and fantasies were so unbearable: they were accompanied by overwhelmingly strong murderous sadistic fantasies. (Ibid., p. 165)

*This patient is obviously suffering from severe bisexual conflict, not knowing from one minute to the next whether she is male or female.*

121    When the patient ate, she thought that her figure altered and
       increased in size and that her breasts became larger. She then
       wanted to destroy her body and tear off her breasts. The
       alcohol addiction seemed to follow these anxieties and
       impulses. The author believes that in this case there was a
       psychotic paranoid hatred of women, which was related to the
       patient's violent hatred of her own body and the rejection of
       her femininity. She thinks that the driving force behind the
       urge was the annihilation of femininity or the need to ward off
       repressed homosexual impulses. (Ibid., p. 233)

           *This patient's "psychotic paranoid hatred of women"*
       *was a projective defense against her repressed homosexual*
       *cravings directed towards them. Her hatred of her femininity*
       *resulted from her unconscious wishes to be a man.*

122    Another patient dreamed of being 'grafted on to another
       person.' The 40-year-old male patient said: 'Why should I be
       on bad terms with my sister? After all I am my sister,' and then
       started in some surprise at what he had heard himself say. A
       young married woman struggling to master a blind compulsive
       longing for a male relative she played with as a child, said:
       'I've always felt he's me and I'm him. I felt a terrible need to
       fuss around him and do everything for him. I want him to be
       touching me all the time. I feel there is no difference between
       him and me.' —Schizoid Phenomena, Object-Relations, and
       the Self, Harry Guntrip, International Universities Press, Inc.,
       New York, 1969, p. 40.

           *These are more examples of the sexual confusion*
       *which is always to be found in schizophrenia.*

123        In the case Winnicot examines he says: 'There was a
       dissociation [of the opposite sexual element] that was on the
       point of breaking down. The dissociation defence was giving

way to an acceptance of bisexuality as a quality of the unit or total self ... I was dealing with what could be called *a pure female element* [i.e. in a male].'

He adds: 'In our theory it is necessary to allow for both a male and a female element in boys and men and girls and women. These elements may be split off to a high degree ... I wish to compare and contrast the unalloyed male and female elements in the contexts of object-relating.' (Ibid., p. 252)

*Every male has "a pure feminine element" in him, just as every female has a pure male element in her. When these opposite-sexed elements become more powerful than they naturally should be, due to noxious societal (parental) influences, the affected person either becomes homosexual, or, if these feelings are repressed (dissociated), emotionally disturbed (schizophrenic).*

124 Thus a female patient, a spinster in her early fifties, when anxiously depressed, or when she felt she was being 'made into nothing' at work by coercion or undervaluation, would fly into violent rages to master her fears, and scream out: 'I'm not a woman, I'm a man, a man. They cut off my penis and left me with a filthy hole.' It emerged that this 'hole' symbolized her pathological version of the female element, a sense not only of her weakness but of her sense of 'non-being,' of there being nothing there, an emptiness at the heart of her. (Ibid., p. 256)

*Each neurotic or psychotic woman feels somewhere deep in her unconscious that "they" have cut off her penis and left her with "a filthy hole." In this particular patient, it is her lack of a penis and her possession of an abhorred vagina which form the core of her feeling that there is "an emptiness at the heart of her."*

125          Concurrently, he devalued Drs. Clark and Gibson and
tried to avoid them. He would say, 'Go away. I'm too busy
writing to Lt. Grant to see you.' He accused the doctors of
wanting to kill him, of having sexual interests in him and in
each other, and of being women who pretended to be men. He
complained that Dr. Gibson was dominated by the charge
nurse, and said, 'She's more of a man than you are.'   —
Schizophrenia and the Need-Fear Dilemma, Donald L.
Burnham,   Arthur   I.   Gladstone,   Robert   W.   Gibson,
International Universities Press, Inc., New York, 1969, p. 127.

        *In accusing his doctors of having "sexual interests" in
him, this patient is making the paranoid projection onto the
doctors of his own homosexual interests in them. And in
saying that the charge nurse was "more of a man than" the
doctor, the patient is intuitively recognizing and commenting
on the nurse's strong masculine component.*

126     He   was   similarly   jealous   of   Dr.   Clark's   other   patients,
particularly an older man who had been the doctor's patient
longer than himself. He accused this man and Dr. Clark of
having a sexual relationship.
        Another bout of jealousy was set off when Dr. Gibson
became the psychotherapist of Frank Sacco, another Third
Floor   patient,   whose   severe   autism   and   limited   verbal
communicative   capacity   called   for   therapy   tactics   which
included   play   and   physical   contact.   Glen   expressed   his
jealousy of Frank to one of the aides: 'Do you like Frank better
than me?' To another he said, 'I don't bother you by asking you
to go for a walk with me. Mrs. (sic) Sacco has already
bothered you enough by his hollering.' (Ibid., p. 144)

        *Again we see the paranoid projection of the patient's
own repressed homosexual cravings onto the doctor and
another patient. He then calls another male patient "Mrs.," a*

*title which could very well apply to his own unconscious image of himself.*

127    His bitter complaints about overprotection were counterbalanced by conscious wishes for guidance and regulation by others, as in his stating, 'I feel more my real self when someone gives me clear, strict orders.'

Dan's belief that others literally determined who he was far exceeded normal need for identity confirmation. He said, 'I have a true self and a phony self, and others determine which one I am at any particular time.' This included whether he was man or boy, male or female, and strong or weak, as if these identity elements were fed into him from the outside. He said that rough or insulting responses made him feel more real and manly because they demonstrated that he had no need or wish to be tenderly handled or to return to the sheltered existence of a little boy. (Ibid., p. 182)

Dan was further troubled by his father's inconsistencies, such as dressing impeccably in public but sloppily at home, and proclaiming the ideals of strength and self-determination while deferring to his mother-in-law as the head of the family. Adding to Dan's confusion about masculine and feminine roles was his observation that his father indulged and protected his mother in a manner that Dan envied and desired for himself. (Ibid., p. 188)

*Dan's confusion about his sexual identity is glaringly obvious. The fact his father defers to his mother-in-law as head of the family demonstrates the father's own lack of confidence in his masculinity, a trait invariably to be found in the fathers of schizophrenic children of either sex. For children to grow up to have confidence in their biological sexual roles, they need to identify with parents who are comfortable and happy in their own sexuality. The parents of schizophrenic children invariably show evidence of insecurity and dissatisfaction in this vital area.*

128          He continued manifold expressions of need toward Dr. Hein. For a time these included undisguised sexual overtures and attempts to embrace the doctor, who, after trying gentle dissuasion, finally quite brusquely repulsed these advances. With a hurt, hangdog look, Alberto responded, 'You needn't be so nasty about it.' Thereafter his sexual overtures were rare, and usually he would stop himself, often by saying, 'I guess I smell bad; I need a bath.' (Ibid., p. 208)

*Alberto's powerful homosexual cravings have begun to surface in his transference relationship with Dr. Hein. Once he is consciously able to acknowledge these "perverse" feelings, he will no longer be "schizophrenic," since basically schizophrenia is <u>the negation of</u> homosexuality.*

129     At home he repeatedly asked his father to pray with him. Harvey asked his father whether he (Harvey) had had any kind of accident or illness as a child which might have caused the confused feelings he was experiencing. He also said or did something which the father interpreted as a homosexual advance, and which shocked him violently.
          The following day Harvey was admitted to a sanitarium in his home town. During an evaluation interview held a week or so earlier with Dr. Wallis, a psychiatrist at the sanitarium, Harvey had described an organized ring of homosexuals who were trying to influence him. He believed that the ring included social acquaintances and the bartender at his club, and used an elaborate system of hand signals to communicate. When Dr. Wallis had told Harvey that he needed psychiatric hospitalization, Harvey had become angry and stalked out of the office. (Ibid., p. 223)

> *Harvey's paranoia is fueled by his repressed homosexual feelings.*

130    Sarah had become emotionally upset at examination time and had experienced some delusional ideas, such as being the counterpart of Jesus Christ and receiving undeserved help from others. She never told her parents about this experience. (Ibid., p. 242)

> *Sarah's delusion that she is the "counterpart of Jesus Christ" means she has now identified herself as a Christ-like <u>man</u>, thus fulfilling her unconscious wishes to be male.*

131    During his period of identity diffusion, Pete expressed grave uncertainty regarding his sexual identity. He feared that he was being changed into a woman. In rapid sequence during the same day he made a clumsy effort to rape a woman activities worker to whom he had become quite attached and whom he occasionally had addressed as 'Mother,' and a frightened venture into homosexual play with Tom. He also occasionally brushed against his therapist in a vaguely sexually suggestive manner. His uncertainty about sexual identity undoubtedly was associated with conflicts of activity versus passivity, and dominance versus submission. Many of his attacks on others seemed prompted by a desperate urge to break out from the mire of passivity and to assert manliness. (Ibid., p. 348)

> *Pete is another obvious victim of the "bearded lady" disease.*

132    A few weeks after his return to duty, John began to act peculiarly. He stared fixedly at the post nurses and was convinced of their sexual interest in him. At the same time he startled his commanding officer by the question, 'Are you a

woman? Are you what you think you are?' Hospitalization
followed shortly with a diagnosis of paranoid schizophrenia.
Hallucinated voices accused him of weakness, homosexuality,
and failure. He attempted to hang himself. His uncertainty
regarding the masculine-feminine component of his identity
was strikingly indicated by his hearing voices which classified
his gender after each of his actions. Because his every
movement was followed by the hallucinated comment, 'That's
a man' or 'That's a woman,' he felt that his slightest gesture
might alter the judgment of his sexual identity. (Ibid., p. 360)

    … A further gross contradiction of John's assertion of
a strong masculine identity was evidenced in his periodic open
statements that he wished to be transformed into a woman. He
said that women have a better life than men and occupy a
position of dominance over everything. Somewhat
incoherently he described having attempted between
hospitalizations at the Lodge to transform himself by
consuming huge quantities of cream and other soft, fattening,
and to John, feminizing foods. He had also purchased a large
supply of soft pencils with which to 'scratch the muscle fibers
to make them female.' The wish to change to a woman was
mixed in varying proportions with a fear of such a change. It
might be noted parenthetically that in the subsequent course of
John's illness the wish gradually predominated over the fear.
He seemed progressively to abandon his struggle to achieve a
masculine identity patterned after his father and instead to
helplessly accept identification with his sick mother.
Increasingly his behavior resembles that of his mother in her
illness 17 years before, especially in the features of helpless
passivity and retreat to bed. (Ibid., p. 363)

    *John is another obvious victim of the "bearded lady"
disease.*

133    From the beginning of the illness, patients may seem suspicious and bound to misinterpret things and events in a way derogatory to themselves. The underlying feeling about oneself is immediately lost and transformed into a symptomatology where <u>projection</u> occurs (that is, attributing to others a negative feeling about the patient). For instance, a patient may consider himself clumsy and ridiculously inadequate. He develops the impression that people are laughing at him. The impression soon becomes certainty. He is sure they think he is no good and inadequate. But to be no good and inadequate means to be homosexual. That is why they refer to him as 'she.' The patient, for instance, heard co-workers saying, 'She is not doing her work as she should.' They used the word <u>she</u> because they think the patient is not a man.   —<u>Interpretation of Schizophrenia</u>, Silvano Arieti, M. D., Basic Books, Inc., New York, $2^{nd}$ ed., 1974, p. 35

*This patient is another obvious victim of the "bearded lady" disease.*

134    The delusion of being Moses occurs in both male and female Jewish patients. (Ibid., p. 36)

*For a female to believe she is Moses is for her to believe she is a man, which unconsciously is what she would like to be in reality.*

135    As many authors have described, quite often the preschizophrenic child has also some indecision as to what his sex is going to be . . . In children who tend to become schizophrenic in adult life, the uncertainty about sexuality is of a different nature. It concerns the sex and gender identity. Some of these children do not know what their sex is going to be. Although they know that they are boys or girls, they are not sure that they will maintain their sex throughout their

lives. Boys may lose a penis. Girls may grow one. Although even normal children or children who later develop less serious psychiatric conditions occasionally have these thoughts, in the preschizophrenic they assume the form of serious and disturbing doubt. In many cases the doubts are related to the fact that children somehow connect a sense of hostility coming from others with their belonging to a given sex. If they were girls instead of boys, or boys instead of girls, they think their parents would be more pleased with them. If the most disturbing parent is of the opposite sex, the child would like to be of the same sex as this parent, so that he could resist him or her better. (Ibid., p. 92)

*More proof of the fact that schizophrenia results from confused gender identity resulting in severe bisexual conflict.*

136    The child will have difficulties in identifying with the significant adults. Nevertheless he will be able to build up some kind of less undesirable self-image, including identification with one sex rather than the other. Sexual confusion or homosexual tendencies are repressed, and the child's identification with his own sex is achieved. However, this patched-up self-image and these identifications are not deeply rooted in the core of his being. They are more superficial reflections of how he feels people deal with him, rather than a well-integrated vision of the self. (Ibid., p. 101)

*In today's society it is the norm rather than the exception for a person to be repressing some sexual confusion with attendant homosexual tendencies. This person is labelled "neurotic." It is only when the repressed sexual confusion is of a more severe nature that the person comes to be labelled "schizophrenic." A healthy, mature individual would be one who has a "well-integrated vision" of the self, that is, of his correct biological sexual identity and that this sexual identity* is *"deeply rooted in the core of his being" and is not dependent on "superficial reflections of how he feels people deal with him."*

137   The child who develops a stormy personality has a greater difficulty in preserving a sense of self than does the schizoid person. Like the child who develops a schizoid personality, he could not properly identify with either of his parents, and his sex and gender identity were in many cases not well defined. (Ibid., p. 107)

*Here we see that both so-called "stormy" and "schizoid" personalities are linked to bisexual conflict and confusion. In fact, all emotional disturbance is linked to this same pathogen.*

138   We have already mentioned that one of the most common sexual difficulties consists of the inability on the part of the future schizophrenic to establish a definite and stable sexual identity. Although the occurrence of this difficulty cannot be evaluated statistically with accuracy, I would roughly estimate that it is one of the most common, if not the most common.

   In the second period of development, as described in chapter 6, the young individual succeeded in hiding the sexual uncertainty transmitted from the first period and reached some kind of sexual identity; but, as we have already mentioned, this identity was not deeply grounded and was later easily shaken by the events of life. The unfavorable dealings with the world reinforce in the patient the feeling that he or she is not really a man or a woman. He sees himself in an ambiguous position.*

   *After the onset of the psychosis, this lack of definite sexual identity becomes manifest in the overt schizophrenic symptomatology. The different gender identity that the patient may assume and his drawings of human figures with characteristics of both sexes are expressions of this psychosexual conflict. (Ibid., p. 117)

*The author of this quotation should have said that "the inability on the part of the future schizophrenic to establish a definite and stable sexual identity" is not just "one of the most common difficulties" of the future schizophrenic, but in fact is the <u>invariable cause</u> of schizophrenia.*

139    Things are often seen as a composite of A and B. For instance, in schizophrenic drawings one often sees a human figure who is half man and half woman. The person represented in the drawing may be conceived by the schizophrenic as having a characteristic of the opposite sex. Also the emotional difficulty the schizophrenic has in identifying himself with one sex may be revealed formally by his nonadherence to the third law of thought. (Ibid., p. 238)

*Again, the "bearded lady" syndrome in schizophrenia is firmly emphasized. However, the author's reference to the "third law of thought" is unclear to the compiler of these quotations.*

140    In many cases the self-mutilating act has a more specific symbolic meaning. Castrations play a prominent role (Hemphill, 1951). By cutting, or burning, or injuring in any way the arms, legs, fingers, toes, penis, and testicles, often male patients want to castrate themselves in order to punish themselves or because 'they prefer to belong to the other sex.' (Ibid., p. 308)

*The fact a schizophrenic patient would actually castrate himself demonstrates the depth of his unconscious hatred for and dissatisfaction with his masculine sexual identity.*

141    It is common clinical experience to treat schizophrenic patients who have distorted ideas about their own bodies. The face is the most common cause of complaint and preoccupation. A 23-year-old girl described her experience as follows: 'I look at myself in the mirror, and it is not really me that I see. I don't have any definite image of myself, but many different ones, all of them horrible to me. I look like a man.' She demanded that plastic surgery be done on her. (Ibid., p. 328)

   *This patient unconsciously feels like a man and perceives herself as such when she looks in the mirror.*

142         Some authors (for instance, Meth, 1974) have reported among Chinese and Indonesians a phobic condition called <u>Koro</u>. The patient becomes fearful that his penis will disappear into his abdomen and he will die. I have seen in schizophrenics a related delusion (that the penis or testicles have already entered into the abdomen), at times because of some medical treatment allegedly received from unscrupulous doctors. The patient is not afraid to die but to lose his masculinity. Generally the patient with this or similar delusions is afraid of being homosexual, or of being considered homosexual, of having lost his potency. (Ibid., p. 331)

   *This "phobic" condition called "<u>Koro</u>" is but another name for the so-called "homosexual panic" that many schizophrenics, of both sexes, experience during the course of their illness. In Freud's famous Schreber case, Daniel Paul Schreber experienced similar delusions that his penis was disappearing into his abdomen and that he was becoming a* *woman, which, of course, was his fondest unconscious wish and the source of his mental illness, as it is also in all victims of "Koro."*

143          Lucille portrayed also a desire to escape into a fairy-tale world different from her reality. In Figure 16, castle and ships, friendly waves, sirens, and moons are put together to signify a world without anxiety, a place where we too, like the girl on the ship, would like to land. But the patient did not land there. Figure 17, made at the beginning of the illness, portrays already the patient's conflict. Woman is the protagonist. The theatrical setting discloses the drama of woman, as lived by the patient. Woman appears in various poses that reveal grace and beauty in the majesty of the stage of life. But let us look at the two couples in the center of the picture. Strangely, each couple does not consist of a woman and a man, but of two women: one more energetic, not fully dressed, and another one typically feminine in a beautiful evening gown.

          The illness progresses, as shown by Figure 18. Here athletic women have incongruously masculine physical characteristics. Now the desire to be a man can no longer be repressed by the patient, who has tried to fight her own homosexuality. At this point Lucille ceases to be an artist and becomes a schizophrenic patient. (Ibid., p. 359)

          *The formula for schizophrenia is this: "Now the desire to be a man (woman) can no longer be repressed by the patient, who has tried to fight his (her) own homosexuality. At this point [name] ceases to be a [occupation] and becomes a schizophrenic patient."*

144          To some patients who injure themselves to substitute a physical pain for an emotional one, we may say, 'You want to hurt yourself to remove your anguish. If we talk about it, we share the pain; the pain will decrease.' This explanation has to

be given with some cautiousness because self-injury is not always an attempted concretization of mental pain or a way to make the pain 'more real.' At other times it is exclusively or predominantly an expression of need for punishment or a way to achieve change in gender or to inflict bodily disfigurations that have a symbolic meaning. (Ibid., p. 579)

*The extreme self-injury is suicide, which has been called, with good reason, the most serious syndrome of schizophrenia. It could be said that suicide is the ultimate castration, and is only performed by those who hate their genitals and wish to be of the opposite sex, even though this wish has been repressed and is unconscious.*

145        While she was being taken by car to the hospital, she knew that she was going to be committed but felt that her mother, not she, was insane. As John drove, she saw him as a mad monster, a hollow shell of a man whose voice reverberated eerily in his empty skull, a mindless automaton. The first few days that she was in the hospital she felt she had died; as a matter of fact, one day she heard 'the ruffled drums of a large military funeral in her honor.' Lifting her hand, she waved to her admirers....

One night, while she was locked in her cell, she stood at the window with her arms raised to make herself a target, shaped like a cross. She began to think of herself as a Christ, sacrificing herself for others, particularly for her mother and John. (Ibid., p. 625)

While, from the window of her cell, she was looking at the bushes that surrounded the hospital, she believed that some soldiers were hiding behind the bushes, ready to free her because she was their leader. (Ibid., p. 628)

*This patient's desire to be a man is shown by her identification with Christ and by her identification as a leader of troops.*

146     The patient appeared apathetic, withdrawn, and could not even express his delusions. Occasionally, however, he would make remarks that were very revealing. He could not look people in the eyes because they would find out things of which he was ashamed. He felt he could not get along with people in the hospital; they would laugh at him or make unpleasant remarks about him. They would refer to him as a 'she,' not 'he.' At times they were saying what he was thinking. (Ibid., p. 638)

*This patient's deep-seated sexual confusion is apparent from his concern that people would refer to him as a "she" rather than a "he."*

147     One procedure employed in exploring this area involves the matching of abstract figures with personal names. If elongated and pointed figures are matched with male names and rounded or containing figures with female names, sexual symbolism is said to be demonstrated. In studies by Starer (120) and Jones (121), there were associations of figures and names as predicted. Normals assessed the figures more 'accurately' than the patients, most of whom were schizophrenics. This could be interpreted as evidence of inadequate social learning, or a deficit in abstract thinking could be emphasized as the basis of the performance. Starer makes the comment that greater clinical severity of psychosis is correlated with less success in this symbolism test.  —"Some Psychological Studies of Schizophrenics," C. L. Winder (in The Etiology of Schizophrenia, edited by Don D. Jackson, M. D., Basic Books, Inc., New York, 1960, p. 217).

*The reason the schizophrenics did not assess the male and female symbolic figures more accurately is because they are so deeply confused about their own sexual identities.*

148    In each family at least one parent suffered from serious and crippling psychopathology, and in many both were markedly disturbed. Although none of these parents had ever been in a mental hospital, at least 10 of the 16 families contained a parent who was an ambulatory schizophrenic or clearly paranoid, and our diagnostic cut-off point was arbitrary and conservative. Still others were chronic alcoholics, severe obsessives, or so extremely passive-dependent that they were virtually children of their spouses rather than another parent. Many parents constantly required support for their tottering narcissism that could not be gained from the spouse, and they chronically distorted situations to maintain their self-image and the single, narrow way of life that constituted their adjustment. Insecurity and confusion concerning sexual identity, often with fairly obvious homosexual trends, were common, and many of these parents had difficulty in controlling their incestuous impulses, both heterosexual and homosexual. —"Schizophrenia, Human Integration, and the Role of the Family," Theodore Lidz and Stephen Fleck, (in The Etiology of Schizophrenia, edited by Don D. Jackson, M. D., Ibid., p. 333).

*This is probably the most accurate description of the schizophrenogenic parental constellation that has ever been produced by any investigators. As Lidz and Fleck so clearly show, the parents of schizophrenics have serious disturbances of their own with regard to their sexual identities, which insecurity is markedly magnified in their offspring, leading to the development of schizophrenic symptomatology.*

149     The family member who becomes the patient may exhibit more distorted communication, and, in his behavior, more irrationality than do his siblings or parents. But it is the parents who chronically distorted meanings and communications to defend a precarious equilibrium, either within one of them, or within the marriage, or within the family, or in all three spheres, providing, in a sense, training in irrationality.

Confusion of sexual identity is common among the patients, noted particularly in homosexual trends and fears and in delusions of impending change of sex. The parents also suffer from faulty sexual identity, often with apparent latent homosexual tendencies and with some degree of reversal of sex-linked social and parental roles. The parent of the same sex as the patient rarely provided an adequate model for identification; and, even if he could have done so, the worth of this parent as man or woman, husband or wife, father or mother often was seriously undercut by the spouse. Patients' needs to seek to fill the emotional needs of a parent in crossed sexual or asexual ways compounded the difficulties. (Ibid., Lidz and Fleck, p. 340)

*Lidz and Fleck again emphasize the role the parents' own sexual confusion plays in creating an even more severe state of sexual identity confusion in their children who become schizophrenic.*

150     Observation 6. Age 28, eighth grade, public school education, and was considered to be a quiet, peaceable person of good habits making a satisfactory adjustment in the community until her present age. She suddenly became active, loud, boisterous, sang and talked, misidentified strangers as relatives and friends, and made extravagant claims. At the hospital she promised the doctors and nurses large sums of money, showed flight of ideas with distractibility, and was

profane and obscene. At times she was depressed and had visual hallucinations of persons being in the room, and thought that the women patients on the ward were men in disguise. —Research in Dementia Praecox, Nolan D. C. Lewis, M. D., Northern Masonic Jurisdiction of the Scottish Rite, 1936, p. 217.

*Here we see yet another example of severe sexual confusion in a schizophrenic patient, who thought that women patients on her ward were men in disguise. This patient had been behaving in a normal female manner when suddenly her personality changed and she became "active, loud, boisterous," etc. In other words, she started acting in a very "unfeminine" manner. The cause of this change was a strong masculine identification, which previously had been repressed but which had now broken through this repression and was asserting itself by causing her to act in a masculine, aggressive fashion.*

151         *Observation 1.* Age 71 years, no formal education, was married several times. Was said to have been 'queer' for a number of years, and for past 10 or 12 years had had periodic spells of praying and singing excessively. In her 60's she was hospitalized for two months, and discharged as improved from paranoid condition. During this period she was hallucinated as to voices and also thought gas had been pumped into her house for purposes of persecution. At the time of her last admission, elation and grandiosity were predominating with pressure of speech, utilizing an extensive but incorrect vocabulary. She had persecutory delusions, thinking her sister had attempted to murder her, and that someone was trying to poison her with paris green. She was keen minded, emotionally active, and for a period of time went about with a powder can tied in her pocket in the position of a penis, which she tried to use on other patients. Later she patted her own

abdomen and stated 'there is no little baby in there. There is no p--- – there. There was a little p--- – there once, but my brother cut it off, and didn't take proper care of it, so it grew inwardly and that is what is in there now.' (Ibid., p. 222)

*This patient's wish to be a man is glaringly obvious. She is using her powder-can "penis" as a replacement for the penis she believes she once had but which was cut off by her brother and is now inside her stomach. Her homosexuality is also very apparent, in that she tries to use her new-found penis on other female patients.*

152     Patient was rather poorly adjusted in her early years, was said to be extroverted in her activities. She made her own living from an early age but changed jobs frequently, usually getting into difficulty with her employers and later becoming heavily addicted to alcohol. Her first actual psychosis occurred at the age of 50 and she had four hospitalizations in rather rapid succession with what were called manic attacks of comparatively short duration and always discharged as recovered with the exception of the last or present admission at the age of 65. On this admission the patient was very threatening and destructive, showing irritability and resistiveness with noisy shouting and scolding. She attempted to bite the nurses and other patients at times. The content of her speech was very religious and she heard voices of the dead. She later took up some work and became comparatively quiet although she could still hear voices at times. She thought she could talk with living people who were located at a great distance. Once she produced a coat hanger, one end of which was wrapped with a bandage until it was phallus shaped. The end was tipped with blood. This she declared came out of her own body. She said she was going to thrust it into the abdomen of the female physician in charge. (Ibid., p. 241)

*This patient's powerful homosexual strivings and desires to be a man, hitherto repressed, are represented by the artificial penis she has constructed from a coat hanger and which she now wishes to thrust into the "abdomen" of her female physician, "abdomen" obviously being the equivalent of "vagina."*

153    At the age of 28 after a series of quarrels with her husband she attempted suicide by cutting her throat. At the time she was admitted to the hospital she was excited, sang and talked under pressure, and was generally difficult to manage. She was partly out of touch with things, spoke meaningless phrases, was manneristic and irritable and had hallucinations principally of devils and bogies. She remarked, 'Someone has tried to gas me – put croton oil in my cabbage and rose water in my tea.' Her trouble began when 'bulldike' (neologism) 'smashed a devil into me in a lunchroom. Ever since then bulldikes have been bothering me. They would first love me up and then when I did not love them they would bite me inside. I felt shocks like needles in my arms.' Patient was boisterous, vulgar, obscene and abusive most of the time. She expressed a flash of insight when she remarked 'I am crazier than the others in the hospital and want to teach them more about crazy things.' She would urinate on the floor and make designs out of the puddle. She also made homosexual assaults on the other patients and nurses as she was erotic and sadistic most of the time and claimed she could recognize passive homosexuality at a glance and thus knew whom to assault. (Ibid., p. 244)

*This woman's homosexuality is very apparent, even though she is still repressing these feelings, attributing them to others, i.e. the "bulldikes" who keep sexually assaulting her. If she were able to accept her own homosexual feelings on a conscious level, she would no longer be "schizophrenic."*

154          She was hospitalized one year later during an attack of septic arthritis, duration four months. She had active auditory hallucinations, called the doctors missionaries, stating that they were Catholics and at the same time robbing friends and acquaintances. At times she was noisy, talkative, sang, cried, broke furniture and tried to march about like a soldier. This reaction changed into a quiet, more depressive mood with thoughts of world destruction. (Ibid., p. 259)

*The patient's wish to be a man is shown by her activity of marching about "like a soldier."*

155          It was the case of a thirty-eight year old woman who manifested the following symptoms: She imagined that her environment had changed, she was no longer respected, she was annoyed, she was watched, and her thoughts were known. Later she thought that she was watched in the evening while undressing. She also experienced sensations in her abdomen which she believed were occasioned by an unseemly thought on the part of the servant girl. Visions then appeared in which she saw female and male genitals. Whenever she was with women alone she had hallucinations of female genitals, and at the same time imagined that the others saw her own genitals. —The Psychology of Dementia Praecox, C. G. Jung, M. D., Nervous and Mental Disease Publishing Company, New York and Washington, D.C, 1936, p. 26.

*The bisexual conflict in this patient of Jung's is very clear. She has strong, repressed homosexual feelings directed towards the servant girl which are manifested as "sensations in her abdomen." Her homosexuality is also demonstrated by the fact that when she is alone with other women she hallucinates female genitalia. These unconscious homosexual desires form the etiological bedrock of her paranoid schizophrenia.*

156     Before the present attack she fell in love with a composer from whom she took singing lessons. Her love soon reached a passionate height accompanied by periods of insane excitement. She was then brought to the Burgholzli Hospital. At first she looked upon her confinement and her new experiences in the hospital as a descent into the underworld. She got this idea from her teacher's last composition which was 'Charon.' Then after this purifying passage through the underworld she interpreted everything happening about her in the sense of vicissitudes and struggles which she had to undergo in order to become united with her lover. Patient then thought another patient her lover and for a couple of nights went into her bed. She then thought herself **pregnant**, felt and heard twins in her womb, a girl resembling **herself** and a boy resembling the imaginary father. Later she thought that she gave birth to a child and had hallucinations of having a child in bed. With this the psychosis came to a close. (Ibid., p. 74)

*When the patient thought another patient was her lover and went into this other patient's bed on several different nights, she was expressing her homosexual love for this other patient.*

157     The explanation of her stereotype 'I am Socrates' or 'I am Socratic' lies in the fact that she was the 'best seamstress' 'who never cut a thread' and 'never had piece of cloth on the floor.' She is an 'artist,' a 'professor,' in her line. She is tortured, she is not recognized as world proprietress, etc., she is considered sick which is a 'slander.' She is 'wise' and 'modest.' She has performed the 'highest.' All these analogies to the life and end of Socrates. She therefore wishes to say 'I am and suffer like Socrates.' With a certain poetic license, characteristic in a moment of strong affect, she says directly 'I am Socrates.' The pathological part of this lies in the fact that her identification with Socrates is such that she cannot free herself from it. She

takes her identification somehow as self-evident, and she assumes so much reality for the metonymy that she expects everybody else to understand it. (Ibid., p. 104)

... By this the patient has reference to the pass key carried by the physicians. With the stereotype 'I am the main key' she solves the complex of her confinement. Here it can very well be seen how obscure her ideas as well as her expressions are; now she is the main key, now she only affirms it; likewise she is not the house, and now it belongs to her. This key, which opens everything and frees her, gives her also the occasion for the analogy with the key to heaven, which opens for her the entrance to bliss. (Ibid., p. 109)

A remarkable figure in this analysis is the 'Roman Mr. St., the most potent deity in heaven.' We have seen above that the patient bestows upon herself the title, 'God,' we have therefore in this connection a firm association with the idea of deity. Here we get another link, the name of the highest deity is 'St.' as is also the name of the patient. The adjective 'Roman' probably has to thank for its origin the vague analogy to 'Pope.' The deity of the Pope is of masculine gender and differentiates itself from the patient as 'God.' (Ibid., p. 125)

... [4] *Maria Theresa* – I belong to the synagogue in Lowen Street since 1886, I am a Jewess since 1886 – world proprietress – I am therefore three empresses – I am also Maria Theresa as von Planta – that is conclusion – in my dream I was at a table with omelets and dried plums – then there was a dam with speaking trumpets in it – then there were four horses with mustaches over their tails – they stood near the speaking trumpets – the third Emperor has already legalized this – I am Emperor Francis from the city of Vienna – in spite of that I am a woman – my Liesel rises early and yodels in the morning – it is also there – every horse stood near a speaking trumpet – (Patient suddenly goes through the gestures of embracing someone and on being questioned she states that she once dreamed that a man took her in his arms.)

... By 'Maria Theresa' patient again understands a particular quality of her greatness. This part of the analysis therefore interests us no longer. We have here a peculiar formation which ends with 'I am Emperor Francis.' Emperor Francis was the husband of Maria Theresa. The patient is Maria Theresa and at the same time Emperor Francis, 'in spite of her being a woman.' She fuses therefore the relations of both persons into her own, which in her hazy way of talking probably signifies nothing more than that both persons stand in association to each other and that this has some resemblance to her. (Ibid., p. 129)

*This schizophrenic patient identifies herself both as a woman – "best seamstress" – and as a man – "I am Socrates." In fact, her masculine identification seems much stronger than her feminine one. She is also an "artist," a "professor," "God," the "Pope" and the "Emperor Francis." When she says she is the "main key," she is referring to the pass key carried by physicians, which also indicates an identification with them. Symbolically, this key could also stand for the penis she wishes she possessed and which "opens for her the entrance to bliss," a possible allusion to having sexual intercourse with another woman.*

*When she says "I am Emperor Francis from the city of Vienna – in spite of that I am a woman – my Liesel rises early in the morning – it is also there" – etc., she is showing immense confusion in her sexual identity. First she is a man, then she is a woman, then her "Liesel rises early in the morning" – which is a direct, jocular reference to the well-known fact that men often experience early morning penile erections.*

*When Dr. Jung says this patient's tendency to fuse both male and female figures into her own persona "probably signifies nothing more than that both persons stand in association to each other and that this has some resemblance to her," he totally misjudges the significance of this woman's severe bisexual conflict and the critical etiological role it plays in her schizophrenic symptomatology.*

158    Ambivalence is part of being human, but to be immobilized by the ambivalence, to be caught up in the ambitendency of two opposing pressures for action, to be, like the Cartesian donkey, stuck between two haystacks while starving to death, is truly schizophrenic. —Schizophrenia, (The Experience and It's Treatment), Werner M. Mendel, Jossey-Bass Publishers, San Francisco, CA, Washington, D.C. and London, 1976, p. 24.

   *To paraphrase this quotation: "Ambivalence is part of being human, but to be immobilized by the ambivalence, to be caught up in the ambivalency of two opposing pressures for action – the heterosexual and the homosexual – to be, like the Cartesian donkey, stuck between two haystacks – heterosexual love and homosexual love – while starving to death – i.e., not receiving sexual satisfaction from either source – is truly schizophrenic."*

159    Some other of the major psychotic symptoms can also be understood as attempts at restitution. These symptoms include the megalomania and delusions of grandeur that are restitutive attempts at dealing with severely impaired self-esteem. Bizarre behavior frequently is used as an explanation for impaired interpersonal relationship, thus making meaning out of nonmeaning. Polymorphous sexual perversion represents a clumsy restitutional attempt, and hopelessness and catatonia become a final and bizarre way in which the individual removes himself from the arena of interpersonal transactions in which he suffers so much pain and failure. (Ibid., p. 27)

   *The source of the "severely impaired self-esteem" in schizophrenia is the unconscious knowledge of one's "perverse" or "unnatural" homosexual impulses. The megalomania and delusions of grandeur compensate for these feelings by denying the perversity: "No, I am not a pervert, I am the most important man (woman) in the world." In this way schizophrenics of both sexes try to retain some semblance of their self-respect.*

*"Polymorphous sexual perversion" represents a great deal more than "a clumsy restitutional attempt" on the part of the schizophrenic patient. It represents his or her only avenue of escape from the bonds of madness, because only by consciously acknowledging their homosexuality and "working through" these feelings – either in actual practice or in phantasy – can schizophrenics be cured of their mental illness.*

160      The symptom described as <u>panneurosis,</u> the condition in which many normal techniques of managing anxiety are used at the same time, is a clinical condition characteristic of certain stages of schizophrenia. In this condition the human being is depressed, withdrawn, obsessive, compulsive, paranoid (projecting), and somatizing; he has hysterical symptoms and none of them works. In the area of sexuality, we see the picture of polymorphous sexual perversion. The patient, frequently in a short span of time, enters into heterosexual, homosexual, exhibitionistic, voyeuristic, sadistic, and masochistic relationships. All of them are inadequate. None leads to sexual satisfaction. All of them culminate in interpersonal disasters. (Ibid., p. 34)

*This is another pertinent observation on how the schizophrenic, in trying to relieve his (or her) symptoms, engages in homosexual activity. Since the repression of his homosexuality is what caused him to become mentally ill in the first place, to actually engage in this previously abhorred activity is a great step forward in coming to grips with his psychological reality. He can then cease dissociating these "perverse" feelings from his ego and accept them as a part of himself. When this stage is reached, the schizophrenic no longer has need for the many defenses or symptoms that his mental illness has provided him with, and he can thereby dispense with them and proceed down the road leading to mental health.*

161             Then in the midst of all this despair and desolation there arose improbably a Joan of Arc of the Kongo. Her name was Kimpa Vita, baptized Beatriz, and the Capuchin Father de Lucqués describes her for us in this way:

'This young woman was about twenty-two years old. She was rather slender and fine-featured. Externally she appeared very devout. She spoke with gravity, and seemed to weigh each word. She foretold the future and predicted, among other things, that the day of Judgement was near.'

His confrère, a Father Bernardo de Gallo, from an interview he conducted with Beatriz, provides us with her own account of how she discovered her mission:

The event occurred in this manner, she said. When she was sick and on the point of death, at the last gasp, a brother dressed as a Capuchin appeared to her. He told her he was Saint Anthony, sent by God through her person to preach to the people, hasten the restoration of the Kingdom, and threaten all those who tried to oppose it with severe punishments. She died, because in place of her soul, Saint Anthony had entered her head; without knowing how, she felt herself revive ... She arose then and calling her parents, explained the divine commandment to go and preach, teach the people, and hasten the departure toward Sao Salvador. So as to do everything properly, she began by distributing the few things she possessed, renouncing the things of this world, as the apostolic missionaries do. Having done this she went up into the mountain and in complete liberty fulfilled her duty, as God had commanded her to do, and with great success.

Thus, in the early eighteenth century, the sect of the Antonians was born. Within two years this extraordinary young woman developed a dogma and doctrine, established a rudimentary church, and gathered an immense following. She claimed Saint Anthony was the second God, who held the keys to heaven and was eager to restore the Kongo kingdom. She herself, as Father de Gallo tells us, 'was in the habit of dying every Friday,' in imitation of the passion of Christ, and going up to heaven 'to dine with God and plead the cause of the Negroes, especially the restoration of the Kongo' and being 'born again on Saturday.' She imitated the virgin as well, and when she had a son she told Father de Lucqués, 'I cannot deny that he is mine but how I had him I do not know: I know however that he came to me from heaven.' —The River Congo, Peter Forbath, E. P. Dutton, New York, 1979, p. 137.

*Kimpa Vita is a classic case of religious paranoia. She relates how she died and in place of her soul St. Anthony entered into her and in effect became her. In psychological terms, she gave up her feminine identification and replaced it with a masculine one. This change of sexual identity resulted in a severe bisexual conflict, leading to the development of paranoid delusions of grandeur and omnipotence. Her bisexual conflict is also demonstrated by the fact she further identified with Christ by "dying every Friday" and being "born again on Saturday," while simultaneously identifying with the Virgin Mary by stating her son must have come to her from heaven, implying an "immaculate conception."*

*Thus this young woman, suffering from a severe case of paranoid schizophrenia caused by her bisexual conflict, was driven to establish a new church and became a very powerful figure in her environment.*

162    A parent of the same sex with whom the child should identify during latency and adolescence, who is not an acceptable love

object to the other parent but is hated and despised, cannot provide a model through which a child can achieve mature identity. Potential homosexual trends, which play a large role in schizophrenia, are opened. —Schizophrenia and the Family, Theodore Lidz, M. D., Stephen Fleck, M. D., and Alice R. Cornelison, M.S.S., International Universities Press, Inc., New York, 1965, p. 146.

*Again, the key role which homosexuality, or bisexual conflict, plays in the genesis of schizophrenia is noted by three very astute investigators.*

163     Although Mrs. Newcomb expressed some ideas that she would have liked a husband to provide more guidance, there was ample evidence that she could not relinquish the direction of the family. The sex-linked roles of the parents obviously went askew because of the subsidiary role filled by the husband. In addition, Mrs. Newcomb's own confusions concerning sexual identity and her deep-seated lack of self-esteem as a woman created further complications for her children. (Ibid., p. 303)

*Mrs. Newcomb is the typical schizophrenogenic mother, that is, a woman who is very confused concerning her own sexual identity and shows definite signs of homosexual interests. The children of such a mother always tend to evidence even greater confusion in their sexual identity, to such an extent that their severe bisexual conflict leads to the development of schizophrenic symptomatology.*

164     The problems presented by fathers who are passive adjuncts of their wives, or mothers who assume the prerogatives of fathers, lead to the topic of the importance of the parents' maintenance of gender-linked roles. The parental adherence to appropriate sex-linked roles not only serves as a guide for the achievement of reciprocal role relationships by

parents but also plays a major part in guiding the child's development as a male or female. Of all factors entering into formation of personality characteristics, the sex of the child is the most decisive; and security of sexual identity is a cardinal factor in the achievement of a stable ego identity. Probably all schizophrenic patients are seriously confused in their sexual identity. Clear-cut role reversals in parents can obviously distort the child's development as when a parent is overtly homosexual or when they concern the division of major tasks between the parents. However, the inability of a mother to fill an affectional-expressive role, or of a father to provide instrumental leadership for the family also creates difficulties. Either a cold and unyielding mother or a weak and ineffectual father is apt to distort the family structure and a child's development. Failures to maintain gender-linked roles by parents as well as failures of one parent to support the spouse's gender role were very striking in these families – failures ranging from strong homosexual tendencies through assumptions of male roles by mothers and female roles by fathers to absence of effective parental leadership and maternal coldness and aloofness.

Although the various complications that arise from such deficiencies in parents' adherence to sex-linked roles deserve more discussion, we should note that if a mother is consciously or unconsciously rivalrous with men and denigrating of her husband, a son can readily learn that masculinity will evoke rebuff from her, and fear of engulfment or castration by the mother can outweigh fears of retaliatory castration by the father. The schizophrenic patients' faulty sexual identity, including homosexual tendencies and concerns, are related to the parents' confused gender roles and the resultant imbalances in the family's dynamic structure. (Ibid., pp. 370-371)

*This quotation speaks for itself. It would be hard to find a more unerring description of the personalities of parents whose children become schizophrenic.*

165    The often-observed fluidity of boundaries between generations and of sexual identity in schizophrenics' families (Lidz, 1963b) seem like further reflections of problems with self definition. (Ibid., p. 420)

*Again, note is made of the ubiquitous presence of sexual identity problems in the families of schizophrenics.*

166    Simply to indicate the scope of the expansion and reorganization of psychoanalytic theory and psychopathology that appears to be required, we shall briefly consider problems of sexual identity. Whether a person is a male or a female is probably the most important determinant of personality characteristics, and security of gender identity is of critical moment to harmonious personality development. Confusions of sexual identity are basic to most of the perversions, and thereby, if we accept Freud's dicta, contribute to the causation of the neuroses. We have already adequately emphasized the critical role of gender identity confusion in schizophrenia. (Ibid., p. 427)

*The truth would have been better served if the authors had said that confusion of sexual identity, or bisexual conflict, is basic to all, not most, of the perversions, and, going beyond Freud's dicta, that this factor plays the basic etiological role not only in the causation of all the neuroses but of all the psychoses as well. In fact, functional mental illness, i.e. the neuroses and psychoses, is but one "disease" process with one fundamental etiological trigger – bisexual conflict. (See Quotation 001 by Dr. Edward J. Kempf.)*

167   c: The hypothesis concerning the confused gender identities and faulty sexual role assumptions of parents of schizophrenic patients should also be amenable to experimental testing. Currently, a group of colleagues is seeking suitable ways of measuring objectively confusions in sexual identity, reviewing existing tests and experimenting with new procedures. (Ibid., p. 434)

   *This hypotheses should certainly be tested, if for no other reason than to convince any doubters of its irrefutable truth.*

168 In those societies in which religious functions are marked by ecstatic trance behavior and cross-dressing for both sexes, 'early occurrence of states of catalepsy, dissociation, or hallucinatory experiences may trigger that sex role assignment' (Mead, 1961). —<u>Sexual Identity Conflict in Children and Adults</u>, Richard Green, M. D., Basic Books, Inc., New York, 1974, p. 26.

   *This "early occurrence of states of catalepsy, dissociation, or hallucinatory experiences" is actually the early occurrence of schizophrenic symptomatology. The fact that these symptoms may "trigger" opposite-sex role behavior coincides exactly with the "bearded lady" theory of schizophrenia as being caused by severe bisexual conflict.*

169   I do have a pencil and enough sheets of paper to last for a while – and as long as this crazy woman that I have become, wants to rave – what matter if the sound of her raving falls into words on the paper – or goes off into air, and mixes with all the other tumult and uproar that goes on down here. Her thinking is wild – but I have the wilder idea that if I can force her to keep it hitched to a pencil, and hold it down to the slow rhythm of writing things out in long hand – the practice

might tame her somewhat. I would rather try to tame a wild bull in a pasture. I know not how to deal with her because she is a maniac. Because she is I – and because I still have myself on my hands, even if I am a maniac, I must deal with me somehow.

The nurse just now picked up one of the sheets I have written. She read it – looked at me oddly – and asked what in the hell I thought I was doing. And because she expected an answer in keeping with my strange occupation – I did not have the heart to disappoint her. So I gave her an answer that fitted. I told her that I was Shakespeare, the reincarnation of Shakespeare trying to sidestep a strait-jacket. (I'll admit that I feel queer enough to be the reincarnation of something but I doubt if Shakespeare would claim me.) But hurray! She came back down the aisle with a whole ream of paper and said to me: 'Go to it, Shakespeare.'

Verily, verily, Shakespeare, I had no idea you could be called from your quiet English grave with so little effort. In my present predicament, I know of no one who could be quite such a fortunate choice for a delusion of grandeur. So welcome! I hope you will be as pleased with the arrangement as I am. Poor fellow, this is surely a come-down from your former position.   —The Inner Word of Mental Illness (A Series of First-Person Accounts of What It Was Like), edited by Bert Kaplan, Harper and Row, New York, Evanston, IL and London, 1964, p. 12.

*This patient, in writing that she "would rather try to tame a wild bull in a pasture" than herself, is saying, in effect, she is even wilder than a wild bull, which could also be understood as being more masculine than a bull. An astute therapist at this juncture would definitely want to point out to the patient her very strong unconscious masculine identification, as made clear by her comparison of herself with a wild bull.*

*Furthermore, this patient then proceeds to identify herself with William Shakespeare, certainly another very strong masculine identification on her part.*

170      I feel so close to God, so inspired by His Spirit that in a sense I am God. I see the future, plan the Universe, save mankind; I am utterly and completely immortal; I am even male and female. The whole Universe, animate and inanimate, past, present and future, is within me. [John Custance] (Ibid., p. 53)

*John Custance here states unequivocally that he is a "bearded lady" figure when he claims that "I am even male and female." Custance suffered from a very severe case of "manic-depressive" schizophrenia.*

171      But once again the causes that had flung me into my own sky continued to eat me up. Sexually unconfident, I went to whores, ate my meals alone, and forced myself to write a few pieces in the loneliest of places, a tiny blank hotelroom in the middle of nowhere. For the first time in my life the incentive to live, the isolation and frustration of my existence, grew dim; while the psychologist smiled and smoked his pipe – and did the well-adjusted, tweedy, urbane act behind his tastefully battered desk as he ladled out platitudes – I was saving up the sleeping bombs, and when I had enough to do the trick I burned the letters I had received through the years from the several men and women I had loved, destroyed my journal of 15 years' standing, and one carefully chosen night went to a hotel in Newark, NJ. [Seymour Krim] (Ibid., 65)

*There are two clues here which point to bisexual conflict in the writer. The first is when he says he is "sexually unconfident" and visits "whores." A man who is confident in his masculinity and thus without bisexual conflict does not need to rely on "whores" for his sexual satisfaction. The second clue is where he writes that he had burned the letters he had received over the years "from the several men and women" he had loved. It is interesting he put "men" before "women," and that he had "loved" them both, seemingly equally. Combined with the first clue, this definitely points to a bisexual conflict with consequent homosexual overtones. Furthermore, the fact the writer was suicidal means he was suffering from the most dangerous and serious symptom of schizophrenia, i.e. self-destruction.*

172         That morning I was transferred to Ward 4. Here I was subjected to a lot of personal questions by a nice-looking young fellow who did not have on a white coat. I was introduced to another patient who was said to be a Harvard professor. His name, I believe, was Nicholls. But I kept getting more and more excited. I was invited to play checkers and started to do so, but I could not go on. I was too much absorbed in my own thoughts, particularly those regarding the approaching end of the world and those responsible for the use of force and for the charge of homicidal intent. By nightfall my head was all in a whirl. It seemed to be the Day of Judgement and all humanity came streaming in from four different directions as in the accompanying diagram. They all came in to a common center. There they were brought before the judgment seat. But it seemed to be an automatic sort of judgment. Each individual judged himself. There were certain passwords and they made certain choices. Each person had three chances: a difficult 'right the first time affair,' a second choice which involved an element of sacrifice and meant that one would become a woman and not a man. The other was only a seeming chance which sent one at once to the lower regions. These lower regions did not seem to be anything very fixed. [Anton Boisen] (Ibid., p. 118)

Then I found myself in the Moon. The idea of being in the Moon had been present almost from the beginning of the week. Now this became an outstanding feature. The Moon seemed ordinarily quite far away, but really it was very near. The medical men knew about it and they had perfected a way of spiriting people away and burying them alive in a cell in the Moon, while in the meantime some designing person, a sort of double, would take their place in this world. Everything was run in a very strange way in the Moon. It was done in the most scientific manner. It seemed that it was the abode of departed spirits and all the interests were frankly and openly concerned with the problem of reproduction and of sex. Really it was quite appalling. It seemed that upon one's advent in the Moon the sex was likely to change and one of the first things the doctors tried to determine was whether you were a man or a woman. They had certain delicate instruments for determining that. When they examined me I heard them say in great surprise, 'He is a perfect neutral.' It seemed that the needle was not deflected in either direction. I was thus not consignable to either side and thus they had no power over me. [Anton Boisen] (Ibid., p. 122)

*In the midst of his psychosis, Anton Boisen finds himself in a delusional situation where he has "a second choice which involved an element of sacrifice and meant that one would become a woman and not a man." In other words, he could choose castration (the element of sacrifice) and become a woman, which the feminine part of himself was strongly tempted to do, or else he could remain a man.*

*Later, when he imagines that he is examined by doctors on the moon, where upon one's arrival a person's sex "was likely to change," he is found to be neither male nor female, but a "perfect neutral." In other words, he was a perfect "bearded lady," suffering from the "bearded lady" disease – schizophrenia.*

173   I am almost convinced that natural instinct could lead a
      schizophrenic to a cure, when tempered with common sense
      and a learned ability to test reality. It is another interesting
      paradox. Living with this illness is a matter of balancing
      opposites which are enormously incompatible. [Norma
      MacDonald] (Ibid., p. 179)

*Norma MacDonald has intuitively uncovered some
basic truths about schizophrenia. First, natural instinct does
try to cure the schizophrenic by means of psychosis. For
psychosis is nature's way of trying to abreact the repressed
homosexual cravings that the schizophrenic has gone crazy
trying to deny. It is a well known fact that psychotic people
often "change sex," i.e., assume the roles and actions of the
opposite sex or in other ways display confusion of sexual
identity during their psychosis. By living through these
feelings, healing occurs, because it is the denial by the ego of
these perverse cravings that has brought on the mental illness
in the first place.*

*A good analogy would be the process of lancing a boil
(in this case the mass of repressed "perverse" fantasies and
cravings) which has the effect of diminishing their pressure
and thus their ability to shatter the defending ego. Once this
material is allowed to escape through being abreacted in the
psychosis, just as the pathogenic pus from the lanced boil
drains away, healing begins to take place. Hopefully the ego
can now begin to accept the reality of its heretofore repressed,
ego-dystonic wishes and begin the process of assimilating all
these conflicting cravings into the now strengthened and
healthier self.*

*Secondly, Norma MacDonald is correct when she says
of her schizophrenia that "living with this illness is a matter of
balancing opposites which are enormously incompatible" –
actually, her male and female selves, or her homosexual and
heterosexual selves. The cure for schizophrenia is to <u>stop</u>*

*balancing them and allow either one or the other to gain ascendency, so that the schizophrenic person can begin to enjoy simple sexual gratification again, thereby dispensing with the severe bisexual conflict which has fueled the schizophrenia. Of course, it would take much psychotherapy for the schizophrenic to arrive at this happy conclusion, since it would mean his or her having to make a conscious, rational decision on whether to live as a man or a woman, or as a homosexual or a heterosexual.*

174     Mental illness is a emotion the person can not under why he did some things he or she did or craved and could not understand But with God help an a doctors help they can become well and never will be sick again.

[Names of six men patients found attractive.] I am look for someone to love in the wrong sex. Between the Drotors and God we that is I will be able to over come my sex love and be able to live in reality all the time., [Unnamed patient of E. Robert Sinnett, M. D.] (Ibid., p. 187)

… A schizoid person is a person who has two typ's of forse's going on an unable to make up his mind. [Unnamed Patient of E. Robert Sinnett, M. D.] (Ibid., p. 189)

*"I am looking for someone to love in the wrong sex." This simple sentence tells us what lies at the heart of schizophrenia – bisexual conflict and confusion, with powerful homosexual cravings. This patient has been his own best doctor, for he knows what has driven him crazy without anyone else telling him. Furthermore, when he describes "a schizoid person" as one who has "two typ's of forse's going on and unable to make up his mind," he is truthfully describing the pathogenic effect of having both homosexual and heterosexual desires and wishes, both equally powerful, to the point the "schizoid" person becomes "paralyzed" and unable to receive sexual satisfaction in either direction. This leads to*

*the extreme buildup of orgasmically undischarged sexual excitement, which is the actual pathogen leading to schizophrenic symptomatology, or that which drives a person "crazy."*

175          A group of us were trotted off once a week for mysterious injections and blood tests. There was an absolute campaign to find out what they were all about, but nobody ever did. One girl was so oppressed by the dark mystery she left the dinner table one day and sought out Sister. She returned with round eyes and breathed one word: 'Hormones.' There was a concerned clucking and one youngster said softly: 'Oo er.' The gay little nurse I pestered for information told me the idea was to change our sex. In that case, the experiment was a wash-out, though nothing would have surprised me at the time. [Mary Cecil] (Ibid., p. 228)

          *This patient says the nurse told her the purpose of her treatment was to "change our sex." It is hard to believe a nurse would actually have told a patient this, except jokingly. More likely the idea came from the patient's own unconscious, where precisely the wish to change sex was operative and was the pathogenic factor in her mental illness, as is invariably the case.*

176          It is true that life is a tragedy to those who feel. When my Happiness is given me life will be an ineffable, a nameless thing.
          It will seethe and roar; it will plunge and whirl; it will leap and shriek in convulsion; it will quiver in delicate fantasy; it will writhe and twist; it will glitter and flash and shine; it will sing gently; it will shout in exquisite excitement; it will vibrate to the roots like a great oak in a storm; it will dance; it will glide; it will gallop; it will rush; it will swell and surge; it will fly; it will soar high-high: it will go down into

depths unexplored; it will rage and rave; it will yell in utter joy; it will melt; it will blaze; it will ride triumphant; it will grovel in the dust of entire pleasure; it will sound out like a terrific blare of trumpets; it will chime faintly, faintly like the remote tinkling notes of a harp; it will sob and grieve and weep; it will revel and carouse; it will shrink; it will go in pride; it will lie prone like the dead; it will float buoyantly on air; it will moan, shiver, burst – oh, it will reek with Love and Light! [Mary Maclane] (Ibid., p. 271)

*The reason the compiler of these quotations added this particular one to the collection is because he feels it is a powerful example of the way the unconscious works, in this case the unconscious of Mary Maclane, and of the role it plays in her mental illness.*

*For it would seem that with the substitution of the word "penis" in the second sentence for the word "happiness," the meaning of her words becomes much clearer. To paraphrase: "When my Penis is given me life will be an ineffable, a nameless thing." Actually, penis and happiness are synonymous in her unconscious. That is, she can only find happiness in life by being a man with a penis. And the next paragraph could be called one of the greatest "poetic" descriptions of the various functions and manifestations of a penis that has ever been written. All that needs to be done is to replace "it" with "penis" and the meaning of her words becomes understandable. The fact Mary Maclane is a mental patient, who would not be emotionally disturbed were she not plagued by severe bisexual conflict, makes the interpretation of "penis" as being the equivalent of "Happiness" and "it" extremely plausible.*

177    He said he was with a woman that night ... Tom went the limit that night, but I did not, thank God ... For the first time in my life I had the desire to kill, to plunge a dagger in her [the other

woman's] heart. She's innocent. She didn't know he was married, and even so, she is not to blame. He is all wrong. I wonder if what I feel is jealousy. I think not. It is simply repugnance for the whole human race and their ideas, their unjustness. This is a man's world, ruled by men because they made it. Woman simply fits in for man's convenience ... Why cannot a woman do all a man does? Because she is supported by him. If she rebels she is put out of her home and her children are taken away from her ... My God, a woman is a fool and a coward, and by God, sometimes I do believe these puppets of women who bow down to their lord and master ought to be treated as they are. If they don't know enough to stand up for their rights. But how can they stand up for their rights? They have none, or only those men give them ... Oh, God, why can't these things be made clear to me? Why cannot woman do as man does, or rather man do as woman does? How can the world go on? Oh, God, tell me. Let someone explain ... Is there any answer but the one, 'Man makes it so?' Doesn't woman count for anything? Is she nothing? What is there a woman can do that a man cannot do? Bearing a child is the only thing I can think of. All this is killing me, but thank God, I want to go. I want and beg to go home, to drop out of this earth where there is no place for me – where I don't want a place ... I wish to God I could drop off the earth and just end my life, but it is not so. [R. S. Cavan] (Ibid., p. 297-98)

... Twice during this period of disturbance she wrote of wishing to kill Tom, and almost every entry is filled with questions regarding the inequality of standards of morality between the sexes and requests to God to take her. They decided to separate in May and Marion asked God to take her before she should sink into the mire. (Ibid., p. 299)

'Only trouble, only heartaches. Tom's trunk is on the back porch, waiting to be taken away. He left this A.M. without a word, and don't know where he is going or anything ... After Tom left it seemed as though the world would end, or as though there would be no end to my pain. Do I want him? Do I want Roy [her most constant man friend]? Do I want both or either? Or am I crazy or am I unhappy simply because I don't love either one? Sometimes I believe that is it. My mind tells me I must love Roy, he is so good.'

Two months later, of Roy she wrote that he 'does so many things I don't like, and never will learn.' Then Marion met Albert Cummings, a married man, and soon her old friends had been discarded in his exclusive favor. (Ibid., p. 301)

April 24, Sunday, 1 A.M. ... Money, of course, is the all-important thing. I have got to have it. Things are not running smoothly. I don't know how I am going to make enough to keep me, and I can't do what I have done, to love Bert and give myself, or rather sell myself to someone else whom I loathe. I do all men, but my Bert would kill me. I couldn't get drunk enough ever to slip, thank God; and I won't drink without him. The past few days I have been ready to cry any time. (Ibid., p. 304)

'May 6, Saturday, 9:40 A.M. Thursday A.M. Bert phoned, swore at me furiously about phoning the night before. Marjorie raised cain, he said. I listened to nothing but oaths and hung up. I did not phone yesterday, nor did he. I thought I'd let him cool down, and he knew I had only $6 Tuesday night. Just now he phoned and said he wanted to send me some money, and I said I was going downtown and would meet him for lunch. I'm glad I didn't phone first. I am all broken up about Bert. My sense of honor (Oh, God, how ridiculous that sounds, for me) tells me to leave my Bert, who belongs to another. Some day I will have the strength.'

The foregoing is the last entry in the diary. What happened between Marion and Bert when they met is not known, but Bert stayed with her the night of May 6 and sometime while he slept Marion shot and killed him and then killed herself. (Ibid., p. 310)

*This highly disturbed woman suffers from a very intense case of Freudian "penis envy," or desire to be a man. Her bisexual conflict eventually leads to murder and suicide, as this quotation reveals. Marion only once becomes completely honest with herself when, after stating she can no longer "sell" herself to somebody whom she loathes, adds, "I do all men, but my Bert would kill me." She finally admits her deepest feelings about men – she loathes them all. She soon proves this by murdering her supposedly beloved Bert.*

178          Patients laugh and posture when they see through the doctor who says he will help but really won't or can't. Posturing, for a girl, is seductive, but it's also an effort to distract the doctor away from all her pelvic functions. The patients try to divert and distract him. They try to please the doctor but also confuse him so he won't go into anything important. When you find people who will really help, you don't need to distract them. You can act in a normal way. I can sense if the doctor not only wants to help but also can and will help. [The patient stressed this.]

          (What kind of help did you need?) Well, one thing was getting down to my need to be a boy. The very first interview you said something about a prick. I was terrified but it really was a great relief, even though I felt like an old rag in a gun closet. Most of my doctors had avoided it with me. You showed that you felt it was a problem that had to be cleared up. You knew I was terrified, but I knew you would go down to the depth with me. All my other doctors sat on the edge and fished. They waited for me to say things. That's not fair. You went right ahead. You were willing to get in with me. [M.L. Hayward and J. E. Taylor] (Ibid., p. 327)

          The reference to a 'prick,' in the second paragraph, relates to the fact that Joan had always carried a knitting needle with her to the early interviews. The therapist made the suggestion, 'Perhaps you feel safer if you have something to prick with.' As discussed in an earlier paper, this type of clarification gives the patient the enormous encouragement of realizing that the doctor can understand and accept his problems. Joan also points out the futility of 'fishing'; that is, asking questions.

Her comparison of herself to a rag in a gun closet seems a particularly vivid example of the intense overvaluation of the phallus that is seen as a major problem in many girls suffering from schizophrenia. (Ibid., p. 327)

The toy penguin mentioned in the text is related to an extraordinary episode which occurred at the time of Joan's first visit home, after the clearing of the overt psychosis. In spite of the fact that Joan was a tall, handsome young woman of 19, her father brought this doll as a present and insisted she carry it on the trip home. From this episode one can see the father's overwhelming unconscious need to convert her from a growing woman to a male child. (Ibid., p. 328)

I needed to be controlled and know what you wanted me to be. Then I'd be sure you would want me. With my parents I couldn't be a boy and they never made it clear what else they wanted me to be except that. So I tried to die by being catatonic. You should never have let me wear slacks. You even said I looked nice in them. I was sure you loved me like that and would be like my parents.

I would go into these violent rages at you, early in treatment, because of a sense of desperate frustration. I longed for you to take care of me and love me, but I was sure I wasn't lovable as a girl, and I knew I couldn't really become a boy. I felt sure you would soon realize I wasn't a boy and then you would go away. You seemed ready to feed me but then you never would. (Ibid., p. 333)

Joan's outstanding problem throughout treatment was a feeling that she could be more lovable as a boy. Apparently this idea had its roots in her earliest relationship with her mother.

Treatment had to prove to her that she was a girl and could be loved as a girl; starting with her existence only as a wish in the therapist's mind. Eventually, as described in Section XXV, she could test the therapist out more and more completely; thereby convincing herself that as a girl she did have power to please and attract people. Sechehaye describes this growth of self-esteem very well. (Ibid., p. 334)

The majority of schizophrenics are struggling with three conflicting drives. Part of these drives wants to be a boy, part wants to be a girl, and part a baby. As Joan has pointed out, the simultaneous presence of all these drives leads to immense confusion. (Ibid., p. 335)

When a girl doesn't want to walk, it's because she doesn't want to realize that there is nothing swinging between her legs. She would like to be paralyzed from the waist down. If her legs are dead, then her genitals are dead too. She won't have to think of them again. I hated to walk. I could feel my thighs rubbing and that made me remember my genitals. I hated you for making me walk. (Ibid., p. 340)

Hindsight shows that in this case the therapy of the period of overt psychosis fell into three principal phases. At the start, Joan presented chiefly the picture of catatonic withdrawal or of belligerent masculine identification, so that the work of therapy centered around efforts to help her control her aggression and overcome her fear of being hurt again if she established a human relationship. The therapist had to be tested at length until he proved he was dependable and would always strive to do what was necessary for her welfare.

Once Joan was sure she could depend on the therapist, she began a process of replacing the deprivations of the original oral period through a new mother-infant experience. This she describes as the really vital relationship which enabled her to feel like a girl. She could only be a girl if she started with a mother who could love her as a girl.

The third phase, or period of growth, went on slowly and almost imperceptibly. Joan was free of overt psychosis by the time she began to use the therapist, less as a mother and more as a good father who could convince her of her ability to be attractive and successful as a woman. She entered reality solidly, when she could again see the therapist as a doctor and the relationship became more co-operative and adult. (Ibid., p. 344)

*Much has been written about the "schizophrenogenic mother" in the genesis of schizophrenia, but little about the "schizophrenogenic father." In one brief sentence in this quotation, the psychodynamics of this kind of father is disclosed. "From this episode," it reads, "one can see the father's overwhelming unconscious need to convert her from a growing woman to a male child." Daughters who become schizophrenic invariably have fathers possessed of a pathological emotional need to squelch their daughters' femininity and encourage their masculinity. Thus they compete with their daughters and subtly encourage them to become masculine. Furthermore, these fathers are basically homosexual and prefer boys to girls. With a father like this and a mother who hates her own femaleness, the daughter will have a very difficult, if not impossible, task in trying to establish for herself a comfortable sexual identity as a woman.*

*In the same manner as "Schreber's name is legion," so is Joan's. Joan's case history as revealed in this quotation is basically the case history of every schizophrenic, or mentally ill, woman.*

179    No student of human behavior, no matter what his point of view, can, for one moment, afford to lose sight of the fact that all men and women are bisexual in their anatomical construction and in their affective cravings, and that all the segments contribute to the affections and wishes of the

personality. —Psychopathology, Edward J. Kempf, M. D., C. V. Mosby Co., St. Louis, Missouri, 1920, p. 14.

*Dr. Kempf should have added that when these bisexual segments of the human personality come into conflict, the stage is set for the development of functional mental illness – from slight neurosis up to and including the most severe forms of schizophrenia – the degree of severity of the mental illness depending solely upon the degree of severity of the person's bisexual conflict.*

180      A brilliant, paranoid army surgeon amputated his penis to prevent young women, whom he hallucinated, from using him for sexual purposes. The erotic segments continued to exercise a pathological effect upon the personality even though partly destroyed. He now begs to have his testicles excised for the same purpose. (Ibid., p. 70)

*The true motivation, albeit unconscious, behind this man's desire for castration is not to protect himself from fantasied young women but to become a young woman himself, or at least a female in preference to his male self which he despises.*

181      During the convalescence [from her third labor], following a sudden conflict with her mother, she passed into a psychosis in which she became crucified as a hermaphrodite Christ – becoming both male and female in that she believed she was masculine sometimes and feminine others. (Ibid., p. 103)

*This patient is obviously in the grip of a very severe bisexual conflict which has driven her insane.*

182      The patient insisted that he had 'feminine' qualities, but, spontaneously, with undue earnestness and repeated efforts, he

tried to establish that he was not 'effeminate.' No homosexual relations had ever occurred, and no perversions.

He *dreamed* of a knight in beautiful armor who appeared before an audience, and a penetrating light was thrown upon his pelvis which revealed the genitalia of a female. He recognized himself as this knight. This was a reaction to the light of psycho-analysis. He also *dreamed* of a man singing to an appreciative audience. The man had a baritone voice, but it changed to contralto and then to soprano. The hair became long, although his mustache remained; the breast was a man's but the manners were a woman's. The singer showed embarrassment, then distress, and, finally broke down in tears. The audience sympathized with him. The patient awakened 'in strong agitation,' and recognized the singer as himself. At one time he had a pleasing baritone voice. He never shaved his mustache in order not to look effeminate. [This man had become homicidal before being admitted to St. Elisabeth's Hospital.] (Ibid., p. 281)

*This quotation illustrates the fact that "homosexual panic" is often the motivating factor behind homicidal male behavior. It is noted that this particular patient was homicidal before being admitted to St. Elisabeth's Hospital.*

183    She repeatedly protruded her tongue, covered with foaming saliva, during the conversation and, in reply to my questions, she explained that this meant 'passion.' ... From the time of her admission she had complained of being afraid of an 'old, grey-haired woman,' described her as naked, trying to get into her bed to perform sexual acts on her with 'her mouth.' For this reason she was afraid of the women when they entered the room and attacked them. ... The patient's <u>anxiety</u> about her perverse eroticism was unquestionable. She was terrified and begged to be saved from insanity. (Ibid., p. 341)

> *Anxiety of such intensity that it leads to mental illness is always anxiety about "perverse eroticism," i.e. homosexual phantasies and feelings, desires to be of the opposite sex and identification with the opposite sex.*

184    She said that a voice told her she would see Christ and that she herself was the Christ Child Jesus. ... She was inclined to feel that in some respects the psychosis did her good. (Ibid., p. 343)

> *As a direct result of her psychosis, this woman's masculine identification (with Jesus Christ) was brought into her conscious awareness. Hitherto it had been repressed and was the cause of the severe bisexual conflict which formed the etiological core of her psychosis.*
> *In expressing the opinion that "in some respects the psychosis did her good," she intuitively recognizes the fact that only by admitting and coming to grips with this masculine identification could she regain her mental health.*

185    She rubbed and plucked her skin like the autoerotic patient, but denied masturbation. During the erotic period I observed her to grab her finger and, unmistakably, make the masturbatory movement of the male, without apparently being aware of it. (Ibid., p. 363)

> *This patient's unconscious identification as a male is very obvious.*

186    She complained almost constantly about the two balls of hair in her throat, frequently palpable and enlarged submaxillary glands, which, she said, was one of the balls, and wanted to have her throat cut or an operation performed to remove it ... she said she couldn't control herself and felt compelled to

scream her denunciations of God, and wanted to know why she shouted: 'If I had it I would bite it off.' (Ibid., p. 376)

*Here the unconscious desire to be a man is so powerful that it has deluded the patient into believing she has two testicles lodged in her throat, and that if she actually did possess a longed-for penis, she would prove that she really didn't want it by the act of biting it off.*

187    She talked a great deal about love, heard 'false voices' call her 'baby dear,' and suddenly attacked a male physician to show him that she was 'innocent.' She said his eyes made her feel excited. She misidentified the woman physician as a man when she examined the patient's heart, and accused the woman physician of making her feel 'passionate.' Masons tried to initiate her into a secret. ... 'I never look into the eyes of a man; but a woman, that is different.' ... quite characteristically, she held some little object in her hand and sat, mute, dreaming, indifferent. (Ibid., p. 380)

*The patient was homosexually excited by the woman physician who examined her, but in order to deny this fact she delusionally changed the woman physician into a man, thus making her erotic feelings acceptable to herself by transforming them from homosexual into heterosexual ones. She confirms her homosexuality, however, when she states that "I never look into the eyes of a man; but a woman, that is different." Finally, the "little object" she "characteristically" held in her hand was undoubtedly a penis symbol.*

188    Another woman, who had rubbed all the hair from her scalp so that she was perfectly bald, occupied a bed in the same ward. The patient forced herself into this woman's bed calling her a 'man,' and it was with difficulty that she was removed. Then she began an unusually unbridled, vicious

attack upon her own genitals, masturbating without restraint and regardless of all the women on the ward; stuffing pieces of cloth, and other things, into her vagina. (Ibid., p. 373)

*This patient tries to defend herself against her powerful homosexual strivings by her delusion that the object of her affections is a man rather than the woman she in reality is.*

189   Case M.D.-9 is an unmarried woman of sixty, who has for three years been trying to dominate her environment by claiming to be 'The Lord,' 'God Almighty,' 'The King,' 'The President,' 'Secretary of the Navy,' and so on. She proclaims that she is the maker of a cannon that shoots 6,000 cannon balls which will destroy everything and shoot into the uterus of her physician, who is a 'she devil.' She threatens to cut off anyone's head who comes near her, damns everybody, and does it with such vicious emphasis that she makes one feel decidedly like leaving her alone.

With hair flowing, gown often exhibitionistically adjusted, exophthalmic stare, stern masculine countenance, mannish voice, and hypertrichosis, she makes a formidable impression.

At about thirty-five she had a serious depression, lasting 17 months, following the death of her sister.

At fifty, she had a manic attack, lasting a year.

At fifty four, she had a similar psychosis which lasted about 8 months. (Ibid., p. 407)

*This woman's unconscious desire to be a man is so powerful and overwhelming that it has not only driven her insane but has caused her to become a fearsome force in her environment.*

*The "cannon" she claims to have made is an obvious penis symbol, as the "balls" are symbolic of testicles. She would like to use her "cannon" to shoot "balls" into the uterus of her female physician, which is to say she would like to have a penis and testicles and use this penis to have sexual intercourse with the physician and "shoot" semen into the latter's uterus.*

190    Often at night, he pounded on the door and called for help. He would usually be in a panic because of his terrifying sensory hallucinations, such as having holes pounded into his abdomen, drawing sensations at his heart and umbilicus, and pounding electricity into his head. Sometimes he tied a handkerchief about his head because of head pains, and another time he pasted a piece of paper over his abdomen and asked for treatment for a hole there.

    The voices talked of making a 'hermaphrodite' out of him. (Ibid., p. 501)

*This "hole" this patient believed was in his abdomen was a much-desired vagina, possession of which would make him the woman he had longed to be.*

191    He impulsively attacked other patients, and, one time, while lying sullen and brooding on a couch, and a physician bent over him to ask how he felt, he struck the physician in the face, shattering his glasses. He would give no explanation for this act. It looked 'impulsive,' but later he explained that he thought homosexual insinuations were meant by the question of 'how he felt.' (Ibid., p. 521)

    ... About the fifth month, his work had to be stopped because he began openly to accuse different men of making sexual advances to him. ... At this time he was very erotic and one morning he indignantly demanded the protection of his physician, and with great bitterness, he insisted that while asleep some men had forced him to submit to an oral sexual assault. Despite the most earnest persuasions, he could not be made to doubt the reality of this vivid dream experience. Fear of sexual assault by men continued almost nightly for the next two months. During this time, he slept very little and used many precautions to protect himself from the assaults. He barricaded the door of his room with all the furniture available, and kept chewed paper in his mouth, which, he thought, would catch the semen and prove that he had been mistreated while asleep. Unfortunately, one morning, he found a hair in the paper, and this firmly convinced him that his hallucinations were realities. Conversations or questions had 'double meanings.' One night, the attendant legitimately asked him if he wished to have a sheet. The patient interpreted this to mean something 'to spit in,' and promptly assaulted the attendant. He was sure he heard the attendant say he had chancres in his throat. (Ibid., p. 522)

*The incredible lengths the mind will go to guard itself against unwanted insight is vividly illustrated by this case. The patient is fighting desperately against consciously accepting the glaringly obvious fact that he has very powerful oral homosexual desires.*

192    He said: 'I would rather die than become a cocksucker.' ... Either attempts at suicide, or, as he expressed himself before his discharge, 'I'd rather go crazy before I'd become a cocksucker.' ... The fear of the shrinking penis becoming invaginated into the abdomen was apparently due to an uncontrollable effeminate attachment to his companion. (Ibid., p. 498)

*This patient is really saying he would rather die than admit to having homosexual desires. Thousands of people actually do die yearly for this very reason, by means of direct suicide, indirect suicide (alcoholism, drug addiction, etc.) and the myriad of other forms of self-destructive behavior man engages in, all in an effort to deny their bisexual conflict.*

*A note of interest here is the reference to "the fear of the shrinking penis becoming invaginated into the abdomen." This same fear is found in a condition called "Koro" in certain Asian societies. Koro, in reality, is nothing more than a schizophrenic psychosis caused by severe bisexual conflict, as clearly illustrated by the above case.*

193        That he will be able to maintain a biologically satisfactory heterosexual adjustment is very unlikely, and his homosexual cravings being intolerable, a latent sustained chronic dissociation of the personality with consequent deterioration, because of the future hallucinatory gratification of his homosexual needs, will probably be the ultimate course of his biological career. (Ibid., p. 500)

*In reality, a psychosis is nature's way of trying to heal the mentally disturbed individual by providing him or her the hallucinatory gratification of the long-repressed homosexual cravings. Since the schizophrenic's ego is too highly defended and inflexible to allow these wishes to enter conscious awareness, they have no other means of obtaining satisfaction except through the hallucinations, which are the healing agency of the psychosis. Since the repressed homosexual cravings are what drive the person insane, the sole cure is to bring these wishes into conscious awareness and allow them to experience the sexual excitement and orgasmic discharge they have been longing for. If the ego will not allow this abreaction to take place, then the only alternative for the gratification of these "perverse" sexual cravings lies in the development of a psychosis with its accompanying hallucinatory discharge and consequent satisfaction of these cravings.*

194     Case PD-26 was the only son of an overworked, uneducated
        mother who suffered from neglect and the need of the simple
        comforts necessary to make life worth living. He was a typical
        'mama's boy,' seriously pampered, effeminate, dainty in his
        manners, tenor voice, and generally submissive in his make-
        up.
                He was an ordinary seaman in the navy when a typical
        homosexual panic developed in which he was obsessed with
        fears that men plotted to sexually assault him. He had to be
        tube-fed, and when he resisted, and his arms were forcibly
        drawn behind him, he had a 'vision of Jesus Christ and the
        thieves on the cross,' feeling that he was being crucified as one
        of the thieves. Later, he realized that it was 'imagination.'
        (Ibid., p. 502)

                *Every male who suffers from schizophrenia is basically
        a "mama's boy" at heart, for the "typical 'mama's boy'" is
        faced with either becoming an overt homosexual or else
        repressing these feelings and consequently being driven crazy
        (schizophrenic), as this case so aptly illustrates.*

195     The factor of this man's anal eroticism and its capacity to take
        his senses away, make him unconscious, will be referred to in
        the chapter on the anal erotic group and their convulsions and
        stupors. (Ibid., p. 533)

                *Dr. Kempf here emphasizes the tremendous power of
        repressed, passive anal (homosexual) cravings over the male
        individual who is so inclined. It brings to mind Freud's dictum
        that what man represses at his deepest level are his passive
        pederastic instincts.*

196     All night long he remained in his room (9th floor) in a panic
        expecting the Masons to rush into his room. He prepared the
        window so that he could jump if the door was opened. (His

behavior suggests an explanation for some impulsive leaps from windows by panic-stricken travelers in hotels.)

He was then sent to a sanatorium and the physicians, he said, put 'poison,' 'spue' (semen) into his food and wanted him to marry an immoral woman. The physician, he fancied, tried to hypnotize him and promised to release him if he would perform fellatio. He eloped from the sanatorium in a panic and was committed to St. Eliz. Hospital. (The cause of the panic and delusions must be seen in the patient himself – in his uncontrollable homosexual cravings.) ... He finally confided that he was controlled by a stronger will which masturbated him and forced him to submit to oral perversions. ... He described Dr. – as trying to make him submit to a sexual assault and in it he made a significant error; 'Then I begged him not *to let me*. I mean not *to make me do it*. He kept me from eating and tried to weaken my will.' (The oral erotic act often has the significance of a religious act, a crucifixion of the rival son to the virile father ... Homosexual perverts sometimes speak of their oral-erotic submission as a crucifixion. Biologically, this is quite true.)

For a year or more previous to this analysis, he had complained of being masturbated and orally seduced by hypnotic powers, etc., and spit continuously in any direction and on anything. His face was chapped and raw from the constant application of a towel over his mouth to keep out 'something.' He used great quantities of toothpaste to keep his mouth clean and would not explain to us why he persisted in these prophylactic measures.

He had an occasional tic, jerking his head back as if something sharp were being thrust into him, but would never discuss this, usually only muttered and cursed to himself when it occurred. (Ibid., p. 541)

*When Dr. Kempf states that the cause of this man's panic and delusions was his "uncontrollable homosexual cravings," he should have added that this factor is the cause of all such panics and delusions in both men and women, of whatever age, social rank or culture.*

197    The crucifixion cravings soon dominated everything, and he had to be isolated because he persisted in removing his clothing and being crucified. ... From about the fourth week to about the thirty-fifth week, except for a brief interval, his personality was markedly dissociated, and he seemed unable to prevent himself from submitting to the hallucinations. ... but he later abandoned himself to the affective wave that swept the ego under. ... During this catatonic period he used manneristic expressions and symbols, and entertained classical crucifixion fancies. He also informed the nurse that he had given birth to a child, and actually simulated labor pains. Then followed the birth of many children. When, during this apparently profound stupor, he protested that his nurse was killing his child, he spoke the nurse's correct name. ... He said his body was destroyed, bones broken, he died, was female and male in one, had all the thoughts of the world to care for, etc. (Ibid., p. 562)

*This patient is a prime example of the "bearded lady" syndrome in schizophrenia.*

198    She recalled during the analysis that while at the sanatorium she looked over some pictures of priests and thought of herself as being like one of the priests who was effeminate-looking. (This bisexual interest should be compared to the bisexual interests of the previous case.) ... The nurse reported that when she dressed herself after the physical exmaination she tucked her skirts inside of her drawers like a boy. (Again the bisexual.)

       She had no difficulty in recalling the important features of her illness which were essentially relative to the crucifixion, death of her personality, and the rebirth. (Ibid., p. 575)

The father and mother situation had to be handled tactfully until she had brought out the details of her psychosis and her life.

The father appeared (hallucinated) in the disguise of elderly women. She said, that when he appeared in the reception room, 'He or she said' (laughs), 'It was up to me to make him happy.' He said: 'I hope you can do it, son Harry,' and 'Welcome, son Harry.' In the dormitory, 'He, she or it' (laughs) was taken out of the room, and she looked at me and said: 'You will be sorry some day.' ... That her father should call her Harry, was due to the fact that this was her nickname with some playmates when she was a child.

That her father should be associated with women and be spoken of as 'he, she or it ... '

The mother's attitude was so subtly ingratiating, and yet domineering, that she would almost have to be destroyed as a mother if the patient were to free herself from its terrible influence and win her own womanhood and independence.

Why should this patient have become masculine ('son Harry') during her stuporous state? Christ and the young priest had marked effeminate traits, as do many crucified heroes: and males who go through the crucifixion, complain of being effeminate and even of losing all masculine attributes. The renunciation of all competitive sexual interests in order that the rival parent shall dominate, may perhaps be compensated for by the development of a complete sexual cycle within the self. The female, developing masculine traits, and the male, developing female traits, are protected, like Buddha, from the more virile members of their sex who would dominate them. This conjecture is based upon observations of the completely autoerotic who are physically of one sex and fancifully develop the attributes of the other sex, thereby perfecting the autoerotic cycle. Some of our autoerotic patients complain of being male at one time and female at others. (Ibid., p. 577)

*Dr. Kempf gives an excellent description of the typical "schizophrenogenic" mother when he states that her attitude "was so subtly ingratiating, and yet domineering, that she would almost have to be destroyed as a mother if the patient were to free herself from its terrible influence and win her own womanhood and independence." He might also have added that a schizophrenic* <u>son</u> *could have been substituted for the patient in this same context, making the last part of the quotation read"... if the patient were to free* <u>himself</u> *from its terrible influence and win* <u>his</u> *own* <u>manhood</u> *and independence." Note also the effeminancy of the patient's father, who treats his daughter like a son.*

199    Case CD-5 was an uneducated Russian immigrant who was sent to St. Eliz. Hospital after having excised one of his testicles. He said it did not stop masturbating, but his behavior otherwise showed unmistakable religious fanaticism and the desire to be crucified. He tried to raise a beard like Christ, and his prayers and uplifted eyes, ecstatic crucifixion countenance, his tears and impulsive giggles, revealing pleasure at the physician's approach on the ward, showed, as he persisted in attempts to bow and kiss the physician's hand, not only his appreciation, but also an intense desire to subject himself to the physician's domination. The homosexual eroticism of this was suspected at first, but later it became confirmed when we had to watch him continually to prevent him from getting into homosexual embraces with other erotic men. (Ibid., p. 600)

*This patient's severe bisexual conflict is glaringly apparent.*

200   Horses, bulls, negroes, 'morphrodites with three penises and large breasts,' her husband with two penises, her father, brother, mother and sister would have intercourse with her. ... She had become a 'morphrodite' and would have intercourse with herself and use a horse's penis. ... 'When you speak [Dr. Kempf] I think I speak.' ... 'I am trying to do everything.' ... She believed she was everybody. (Ibid., p. 639)

*Again, an obvious "bearded lady" example.*

201   A severe <u>panic</u> about having circumcised, eaten and killed her infant continued about three weeks. She was sad and cried as if her baby were really dead. (The identification is made here of the entire baby with the baby's penis which actually was circumcised. Later the identification of the penis as a baby came out frankly and the feeling that she had eaten her baby became recognizable as an erotic wish-fulfillment.)

When I asked, 'Why do you think you <u>ate</u> your baby?,' she gave me to understand that she did not 'hate' her baby. The burdensome baby was disposed of in her dreams and hallucinations in the form of abortions.

She thought she threw her infant down a shaft and burned it to death.

When she was in bed she would lie half exposed and as a man approached she made little movements to uncover herself. (To submit herself) and yet looked at him in great fear. ... She still had erotic dreams and would have to awaken to keep from masturbating. Her social interests were decidedly homosexual. She delighted in dancing with certain women, dreamed of being in continuous tubs with them and being tempted to masturbate by them.

She began to quarrel with the other patients, and derived special delight out of 'cussing.' She used profanity liberally for almost everything, and was very much like a tomboy in her vulgarity and heedlessness. ... 'I remember when I was lying with my head on my nurse's knee I determined not to commit masturbation, but I would have anything for happiness, so I let my imagination go and it got bigger and worse all the time.' (Ibid., p. 642)

She wrote several letters filled with vulgar sexual phrases, references to feces and her love for the nurse. ... She was fond of resting her <u>back</u> against the electric light switch and turning on the light. Sometimes she assumed the female sexual position on the floor and then assumed the male sexual position and initiated coitus: she usually left her slippers in the office when she started to leave. ... Since her return to the hospital she will not wear clothing, but tears her dresses, wraps them around her body like a blanket, sits on the floor for hours with her head buried in her arms and her knees pulled up to her chest – a very common dementia praecox position in which such patients freely play with their <u>pelvic</u> orifices. (Ibid., p. 657)

*It is very obvious, from all these cases of schizophrenia which are reported on by Dr. Kempf, why he was driven to the conclusion that bisexual conflict is invariably the basic etiological factor in "every case of emotional neurosis or psychosis" in man. This factor appears with such monotonous regularity in all these cases that it is inconceivable that any objective investigator would not reach the identical conclusion.*

202    He became very slovenly, worried about having been subjected to sodomy and his feelings of an enlarging abdomen. He walked so that his abdomen was protruded forcefully, a distinct effort to have a pregnant abdomen.

He complained frequently that 'this patient in my stomach talks to me all the time and mixes me up. Water or something moves up and down in here. It might be a rupture or something.' He said it took him all over the country and showed him many things and talked 'plainly' to him. He would not talk freely about it because it might get him into trouble. He seemed to believe that the feelings were the result of some form of pregnancy and explained it by 'someone stuck a stick of dynamite in there,' and stuck needles into his 'back.' (Ibid., p. 677)

He later felt compelled to remove his clothing and without explanation stood about naked. He persisted in fondling certain other patients and became extremely persistent in getting into physical contact with them. He had a particular attachment to another patient who had similar difficulties and frequently hallucinated someone trying to perform sodomy on him. (Ibid., p. 678)

*The needles this patient believes have been thrust into his "back" and the stick of dynamite he believes someone has "stuck" into his stomach are obvious phallic symbols, representing the symbolic fulfillment of repressed homosexual cravings to indulge in passive pederastic intercourse.*

203     This was only intelligible from what followed in the sense that he was resisting his feminine cravings to marry a man. ... He always slept in a bed with his back to the wall, and watched the men so that they could not secretly perform sodomy upon him while he slept. He had a characteristic walk. Passing along through the ward for several steps, then turning to look down close behind him, as if sensory disturbances made him feel that someone was approaching him. Such back and anal sensations persisted more or less vividly for about ten months, as his behavior indicated.

One day he approached me asking if I was a detective and adding, 'I am carved from here to here.' (passing his hand from anus to scrotum.) ... During most of this period, frank sodomistic interests and fancies occupied his entire time. He could not be interested in anything.

Whenever I met him on the ward he would come up to me, grinning and shaking his head oddly, to say that he was not sure that anyone had performed sodomy on him, but that he would watch out for them. (Ibid., p. 681)

*This patient's passive anal erotic urges, which had existed previously in a state of unconscious repression and had consequently driven him "crazy," have now broken through into conscious awareness where they can more easily be dealt with. His being "carved from here to here" emphasizes his primary identification as a woman.*

204    Another patient, who passed through a psychosis and panic because of fear of being destroyed and sexually misused, finally recovered and returned to work. A few years later he voluntarily sought admission to St. Eliz. Hospital. He said his genitalia were disappearing and his rectum was changing into a vagina. He was decidedly pleased and lived his belief, devoting his time to erotic fancies about his hermaphrodite nature, not caring to return to society, but probably better pleased with the men on the wards. (Ibid., p. 690)

*This is another obvious "bearded lady" case.*

205    (Case HD-16) – He was sent to St. Eliz. Hospital because of his unfitness to remain in the Soldier's Home. He says: 'I represented the Spirit of American Service, the Navy Service and the Department of Justice, through a method of transfiguration, the purity of the Church represented in it.' (Grand compensation).

On the wards he often shouted 'get out of my stomach,' and rubbed his left hand on the right side of his abdomen. When asked about the trouble, he said it was a 'composition' put in by magnetism through a transfiguration, and a 'divorced woman, a whore, is trying to get inside.'

He said he had been bothered considerably more than usual the past ten months or year. He earnestly asked the physicians to feel his abdomen and note the movements in it. Sometimes he insists that there is something 'alive' in his 'stomach'.

When the remark was passed that ten months was a long time to carry anything there, he looked decidedly pleased and smiled effusively. When asked how he acquired it, he threw back his head and looked upward and smiled knowingly (as if it came from God).

He will not frankly state today that he is pregnant, but he is pleased by such fancies, and characteristically rubs his abdomen. While making this note he suddenly denounced in vigorous language the 'divorced whore' who is trying to get into his abdomen. (Ibid., p. 691)

*This patient's unconscious identification as a female is demonstrated by his delusion of being pregnant.*

206 Fig. 69 – Masculine compensation in a woman. Following the mother's interference with her mating she developed a psychosis in which she solved her unhappiness by becoming male, the priest of an elaborate new religion and philosophy. Her attitude is that of aggressive homosexuality. She made the costume. (Ibid., p. 701)

*Why did the mother of this patient interfere "with her mating?" Undoubtedly because the mother unconsciously was homosexually attracted to the daughter and resented any competition from men for the daughter's affections.*

207 On the other hand, the individuals, who finally yield to their perverse erotic cravings and resign themselves to live at the level of non-resistance to it, may be found on the wards by the hundreds as so-called chronic dementia praecox types. A study

of these people shows that they are preoccupied with an incessant stream of lurid, weird polymorphous perverse sexual thoughts and sensations, and a most grotesque, primitive estimation of their place in the social herd. Their slovenly appearance and characteristically relaxed, slouchly carriage reveal the marked indifference of the erotic affect to social esteem ... (Ibid., p. 706)

*With the proper guidance and psychotherapy, the individuals described here by Dr. Kempf would have a good chance of eventually regaining a useful place in society, rather than being relegated to the back wards of mental hospitals. For by yielding to "their perverse erotic cravings" and resigning themselves to "live at the level of non-resistance" to them, these patients have already accomplished the fundamental task which is indispensable for the cure of their mental illness, namely, the admitting into conscious awareness of these heretofore repressed erotic cravings, the denial of which has caused them to become insane.*

208   Another patient would break out into wild rage at each visit from the doctor, grinding his teeth and threatening to assault so that he had to be restrained. Yet, shortly after he would jump into his bed and with an elegant gesture send the physician a 'kiss of forgiveness.' —Dementia Praecox or the Group of Schizophrenias, Eugen Bleuler (Ibid., p. 45)

*The "kiss of forgiveness" which this patient sent his physician is definitely an effeminate gesture, and is indicative of the patient's bisexual conflict.*

209   A woman patient is 'Christ and the Lord of the World.' ... She is the Savior's Housekeeper, the Bride of Christ, 'the five-hundredth messiah, God's Golden Book and must be rewarded.' The patient is like God at least inasmuch as

everything which she even dares to think comes to pass at once. In women, these religious, grandiose ideas usually have an erotic character. Rarely is it simply a sublimation of sexual love in religious ideas. More frequently, there is a condensation of vague religious ideas in certain definite forms. The Lord or Savior to whom the patient is related or with whom she identifies is usually characterized by certain traits of a real man who had played some part in the patient's life. (Ibid., p. 120)

*This patient's bisexual conflict is illustrated by her female identification – the "Savior's Housekeeper" and the "Bride of Christ" – and her simultaneous male identification – "Christ and the Lord of the World" and the "five hundredth messiah."*

210 Thus a patient says that he is being 'subjected to rape,' although his confinement in a mental hospital constitutes a different kind of violation of his person. (Ibid., p. 151)

*For a male patient to say he is being "subjected to rape" indicates a very strong feminine identification.*

211 The delusion of being possessed is very commonly seen as a specific type of 'double personality.' Nowadays we rarely see it in its ancient religious form or sense. Instead of the Devil, God may be the commanding spirit; or 'God has hurled a spirit at the patient's head. His spirit is then possessed.' Now and then the patient's sex appears altered delusionally. The male patient may feel himself at times, or even continually, a woman, or vice-versa. (Ibid., p. 123)

*When Dr. Bleuler, the man who originated the name "schizophrenia," states that "now and then the patient's sex appears altered delusionally," he would have been more* *accurate had he stated that in schizophrenia the patient's sex is <u>always</u> altered delusionally, even if in some cases this phenomenon is not quite as apparent as it is in others, for it is always severe bisexual conflict which forms the core of the disease.*

212     Frequently the patient considers his entire environment as transformed, "shammed." We also find that people's characteristics and station in life are being changed. The patient's sister has become engaged. The doctor is divorced from his wife and the nurse becomes a man in disguise. The patient's late mother continues living as a bull in his stable. (Ibid., p. 124)

*The fact the patient believes his female nurse is a man in disguise shows the depth of his bisexual conflict and confusion. However, intuitively he may realize the nurse is somewhat "mannish." Likewise, in his schizophrenic delusion he believes his mother lives on as a "bull in his stable," implying that she too was a very masculine woman. In fact the mothers of all schizophrenic patients, both male <u>and</u> female, display strong masculine characteristics either openly or subtly.*

213     A female patient adores both a music teacher (a woman) and a minister. Occasionally she identifies with both. [22] In her hallucinations the patient obtains sexual satisfaction from the minister. But occasionally she sees the music teacher and the minister in a sexual embrace and this arouses tremendous excitement in herself. ... [[22]The same thing occurs very frequently in the dreams of normal people. C. F. Kraft-Ebbing's patient who could only love women who limp and could not resist the impulse to imitate such women.] (Ibid., p. 146)

*The female patient "adores" both her music teacher (homosexually) and her minister (heterosexually) and "occasionally she identifies with both." That is, sometimes she identifies herself as being a woman, other times as being a man. Furthermore, she identifies as a man with the minister when he is making love to the music teacher, thereby arousing tremendous homosexual excitement in herself. This is an obvious case of bisexual conflict. Kraft-Ebbing's patient who only loved women who limped, and then compulsively imitated such women, demonstrates clearly his own unconscious feminine identification.*

214   They may come to believe in real people burning them with real fire when their secret love burns within them. The following ideas are somewhat similar: a catatonic makes a certain movement of his eyebrows in exact imitation of a Miss N.; then he insists he had sexual relations with her. Miss N.'s gesture executed by his own body is equated with Miss N. herself. (Ibid., p. 76)

*This patient, like the one in quotation 211, imitates a woman. He makes the same eyebrow movements as that of a certain female acquaintance. Then he says he had sexual relations with her. First, he identifies as a female with her, then he makes love to her. His bisexual conflict is very apparent.*

215   Just as little can I believe that Wernicke's patient who mistook the attendant for his sister, Laura [24] had forgotten the memory picture of male and female clothing. As a rule lucid schizophrenics have a fairly good grasp of such ideas and memory pictures. (Ibid., p. 75)

> *Again, a schizophrenic patient demonstrates his sexual confusion by mistaking a man for a woman, in this case the male attendant for his sister Laura.*

216     A hebephrenic who worked for a time in our office, strutted around carefully togged out, manicured and pomaded and did not in the least seem to mind the teasing which he was subjected to by another uncouth employee. (Ibid., p. 49)

> *This hebephrenic patient was teased by an "uncouth employee" for displaying effeminate mannerisms.*

217     Particularly often, several persons are conceived of as one. A patient is his father and mother, and his children. During an acute, although mildly cloudy episode of his illness, another patient does not distinguish between his children as they now are and as they were as infants. When the conversation turns to sexual matters and the education of children, his wife and his own ego seem to run together into an indivisible concept: likewise he confuses the institution with his home. On questioning or other stimulation it does not make any difference of which part of this conceptual pair he or the observer are talking about since he says the same things about either part and it is quite impossible to force a separation. (Ibid., p. 75)

> *Bisexual confusion is shown by the first patient who is both "his father and his mother," as well as his children. The second patient's ego seems to "run together into an indivisible concept" with that of his wife's, and Dr. Bleuler comments that "it is quite impossible to force a separation" between them. In other words, the patient so strongly identifies as a woman with his wife that for all intents and purposes they are one and the same person, a delusional "bearded lady."*

218        The bodily 'influencing' constitutes an especially unbearable torture for these patients. The physician stabs their eyes with a 'knife-voice.' They are dissected, beaten, electrocuted, their brain is sawn to pieces, their muscles are stiffened. A constantly operating machine has been installed in their heads. Someone has injected something in their tear-ducts. Their eyes have been exchanged for those of old women. They are put to sleep. A woman patient is told that her flesh would make delicious veal chops, which are then devoured by wolves. Their sexual organs are cut off and exhibited in a neighboring city. (Ibid., p. 118)

*The male patients believe "their eyes have been exchanged for those of old women." That is, unconsciously they identify themselves as being female. And the patients who believe their sexual organs have been cut off and are being exhibited in neighboring cities are merely indulging in unconscious wish fulfillment to exchange their genitals for those of the opposite sex, requiring as a first step the relinquishment of their present equipment.*

219    The patients take no trouble at all about thinking these ideas through. They can be simultaneously or alternately not only the King of Britain, but Brittania herself. (Ibid., p. 120)

*The patients who are both "King of Britain" and "Brittania herself" are definitely "bearded ladies."*

220    Some of these patients are at any one time so consistently and completely the one personality or the other, that they do not even think of the other person when they assume the part of one, the person whom they represent at the moment is considered as the natural one. Other patients may become conscious of the change. A woman patient may be 'switched, from a virgin to a married woman.' Another woman is 'a man

named Bauman and then again myself.' For the most part, the different conceptions are mixed up in an irregular way, occasionally even in the very same sentence.

The delusion of sex transformation also alters the personality. (Ibid., p. 144)

*This patient sometimes is "a man named Bauman and then again myself." She is afflicted with the schizophrenic "delusion of sex transformation" which also "alters the personality," changing one from woman to man, or vice versa. The delusional sex transformation is the psychotic manifestation of powerful unconscious wishes.*

221     Frequently the patients will blame their surroundings or attendants for what they themselves have done. A patient hits the attendant on the head and screams, 'Oh, my poor little head!' Another seeing the attendant calls out, 'There goes the maid with the lantern. I am the maid with the lantern.' (Ibid., p. 145)

*The patient who mistakes the male attendant for the "maid with the lantern" and then states that he himself is "the maid with the lantern" is demonstrating a severe degree of bisexual confusion and conflict.*

222     The patient's wife must not use eggs in cooking, otherwise he will grow feathers. Hair is growing down his back. He has no nose anymore; he has become a rubber ball. His genitals are gone; they were destroyed by fire. His spinal marrow runs out in his sperm. (Ibid., p. 123)

*The patient's unconscious wish to be a female is greatly facilitated by having his male genitalia destroyed by fire, thus symbolizing the longed-for castration which must precede any transformation into a female.*

223         Silk weaver: intelligent. At the age of fifteen: religious ideas of grandeur. At twenty: catatonic frenzy, improvement. At age of twenty-seven: diagnosis of dementia. From ages twenty-nine to thirty-one, catatonic. Until the age of fifty-five, he continued as a diligent, quiet weaver who supported his parents and himself. At the age of fifty-five, auto-castration; since then he has been in the hospital with some catatonic symptoms. (Ibid., p. 247)

*This patient went a step further than the one in quotation 220 by actually castrating himself rather than merely having delusions of such, i.e. of having lost his genitals in a fire. With the loss of his male genitals he is a step closer to fulfilling his deepest wish, namely, that of becoming female.*

224   The clearer the patient's state of consciousness and the fewer reasons there are for the presence of affects, the milder may the symptoms be which permit a diagnosis of schizophrenia. The same applies to the differential diagnosis: epileptics may create symbols; they may confuse concepts such as man and woman, or coin neologisms, but only when their consciousness is clouded. (Ibid., p. 295)

*Dr. Bleuler again emphasizes how schizophrenics "may confuse concepts such as man and woman," much as do certain persons suffering from so-called "epilepsy," which in reality is frequently but one of the symptoms of schizophrenia.*

225         In schizophrenia, the habitual well-worn pathways of association have lost their cohesiveness. ... In a certain context, the father believes that he is the mother of his children, by ignoring existing attributes of his own person and substituting attributes that belong to his wife. (Ibid., p. 355)

*Again, attention is drawn to the bisexual conflict in schizophrenics by the example of the father who may now believe "he is the mother of his children."*

226    Probably, too, the delusions like the dreams often express precisely the opposite of what the patient really wants. A catatonic has homosexual tendencies; he builds a delusion that a woman of high society (whom he does not really know) is in love with him, and he insists that he is in love with her. Under such conditions, it is understandable that there is no affect bound up with the delusion. He does not love the woman at all; the idea is obviously only the reaction to the unpleasant consciousness of his homosexuality. (Ibid., p. 369)

*This is an excellent example of how repressed homosexuality leads to schizophrenic symptomatology. To defend himself against his homosexual cravings, the patient creates the psychotic delusion that he both loves and is loved by a woman whom in fact he doesn't even know. As long as he can keep this delusion alive, he can evade the reality of his "perverse" sexual longings.*

227    A certain type of facial expression can lead us to conclude that the patient practices fellatio; a delusion may reveal the bad conscience of a pederast. Our findings are confirmed by the patients without any attempt at suggestion. (Ibid., p. 391)

*Dr. Bleuler points out the existence of certain "perverse" sexual practices in some of his hospitalized schizophrenic patients, specifically – oral and anal homosexual intercourse.*

228    A sexually aroused hospitalized patient thinks that he is in a convent and uses his mattress as a sexual object. (Ibid., p. 393)

*Since only women are allowed to be in convents, it could be construed that Dr. Bleuler's patient believes he is a woman.*

229       One husband is ashamed before his wife and therefore must depreciate her; another throws the blame on her; a third surrenders his masculinity and becomes a woman. [44] For the most part, the delusion is a combined one in which all three forms appear in the same patient, but one usually occupies the foreground. [[44] Schreber's desire to have children was not satisfied. In the process of becoming a woman he is made pregnant by God and will renew humanity.] (Ibid., p. 399)

*The husband (the patient) "surrenders his masculinity and becomes a woman," precisely as did Daniel Paul Schreber, Dr. Bleuler points out. As Drs. Macalpine and Hunter so aptly phrased it: "Schreber's name is legion."*

230       A workingman felt his childishness very keenly. However, he had never been very active sexually, and of late was almost entirely impotent or suffered from ejaculatio praecox. Because of his hebephrenia, he has been incapable of working at his trade for many years. Therefore, he does all the womanly tasks at home while his wife conducts a business. (Ibid., p. 399)

*This hebephrenic patient has "surrendered his masculinity" and become a woman in all but name only. If his ego had been unable to accept his strong feminine strivings and had resisted them, he would have become a "paranoid" schizophrenic rather than the "hebephrenic" schizophrenic he is classified as by Dr. Bleuler.*

231       Metamorphosis sexualis paranoica may have other sources than that of impotence, particularly a complicating

homosexuality. In one such case, which unfortunately I was unable to analyze, I had reason to suspect that the patient considered herself to be a man because only as a man she could hope to realize her scholastic aspirations. Occasionally, such a delusion is an accidental by-product of further elaborated and displaced delusional ideas: one patient had been in love with a minister some fifty years previously; gradually, the woman patient (like many another under the same conditions) became Christ, proving this transformation by demonstrating a femoral hernia as a scrotum. (Ibid., p. 400)

*Dr. Bleuler again emphasizes the vital role played by bisexual conflict and confusion among his schizophrenic patients.*

232    Perversions, alongside the manifestations of normal drives, are much more pronounced in schizophrenics than in neurotics. The homosexual components, especially, play an unsuspectedly large role. But we will not go into further details at this point. (Ibid., pp. 410-411)

*It was most unfortunate that Dr. Bleuler decided not to "go into further details at this point" on the "unsuspectedly large role" that homosexuality plays in the genesis of schizophrenia, for by not doing so – then or later – he threw off the scent the vast majority of investigators who followed in his footsteps.*

233    Another catatonic woman, also in love with a preacher, writes in a letter: 'The preacher of the Reformed Church must annihilate me.' At times the nurse – <u>faute de mieux</u> – serves as the patient's love object. In this sense she once said she would love to squeeze the nurse against her own body till the nurse got so thin that she could kindle her. (Ibid., p. 415)

*This patient's nurse "kindles" the latter's powerful homosexual feelings, the prior repression of which have driven her insane.*

234         Among the male patients, a female saint generally represents the love object. Yet schizophrenic men are not in the least embarrassed to be married even to God or Christ. Thus in the patient mentioned above whose first erotic feelings were directed to his sister, Christ appeared to him as a very pretty girl who looked just like his sister. (Ibid., p. 420)

*The fact that schizophrenic male patients "are not in the least embarrassed to be married even to God or Christ" is evidence of their bisexual conflict and homosexual inclinations.*

235         The eye also serves as a symbol of the female genitalia; whereas the nose can be both the male and female organ, even in the same patient. Women who have to be tube-fed through the nasal passage often complain that they are being sexually abused. Whenever someone touches his nose, a patient proclaims this to mean that he himself is masturbating; he sticks cigarettes up his nose which for him is a conscious symbolic act representing intercourse.[70] (Ibid., p. 424)

*By sticking a cigarette up his nose, this patient is symbolically playing the part of a female having sexual intercourse with a male, the nose representing a vagina and the cigarette a penis.*

236    A man ran about looking for his (imaginary) wife. Then, for a long time he stared at the doctor whom he recognized as such, finally blurting out: 'But you are really my beloved.' Afterwards he asked one of the other doctors whether he was not his wife, unbuttoning his trousers as he spoke. On the

following day the patient said to the same physician: 'I don't know whether you are a representative of a young lady. Yesterday, I saw one here who looked very much like you.' When his attention was called to the doctor's beard, he looked closely at the doctor and then said: 'In the theater women often play the roles of men.' Some time later he grasped the doctor's hand and exclaimed, filled with rapture: 'Aren't you the young girl who took lessons from me?' Later, he approached other patients in the same way. (Ibid., p. 427)

*This is a striking example of the intensity of the sexual confusion and conflict in a schizophrenic.*

237    The displacement went much farther in the previously mentioned woman who thought she was a man and possessed testicles which meant that, via Christ, she was in love with a priest. Another patient had the same original delusion. But in place of the priest, there were successively substituted the Holy Ghost, God the Father, and Christ who in turn was represented by a lamb. Now a lamb belongs to a ram. Therefore, 'I am a ram,' in this case originally meant: 'I have obtained my priest.' (Ibid., p. 436)

*This schizophrenic patient thought she was a man who possessed testicles, and also thought of herself as a "ram," a powerful symbol of male sexuality.*

238             … I recall very vividly four castrated schizophrenics. One of them had cut off his own testicles. Two had their ovaries removed for 'nervous troubles;' i.e., in reality, because of the psychosis. A fourth had an ovariectomy because of an inflammatory process of the internal genitalia. In none of these cases could we detect a beneficial effect on the course of the disease. In two cases, castration was followed by the actual outbreak of the illness, giving rise to the patients' notion that

they were no longer 'complete' human beings, thus constituting an integral part of the disease symptoms. Unilateral castration was also of no help in another male case. (Ibid., p. 473)

*These four schizophrenics had strong unconscious desires to be of the opposite sex and consequently were instrumental in bringing about their own castration.*

239     Dear Dr. ... I do not want to be a boy. I wemt to be a girl just my sister is ... Fae M. Stamtey. (Anonymous)

*This boy "Fae," who wants to be a girl like his "sister is," demonstrates at what an early age these opposite-sex feelings can develop and how overwhelming they can be.*

240     On Christmas morning oranges are going to turn blue
        On Christmas morning girls are going to turn into boys
and
        vice versa
        On Christmas morning football scores will start at one
hundred
        On Christmas morning night will turn into day.
            —Jeanne Turner, sixth grade

*This young lady is obviously entertaining fantasies of becoming a boy.*

241     All through his childhood he had been very fond of playing parts in front of the mirror. Now in front of the mirror he continued to play parts, but in this one special instance he allowed himself to become absorbed into the part he played (to be spontaneous). This he felt was his undoing. The parts he played in front of the mirror were always women's parts. He dressed himself up in his mother's clothes, which had been

kept. He rehearsed female parts from the great tragedies. But then he found he could not stop playing the part of a woman. He caught himself compulsively walking like a woman, talking like a woman, even seeing and thinking as a woman might see and think. This was his present position, and this was his explanation for his fantastic get-up. For, he said, he found that he was driven to dress up and act in his present manner as the only way to arrest the womanish part that threatened to engulf not only his actions but even his 'own' self as well, and to rob him of his much cherished control and mastery of his being. Why he was driven into playing this role, which he hated and which he knew everyone laughed at, he could not understand. But this 'schizophrenic' role was the only refuge he knew from being entirely engulfed by the woman who was inside him, and always seemed to be coming out of him. —<u>The Divided Self,</u> R. D. Laing, Penguin Books, Baltimore, Maryland, 1965, p. 72.

*R. D. Laing sketches a vivid picture of the intensity of the homosexual feelings a schizophrenic youth is vainly attempting to hold in abeyance.*

242   The first step in the process of increasing barrenness of his existence was that the woman lost her love transparency, being a completely different, remote 'foreign' pole of existence; she became 'pale,' a 'mirage,' then she represented 'undigestible food' and finally she dropped entirely out of the frame of his world. When his progressing schizophrenia 'depleted his masculinity,' when most of his own male feelings 'had run out,' he suddenly and for the first time in his life felt driven to 'open himself' to a certain form of homosexual love. He described most vividly how in this homosexual love he succeeded in experiencing at least half of the fullness of existence. He did not have to 'exert' himself very much to attain this semi-fullness, there was little danger of 'losing

himself' and of 'running out' into boundlessness in this limited extent and depth. On the contrary, the homosexual love could 'replenish' his existence 'to a whole man.' (Ibid., p. 146)

*This is an excellent description of the only way a schizophrenic can be cured of his "disease," and that is by consciously allowing himself to experience to the fullest all those homosexual feelings and desires whose prior repression is the factor which has led to his insanity, or "schizophrenia." (This process applies equally to schizophrenic women.)*

243         We shall attempt to characterize the nature of this 'self' by statements made not only by this 'self' directly but also by statements that appear to originate in other systems. There are not a great many of these statements, at least by the 'self' in person as it were. During her years in hospital, many of them probably had become run together to result in constantly reiterated short telegraphic statements containing a great wealth of implications.

As we saw above, she said she had the Tree of Life inside her. The apples of this tree were her breasts. She had ten nipples (her fingers). She had 'all the bones of a brigade of the Highland Light Infantry.' She had everything she could think of. Anything she wanted, she had and she had not, immediately, at the one time. Reality did not cast its shadow or its light over any wish or fear. Every wish met with instantaneous phantom fulfillment and every dread likewise instantaneously came to pass in a phantom way. Thus she could be anyone, anywhere, any time. 'I'm Rita Hayworth, I'm Joan Blondell, I'm a royal queen. My royal name is Julianne.' 'She's self-sufficient,' she told me. 'She's the self-possessed.' But this self-possession was double-edged. It had also its dark side. She was a girl 'possessed' by the phantom of her own being. Her self had no freedom, autonomy, or power in the real world. Since she was anyone she cared to mention, she

was no *one*. 'I'm thousands. I'm an in divide you all. I'm a no
un' (i.e. a nun: a noun: no one single person). Being a nun had
very many meanings. One of them was contrasted with being a
bride. She usually regarded me as her brother and called
herself my bride or the bride of 'leally lovely lifey life.' Of
course since life and me were sometimes identical for her, she
was terrified of Life, or me. Life (me) would mash her to pulp,
burn her heart with a red-hot iron, cut off her legs, hands,
tongue, breasts. Life was conceived in the most violent and
fiercely destructive terms imaginable. It was not some quality
about me, or something I had (e.g. a phallus = a red-hot iron).
It was what I was. I was life. Notwithstanding having the Tree
of Life inside her, she generally felt that she was the Destroyer
of Life. It was understandable, therefore, that she was terrified
that life would destroy her. Life was usually depicted by a
male or phallic symbol, but what she seemed to wish for was
not simply to be a male herself but to have a heavy
armamentarium of the sexual equipment of both sexes, all the
bones of a brigade of the Highland Light Infantry and ten
nipples, etc.

> She was born under a black sun.
> She's the occidental sun.

The ancient and very sinister image of the black sun
arose quite independently of any reading. Julie had left school
at fourteen, had read very little, and was not particularly
clever. It was extremely unlikely that she would have come
across any reference to it, but we shall forgo discussion of the
origin of the symbol and restrict ourselves to seeing her
language as an expression of the way she experienced being-
in-the-world.

She always insisted that her mother had never wanted
her, and had crushed her out in some monstrous way rather
than give birth to her normally. Her mother had 'wanted and

not wanted' a son. She was 'an accidental sun,' i.e. an accidental son whom her mother out of hate had turned into a girl. The rays of the black sun scorched and shrivelled her. Under the black sun she existed as a dead thing. (Ibid., p. 203)

*The graphic illustration of bisexual confusion in a schizophrenic woman that is portrayed here by Dr. Laing should convince even the most skeptical of the enormous potential this conflict has for causing severe emotional distress and illness.*

244     They forgot that, amidst all my lunatic childishness and simplicity, I was a grown-up man, and probably knew not myself. And if it is true of any creature, that he knoweth not of what spirit he is, it is strikingly true of a lunatic. —Perceval's Narrative (A Patient's Account of His Psychosis), 1830-1832, edited by Gregory Bateson, Stanford University Press, Stanford, California, 1961, p. 123.

*When Perceval writes that "it is strikingly true of a lunatic" that "he knoweth not of what spirit he is," he could as well have written that "he knoweth not of what gender he is."*

245     What was true of Goethe is true of me. I have two souls. What are they? They are male and female, positive and negative, destructive and inductive, Yang and Yin. And they want to divide in a sort of eternal schizophrenia. Well, let them go. I, quite an ordinary person, have reunited them and I tell them to go where they will. I have a split mind. I was a manic-depressive; let us say for the sake of the argument that I am now a schizophrenic. —Wisdom, Madness and Folly (The Philosophy of a Lunatic), John Custance, Pellegrini & Cudahy, New York, 1952, p. 135.

*John Custance, in this short sentence, has given the world the key to understanding mental illness. His "split mind" is caused by conflict between his male and female selves, his "Yang and Yin." Goethe himself recognized this same conflict when he lamented that "Alas, two souls" were housed within his breast. It is invariably the conflict of these two souls, the male and the female, which forms the etiological basis of all functional mental illness.*

246            I was a combination of Oliver Twist and Little Nell. —
On Being Different, Merle Miller, Random House, New York, 1971, p. 15.

*Merle Miller, a writer whose sexual orientation is homosexual, grew up knowing he was "different" from other boys. When he states he was a "combination of Oliver Twist and Little Nell," he is also describing the <u>unconscious</u> bisexual conflict of every schizophrenic person, or one who is afflicted with the "bearded lady" disease.*

247            I look at my hands and feet. They're big. Sometimes I feel big. Sometimes I look at me and I look big. But then I feel a thing about me. It's a hard thing to call by a name. It's a delicate thing. Maybe that's it, a delicacy and already I don't like the word. But it fits. So I go around feeling this here delicacy. In the middle of a bigness and a gawkiness I feel this delicacy. I heard them talk, my mother and father. 'Awkward,' I heard and this was about me. 'Gawky,' I heard and this was also about me. 'Skinny,' I heard and something about a nice face and maybe that was also supposed to be about me. But in the middle of all this I sometimes have the delicacy thing. I watch myself, my hands, the way I move them, and I swear there's a delicate thing to it. Sometimes it's mixed. I mean this: all at the same time I'm a turbine, Arthur Turbitzky and this delicacy thing.

The delicacy. There's a girl-like thing about it that I could be happy to skip. But sometimes it's there and all the time while I'm a turbine, a dynamo, a dynamic turbine, I see me moving my hands so delicately that it's crazy. —<u>Platzo and the Mexican Pony Rider</u>, Theodore Isaac Rubin, M. D., Ballantine Books, New York, 1965, pp. 32-33.

*Dr. Rubin gives a wonderful description here of a young man's bisexual turmoil.*

248    Whereas the older one 'has no nerves' and is very well adjusted and cheerful, the younger is 'a bundle of nerves' and is a soft [3] and womanish aesthete. At seventeen he was in a psychiatric clinic for some weeks on account of a mental ailment with suicidal ideas, and even after his recovery he remained easily excitable. He has married. [[3] The word <u>soft</u> implies in this context all the varied meanings of the german <u>weich</u> – a frequently used and important term in this paper – including physically soft as well as tender-hearted, delicate, effeminate, weak, or malleable – translators] —"The Case of Ellen West (An Anthropological-Clinical Study)", Ludwig Binswanger (in <u>Existence</u>, edited by Rollo May, Ernest Angel and Henri F. Ellenberger, Simon & Schuster, New York, 1958, p. 237).

*The younger brother has had a "schizophrenic break" due to his repressed homosexual tendencies. His effeminacy is remarked on by the writer, Dr. Binswanger.*

249    At this time too she was of a lively temperament, but still self-willed. She had already chosen the motto: <u>aut Caesar aut nihil</u>! [5] [Literally, 'Either Caesar or nothing!' – translated.] Up to her sixteenth year her games were boyish. She preferred to wear trousers. From her babyhood Ellen West had been a thumb-sucker; at sixteen she suddenly gave that up, along with

her boyish games, at the onset of an infatuation which lasted two years. In a poem written in her seventeenth year, however, she still expressed the ardent desire to be a boy, for then she would be a soldier, fear no foe, and die joyously, sword in hand. (Ibid., p. 239)

On the third day of being home she is as if transformed. At breakfast she eats butter and sugar, at noon she eats so much that – for the first time in thirteen years! – she is satisfied by her food and gets really full. At afternoon coffee she eats chocolate creams and Easter eggs. She takes a walk with her husband, reads poems by Rilke, Storm, Goethe, and Tennyson, is amused by the first chapter of Mark Twain's 'Christian Science,' is in a positively festive mood, and all heaviness seems to have fallen away from her. She writes letters, the last one a letter to the fellow patient here to whom she had become so attached. In the evening she takes a lethal dose of poison, and on the following morning she is dead. 'She looked as she had never looked in life – calm and happy and peaceful.' (Ibid., p. 267)

*Ellen West's intense bisexual conflict eventually triggered her death by suicide. As has been said before, suicide is the most serious symptom of schizophrenia.*

250    Letailleur, Morin and Le Borgne (1958) write of a reversal of the sex role in schizophrenia, suggesting that this reversal results from the delusions and hallucinations accompanying schizophrenia and somatic and psychological predispositions. —"A Serendipitous Finding: Sex Roles and Schizophrenia", Frances E. Cheek, <u>Journal of Abnormal and Social Psychology</u>, Vol. 69, No. 4, 1964, p. 393.

We had expected that females as a group would be lower than males on task behaviors, and for the normal females the pattern is fairly well exhibited; on procedural suggestions, for instance, a measure of dominance, they are certainly lower. However, the schizophrenic females show the reverse pattern. They clearly reveal their activity, being higher than the normal females on procedural suggestions and notably on giving opinion (category 8) and clarification (category 12). The schizophrenic males are much lower in general on task behaviors than the normal males.

The male schizophrenics, as we have anticipated, have presented an interaction equivalent of withdrawal – low total activity rates, low rates of dominance behavior, low rates of disagreement and projected hostility – although they are close to the normal males in rates of overt hostility and higher on ego defensiveness.

However, the female schizophrenics present a marked contrast to the males. They are revealed in the interaction as more active and dominating than the female normals. ...

Our earlier observations regarding the overactivity of the female schizophrenics as suggested by their more active recreational patterns in the developmental data, the number of problems which they presented to their families, and their lack of conformity as perceived by their parents in the questionnaire study are thus corroborated.

Also, it appears that the sex differences in release rates, marital status, pupil size, and the MMPI findings of Gross (1959), which revealed withdrawal and intratensive behaviors in the male schizophrenics and more overtly emotional behavior patterns in the female, could well have been reflections of these differences in activity which we have observed. The reversal of sex roles hypothesized by Letailleur (1958) also fits this picture, for the overactive, dominating female and underactive, passive male are cultural anomalies.

Indeed, these sex-linked differences in schizophrenics would seem to be an unstated but not unfamiliar psychiatric observation. In discussing this finding with psychiatrists who have handled male and female wards we find an immediate recognition in typical comments that female wards are always noisier and more disturbed, require more attendants, etc. This would appear to be one of those glaring apparent facts which must have a clear, cold eye, such as the interaction categories, cast upon them before they can be truly seen. . . .

It is of considerable interest to speculate as to the significance of these findings for our understanding of the nature and etiology of schizophrenia. Does schizophrenia make females more active and males more passive? This would fit the notion of Letailleur and his associates (1958) of the reversal of sex roles as a function of the disease process. However, probably this is not the case as our developmental data suggest that the females have been more active and the males more passive from early childhood. (Ibid., pp. 398-99)

*This article on schizophrenia by Frances E. Cheek documents the fact of sexual role reversal in male and female schizophrenics. In other words, male schizophrenics exhibit more feminine behavior than do "normal" males, while female schizophrenics exhibit more masculine behavior than do "normal" females. The author also makes the point that this sexual role reversal is not so much the product of the disease as it is the precondition for the disease, correctly implying, thereby, a direct etiological connection.*

251          As a preliminary exercise in understanding the possibilities in such a situation, a case reported from the literature on mental illness may be considered.

It is that of a man who has been hospitalized for a long time because of some rather weird ideas. He thinks that certain persecutors, by exerting extraordinary influence upon him, are causing him to be tormented with sexual sensations and feelings which he finds, or professes to find, revolting. The 'influences' by which this is achieved are invisible, and act over long distances. Of main interest here is the kind of experience that could lead to such a disorder, and the kind of person to whom it could happen.

Important, first of all, is a particular <u>build</u> of personality. The man is described, at the outset, as exaggerated in his self-esteem, confident to the point of arrogance. In the midst of his exalted pretensions and a feeling of contemptuous superiority towards others, he now discovers within himself, not only that he is timid and inadequate in the region of sexual behavior, but that he has a natural disposition toward effeminacy.

In a society such as ours, in which 'real manhood' is so closely linked with sex virility and masculine courage, such a discovery might well be catastrophic, especially to a person who tends strongly toward vanity. It may easily be believed that the conflict was completely unbearable. Here, where the most exalted ago was confronted with the most degrading and shameful defect, is something approaching the ultimate degree of human internal crisis. The effect of directly facing the facts would be like an explosion in a locked room.

That such a person should begin to feel himself regarded as an object of contempt is understandable enough; likewise that the onset of his disorder should show the familiar mistaken interpretation of remarks in which he finds the accusation that he is queer and lacking in masculinity.

In the next phase the idea develops that he has become the object of a plot in which certain evil persons (through motives which need not be detailed) are causing him, or forcing him, to experience the emotions, thoughts and desires of a woman. The extraordinary means by which these influences are exerted, he believes, involve not only supernatural forces, but also electrical action, in which the nerves of his skin are likened to 'tiny radio antennae capable of receiving sensations.'

While the delusional system here includes some rather strange notions, to be later considered, its meaning is clear enough. Through the belief that <u>others</u> are working these criminal effects upon him, he is able to enjoy otherwise forbidden and shameful erotic sensations and emotions with the excuse that he is a passive and helpless victim. Feminine feelings, homosexual desires, the impulse to masturbate, all now become tolerable since full responsibility can be charged to the persecutors. The delusions are thus, in effect, a denial of ownership. The patient has 'pointed the finger' elsewhere. He has made the <u>paranoid shift</u>. —<u>This is Mental Illness (How it Feels and What it Means)</u>, Vernon W. Grant, Ph. D., Beacon Press, Boston, 1966, pp. 92-94.

*This is an excellent example of the indispensable role played by repressed homosexual tendencies in the genesis of schizophrenia. "Schreber's name is legion."*

252          Sylvia felt interested in certain girls in her office. It seemed to her that these girls appeared slightly confused in her presence, that they blushed or paled slightly when they saw her. From this she inferred that they were attracted to her. She once phoned one of these 'smitten' girls and asked if she would like to spend the night together. In explaining her motive, Sylvia said: 'She had to be made to realize what it was she wanted of me. When I called her up all I wanted was for her to realize that this thing was abnormal and must stop. I thought she did not know her impulses were homosexual, or rather that she could not face them. I wanted her to know where her impulses would lead, and that she was playing with fire. It worked, and she refused, and was walking around blushing for several days.'

This is an excellent example of the kind of thinking called rationalization. Sylvia herself made the advance, but managed to persuade herself that her sole motive was to make the girl aware it was *she* who was attracted to Sylvia. It was a neat way of shifting, or reversing the fact that she herself was the attracted one.

The social shyness of the schizophrenic is well illustrated in Sylvia's behavior. Thus, in this instance, an outright advance would have been impossible for her. Only by disguising her motive was she able to be so daring. Typically, she was more round-about in her approaches. One Christmas the girls exchanged gifts. Sylvia gave one girl a book dealing with the Kinsey report. This she did because: 'I thought that since it would get around to everyone that I had given Mary the Kinsey book it would get to Lila too, and she would realize that she might have Lesbian qualities.' Lila was the goal of this maneuver. Sylvia commented, 'Yes, I realize it was indirect, but it was about as direct as I can be. I'm pretty cautious in such matters.'

Sylvia is tall, rather slender, with black hair and grayish eyes. While her features are good, there is a slightly masculine quality about them. During experiences such as those reported above, she feels that she may be homosexual. She has had rather strongly negative feelings toward men. (Ibid., p. 30)

*Sylvia is described by the author as being "schizophrenic," whereas in fact she has avoided this fate by admitting to herself that "she may be homosexual." Her homosexuality has always been close to the surface, as indicated here, and her conscious awareness of the possibility she might be homosexual has saved her from becoming more seriously mentally ill.*

253  I felt the old surge of hatred as I had against my father this last summer in Spain when money didn't come ... when love didn't come ... Everybody knows or accepts by now that such things 'the jargon' homosexual conflicts etc. are within them ... everyone knows that what they do every day has something to

do with that jargon, but very few are willing to find out
EXACTLY what the connecting links are, what the psychic
energy has to do with its product ... most don't have to until
they are shown by some disaster that what they do is foolish,
or harmful or too painful for themselves to bear and only then
do they ask themselves what those connecting links are, HOW
EXACTLY they have been exteriorizing ... John is driving me
crazy (scaring me, still threatening) I called to get that lift
down to New York I stumbled on some word (inside myself,
still inside myself) and he jumped on it said 'Do you feel
guilty about something, daddy?' for himself he meant guilty
about trying to escape him last night, refusing to let him
bother me ... whatever he meant by Daddy is his problem I
suppose the guy you want to make love to has to resemble
your father. It's just too uncanny having him take me down to
try and come to terms with Laura. I had a fear a while back
that something inside him would make us crash and although
objectively that may yet be my own fear comes from a desire
that that should be so, that I should go no further with this
analysis but instead give myself up to him as he desires
(desires ... desires ... there's another word I used in that letter
to Nathan.) ... Acquiesce to my desires I want to beat (love)
you that damn letter was in part a love letter ... (No no it can't
be that just stated them in their undeniable form so that I had
to face it both the wish to beat and love my father and the wish
to love healthily, heterosexually) I mustn't shake John's grip if
I'm going to ride in the same car with him that's silly you have
to go pretty far crazy to kill yourself even subconsciously
directed because you are threatened he probably believes there
are plenty of others besides me the fact is I MUST shake
John's grip on myself and not scare myself with eery
consequences ... the newspaper odds are AGAINST
automobile deaths, that was the resistance mechanism trying
to stop me again I'm hot on your tail blue bear that doesn't
mean anything what does that mean it means that I'm feeling

the denied homosexual instincts feeling the woman in me and getting over her that's it that's what Faulkner's bear was a woman I have the quotes up on my wall I wrote them down a week ago ... woman is a bear you must kill the bear to be a man no that isn't what I've got on my wall the quotes go 'Anyone could be upset by his first lion.' —"The Onset of Psychosis – A Diary Account," Malcolm Bowers, <u>Psychiatry</u>, Vol 28, 1965, p. 356.

*Malcolm Bowers, even in the very grip of madness, has been able to gain insight into the bisexual conflict which provoked it.*

254  There is a hint here, but only a hint, that Orestes has to combat a feminine side of himself. But what is clearly in focus is the sense that Orestes' madness is inevitable.

In an important sense the conflict is an external one, though he may suffer internally because of it. Orestes is caught up in a conflict he did not create. Aeschylus' portrayal of Orestes is different from Euripides' version, where we find that the external conflict between Apollo and the Furies mirrors the inner conflicts between the male and female parts of his character. —<u>Mind and Madness in Ancient Greece</u>, Bennett Simon, M. D., Cornell University Press, Ithaca, NY and London, 1978, pp. 103-104.

*Aeschylus and Euripides were intuitive psychologists as well as great playwrights, for both could sense Orestes' bisexual conflict and knew it was somehow connected with his growing madness.*

255  Dionysus is the god who induces madness, and in some mythic versions was himself driven mad by Hera in revenge against Zeus. Hera is also said to have caused his

effeminacy, which is closely related to the theme of madness.[57] (Ibid., p. 115)

> *The fact that the Greek playwrights were able to relate a man's effeminacy to his madness shows acute psychological insight on their part. Were they also perceptive enough to link a woman's <u>masculinity</u> to her madness? If so, they would have been among the very first to have developed the "bearded lady" concept of mental illness.*

256              Let us first consider the madness of Pentheus. It is shown step by step to take place in an interpersonal process. Dionysus, the other 'person' in this process, embodies the urges for release, the yearning for ecstatic orgy, the repressed sexuality, and the warded-off, dreaded wishes to be feminine. [58] ... Pentheus looks to his armor and spear to defend himself against <u>inner</u> threats, which include his wishes to become a woman among the women and his fears of the Maenads as phallic destroyers. (Ibid., pp. 116-17)

... Finally, in Euripides' <u>Bacchae</u>, which is full of illusions, theater and madness are joined in the person of Pentheus dressing up as a woman. He does on stage what a typical greek male actor playing a woman must do offstage – get his costume just right, ask for help in final adjustment, and get last-minute coaching on how to walk and hold himself as a woman.

... In the <u>Bacchae</u> Pentheus starts out at one extreme – he will brook no illusions or convenient fictions. By the end of the play, this insistence on brute reality has turned out to be quite brittle, and he gradually goes mad. The boundary between reality and madness is marked by the scene in which he dresses as a woman, deluding himself that he is not deluded. (Ibid., p. 147)

> *Euripides correctly attributes Pentheus' growing madness to his severe bisexual conflict, which is vividly illustrated by his actions on the stage.*

257         A particularly vivid example of this kind of attack and the associated ritual healing is supplied by Grace Harris in her description of saka, a possession hysteria in women in an East African tribe. [38] These women at first show signs of a general restlessness or anxiety, and then suddenly begin the characteristic convulsive movements. The shoulders shake rapidly while the head moves rhythmically from side to side. Often the eyes are closed and the face is expressionless, and the woman seemingly loses consciousness. Some women perform monotonous repetitive acts, while others repeat strange sounds that mimic foreign words. The people of the tribe consider this a disease of 'the heart' which involves abnormal urges and cravings as well as fears. One disease related to *saka* is a form of kleptomania. *Saka* is an illness of 'wanting and wanting.' The attacks are frequently triggered by a desire for something belonging to the victim's husband or something (usually requiring cash) that he has been unwilling or unable to procure for her. The healing takes place at a public or semipublic ritual, with other women present, and involves dance and drums. The spirit that allegedly possesses the woman demands that she be given the objects she craves, often items associated with the activities of men. During the ritual the woman wears male garb and carries a man's walking stick. The items that the husband must provide seem unexotic but are important to her: cigarettes, bananas (from the foreign-owned plantations where the men work), manufactured cloth. Recovery from the illness is usually rapid if the husband provides these items, and harmony seems to be restored. In this culture, boundaries between the roles of men and women are sharply demarcated. Men work outside the village and have cash to spend. Women have very limited rights and

limited scope in dealing with land and cattle, the mainstays of the tribal life. They cannot inherit or dispose of land or cattle without their husband's consent. ...

... In sum, we have good reason to believe that both hysteria described in Greek literature and the group ecstasy of the Dionysiac rituals served to express and potentially to redress a certain imbalance in the relationships between men and women. Both served as a socially contained (more or less) and socially acceptable way of presenting, negotiating and readjusting serious disturbances in intra-psychic equilibrium. (Ibid., p. 254)

> *The people of this tribe demonstrate acute psychological insight when they describe the mental illness which afflicts certain of its members as being "a disease of the 'heart' which involves abnormal urges and cravings as well as fears." For that is exactly what mental illness is – a disease of the emotions and feelings, emotions and feelings which are always "abnormal" in that they are considered "perverse" or "unnatural" by all societies and therefore repressed by most people. And it is the repression of these feelings, which are always of a bisexual, or opposite-sex, nature, which leads directly to mental illness.*
>
> *In this particular case, this is illustrated by the fact that the "cure" for the mental illness afflicting these females is to allow them to behave in a manner more appropriate to that displayed by the male members of their tribe. These woman with "<u>saka</u>" are in reality suffering from schizophrenic symptoms, among which are included hysterical reactions.*

258        Miss Michels occupied a constant peripheral position because of her ambivalence toward the group and the group's ambivalence toward her. Her tendency to expose herself, her buffoonery and constant chattering, precluded full acceptance. This unacceptability was especially emphasized when she

made vicious verbal attacks on other patients who were upset. On the other hand, her verbal facility, her sense of humor, her ability to retaliate, and her intelligence were viewed with favor … When she disparaged herself by saying she had no mind, had an ugly body, or her words had no significance, the others tried to counter this picture of herself. The following extract records an unsuccessful attempt of this kind by Mrs. Stillman.

Miss Michels: I have a lot of hair [on my body].

Mrs. Stillman: I have, too!

Miss Michels: But I have more than anyone else.

Mrs. Stillman: Oh no. I've seen women with more hair than you have.

Miss Michels: Oh, no, you haven't! They weren't women. They must be apes!

Mrs. Stillman: One of the happiest and best-adjusted girls I know has electrolysis done time and time again.

Miss Michels: There are many hairy women, but no one has as much as I have. I got it all over my chest, my hands, my legs, and my face.

Mrs. Stillman: You look attractive, you know.

Miss Michels: I'm not attractive. If you don't look too close, you might think so, but if you look twice, you'll know differently.

Mrs. Stillman: I'm a woman and I can tell.

Miss Michels: It's nice of you to speak that way, but I'm not attractive.

Mrs. Stillman: But, what motive would I have for telling you that if I didn't mean it?

Miss Michels: I don't know, but I'm not attractive.

—The Mental Hospital (A Study of Institutional Participation in Psychiatric Illness and Treatment), Alfred H. Stanton, M. D., and Morris S. Schwartz, Ph. D. , Basic Books, Inc., New York, 1954, p. 187.

> *Miss Michel's homosexual nature is confirmed by her actions of exposing herself to other women, and by the fact she is obsessed with her own hairiness, which is commonly considered a masculine attribute.*

259 Role-playing can be disorganized not only in this way, but, as psychiatric experience indicates, in other ways; particularly relevant to psychiatric practice are the continuous playing of complementary roles, especially man and woman or adult and child, simultaneously by the same person, and the more massive disorganization of role-playing which may occur in confused states, although even here there is evidence of much residual intact role-playing. (Ibid., p. 473)

> *Any person who simultaneously plays the role of a man and a woman is suffering from severe bisexual conflict and confusion and is indisputably schizophrenic as a result.*

260 The more the work of the past year recedes into perspective, the better pleased I am with it. Now for bisexuality! I am sure you are right about it. And I am accustoming myself to the idea of regarding every sexual act as a process in which four persons are involved. We shall have a lot to discuss about that. —The Origins of Psychoanalysis (Letters to Wilhelm Fliess, Drafts and Notes: 1887-1902), Sigmund Freud, Basic Books, Inc., New York, 1954, p. 289.

> *This letter proves that Wilhelm Fliess was the person who first alerted Sigmund Freud to the theoretical importance of the fact of humanity's innate bisexual constitution.*

261 I do not understand your answer about bisexuality. It is obviously very difficult to understand one another. I certainly had no intention of doing anything but get to grips, as my contribution to the theory of bisexuality, with the thesis that

repression and the neuroses, and thus the independence of the unconscious, presuppose bisexuality. (Ibid., p. 337)

*Here Freud tries to counter Fliess' implied accusation that he has appropriated Fliess's theory of bisexuality for his own uses, without first giving him credit for having brought it to his attention. In fact Fliess was correct in his assessment of this matter, for Freud continued throughout his life to deny Fliess the credit he was due for having been the first to introduce him to this idea, or theory, which was to assume such a vital role in all of Freud's later work.*

262 We must recognize that the sexual affections are still the greatest constructive forces of the personality if properly conditioned and adjusted, but also that they may become the most insidiously, irresistibly destructive if perverted or unconditionally repressed. This statement is based upon the study of more than two thousand psychopathic and criminal personalities of many nationalities and intellectual levels. — Psychopathology, Edward J. Kempf, M. D., (Ibid., p. 749)

*The "sexual affections" which Dr. Kempf speaks of here are almost always "unconditionally repressed" if they become "perverted," with consequent malignant effect upon the person instituting the repression. Every case of functional mental illness, from slight hysteria to the most virulent forms of schizophrenia, has as its etiological core this repression of perverted "sexual affections," which are always of a homosexual nature.*

263 Another important phantasy in which imprisonment and changing were connected was the phantasy of pregnancy. ... Gradually it became clear that he had felt envious of both the mother and the baby, and that he identified with both.

My interpretations were felt to be actual castrations. For the wish to be a pregnant woman or a baby made him become a pregnant woman or a baby, and that implied his not being a man. It follows that interpreting such a wish to him meant castrating him.

In the pregnancy phantasy the change in the external world, the mother, led to a change in himself. He was both the pregnant mother, the big tummy full of babies – voices inside him – and the embryo imprisoned in her womb, castrated, helpless, all tummy and no limbs. —"Some Aspects of the Analysis of a Schizophrenic," Hanna Segal, <u>International Journal of Psycho-Analysis</u>, Vol. 31, 1950, pp. 270–271.

*This schizophrenic man is obviously afflicted with a very serious case of the "bearded lady" disease.*

264        In all three cases, the mother's relationship to the daughter who became schizophrenic contained an erotic quality, including sensuous physical intimacies. None of the mothers had been able to provide good nurturant care to the patient as a child but, at the same time, did not establish clear boundaries between herself and the child. The vacillations between disinterested aloofness and inappropriate physical intimacies that continued into adolescence or even adult life perplexed these patients. The mothers confused their daughters' needs with their own, transferred their anxieties to their daughters, and seemed to need the daughter's dependence upon them. Still, they gained little pleasure or gratification from a daughter but related by being concerned – and conveyed concerns that undermined the daughter's self-esteem and autonomy.

Studies have indicated that the homosexual concerns and tendencies of schizophrenic patients, as well as their incestuous strivings and fears, reflect the incestuous or homosexual proclivities of a parent and, concomitantly, the failure of parents to maintain their own gender-linked roles and the essential boundaries between the two generations in the nuclear family (3). The child's development becomes confused when identification with the parent of the same sex does not promote formation of a proper gender identity that is fundamental to the achievement of a stable and coherent ego identity. The de-erotization of the child-parent relationship is one of the cardinal functions of the family. —"Homosexual Tendencies in Mothers of Schizophrenic Women," Ruth Wilmanns Lidz, M. D. and Theodore Lidz, M. D., The Journal of Nervous and Mental Diseases, Vol. 149, No. 2, Williams and Wilkins Co., p. 232.

*This paper by Doctors Ruth and Theodore Lidz should have been titled "Homosexual Tendencies in the Mothers of Schizophrenics," for the type of mother described here by the authors produces not only schizophrenic daughters but schizophrenic sons as well. Beyond that small criticism, their paper is a masterpiece of psychological insight and erudition. For truly these mothers of schizophrenics definitely do exhibit noticeable homosexual tendencies, which they in turn "inherited" from their own mothers, the grandmothers of their ill children. It appears that the tendency to sexual inversion becomes more pronounced as it is passed down through the generations, until finally the last generation becomes so very mentally ill as a result of trying to repress or dissociate these tendencies that it either does not marry, or else heals itself by becoming openly homosexual, in either case bringing to an end what from nature's standpoint has become a very unprofitable enterprise.*

265        'Schreber's basic bisexuality had developed into a true manifest ambisexuality, male and female potentials being equally matched. Thus he developed fantasies of self-

impregnation while he was acting the part of the woman having intercourse with himself.' [6]

This penetrating reanalysis of Schreber's material reminds us of elements described in some former detailed observations of schizophrenia, in particular the classic publications of Nunberg. [7]

The role of ambisexuality, with its far-reaching consequences in the clinical picture of advanced schizophrenia, has been evident for a long time. From a clinical point of view, one should bear in mind that Schreber not only went through periods of deep paranoid aggression and extensive elaboration but also long periods of catatonia. We know especially, from detailed observations of catatonic attacks and catatonic stupor, that phantasies of self-procreation frequently play an important part.

It is also generally recognized that confusion about one's own sexual identity is a frequent and important part of schizophrenic symptomology. It may occur at a relatively early stage of the illness and, at times, may be detected by psychological testing prior to becoming manifest clinically. In my opinion, this symptom reflects a significant change in the patient's ego and may be described as a struggle of the feminine and masculine identification or, in other words, generally speaking, of the paternal versus the maternal introject. —Homosexuality and Psychosis in Perversions, Psychodynamics and Therapy, Gustav Bychowski, M. D., edited by Sandor Lorand, M. D., Random House, Inc., New York, 1956, p. 98.

*Probably the most accurate definition of schizophrenia one could give would be to describe it as resulting from the "struggle of the feminine and masculine identification or, in other words, generally speaking, of the paternal versus the maternal introject." For a schizophrenic is his mother and his father in equal parts, with neither one able to gain ascendancy over the other. This condition of "manifest ambisexuality" results in a total blockage of sexual and emotional satisfaction for the afflicted person and consequently he or she is driven mad – or "schizophrenic" – by the immense undischarged libidinal tension.*

*Dr. Bychowski would have been more accurate had he stated that it is "generally recognized that confusion about one's own sexual identity is an <u>invariable</u> and <u>indispensable</u> part of schizophrenic symptomology," rather than a "frequent and important part."*

266        Psychoanalytic observations of schizophrenics subjected to insulin shock therapy provide another opportunity for an understanding of the role of latent homosexuality in the origin of paranoid schizophrenia. In particular, these observations illustrate the important role played by the homosexual disappointment and the homosexual panic. The cathartic discharge provoked by the insulin coma creates a release of repressed libidinal impulses. The ambivalent homosexual attitude becomes split into its two components, with the positive one invested ideally in the transference reaction and thus accessible to analytic interpretations and working through.

Psychoanalytic investigations have demonstrated the affinity between homosexuality and the schizophrenic break. In certain complex cases of latent homosexuality, the counter-cathexis, built by the ego in order to maintain the dissociation of the psychotic core from the rest of the ego, is so precarious that the psychotic invasion occurs, as it were, spontaneously and periodically. (Ibid., p. 105)

*Dr. Bychowski emphasizes the vital role played by repressed homosexuality in the genesis of schizophrenia.*

267          Sex-typed reactions are contrasted in male and female
normals and chronic schizophrenics. In general, the
schizophrenic shows sex-role alienation on tests which contain
a self-image reference (a Role Playing Test, a Body Parts
Acceptance Test, and a Figure Preference Test). Female
schizophrenics tend to react in a more assertive manner like
normal males, and male schizophrenics in a more sensitive
manner like normal females. In a direct test of assertive vs.
yielding story sequences on the TAT, the sex-difference
reversal is significant only if housewives are used as normal
female controls. The inclination of female schizophrenics
toward assertive story sequences is matched by a similar
inclination in career women, suggesting this role reversal is
not as critical to the schizophrenic condition as the self-image
disturbance. In conscious sex-typed interests and attitudes,
schizophrenics do not differ from normals. A theory is
proposed relating schizophrenia to sex-identity alienation in
the early years of life. —"Sex-Role Alienation in
Schizophrenia," David C. McClelland and Norman F. Watt,
Journal of Abnormal Psychology, Vol. 73, No. 3, 1968, p.
226.

*It could easily be argued that the most important
sentence ever written in the annals of psychology or
psychiatry is to be found in this quotation, and it reads as
follows: "A theory is proposed relating schizophrenia to sex-
identity alienation in the early years of life." With that brief
statement McClelland and Watt have answered the question
which has plagued mankind down through the ages, namely,
why do people become insane? And in this brilliant paper by
these two extremely astute investigators, we learn the
definitive answer to this mystery.*

268   It has been a recurring clinical observation that female
schizophrenic wards are much noisier than male wards. In fact

the common picture of the schizophrenic as withdrawn applies much better to men than it does to women. Lorr and Klett (1965) have recently found statistical support for this observation in a large-scale survey in which psychotic women were shown to exhibit more excitement than psychotic men, whereas the men manifested a higher degree of retardation and apathy. In a related study using a Ward Behavior Scale, Lorr, O'Connor, and Stafford (1960) reported women were higher on a measure of *hostile belligerence,* defined as hostile, irritable, resistive, noisy, bossy, and paranoid behavior. That is, women showed assertive and interpersonally disruptive behavior that is quite the opposite of expected female sex-role behavior. (Ibid., p. 226)

*The function of the psychosis is to make it possible for a person to express deeply repressed but very powerful opposite-sex feelings, the very feelings which have driven that person crazy, or psychotic, in the first place. Thus it should come as no surprise that psychotic women tend to demonstrate "masculine" feelings and actions and psychotic men "feminine" ones.*

269    Cheek's (1964) study demonstrated sex-role alienation in schizophrenics in the most theoretically relevant way. She used the Bales' (1950) Interaction Process Analysis coding system for small group behavior in observing discussions that normals and schizophrenics of both sexes had with their parents. Schizophrenic women were more active and schizophrenic men less active than their normal counterparts. Female schizophrenics exceeded all three other groups in the *instrumental* conversational categories (giving opinion and explaining – clarification) which are normally male specialties. While she questions whether this may be due to a selection factor in hospitalization which allows overactive males and underactive females to stay in society, the finding

adds to the impression that schizophrenic men and women are alienated from their normal sex roles.

Kagan and Moss (1962) report findings that suggest the etiology of this shift. They found that male children (age 0-3) to whom mothers were hostile tended to grow up to be withdrawn, non-achievement-oriented, and socially anxious (showing the schizoid, non-assertive type of adjustment in males). In contrast, female children to whom mothers were hostile tended to grow up into active, competitive, assertive women (showing an atypical pattern with some components of a schizoid type of adjustment in females). It is conceivable that maternal hostility created sex-identity problems in the children which were solved by opting in part for the opposite sex approach to life. (Ibid., p. 227)

*The authors state that it is "conceivable that maternal hostility created sex-identity problems in the children which were solved by opting in part for the opposite sex approach to life." "Conceivable" is too weak a word to use in this regard, for in reality it is a fact that maternal hostility has just such an effect. It is the primary cause of the development of either a homosexual way of life in the children of such a mother or of a schizophrenic, or schizoid, development – the latter being the negation of the former. Furthermore, the hostile mother is the mother who is unhappy in her own female sexual role and exhibits strong masculine and homosexual leanings, the frustration of which breeds both bitterness, hostility, and a paranoid outlook. These latter emotions she discharges onto those closest to her – her children – with disastrous effect.*

270          The same effect is more noticeable in the marriage-rate figures. Fewer schizophrenics than normals had married ($x^2 = 6.48$, p < .02) and, in a significant Sex X Diagnosis interaction, relatively more schizophrenic males were single than schizophrenic females (interaction $x^2 = 5.79$, p < .02), as

Hollingshead and Redlich (1958) have also shown in larger, more representative samples. They report 42% of the male and 58% of the female mental-patient populations had married as compared with about 80% of both sexes among normals. The interaction $x^2 = 14.03$, p < .01. It seems reasonable to infer that at least part of this difference is due to the lack of normal assertiveness in male schizophrenics. (Ibid., p. 232)

*The low marriage rate among schizophrenics as compared to normals is due to the former's basic sex-role alienation. This alienation leads directly to the severe bisexual conflict and confusion which is at the very core of every schizophrenic's illness, and which makes it so difficult for a schizophrenic to sustain a heterosexual relationship of any type.*

271    The only exception was that the schizophrenic women scored lower on affiliation – nurturance than the female employees ($x^2 = 4.98$, p < .05). (Ibid., p. 232)

*The reason schizophrenic women score poorly on affiliation-nurturance tests is because at a deep, unconscious level they identify with the male sex, which throughout nature tends to be less social and nurturing than the female sex.*

272    The inference seems unmistakable that if there is sex-role alienation, the schizophrenics themselves are not very aware of it. Their conscious interests, likes, and fears appear to be normally sex-typed. (Ibid., p. 232)

*Schizophrenics are totally lacking in insight relating to their repressed, or dissociated, opposite-sex feelings. Actually, this remarkable lack of insight is one of the hallmarks of the disease, and is one of the major factors contributing to the enormous effort it requires to aid schizophrenics in their illness. "I would rather die than admit it" would be a fitting motto for the disease.*

273          Table 4 reports some very different results. Both male and female schizophrenics say more often than normals that they would choose to play opposite-sex roles. Nearly half of the schizophrenics made three or more opposite-sex choices whereas only 10% of the normals made as many. (Ibid., p. 232)

*More evidence is presented showing the opposite-sex, or homosexual, proclivities of schizophrenics.*

274          Among the males, cross-sex choices arise particularly with respect to the alternatives: 'secretary vs. policeman' and 'cow vs. bull.' In both cases the male schizophrenics choose the female roles ('secretary' 7/22 times and 'cow' 8/20 times) significantly more often than the normals (0/20 and 1/19 times, respectively). This fits with the general hypothesis that male schizophrenics are avoiding assertive male identities. (Ibid., p. 233)

*Not only are male schizophrenics "avoiding assertive male identities," but here they are actively choosing female ones. Yet these same male schizophrenics who choose female test roles would resist with all their might any implication they might have homosexual inclinations.*

275          Normal males clearly show less concern with their bodies than normal females. Nearly three-fourths of the males express satisfaction with about three-fourths of the parts listed, as contrasted with less than one-fifth of the females ($x^2 = 10.10$, $p < .01$). Note that both groups of normal women show the same pattern, with the housewives being, if anything, even more concerned about their bodies than the working women.

Among schizophrenics there is a decided reversal, females are <u>less</u> concerned, males more so, and the interaction chi-square is highly significant. The result is all the more impressive because it replicates a Sex X Diagnosis interaction found in a similar experiment by Holzberg and Plummer (1964). The reversal shows up markedly for female body parts. Among normals, females care more about them and males less, but among schizophrenics, males care more than females. These parts have to do essentially with the <u>appearance</u> of the body – it's presenting aspects (face, lips, hips, etc.). It is as if female schizophrenics have become insensitive to their appearance (like normal males), and male schizophrenics have become more sensitive to how they look (like normal females).

For the male body parts, the interaction is not significant. The female schizophrenics continue to be more satisfied than their normal counterparts, but both groups of males are equally satisfied. However, there is another interesting and significant reversal among the males. Normal males care more about their male (or strength) body parts than their female (or appearance) parts, but the trend is reversed for the male schizophrenics (interaction $x^2 = 4.33$, $p < .05$). The same reversal does not appear for the females.

To summarize these findings: schizophrenic males have replaced the normal male concern for masculine body parts with a greater concern for their appearance, like normal females. Schizophrenic females simply show less concern for all parts of their bodies, whether masculine or feminine. By itself, such indifference might be attributable to long hospitalization, but this explanation would not account for the differential results for the schizophrenic males. It seems plausible to conclude that some part of the schizophrenic woman's unconscious self-image is insensitive and more masculine, whereas some part of the schizophrenic man's self-image is sensitive and more feminine. Whether this difference predates their entry to mental hospitals is a question for further research. (Ibid., p. 234)

> *It is not only "plausible" but absolutely correct to "conclude that some part of the schizophrenic woman's unconscious self-image is insensitive and more masculine, whereas some part of the schizophrenic man's self-image is sensitive and more feminine." Furthermore, to answer the author's last question, yes, this difference does predate the entrance of the schizophrenic to the mental hospital, and is observable in the very first years of life, where it is molded by the unconscious, or even conscious, sexual attitudes and wishes of the "schizophrenogenic" parent(s).*

276        On the other hand the data in line 3 of Table 6 shows a marked interaction effect for the only two items in the Test that suggest entering, intrusion against something else, or penetration (items 11 and 13). The schizophrenic women favor the intruding alternative, as do the normal men, whereas the schizophrenic men prefer the non-intrusion alternatives, like the normal women. Although this finding was not predicted but derived post hoc from inspection of the results, it is nevertheless interesting and consistent with the view that it is some aspect of the body image or 'stance' that may be alienated in schizophrenics. (Ibid., p. 235)

> *Here is more proof of the basic sex-role alienation invariably to be found at the core of every schizophrenic's psyche.*

277        The female schizophrenics are less often feminine than the housewives, and the male schizophrenics more often feminine than the normal male employees. The interaction $x^2 = 6.59$, p < .01. It is fair to say that by this measure the schizophrenics are alienated from sex-role patterns characteristic of

nonworking women and working men, but the measure itself seems to be directly influenced by a normal person's occupational role. If he or she has a career orientation, a proactive type of story sequence (E-D) is more apt to appear, whereas nonworking women show the reactive (D-E) sequence. What remains problematical, if this interpretation is correct, is why the schizophrenic women should show a masculine, proactive style, if in fact they are not working and have generally not been able to, for the most part, for years because of their illness. In a sense the E-D pattern is still inappropriate for them, given their life situation. (Ibid., p. 236)

*The reason schizophrenic women show a "masculine, proactive style," even when they have been ill for many years and not working, is simply because they are masculine and aggressive and assertive, albeit at an unconscious level. The reason they have repressed these traits is because they are directly connected to powerful homosexual drives which they would rather "die than admit" to, thus setting the stage for the development of schizophrenia.*

278        The specificity of the evidence for schizophrenic sex-role alienation suggests the results are not trivial. If it had been found that schizophrenics, whether male or female, simply fail to give normal sex-typed responses, one need only infer that here, as elsewhere, schizophrenics are disorganized. Perhaps they just do not attend to the tests but respond more or less randomly. Such an hypothesis is rendered unlikely by the fact that the schizophrenics give normally sex-typed responses to some tests and not others, and to some items on particular tests and not others.

For instance, schizophrenic females generally care less than normals about all parts of the body, showing no differential for male and female parts, while male schizophrenics are more sensitive than normal males about female parts. This also demonstrates that sex-role alienation is not simply a matter of one sex reacting always *exactly* like the opposite sex. That is, the schizophrenic females are not relatively *more* sensitive about their male than female parts, as the normal males are. It is sex-role *alienation*, not reversal. Alienation often means reacting like normals of the opposite sex because that is the major or only alternative, but such is not always the case.

The results taken together suggest that the components of sex-role identity can be arranged in a hierarchy of importance to normal adjustment. At the most basic primary level, at the center of personality structure, lies something that might be labeled *gender identity*, an unconscious schema representing pride, confidence, and security in one's membership in the male or female sex. Strictly speaking it has little to do with sex-typed *actions* or roles (which exist on the secondary level of the hierarchy) but with the fundamental experience of one's self as male or female. At this level the schizophrenics show the most disturbance: they make opposite-sex choices in the Role Playing Test, and they do not experience their own bodies the way normal men and women do. The Figure Preference Test results also suggest the same kind of disturbance in self-orientation, but they are harder to interpret and obviously need replication either with the original free response test or with figure choices more definitely representing various male and female body parts. Among the female schizophrenics, 82% either make three or more opposite-sex choices in the Role Playing Test or are insensitive to their bodies (accepting 14 or more of 20 parts) in a very unfeminine way. This contrasts with only 28% of all the normal females who showed one or the other of these deviations. Among the male schizophrenics, 95% show either the same degree of disturbance on the Role Playing Test or are especially sensitive to their female parts, in a nonmasculine way (accepts 6 or less out of 8), as contrasted with 35% of the normal males showing one or the other of these gender-alien signs. The instruments were not designed to maximize discrimination of schizophrenics from normals, but even two such simple signs yield very large differences, suggesting that the fundamental problem exists for schizophrenics at this level. (Ibid., pp. 236-237)

*The authors present here indisputable evidence of the deep-seated sex-role alienation which is always to be found at the very core of schizophrenic symptomatology. On the unconscious level schizophrenics invariably have identified themselves with members of the opposite sex, both emotionally and physically, and it is this opposite-sex identification which leads directly to the severe bisexual conflict and confusion which triggers the symptoms of their disease.*

279       The maladaptiveness of the male schizophrenic withdrawal is even more obvious and has been often noted in the literature. For example, Farina, Garmezy, and Barry (1963) report the same differential in marriage rates among male and female schizophrenics noted above and comment that to marry in our culture a man must usually approach, court, and propose to a woman as well as provide a home and financial support for her. Such actions require an assertiveness that male schizophrenics typically lack. However, a woman may marry even though she is sex-role alienated simply because less is required of her. All she has to do is 'go along.' The authors also point out that this explains why among divorced and separated schizophrenics more men than women recovered. The men presumably had to be better sex-adjusted to get married in the first place than the women. (Ibid., p. 238)

*The authors here unknowingly give us a perfect description of the so-called "schizophrenogenic" mother, or the mother whose children become either schizophrenic or* *homosexual – schizophrenia being the <u>negation of</u> homosexuality. This mother is invariably a woman who "may marry even though she is sex-role alienated simply because less is required of her. All she has to do is 'go along.'" She is homosexually oriented at an unconscious level, and accordingly is schizophrenic herself, to a greater or lesser degree, while concurrently operating on a seemingly heterosexual basis. Her children, due to her own sexual confusion, almost invariably become severely confused sexually themselves, to the point of either developing schizophrenia as a defense against their homosexuality or else opting consciously for a homosexual way of life.*

280          Such a differentiation permits a speculative reconstruction of the schizophrenic process which would run as follows. For a variety of reasons – for example, hostility, harshness – the child in the earliest period of life loses confidence in its identity, its worth as a human being of its given sex. Obviously ordinary traumas such as neglect are not sufficient: the hostility or overdemandingness must treat the child like an object with no intrinsic worth of its own. Perhaps the parents unconsciously hate the child's sex or maybe the child senses that to be so despised he must be the wrong sex. Whatever the specific causes may be, one aspect of the general self-disconfirmation the child experiences is to lose (or never gain) confidence in his gender role identity, sometimes feeling like a member of the opposite sex or more often just alien from his own. This lack of gender security tends to influence style of approach to life, especially in the critical adolescent years when the sex roles begin to diverge markedly. Sex-role alienation is manifested primarily in passivity and defective instrumentality among males but is most apparent in the expressive functions among females, taking the form of hostile belligerence and emotional insensitivity when hospitalized. (It remains an open question whether the assertive quality of the

behavior observed in female schizophrenics is a secondary by-product of expressive disruption or represents a fundamental divergence from the classical developmental picture of inhibition and social withdrawal in preschizophrenics.) But at the same time, schizophrenics of both sexes are perceived and treated usually by all at home and at school as members of their correct biological sex groups so that they develop more or less normal interests and opinions characteristic of their sex. What is crucial in schizophrenia is a serious disturbance at the primary or identity stage; conflicts at the secondary level of style of approach to life may lead to neuroses and at the tertiary level of interests to social maladjustments. But at any level, sex-role integration appears to be a crucial factor in adjustment. (Ibid., p. 238)

*The "hostile belligerence and emotional insensitivity" shown by hospitalized schizophrenic women reflect their basic masculine identification. These two traits would be considered masculine rather than feminine in all human cultures.*

281        During his stay in that hospital, he did not show improvement. He was transferred to the Sheppard and Enoch Pratt Hospital on January 27, last. After discussing his life up to the time of his brother's enlistment, in our initial interview, he was asked if he had missed his brother. He replied: 'Oh ... He had his friends and went around with girls, too. I had friends, but ... I could not keep up ... They were a little ahead of me ... Well, socially and ... monetary reasons, too.' Here he referred to a doctor with whom he had had some interviews, saying thereafter 'I slept with my brother 'till the war *** that homosexual feeling H – [the doctor] spoke of. I'd tell him ... anything, and ... it seemed I got worse and worse. All our actions and talks were tensions between us, you see. It was on the morning of the eclipse ... I was relating it to myself ... and the morning it came, I was wild, I thought I was dying or

something. \*\*\* I was supposed to be in hell, I guess ... and
they had a language there; I'd hear things ... I couldn't smoke a
cigarette or drink water \*\*\* The whole thing was like going
through a dream ... I was two persons; one night, a man and a
woman; and the next, two men. \*\*\* Called all sorts of
damnable things – dog, cock-sucker ... everything that I had
ever heard.' Later in the discussion, he volunteered 'Never had
intercourse with a woman; never seen a naked woman: have
fooled around when I was on the road'; the latter had
occasioned two incidents of <u>ejaculatio praecox</u> some short
time before his acute episode. He shied at any discussion of
the homosexual goal, saying amiably but with tension, 'Don't
talk to me about those things, I will get all mixed up again ... I
think I know what ails me ... my feelings have got swung
around.' Inquiry as to what he meant increased his discomfort.
—<u>Schizophrenia as a Human Process</u>, Harry Stack Sullivan,
M. D., W. W. Norton & Company, Inc., New York, 1962, p.
75.

*This patient tells us what schizophrenia is all about in
a few brief words: "I think I know what ails me ... my feelings
have got swung around." And of course the "feelings" he is
talking about are his sexual feelings, which have "got swung
around," that is, changed from heterosexual to homosexual.
His bisexual conflict is what has driven him crazy, i.e.
schizophrenic.*

282   The mother recalled that as a child the patient was 'fascinated
by clothes and loved to dress as a girl. Has always loved
costumes and finery.' (Ibid., p. 130)
    ... Developed an interest in automatic writing and felt
that he was receiving communications from deceased
relatives. An acute disorder of sleep appeared. Became so
uncomfortable that he concluded he was suffering an attack of
brain fever. Went to visit a relative, previously making a

memorandum which he carried with him, as follows: 'I feel under a hypnotic power of someone. And if I should marry, it will be against my will power.' Immediately before this trip he had consulted a physician on the assumption that he had venereal disease. On arriving at the neighboring city he complained that he had a dual personality, that he was hypnotized, and that he was hermaphroditic; 'I know the trouble of the whole matter, it's sex.' He talked much to the physician who was called, of censorship from his father, being married, having attempted Coue's method, and that he was a woman – having been castrated. Great excitement ensued; he became disturbed and combative and much hallucinated. After some weeks of care he was returned to the United States.

On admission to this hospital he was much disturbed and made many attempts to harm himself. There was a great deal of antagonism and pugnacity, this frequently most impulsive. Went nude at times and often refused his meals; had feelings that he was being impersonated by someone outside the hospital. (Ibid., p. 131)

… The male nurses scared me. They came into the room about eight o'clock and gave me paraldehyde. It had a revolting taste and odor. I thought it did funny things to me. On one night, I threw up my supper, and then went to sleep. When I woke up, my nostrils were dirty, and I thought they had made me rub my nose in the vomitus. At times, my stomach would seem to swell up specially when I had indigestion. And also when I was shaved, my spine seemed loose, and when I put my head very far back, it seemed as though my spine buckled up. I also thought I was a hermaphrodite. I thought that I was going to become a woman. When my stomach swelled up from indigestion, I thought that I was pregnant. The doctor explained the term hermaphrodite to me in the second nursing home, when I thought I was pregnant. I had the idea afterwards that my penis would drop off. They gave me paraldehyde at night and salts in the morning, and I didn't know what happened at night. The voices never explained what happened at night. There was no desire on my part to become a woman. I did not have a fear of perversion, because I had never slept with a woman. I was over-suppressed. I had the fear that I would be more attracted by the male. I always thought the male figure more beautiful than the female. At the start of my sickness, the only perverted desire I had was a wish to throw my arms around persons whom I developed a fondness for. (Ibid., p. 135)

*This patient's bisexual conflict has driven him insane.*

283          It is traditional that sexual manifestations, and for that matter the less conventional or more abnormal sexual manifestations, are an outstanding factor in the picture of schizophrenia. It is common belief among the group of psychopathologists most probably really acquainted with schizophrenic phenomena that homosexual manifestations are almost all but invariably conspicuous in some stages of this illness. (Ibid., p. 207)

*Dr. Sullivan, in speaking of schizophrenia, hedges slightly when he states that "homosexual manifestations are almost all but invariably conspicuous in some stages of this illness." It would have been more accurate had he said that "homosexual manifestations are <u>invariably</u> conspicuous in some stages" of schizophrenia, and furthermore that the denial of – or repression of – these homosexual tendencies is what has caused the patient to become mentally ill in the first place.*

284     From what has already been said regarding the obstruction of growth of sexual tendencies by too intimate a linkage with the mother, it might be suspected that these quasi-heterosexual dreams are not all that they seem. We learn that they may

mark a course that culminates in a schizophrenic illness, in which there is intense conflict over homoerotic interests; and they are not uncommon in individuals presently to adopt maladjustive homosexual habits. In fact, it is not uncommon for the dream-life to show a gradual or abrupt change from intercourse with unidentified women to sexual relations with someone who turns out to be, if not in fact clearly of the same sex as that of the dreamer, at least a sexually confused, perhaps hermaphroditic, individual.

From my material, in which negative instances are conspicuously absent, I am forced to the conclusion that schizophrenic illnesses in the male are intimately related as a sequent to unfortunate prolongation of the attachment of the son and the mother. That schizophrenic disorders are but one of the possible outcomes of persisting immature attitudes subtending the mother and son relationship must be evident. The failure of growth of heterosexual interests, with persistence of autoerotic or homoerotic interests in adolescence, is the general formula. The factors that determine a schizophrenic outcome may be clarified by a discussion on the one hand of the situations to which I shall refer as homosexual cravings and acute masturbation conflict – often immediate precursors of grave psychosis – and of the various homoerotic and autoerotic procedures, on the other. (Ibid., p. 326)

*Once again, Dr. Sullivan would have been more accurate if he had stated that: "From my material, in which negative instances are conspicuously absent, I am forced to the conclusion that schizophrenic illnesses <u>in both the male and the female</u> are intimately related as a sequent to unfortunate prolongation of the attachment <u>to the mother</u>. That schizophrenic disorders are but one of the possible outcomes of persisting immature attitudes subtending the <u>mother and son or mother and daughter</u> relationship must be* *evident. The failure of growth of heterosexual interests, with persistence of autoerotic or homoerotic interests in adolescence, is the general formula."*

*Harry Stack Sullivan was world renowned for his work with schizophrenic males, but he would have been the first to admit to his lack of insight into the psychodynamics of schizophrenia in females. Thus he failed to realize that the prolongation of the attachment of mother and daughter, as well as that of mother and son, could lead to the same deleterious consequences as enumerated above.*

285        The third form of limited inquiry is one which I have undertaken in the case of some promising patients already suffering incipient schizophrenia or related disorders. The integration of the intimacy situation between patient and physician often cannot proceed in these cases without <u>mediation</u> because of their strong homosexual cravings which may become intolerable leading to panic, occasionally ending in suicide. The principle is to give them protection by way of the three-group, instead of working with the patient alone. The physician distributes his functions between himself and a clinical assistant, striving thereby to effect a distribution of emotional objectivation such that he can always have a positive balance at his disposal to carry the patient forward. The end achieved is a partial socialization of the subject-personality so that he can live for a while comfortably in a suitable special group. Thereafter, a more thorough investigation may be undertaken.[18]   —<u>Personal Psycho-pathology (Early Formulations</u>), Harry Stack Sullivan, M. D., W. W. Norton & Company, Inc., New York, 1972, p. 353.

*Note is made here of the enormously malignant power of repressed homosexual cravings in the causation of schizophrenic symptomatology.*

286     [18]A considerable measure of success has been achieved by this technique. It might seem a much simpler procedure to avoid the possibility of panic from homosexual cravings by a *heterosexual therapy-situation*. This consideration overlooks the basis for intimacy situations, the tendencies for their integration. The male schizophrenics 'gets on with' the woman physician without anything of the tension characteristic of the monosexual group – until he is entirely divorced from reality, comfortably dilapidated or has deluded himself into believing her a man in disguise, then giving way to excitement, perhaps with frank incest fear. So also with the female schizophrenic and the male physician. The outcome of heterosexual therapy of actually schizophrenic adolescents is entirely discouraging. (Ibid., p. 353)

*Here again we are made aware of the tremendous power of the unacknowledged homosexual cravings in schizophrenia, as shown by the fact that a schizophrenic man will delude himself into believing his female physician is a man in disguise, and a schizophrenic woman that her male physician is a woman in disguise.*

287     *Kvarnes*: Unless you are really doing it in some way you can make use of. Anybody can find fault with his own sexuality and particularly if he has low self-esteem. There's another dimension to that. I'm not sure Sullivan ever spent enough time developing it, but certainly one of his core ideas was the huge problem in the schizophrenic of gender identity and the terminology and the concepts weren't developed very well at that point. It is a problem with all kinds of people but particularly with schizophrenics because they've got it backwards much of the time and the homosexual framework for that is not adequate. It's just simply a scary kind of business where you act out something, but deeper down there is an identification on the part of the male schizophrenic with

the female person and that is what they have such an
enormous problem dealing with. Then when they get to
puberty they may come apart trying to deal with pubescent
sexuality, partly because they now have to assume a masculine
role and masculine identity that they are not prepared for. And
either he mentioned that in this seminar or I read about it
someplace else, but it is something we might keep in mind,
particularly with this patient, because he's got a father who is a
success but not a very capable model for a kid; he's got a
mother he's much closer to but she's crazy. So here's this guy
trying to mold himself with these two unusable models. I think
that may get somewhat clearer as we go on. As I reflect on it,
it certainly seems to be what the problem was for the guy,
although I didn't know it at the time, didn't see it that clearly.
—A Harry Stack Sullivan Case Seminar, Treatment of a
Young Male Schizophrenic, Robert G. Kvarnes, M. D., Editor,
Gloria H. Parloff, Assistant Editor, W. W. Norton &
Company, Inc., New York, 1976, p. 90.

*In a brief but brilliant presentation, Dr. Kvarnes
outlines for us the basic determinants of schizophrenia.
Although in this particular instance he is addressing the
problem of schizophrenia in a male patient, everything he says
applies equally to schizophrenia in the female. For example,
Dr. Kvarnes points out that "deeper down there is an
identification on the part of the male schizophrenic with 'the'
female person and that is what they have such an enormous
problem dealing with." Likewise, the female schizophrenic
deeply identifies at an unconscious level with the male and
that is what she has "such an enormous problem dealing
with." Furthermore, it is this particular "enormous problem"
of opposite-sex identification which forms the pathogenic core
of schizophrenia.*

288         Another of his preoccupations has been his feelings of femininity. He first talked about his skin as being softer and thinner than the average man's skin; he is very sensitive to sunburn and mosquito bites and has had some difficulty related to feeding in his early years. He described himself as being thin-skinned, and when I tried to pursue that a little he recognized its double meaning – that he was speaking literally and that he was also implying that he was more sensitive than the average person. Another thing which suggests femininity to him is that his hips seem to be wider than they should be. When he looks in the mirror he thinks the conformation of his lower body is something like that of a woman. Both in the hospital and previously, he has stood in front of the mirror and challenged himself as being feminine. He said it occurred to him that his mouth looked like the female genitalia, that the way the beard grew around the lips suggested that. In talking about this, we got into a discussion of secondary sexual characteristics. He began to recognize that chronologically he did not actually develop more slowly than others, but that both prior to and during puberty changes, he felt he would not develop as rapidly as the ordinary person, pre-judged himself, and hence looked for evidence that he was developing more slowly. Another thing that led to his feelings was his high voice before puberty, but his voice certainly changed to the normal range for the adult male. (Ibid., p. 102)

*This patient is definitely troubled by uncertainty as to which sex he belongs.*

289         *Sullivan*: I have a hunch you have to get jammed up in problems of masculinity-femininity before you have an aptitude for schizophrenia. (Ibid., p. 110)

*Sullivan is speaking here from personal experience as he himself suffered intermittent schizophrenic episodes due to being "jammed up in problems of masculinity-femininity." Unfortunately, he remained "jammed up" in this conflict throughout his life and it was this which kept him from being able to intellectually formulate a clear and consistent theory of schizophrenia applicable to females as well as males. He was a therapeutic wizard in dealing with young schizophrenic males, having been a young schizophrenic male himself at one point, but he never investigated very deeply into female psychopathology, being much more comfortable and effective in his psychotherapy with males. Had this not been the case, undoubtedly he would have realized that the bisexual conflict which drives males crazy, or "schizophrenic," is precisely the same conflict which drives females crazy.*

290    *Kvarnes*: I would like to add a piece of personal history here. The seminar started about the same time I started my own personal analysis, so I wasn't too savvy about many aspects of myself. The patient's background had many elements that were similar to my own. My mother was an ambitious, driven woman who for many years regretted her marriage. I'm certain her pregnancy with me was resented. My hunch is that the ambivalence of love-hate toward me in the first year contributed to my spending my whole life proving I have a right to existence. Somehow around the end of the first year – I've pieced this together from various sources, including strong hunches, she began to see me as 'smart' or 'precocious' and from then on I became 'her' child. She seemed to form a stronger bond with me than with my father or sister, and I was heavily influenced by her 'estimable qualities.' Fortunately I had formed some identification with my father which came much more into awareness during later adolescence. My evolution from a marked disposition toward my mother's attributes to a more acceptable masculinity was a slow process – the last male figure who strongly affected my achieving a comfortable masculine identity I had met only three years

before the start of the seminar. So in presenting this patient, with his gender quandary, I was also presenting myself. I didn't know then I was also talking about myself, and happily nobody else offered that interpretation. Because I couldn't have handled it – it would have blown the whole seminar. (Ibid., p. 135)

*Kvarnes*: In addition to that, I suspect you'd find that Sullivan's makeup or family configuration had something of this in it too, because he had a very strong mother and a quiet, reserved, retiring, farmer father. Some of the myths about Sullivan obviously came from his mother, that he's the child of the West Wind and that kind of thing. Hadn't thought of that until this moment, but maybe here we have the patient and the presenter and the supervisor all having a similar family configuration. (Ibid., p. 136)

*Dr. Kvarnes states that he, Dr. Sullivan and the patient presented in the seminar were all products of a "similar family configuration," wherein the mother is the dominant personality. Typically this is the mother who tends to have a "schizophrenogenic" effect on one or more of her children, as was obviously the case with the patient, and also with Dr. Sullivan and Dr. Kvarnes, who mentions he had experienced "gender quandary" as the result of his early experiences with his "ambitious" and "driven" mother. "Gender quandary" is invariably the foundation upon which all schizophrenic symptomatology rests.*

291         Perhaps I should digress from the subject of obsessional doubts and mention another element of the larger picture – namely, what we see in the way of real, abiding uncertainties in people. These can be awfully harassing things – sometimes, I think, about as painful mental states as one can chronically have. But they are never expressed in frank doubts and so on. In a typical instance of this, it only gradually occurs

to you that a particular patient must be eternally wondering whether he is 'a boy or a girl' – where, in the masculinity-femininity distribution, he really belongs. Or perhaps his uncertainty is – as we often hear in classic theory – 'Can I be loved? Can anybody love me? Am I not essentially unlovable?' But in such an instance, you hear no rattling off of doubts of the typical harassing, obsessional kind. The patient cannot confront these things clearly, even though he is always preoccupied with them. You fall over the thing in all sorts of subtle, indirect attempts which the patient is making at investigating his problem – and the characteristic of all these attempts is that the approach does not present the problem so clearly that the poor bird has to be aware of what is bothering him. He can't stand it, and yet he can't drop it because it has become involved in the whole structure of the future. Until this is settled, there is no peace, there is no happiness; there is always doubt – real doubt – and there is uncertainty, insecurity, sometimes suspicion, and always caution about what people mean and what their actions mean, and so on. Let us say that in treating one of those people, you finally, as a result of good luck and plenty of alertness, close in on a really probable hypothesis of what lots of little details refer to, and you say, for instance, 'Look, are you unclear as to whether you are mostly a man or a woman?' The patient is likely to look at you as if at last somebody had opened the gates of paradise for a moment, and to say, 'Yes, I think I have always been worried about that.'  —Clinical Studies in Psychiatry, Harry Stack Sullivan, M. D., W. W. Norton & Company, Inc., New York, 1956, p. 252.

*Dr. Sullivan's question "Look, are you unclear as to whether you are mostly a man or a woman?" would have to be answered by every schizophrenic, or mentally ill person, in the affirmative, in light of the fact that bisexual conflict is the basic pathogen in mental illness.*

292                When I first saw this patient, she was an 18-year-old
        girl who had been referred to the Gender Identity Research
        Clinic as a schizophrenic; she had been in treatment at two
        other clinics for the previous two years. She had gradually
        become psychotic, starting at age 14, when she was told by a
        gynecologist that she 'might be a boy.' She had been brought
        for that physical examination because her breasts had not
        started to develop and her periods had not yet begun. Though
        she was concerned about this, she had no question about her
        proper sex. She was then examined gynecologically and found
        to be neuter.* The physician who did the examination talked
        with her and her mother, making every attempt to be honest,
        yet tactful. As many enlightened physicians do, he subscribed
        to the thesis that this information would not be disturbing, and
        that, with proper explanations, no psychological damage
        would result. So the child and her mother were told that she
        had no functioning ovaries and therefore no periods or
        completed secondary sex characteristics, but especially that
        her chromatin staining showed a male pattern and that her
        chromosomes were XO. To the patient, despite all
        accompanying explanations, this meant that she was
        genetically, and therefore in the most biological sense, no
        longer a female but a freak, with both male and female
        qualities. From the day of that pronouncement, she began
        ruminating on whether she was a female or a male; this
        rumination and her unsuccessful attempts to reestablish a fixed
        gender identity led to her gradually thinking and reacting in a
        more and more bizarre manner – the psychosis.

                As soon as she was first brought for psychiatric
        treatment at age 16, after two years of developing bizarreness,
        she was diagnosed as schizophrenic; two years later she was
        still considered psychotic*. Her first therapist described her as
        follows:

                'Frequently her manner and behavior seem bizarre.
        Often she appears disheveled in dress and hairdo. Her

problems are rather clearly expressed through body language and verbalizations. She has often verbalized her suspiciousness of me. In the early interviews, her arms were frequently held back of her, constantly swinging of legs, looking away to the side, and sneaking glances at the worker. As she talked, she would giggle, laugh loudly, cry, pound on the desk or put her head down. There was great vacillation in moods, that seemed either manic or depressed. Her voice would vary from an inaudible whisper to a loud shout.'

She was referred to me because she was still psychotic and because I was interested in seeing intersex patients.

The following quotations are taken from several different periods in the first months of her treatment with me. They exemplify the kind of material that was reported by the other clinics and suggest the moderate psychosis (with hysterical features of hopeful prognostic significance) that was present for the four years from the time she was told of her sexual abnormality until the psychosis died away some months after being in treatment in the Gender Identity Research Clinic.

'As soon as they found out about my condition, I should have been left to die. I am no good to society. I am abnormal. I am different. That is what has always been done since time immemorial. No one can reach me. Not even you. I have to kill myself because society didn't. I am trash of the earth. Not fit to live. The population is cluttered with people like me. Only the tall and the handsome shall live. Little puny people like me shall die. I am God. Did you know I am God? I told you I would have delusions of grandeur. And since I am God I shall kill you. You don't deserve to live either, since you are helping me. I will contaminate you with my disease. Keep away from me. Don't touch me. Don't hurt me. Don't let me go! Don't kill me – save me ... I am a destructive God. Only I can destroy anything I don't like. I have power over everyone in the world.'

As she began feeling better, she described some of her feelings of confused gender identity:

'I had fears of being male. I was acting like a little girl partly because of this and partly because I felt I just wouldn't prove to be a female if I acted like one, and I was terrified of having to face that. One day I had a very vivid picture of my pelvis as being all female like I was told it was, but I thought of one place where I would possibly have a male organ and it seemed quite logical to me, because that was the place I was missing the female one and I didn't know for sure. I finally got up enough courage to ask the doctor. She told me I had nothing but fibers there. She told me I was an it, only I didn't have to look [like] or be one because of my medication. She also told me it was possible that if anything had been there, the other chromosomes – it possibly might have been the Y one. All this was terribly hard to take and digest and I guess I still haven't digested it ...

'I don't want to be a girl. I wish I were a boy. I like being a girl sometimes when men pay attention to me, but I feel I would be more wanted by my parents. My breasts aren't real. Only my vagina is, because it was there before. That is what I meant by my sex feelings originate in only one place like a man's instead of two like a woman's. My breasts were given to me for a time. Who knows when they will be taken away? That is my fear. My terrible fear. Not to be like a woman. ... I must learn appropriate ways to show emotion. It just builds up in me and then I have to escape. All of a sudden I feel very womanly. From way inside of me at the center and at the core. The externals don't matter to me ... I feel like my personality is unique, like no other girl's. No man can touch me. He will never know my inner self, my personality, because I don't have one. It is too odd. He won't understand.'

Following some months of treatment aimed at her finding her sense of femaleness again, and that she truly was a young woman, the psychosis disappeared. What has lingered, but with diminishing intensity, are ruminations about whether a particular thought or act is masculine or feminine. (For example: 'You will never know what it is like to pass a restroom marked 'Boys' and wonder if you should go into that one instead of the women's. It's terrible. I was always afraid I would make this mistake sometime and go in the wrong one.' 'Where do I fit in? If I go to school and work, does it mean I am not a woman? If I am forward at the dances does it mean I am not a woman, or do I have to wait to be asked?') While there was a special intensity in her voice when she discussed such problems, the content is not very different from what we hear in some of our anatomically normal patients. —Sex and Gender, Robert J. Stoller, M. D., Jason Aronson, New York, 2$^{nd}$ ed., 1974, pp. 24-28.

> *Here, from a totally different source, we find confirmation of the validity of Dr. Sullivan's question to his schizophrenic patient, "Look, are you unclear as to whether you are mostly a man or a woman?" (see prior quotation 291.)*
> *Dr. Stoller remarks of his patient that "From the day of that pronouncement, she began ruminating on whether she was a female or a male; this rumination and her unsuccessful attempts to reestablish a fixed gender identity led to her gradually thinking and reacting in a more and more bizarre manner – the psychosis." This uncertainty as to gender identity, with consequent bisexual conflict and confusion, is invariably to be found at the core of every psychosis.*

293     (Again, I want to stress that this is quantitatively very different from, and arises from a matrix of personality very different from, the wishes we analysts commonly hear expressed in our typical patients – for example, women's penis envy or men's breast envy.) (Ibid., p. 149)

> *The "penis envy" in women and "breast envy" in men that Dr. Stoller speaks of here (or the unconscious wish of women to be men, and men to be women) is the basic pathogen in all mental illness, from slight neurosis up to and including the most malignant forms of schizophrenia. The severity of the resulting mental illness caused by this pathogen depends entirely on the strength of the wish – overpowering desire on an unconscious level to be of the opposite sex leads to psychosis, while a lesser desire leads to psychoneurosis or simple neurosis.*

294        Bychowski,[3] who feels that 'bisexuality' (i.e., repressed homosexuality) causes paranoid schizophrenia, lists authors with whom he agrees, who feel that 'bisexuality' is at the root of the etiology of other conditions: melancholia (Abraham), alcoholism (Abraham), alcoholic psychoses (Kielholz), cocaine addiction (Hartman), and bulimia (Bychowski). (Ibid., p. 142)

> *Alcoholism, drug addiction, depression, eating disorders, etc. are all expressions of emotional disturbance whose etiology invariably is to be found in bisexual conflict and confusion. In other words, these conditions are all symptoms of mental illness – or of lesser or greater degrees of the "bearded lady" syndrome.*

295        I had been seeing this man, a typical transvestite, for about a year. He would not consider himself a patient but rather a research subject, though I was aware that his occasional visits were motivated by more than his willingness to assist in the research. As different from most transvestites, he had a clear though mild paranoid quality, which put him into closer contact with some of his psychodynamics than is seen in the typical transvestite. Sometime before his first visit, he had gotten from some reading the idea that transvestism

and homosexuality were connected. To determine if this was true for himself, over a period of several months he talked with homosexuals, visited 'gay' bars, and read increasingly about homosexuality. (I take this to be evidence of homosexual desires, still forbidden but nonetheless moving toward conscious gratification.) Along with this interest, he coerced his wife into sexual games in which homosexual qualities were increasingly manifest. This was accompanied by a crescendo of anxiety, irritability, suspiciousness, depressive fits, and hyperactivity, culminating in a paranoid psychosis precipitated by his having his wife, dressed like a prostitute, attach to herself an artificial penis he had made, with which she then performed anal intercourse upon him. Following this dreadful, and finally quite conscious, gratification of his homosexual desires, he became suicidal and homicidal. As we talked throughout the several hours of this emergency, he vividly expressed his opinion, derived possibly in part from his readings, but mainly from his own psychotic thoughts, that his transvestism had been an attempt to keep himself from sensing his homosexual desires. As he absorbed what he was saying, he became calmer. He also stopped his transvestism. Since that moment, a year ago, he has not practiced it again.

A psychodynamic remission. He now has insight, the product of his psychosis and the cause of his remission. Where formerly a potential psychosis was held in check by the complex character structure we have called transvestism, the psychosis is now contained by insight ... But is that the answer? Is there proof this is so? Would a recurrence of the psychosis prove the theory wrong?

The patient now says that he no longer has any desire to dress. He has given away the clothes, makeup, wigs, transvestite magazines and books, and the clothes catalogues. When he sees a woman wearing articles of clothes the sight of which (clothes) would formerly have excited him, he feels no lust (nor disgust either). His wife corroborates this, although, since she cannot climb into his mind and know all he thinks, she still fears it may start up again. (To what extent do her fears that he may again indulge press him toward doing just that?) (Ibid., p. 244)

*Several very important insights are contained in this passage by Dr. Stoller.*

*First, it is made abundantly clear that the patient's transvestism served as a defense against his repressed homosexual impulses, as it does in all cases of transvestism, notwithstanding the fact this truth would be hotly denied by most practitioners of this activity.*

*Secondly, this case provides a superlative example of the way in which severe bisexual conflict, or repressed homosexual craving, can effect a build-up of undischarged sexual tension sufficiently powerful to trigger a schizophrenic psychosis. By submitting himself to passive pederasty via the agency of his dildo-equipped wife, the patient was able to experience in a realistic fashion homosexual cravings which he had long repressed from conscious awareness, cravings which he had been sublimating through his transvestism. Through the agency of the psychosis he was able to gain insight into his powerful homosexual urges, and this new-found insight enabled him to recover his sanity. Once he had consciously accepted his homosexuality, he was able to begin working through it in a rational manner. This allowed him, among other things, to relinquish the need for his transvestism, which he now realized was a mere cover for the homosexuality.*

*This case illustrates the fact that psychosis is nature's way of attempting to cure a person's mental illness by allowing the repressed homosexual material to become conscious. It can then be dealt with on a rational basis, whereas previously it had been dealt with on an irrational (insane) basis.*

296     She said that when she awakened from this dream the thought hit her for the first time that she really doesn't know who she is, and that she is not certain whether she is a man or a woman. She said she had never thought of such a thing before, and since this dream occurred, over a week ago, she has not been able to make anything of this thought, but felt that it was very important. She said, 'I feel it in my body; I just know that it's right but I don't know why.' The patient tied up the idea of C's transvestism with her own problem of not knowing whether she is male or female, and then she expressed puzzlement that while C has this problem in gender identity, her daughter apparently has none whatsoever. (Ibid., p. 303)

   *The fact both the mother and father have very pronounced gender identity problems makes it a certainty the daughter will also have difficulties in this area, irregardless of the fact the mother feels she "apparently has none whatsoever."*

297     Another patient, Dorothea, a fifteen-year-old colored girl, went around lifting her dress and telling everyone she had a penis (which she called a 'dickie'). In the early weeks of therapy her entire conversation was concerned with sexual ideas. One day, she started the meeting this way:
   D.: 'I know something about you!'
   T.: 'You know my name?'
   D.: 'Oh, I know your name, but Barbara [another patient, whom I had seen for diagnostic psychological examination] told me that you had showed her something when she was up there.'
   T.: 'I showed her a lot of things.'

D.: (Giggling) 'She said you showed her what you have between your legs.'

T.: 'You mean my 'dickie!' '

D.: 'Don't say that' (embarrassed and angry).

T.: 'Well, I have one, because I'm a man; you don't have one, because you're a girl. We're different, you and I!'

D.: 'I'm a girl, but I'm not your girl friend.'

T.: 'Oh! I like you very much!'

D.: As she was speaking she moved to another part of the room and lay on her back on the floor. I went and sat on the floor near her. 'You see these things here?' (Giggling.)

T.: 'Yes, those are your breasts. Girls have breasts, and you're a girl.' She starts moving her body seductively.

D.: 'Do you want to lie on top of me and fuck me?'

T.: 'I guess you know very well now that you're a grown-up girl, and you know that I'm different from you.'

D.: 'Well don't you want to fuck me?'

T.: 'No, I don't want to fuck you, but I'm glad you know that you're a real girl now. You're different from me, I'm a man. You have breasts, and you want to be loved by a man. . . .'

—<u>The Experience of Reality in Childhood Schizo-phrenia</u>, Austin M. Des Lauriers, Ph. D., International Universities Press, Inc., New York, 1962, p. 88.

*This young girl has become schizophrenic as a result of her severe bisexual conflict and confusion.*

298    The hostility toward the mother is more clearly evidenced in this test material, but in general the test results suggest that as she is more able to experience closer feelings toward the father, she is also able to get closer to the mother and handles her hostility by reaction formation. Accompanying these shifts in content preoccupation is a concern and interest in body adequacy. This is interestingly indicated by the Sentence

Completion 'CHILDREN ARE USUALLY CERTAIN THAT, that they are a boy or girl.' There is some suggestion in the test material that she feels fairly inadequate, somewhat like the ugly duckling. (Ibid., p. 168)

*This girl shows definite signs of bisexual confusion.*

299     Wesley sees some people on the Rorschach rather than all mythical or odd creatures, and tells logical stories about the persons depicted on the TAT cards. Clinically, this change is reflected in his quite close and trusting relationship to his therapist, and his gradual 'warming up' to others including the examiner. Yet, the generalized, guarded projective stories he tells and his human figure drawings of fictional persons indicate that he is still rather detached at times and is cautious in his contacts with others. Concomitantly, his relationship with his therapist appears to have facilitated his interaction with men, but the TAT shows he has quite ambivalent feelings towards women. His figure drawings suggest he is not yet sure of his body image or of his own identity. (Ibid., p. 183)

*Wesley is obviously having problems with his sexual identity, being unsure whether he is boy or girl, heterosexual or homosexual.*

300          A young girl returning from her first ball leans against the French window of her room and dreamingly recalls all the pleasant impressions of the evening. She thinks of her ideal, and slowly kisses the rose he gave her, which she was wearing in her bodice. Intoxicated by the spring air, the scent of the rose, she falls asleep on a near-by chair. Suddenly the soul of the rose, an intangible, dreamlike apparition, emerges from the moonlit window, in a single leap behind the dreaming girl, as if blown by a soft caressing wind. Is it the scent of the rose, or the echo of a promising love? We do not know. A slender,

sexless being, ethereal, soft, enfolding, stands before us. Not a flower, not a human being. Both. You cannot tell whether it is a youth or a maiden, a dream, or a wish, something unobtainable – something we can only sense. Slender and beautiful, like an unfolding rose, the warm smoothness of the velvety purple petals, sensuous and pure at the same time. With infinite tenderness a full moment it stands at the sill of the window. *Le Spectre de la Rose*. Then in glorious lightness, it whirls through space. It is not dancing, nor yet a dream. We feel everything pure, lovely, beautiful. Here reality and vision meet.   —<u>Nijinsky</u>, Romola Nijinsky, Pocket Books, New York, 1972, p. 111.

*Vaslav Nijinsky, the famous dancer, slowly succumbed to the ravages of schizophrenia following an ill-advised marriage and died hopelessly insane. Prior to this marriage he had lived in a homosexual union with the noted Russian ballet impresario, Sergei Diaghilev. Following a "lover's quarrel" with Diaghilev, Nijinsky threw himself precipitously into a marriage with a young ballerina who had foolishly set out to win his affections, while being fully cognizant of his former relationship with Diaghilev. This abrupt attempt on Nijinsky's part to disavow and repress his strongly homosexual nature led directly to the development of his malignant schizophrenic symptomatology.*

*In this quotation from his wife's biography of the great dancer, we can feel the intensity of his androgynous nature. Romola writes: "A slender, sexless being, ethereal, soft, enfolding, stands before us. Not a flower, not a human being. Both. You cannot tell whether it is a youth or a maiden, a dream, or a wish, something unobtainable – something we can only sense."*

301      Sometimes he danced for us the gypsy dances of Russia. He would suddenly be transformed into a wild, fierce,

savage girl, trembling all over from the tips of his fingers to his toes, shaking his shoulders as if they were independent of his body. And then he would imitate the different *ballerinas* of the Mariinsky. We often begged him to show us how Kshessinskaya danced. But we loved it most when he showed us how the peasant women flirt whilst dancing. He had an inimitable way of throwing inviting glances, and undulating in such a lascivious manner as to stir up the senses of the spectator almost to frenzy. (Ibid., p. 245)

*In this description of his dancing while imitating various females, Nijinsky's strongly effeminate, or homosexual, nature is revealed most vividly. This is the nature which, when repressed and denied by his marriage to Romola, led directly to severe bisexual conflict and consequent schizophrenia. Nijinsky was truly a "bearded lady."*

302    The straightforward princely role, romantic or heroic, was not really in his line. Whereas most male dancers spent their lives being just that and nothing more – cavaliers always at hand to lift the ballerina and take a secondary place – he had begun to specialize in roles that were more fantastic. There was also something awkward to him in the normal man-woman relationship in ballet. In 'Scheherazade,' though an embodiment of lust, he had been in a way more feminine than Ida Rubinstein.    —Nijinsky, Richard Buckle, Simon & Schuster, New York, 1971, p. 144.

*Again, we are given examples of Nijinsky's effeminate nature.*

303    Nijinsky's next roles two days later were in 'Carnaval' – in which Cecchetti (now sixty-six) replaced the sick Bolm as Pierrot – and in 'Les Sylphides,' in which, according to the *Musical Courier*, 'his persistence in stroking his curls gave a

touch of feminism to his performance ... which was not relished by many of the audience.' [164] (Ibid., p. 360)

*The audience in this particular instance intuited Nijinsky's effeminacy and was not particularly pleased by it.*

304          I am not intelligence, but mind. Tolstoy spoke about the mind, Schopenhauer also. I too write about mind. My philosophy is truth and not invention. Nietzsche became insane because he realized at the end of his life that everything he had written was absurd. He became frightened of people and went mad. I will not be frightened if people throw themselves at me. I understand crowds. I can manage them, although I am not a commander. I like family life; I love all children, and I like to play with them. I understand them. I am a child, and I am a father. I am a married man. I love my wife and want to help her in life. I know why men run after girls. I know what a girl is. Man and woman are one; I prefer married people because they know life. Married people make mistakes but they live. I am husband and wife in one. I love my wife. I love my husband. I do not like a husband and wife to be debauched. I am a physical body but not physical love. I am love for mankind. I want the government to allow me to live where I like. My wife is a good woman, so is my child, and they shall not be hurt. —The Diary of Vaslav Nijinsky, Edited by Romola Nijinsky, University of California Press, Berkeley, Los Angeles, CA, London, 1971, pp. 155-156.

*When Nijinsky states that he is "not a commander," he is admitting he is not a masculine, forceful figure. Then he says, "I am husband and wife in one." Here again, even in the midst of his madness, during which time this diary was written, he has insight into his bisexual, androgynous nature, but unfortunately not into the severe conflict and confusion*

*which result from the clash of these two basically*
*incompatible forces.*

305            Splenditello turned out to be a useful character in more
ways than one. First he deceived Bartolomea, now he might
protect Benedetta from punishment. But does his usefulness
mean that Benedetta intentionally refused to recall what
happened? Was it that she wouldn't or that she couldn't
remember? Did her refusal to acknowledge her sexual
relationship grow out of a cynical desire to manipulate other
people, or was it self-delusion? Perhaps Benedetta was just a
good actress, taking her cue from the plays performed in
Tuscan convents where nuns who dressed and talked like men
played male parts. [22] So good was her performance that over a
period of several years she managed to convince an entire
convent, and many outsiders as well, that a beautiful male
angel sometimes inhabited her body. But it is also possible
that her purpose was to convince herself as well as others that
she was Splenditello. The sheer effort of sustaining her
performance intermittently over many years and the success
with which she transformed her voice and her facial
expression into that of the male angel point to the possibility
that she was part of the intended audience. Benedetta may
have been both deceiver and deceived in her self-created
drama. [23]

            What she concealed in her personification of male
angel was not just her breach of the nun's vow of chastity, but
her transgression of society's gender and sexual roles. Like the
ecclesiastical authorities who heard the case, Benedetta lacked
a cultural and intellectual framework to incorporate her
behavior into her view of reality. Her preference for a sexual
relationship with another woman, despite the fact that she
could easily have secured male partners, as did other
Pesciatine nuns, is not indicative of a clearly articulated
choice. The only sexual relations she seemed to recognize

were those between men and women. Her male identity consequently allowed her to have sexual and emotional relations that she could not conceive between women. But Benedetta was not an ordinary woman, she was a nun, and Splenditello could not be an ordinary male. He had to be an angel in order to be compatible with the sexual prohibitions imposed by the monastic vow. In this double role of male and of angel, Benedetta absolved herself from sin and accepted her society's sexual definitions of gender. Splenditello was thus essential to her sense of self because he allowed her to fashion an identity that at the same time assimilated and circumvented the values of patriarchal society. Through Splenditello, Benedetta could maneuver for a larger personal world within the limitations set by the social order. —Immodest Acts (The Life of a Lesbian Nun in Renaissance Italy), Judith C. Brown, Oxford University Press, New York, Oxford, UK, 1986, p. 126.

*Benedetta's psychotic delusion that her body was sometimes inhabited by a male angel allowed her to gratify her powerful homosexual cravings which otherwise would have remained frustrated. In actuality the angel, Splenditello, was the personification of her masculine, homosexual self, the self her conscious ego disavowed and repressed but which was able to emerge and gain sexual satisfaction with Bartolomea by means of the psychotic delusion.*

306   The universal schizophrenic confusion about sexual identity may be split into two parts in the male. The feminine identification is part of the 'good' magic as in the case of Schreber [2] turned into a woman in order to give birth to a new race of men; while the boy's unreal or fantastic masculine identification belongs to the 'bad' class of defenses. Until the psychotic outbreak, these identifications are either repressed or felt as alien by the patient. —Direct Analysis and

Schizophrenia, (Clinical Observations and Evaluations), O. Spurgeon English, M. D., Warren W. Hampe, Jr., M. D., Catherine Bacon, M. D., Calvin F. Settlage, M. D., Grune & Stratton, New York, London, 1961, p. 58.

*Naturally there is "the universal schizophrenic confusion about sexual identity" since severe bisexual conflict and consequent confusion about sexual identity are the pathogenic factors at the core of the disease.*

307    Dr. Rosen has been known to spend hours with a patient insisting, alternately forcefully and tenderly, that the patient call him by name and admit his psychosis. This insistence forces the patient out of his battle within himself and focuses his attention on Dr. Rosen. With equal force, Dr. Rosen insists on the patient's correct sexual identity. The purpose here is directly to force the patient to become aware of the real roles – doctor and patient – and of his real sexual identity, with all that these realities imply in terms of the object relationship of the two persons. (Ibid., p. 60)

*By forcing the patient to face the reality of his or her actual biological sexual identity, Dr. Rosen brings into sharp focus the bisexual conflict which has led to the patient's schizophrenic break, the conflict which must finally be resolved if the patient is ever to regain a healthy mental equilibrium.*

308    It is to be noted however that ideas of death thought of as inflicted by enemies are not so likely to be accompanied by ideas of cosmic catastrophe and cosmic identification. Such ideas are generally associated with concealment reactions. So also are the ideas of self-importance, when these are limited to earthly power and influence and do not go on to assume cosmic or religious significance. Ideas of change of sex were

found in seven cases distributed among all reaction types. —— The Exploration of The Inner World: A Study of Mental Disorder and Religious Experience, Anton T. Boisen, University of Pennsylvania Press, Philadelphia, 1936, p. 34.

*Upon careful examination, "ideas of change of sex" are to be found in <u>all</u> cases of schizophrenia, irregardless of different "reaction types."*

309          And now the water rushed from the quiet pool of his voice to a stone-cluttered bed uneasy for fishes. The song of the brook soared to a rapid soprano and his voice was changing him into a small boy. Dreadful. She tried not to look, but at last her eyes turned irresistibly and, with horror, saw him a girl. She had suspected him of magic and now she knew. —The Snake Pit, Mary Jane Ward, The New American Library, 1946, p. 5.

*In a book about madness, the mention of a delusion concerning change of sex is very appropriate, considering the fact that bisexual conflict forms the pathogenic core of madness.*

310          But this is awkward. Rosa was speaking in Italian. Virginia did not understand Italian but she could recognize it. And knowing that Rosa was an Italian helped.

          The girl spoke brilliantly and she used magnificent gestures. She raised a fist and beat her chest. Almost at once you caught on that she was imitating Mussolini.

          The two white-capped waitresses didn't reach the speaker right away. They scurried around their steam wagon and ran into each other. One of them knocked a stack of plates from the cart and they stopped to pick them up. The plates did not break. They were metal. They made a frightful clatter and Rosa had to raise her voice. Rosa was not simply imitating

Mussolini, for the time being she was Mussolini. Everyone was much impressed and they frowned at the waitresses. The Nose, the aristocrat who dined at Virginia's right, tapped impatiently on the table and said, 'Quiet, you fools.'

When the waitresses reached the speaker they did not apologize for their rudeness. Great strapping women that they were, they laid hands on the delicate Rosa and took her from the dining room so rapidly that you were not certain if they carried her or walked her. (Ibid., p. 36)

*Rosa, an Italian herself, has become, by means of her psychotic delusion, the most masculine and powerful male figure she can conceive of – the Italian dictator, Benito Mussolini.*

311        The two women who had been with Virginia in the small dining room were now with her in the dayroom. The foreigner attempted to convert her robe into an evening gown and she walked around and around and seemed at times to be welcoming guests to a formal reception. The old toothless one sat on the floor and mumbled. There was another old one. This one had a white beard that would have been stunning on a diplomat, preferably a male diplomat. Sometimes Virginia wondered if the bearded person was a man.

But the days, in spite of the bearded lady and the foreign belle, were extremely dull. Most of the ladies just sat and looked at nothing, at any rate nothing Virginia could see. (Ibid., p. 129)

*This schizophrenic woman with the white beard was a "bearded lady" not only psychologically but also physiologically.*

312        None of the ladies, however, wanted to be at the hospital. Whatever their troubles had been outside they were anxious to

get back to them and with one exception they all knew where they were and approximately why. You would have supposed that the one who had no conception of her surroundings might have been happy, but Tamara was the most wretched of all. She stood off by herself. The nurses warned the others repeatedly to stay away from her and as Tamara was tall and muscular and the owner of a glowering expression, the ladies obeyed. (Ibid., p. 134)

*The description of Tamara as being "tall and muscular and the owner of a glowering expression" emphasizes the fact she is an extremely masculine woman, both physically and emotionally. Such a woman would undoubtedly have a strong homosexual orientation which, if repressed and dissociated, would drive her insane. This is what has happened to Tamara.*

313        She sat down on one of the benches. In one corner a woman was dancing. By studying the woman's feet Virginia discovered that she was doing accurate formal ball room dancing. She did the sort of tango your parents did when you were a little girl. Then a one-step, the kind you learned in dancing school. She danced beautifully. It was too bad she looked so much like a man. Her iron-gray hair was cut exactly like a man's and of course the shapeless dress did nothing for her.

'She was a schoolteacher,' said a lady who was sitting beside Virginia. (Ibid., p. 145)

*Again, we find a schizophrenic woman who appears very masculine, due, of course, to her severe bisexual conflict.*

314        On Saturday, all of the workers, except May and the observer, were somewhat slicked up. Treva had a paper flower in her hair and she was carrying a half-smoked cigar. Treva seldom gave assistance in the work but today she stuck her

cigar through her belt and helped push dirty dishes along the chute. Joe muttered to Virginia that Treva had a guilty conscience on account of the dance. (Ibid., p. 172)

*Treva is yet another excellent example of the "bearded lady" syndrome in schizophrenia, her feminine side being expressed by the flower in her hair, her masculine side by the half-smoked cigar she is carrying.*

315        Crazy Jane had become the typical inhabitant of nineteenth-century Bedlam, not only the image of madness for women but the model of insanity for men as well. In the 1850's, Richard Dadd, a Victorian artist who had murdered his father and spent most of his life in lunatic asylums, painted a male inmate of Bethlem as Crazy Jane, wearing the madwoman's patched robes and crowned with her traditional wildflowers, feathers, rags, and straw (Fig. 7). —<u>The Female Malady  (Women, Madness and English Culture, 1830-1980)</u>, Elaine Showalter, Pantheon Books, New York, 1985, p. 14.

*Richard Dadd, a schizophrenic artist, gave expression to his severe bisexual conflict and sexual confusion by painting a fellow inmate of Bedlam to resemble a female. In reality, every male schizophrenic is, on an unconscious level, a "Crazy Jane," while similarly every female schizophrenic is a "Crazy John." Thus Dadd painted a psychologically accurate portrait not only of his fellow patient but also of himself.*

316        Obviously, puberty was a turbulent period for Victorian girls, a potentially traumatic transition from the freedom of androgynous childhood to the confines of the adult feminine role. (Ibid., p. 56)
       A girl's growing awareness of this social dependence and constraint, the realization of her immobility and

disadvantage as compared with her brothers, and other boys, may well have precipitated an emotional crisis. Case histories of mental breakdown attributed to the biological stresses of puberty suggest both gender conflict and protest against sexual repression. 'Miss J.V.,' for example, described herself as 'a mixture of a nymph and a half-man, half-woman, and a boy.' (Ibid., p. 57)

*Puberty is a "turbulent period" for all children, in all times and in all cultures. It is the time they must give up the "freedom of androgynous childhood" and attempt to establish a firm sexual identity as either male or female. The fact that many children fail in this effort and develop the first signs of schizophrenia at this juncture emphasizes the vital importance of this period in the genesis of mental illness. Before Eugen Bleuler coined the term "schizophrenia," the disease was known as "dementia praecox," or precocious dementia, due to its first appearance in these early years of puberty. For if a child refuses to give up "the freedom of androgynous childhood" and unconsciously persists in a state of "infantile omnipotence," or that of being emotionally both male and female, a state of severe bisexual conflict and confusion is established, leading directly to the malignant symptoms of schizophrenia.*

*The reason puberty is such a critical period in human development is because it is at this time that the biological forces of mature sexuality and lust are first awakened in the human body and psyche, leading either to emotional maturity if there is no bisexual conflict or to schizophrenia if there is. Elaine Showalter has partially recognized this fact when she states that "the biological stresses of puberty suggest both gender conflict and protest against sexual repression" and when she tells us that the patient "Miss J.V." described herself "as 'a mixture of a nymph and a half-man, half-woman, and a boy.' "*

317          But Augustine's cheerful willingness to assume whatever poses her audience desired took its toll on her psyche. During the period when she was being repeatedly photographed, she developed a curious hysterical symptom: she began to see everything in black and white. In 1880, she began to rebel against the hospital regime; she had periods of violence in which she tore her clothes and broke windows. During these angry outbreaks she was anaesthetized with ether or chloroform. In June of that year, the doctors gave up their efforts with her case, and she was put in a locked cell. But Augustine was able to use in her own behalf the histrionic abilities that for a time had made her a star of the asylum. Disguising herself as a man, she managed to escape from the saltpêtrière. Nothing further was ever discovered about her whereabouts. [17]

If Charcot and his staff had listened as closely to Augustine's words as they had watched her gestures, they might have predicted that she would eventually try to run away. The case study records her descriptions of her dreams, which were about fire, blood, rape, hatred of men, revolution, and escape. [18] (Ibid., p. 154)

*When Augustine escaped from the Saltpêtrière asylum dressed as a man and was never heard from again, it was probably because she never gave up that disguise and lived the remainder of her life as a male, which fitted in perfectly with her unconscious wishes and drives, the wishes and drives which, when repressed, had driven her crazy in the first place. By becoming in reality what she unconsciously most wanted to be – a man – she in effect cured herself of her mental illness. The dreams she had while in the asylum "about fire, blood, rape, hatred of men, revolution, and escape[18]" were certainly not the dreams of a woman who was happy and at ease in her femininity and womanhood. They sound much more like the dreams of a blood-thirsty pirate or buccaneer, or of a fierce masculine character of some kind, which of course unconsciously she was.*

318     Conolly noted that it was the female side of the asylum 'where the greatest daily amount of excitement and refractoriness was to be met and managed.' Mortimer Granville was concerned that female lunatics were always 'chattering about their grievances' or else involved in 'an excess of vehement declaration and quarreling.' He recommended that the women be set to work that would keep them too busy to talk. [18] The commissioners visiting Colney Hatch 'regularly remarked that the female department, as is usually the case in all asylums, was the most noisy.' And even a male patient at the Glasgow Royal Asylum felt qualified to complain that 'female lunatics are less susceptible to control than males. They are more troublesome, more noisy, and more abusive in their language.' [19]

      Women's deviations from ladylike behavior were severely punished. At Bethlem, for example, women patients were put in solitary confinement in the basement 'on account of being violent, mischievous, dirty, and using bad language.' At Colney Hatch, they were sedated, given cold baths, and secluded in padded cells, up to five times as frequently as male patients.[20] (Ibid., p. 81)

      *The fact female mental patients are "less susceptible to control than males" and are more troublesome, more noisy, and more abusive in their language than their male counterparts has long been noted and commented upon by witnesses close to the scene.*

      *This is a very important observation in that it emphasizes the "masculine" behavior of the females as compared to the "feminine" behavior of the males, who tend to be more submissive, withdrawn, docile and obedient.*

> *The female mental patient is a "bearded lady" with the emphasis on the "bearded" side, while the male patient is a "bearded lady" with the emphasis on the "lady" side.*

319        It is not surprising that in the female narrative the hectoring spirit of the auditory hallucination, the loquacious demon who jeers, judges, commands, and controls schizophrenics, is almost invariably male. He delivers the running critique of appearance and performance that the woman has grown up with as part of her stream of consciousness, but in psychosis, the assessing voice of the surveyor becomes the voice of the Other, an actual voice that she no longer recognizes as part of herself. Frequently, too, the dictatorial voice of the 'surveyor' is echoed by that of the male therapist. Having wrestled with the nagging, wheedling, abusing spirit she calls her 'resident,' for example, Mary Cecil meets an equally hostile psychiatrist: 'Been behaving very oddly indeed, haven't you?' he thundered contemptuously in exactly the jargon of my resident who was now joining in. [47] (Ibid., p. 213)

> *In the female schizophrenic the "hectoring spirit of the auditory hallucination," says Elaine Showalter, "is almost invariably male." This is true because this male voice is in reality the projected masculine part of herself that the female schizophrenic has attempted to repress. In schizophrenia this repression has always failed and the opposite-sex part of the personality has taken over and expresses itself either through delusions of actual change of sex or through hallucinated opposite-sex voices.*

320        But in terms of her identity as a poet, Plath came more and more to view her recovery from madness through shock treatment as a poetic rebirth in which the split between the feminine and the creative selves was resolved. In her journals

in the late 1950s, she wrote detailed descriptions of her shock treatment, describing the 'deadly sleep of her madness, and ... waking to a new world, with no name, being born again, and not of woman.' [58] In her poetry, Plath mythologized ECT as a possession by a male god who is also the Muse. 'By the roots of my hair some god got hold of me,' she wrote in 'The Hanging Man'; 'I sizzled in his blue volts like a desert prophet.' To be seized by this electric god was to be born again only of <u>man,</u> fathered rather than mothered, and thus, in Plath's imagination, purged of the inheritance of feminine vulnerability. The woman artist achieves her freedom and sanity, Plath seems to argue, by transcending ordinary womanhood not just through madness but also through the terrifying and redemptive ordeal of ECT. (Ibid., p. 217)

*When Sylvia Plath says of her electric shock treatment that a male god possessed her soul and that she "sizzled in his blue volts like a desert prophet," she is making a total masculine identification; likewise when she says she has been reborn from man, not woman, thereby rejecting her hated femininity. The powerful masculine drives in her personality have finally broken free from their repression, as a consequence of her schizophrenic break, and are now able to find expression in her conscious awareness and actions. Unfortunately, she was unable to gain sufficient insight from this experience to prevent a recurrence of her mental illness, and she eventually committed suicide.*

321     Oh, play ball. Bash with Teddy. Roll on the floor. Shout loud. Scream and be wild. Hit with my hands, kick with my feet. Be a boy, all trousers and roughness. Never in those days did I wear a skirt. Within a few weeks of first getting up, all the jewellry and make-up was shed. My feet were always bare and my hair was long. There were a few rare quiet moments, as when I would carefully wrap Teddy in a yellow

counterpane Joan had given me. Then I would sit, on the floor, rocking myself and Teddy. Sometimes Joe had visitors. 'Wait here, I'll be back.' Times passes. What is the matter? Where am I? Oh God, God where's Joe? What have I done? Oh why did I run downstairs, rushing up to Joe? Oh God, why do I 'go against'? Groan and rock. Bang my head on the wall. Curl up. Lay down. I can't move. I'm stuck with 'it.' There's a noise. Is it? Can it be? Really? The noise gets nearer. God. God. 'What's that there?' My legs stretch. 'Well, if it isn't Mary Barnes.'    —Mary Barnes (Two Accounts of a Journey Through Madness), Mary Barnes and Joseph Berke, Harcourt Brace Jovanovich, Inc., New York, 1971, p. 122.

*By means of her psychosis, Mary Barnes is able to get in touch once more with the long-repressed masculine, homosexual side of her nature.*

322        I had an awful dream. Two women were in bed in a house. They had had operations on their breasts and their testes had been removed. I didn't want to be there. A man was bossing me about. I didn't want to do what he wanted. I wanted to be liked but I was hated. In the end one of these women wanted to see my paintings. I got some out and felt better. At this time, my sexual feelings were emphasized in my paintings. (Ibid., p. 145)

*The dream about the two women in bed together is definitely a homosexual dream. The women with their "breasts and their testes" removed signify castration and rejection of the female body. Also note the sexual confusion evidenced by her use of the male term "testes" to represent the female reproductive organs, instead of "ovaries."*

323    Unlike my mother, I didn't want to pride myself on being 'a plain woman.' Yet it felt so shameful to be anything else. If

only I'd been born a boy. Then I'd get married. Girls had to wait to be asked, so my mother reminded me. This used to worry me. How would I know? Will a man just tell me 'I want you to marry me?' When does he give you the ring? (Ibid., p. 16)

*Mary's strong desire to be male rather than female is emphasized by her statement: "If only I'd been born a boy."*

324        Unlike me, Peter was considered very good with his hands. My mother kept his drawings. Some she sent to her mother, our Nannie. Many she showed to other people. I was jealous about this, but as Peter got to school and was excellent at all subjects, I could have eaten him with anger and jealousy. To be a boy, to be chosen. He was chosen to be Australia, with a little girl, not me, on Empire Day. (Ibid., p. 23)

*Here we have more evidence of Mary's very intense "penis envy."*

325    I wanted all my mother's attention and to be looked after as a baby and I wanted to be a boy and have all my brother had that I didn't have. The moment they said, 'Well, he's a boy,' I would have the most terrible anger, and when my body got fat and it got periods and breasts I hated all that. I wouldn't wear a brassiere and I demanded to know why didn't boys have 'it,' periods. ... I looked at other girls and wondered if they got 'it' – periods. I didn't ask them. Then I realized what it was all about, girls 'not being well,' being excused swimming or gym. I was more angry than ever and frightened of my sex. I felt so ashamed. I wanted to be a boy. I had no idea of how a boy might like me because I was a girl. (Ibid., p. 29)

*Every schizophrenic woman could relate to a greater or lesser degree, to the very same feelings Mary expresses so honestly here.*

326          I now realize my destructive suicidal despair was bound up with my denial of my body. As I grew up I loathed my breasts, avoided boys, denied to myself that I wanted a boyfriend, forgot what the friendship of boys was like. I'd wanted to be a boy. I pretended to be feminine but couldn't feel or admit my desire for a man. Eventually, without conscious longing for love, I decided I wanted to have a baby. (Ibid., p. 39)

*Suicide has been called, with good reason, the most serious symptom of schizophrenia. We can see from this quotation how suicide might be considered the ultimate castration, performed only by those who hate their genitals and wish to be of the opposite sex.*

327          She takes me home. I feel I love Elly. She had put her arms around me. Later I shout, 'I'm being pushed out. It's not fair. Why should he push me out. Why do boys get the best of it. I'm only a girl.' (Ibid., p. 63)

*Mary Barnes, homosexually attracted to a female acquaintance, is displaced in the latter's affections by a boy. This causes her great anguish and serves to exacerbate her already intense penis envy and anger towards males in general.*

328          In the spring of '66 my bearing and behavior could be very deceptive to strangers. As I felt, so I appeared. Sulky, excitable, shouting, screaming. My speech always muddled, unclear, when hurried, went from a sheer jumble of running words, into mere sounds. My pronunciation was queer. I was

going back to my real girl self through my pretence layers of girl on boy. (Ibid., p. 143)

*Every schizophrenic woman, to get well, would have to go back to her "real girl self" through her "pretence layers of girl on boy," just as Mary Barnes has done. From her "real girl self" she could then grow into mature womanhood. Vice versa for schizophrenic men – back to their real boy self through pretense layers of boy on girl.*

329     The water was warm. Her hair was like weed. We got quiet. She lay in bed. I boiled an egg, lightly. With her eyes shut she took it, slowly as I fed her. Then there was peace. When the milkman came there was milk, warm from a glass or cold, sucked through a straw. My breast was her bottle. I would kneel over her, and she would put her mouth to my nipple. This was satisfying to me. We both enjoyed it. (Ibid., p. 284)

*Mary is now able to express her homosexuality openly and freely, thus negating any need for her previous psychotic defenses against it.*

330     Joe assured me, 'You will be back before the baby is born. The baby won't push you out. I still care for you very much. Going out with the boys last night – feeling you wanted to be a boy like them makes you have guilt. You feel it's wrong to want to be a boy.' (Ibid., p. 333)

*Mary's wish to be a boy – or a male instead of a female – is very apparent.*

331     When I get very angry because Peter doesn't go into therapy with Joe, this is really me wanting to cure myself, to get united with my masculine part, which is a part of me, not

Peter. He is not really my masculine part. My getting whole is something that happens between me and Joe, with or without Peter going to Joe. (Ibid., p. 334)

*As a result of her psychotherapy with Joe, Mary is getting "united" with her "masculine part," and consequently is being cured of her schizophrenia.*

332     I didn't feel good but I felt better as I lashed my jacket together with some torn strips and got a sort of corset effect. I combed my hair with my fingers. As for a toothbrush, I knew better than to ask for one. All the time I was in that lavatory I was seeing the dead man on the floor. Hallucination or not, he was memorable. —If A Man Be Mad, Harold Maine, Doubleday & Company, Inc., Garden City, New York, 1947, p. 47.

*Unconsciously, Harold Maine would like to be a woman and wear a real corset.*

333     'Look at the stories he writes,' said my stepfather. 'He signs them with some woman's or man's name and goes convincingly into the most revolting crimes. He makes people believe he is actually the woman or man and is going through their experience. Do you call that normal?'
'Maybe he's of the feminine type then,' said the psychiatrist, 'or maybe he has no personal reality.'
'He's been married twice and both wives have loved him,' said my mother.
'He defies typing,' said my stepfather. 'He is capable of being anything but an honest, hard-working man, and capable of doing anything to live as he chooses. His mother is naturally prejudiced in his favor.'
'Does he ever act in any way you consider strange, particularly when he isn't drinking?' asked the psychiatrist.

'Lately he has been coughing all the time,' said my stepfather. 'He coughs merely to irritate people and as if to complain because he isn't the center of interest. When he is writing at the typewriter he talks to himself and grimaces. He'll talk of his successes, such as they are, but he is secretive about his failures. He makes dirty remarks about all the churches in this town.'

I coughed as if to document my stepfather's statement. (Ibid., p. 231)

*Maine's severe bisexual conflict causes him to sign his stories "with some woman's or man's name," corresponding to his unconscious image of himself as either male or female, or both. Another symptom of his bisexual conflict is his alcoholism, which always stems from this source. Furthermore, his step-father's declaration that Harold's mother "is naturally prejudiced in his favor" seems to imply that Harold is something of a "mama's boy," which correlates with the fact of his obvious effeminacy.*

334 Still, their correspondence flourished. Zelda wrote Scott that she hoped his mother would like her. 'I'll be as nice as possible and try to make her – but I'm afraid I'm losing all pretense of femininity, and I imagine she will demand it – .' Then, because he wanted to know exactly what she did with her time, she told him about a 'syndicate' she and Eleanor Browder had formed: '… we're 'best friends' to more college boys than Solomon had wives – Just sorter buddying with 'em and I really am enjoying it – as much as I could anything without you – I have always been inclined toward masculinity. It's such a cheery atmosphere boys radiate – And we do such unique things.' —<u>Zelda</u>, Nancy Milford, Harper & Row, New York, Evanston, IL, and London, 1970, p. 43

*Zelda is very frank with F. Scott Fitzgerald about her masculine leanings. Her statements (that she is "afraid I'm losing all pretense of femininity," that "I have always been inclined toward masculinity" and that "It's such a cheery atmosphere boys radiate – And we do such unique things") leave no doubt about these feelings. When she says that "we do such unique things," she is unconsciously identifying herself as one of these boys.*

335     By the next letter Zelda's mood had again shifted; she told him all about a wild drive to Auburn 'with ten boys to liven things up' and an escapade down on Commerce Street near the river in the worst part of Montgomery, where she had donned men's clothes and gone to the movies with a gang of boys. Fitzgerald was furious. (Ibid., p. 44)

*In this passage Zelda tells of becoming a transvestite, dressing herself in the clothes of the opposite sex, while engaged in masculine adventures.*

336     The trip itself was a series of minor catastrophes: there were blowouts, lost wheels, and broken axles. Zelda, who was to navigate, had no idea how to read a map. Her white knickerbocker suit (which had been made to match Scott's) was considered shocking enough in Virginia almost to keep them out of a good hotel. The manager eventually relented and Zelda compromised at the next stop by putting a skirt on over the outfit. (Ibid., p. 73)

*Again, Zelda dresses in men's clothing, a suit, which perfectly matches Scott's. This was bizarre behavior on the part of a woman of that time and place, as is demonstrated by the hotel manager's shocked reaction to her masculine attire.*

337   But the most exciting event of their visit was a walking tour with Shane Leslie around the waterfronts of London. Scott, Shane Leslie later wrote, 'wanted to see the real Dockland Stepney Limehouse Wapping where there was no taxis no police – We wore tweed caps and slacks. We had to be ready to carry Zelda – but she was light and enjoyed the adventure.' With Zelda dressed in men's clothes and with no money or jewelry, they prowled the haunts of Jack the Ripper. (Ibid., p. 83)

*Zelda once more assumes the costume of a transvestite and engages in masculine behavior with her men friends on the London docks.*

338   In a film taken during the summer there is a glimpse of Zelda sitting with Scott and several friends around a large circular table with a beach parasol over them. She is wearing a brightly striped French sailor's jersey, and her short hair is blowing back from her face and looks springy and dark. Nervously she plays with her hands on the table top, and looking up once into the camera, clearly embarrassed, she waves and laughs. (Ibid., p. 120)

*Here we see Zelda wearing a man's sweater, specifically a French sailor's jersey. Her hair is cut short, which adds to her masculine appearance. Note is made of her nervousness as she "plays with her hands on the table top." ... This "nervousness" will eventually escalate into a full-fledged schizophrenic breakdown.*

339   The Murphys knew the Fitzgeralds at their peak; Scott had finished <u>Gatsby</u> and Zelda was still lovely. 'She was not a legitimate beauty – thank God!' said Gerald Murphy. 'Her beauty was not legitimate at all. It was all in her eyes. They were strange eyes, brooding but not sad, severe, almost

masculine in their directness. She possessed an astounding gaze, one doesn't find it often in women, perfectly level and head on.' (Ibid., p. 124)

*Gerald Murphy comments on Zelda's "strange eyes" which were "almost masculine in their directness" and on her "astounding gaze, one doesn't find it often in women, perfectly level and head on." He seems to find this masculine presence in Zelda somewhat disturbing, and thus worthy of note in his reminiscence of her.*

340          It rained nearly every day from the end of November to mid-December and Zelda wrote that she not only missed Scott and was lonely, but had a 'sore throat, asthma, grippe and indigestion.' On the good days, she said, a joyous release of pent-up excitement was likely to overcome her. She had a pistol without any bullets that she kept in a bureau drawer for protection.

'I love climbing out on the tin roof and brandishing my empty pistol and yelling 'Who's there?' as if I had a mob at bay. But I am, secretly, always the escaping criminal. My bravado instincts do not function on the side of law and order, as do not also a great many other interesting facets of myself: i.e. to me, interesting, of cource.' ...

'I miss my Daddy horribly. I am losing my identity here without men. I would not live two weeks again where there are none, since the first thing that goes is concision, and they give you something to butt your vitality against so it isn't littered over the air like spray[s] of dynamite.' (Ibid., p. 206)

*Zelda's "empty pistol" symbolizes her unconscious, castrated male image of herself, and her "bravado instincts," as she calls them, reflect her bold masculine spirits. Her self-description as "always the escaping criminal" furthermore*

*implies an unconscious masculine self-identification, as
"escaping criminals" are almost always of the male sex.*

*Zelda needed to be around men to bolster her
unconscious identification as one, and to provide her with the
male competition she needed to "butt" her own masculine
"vitality against so it isn't littered over the air like spray[s] of
dynamite." The word "dynamite" aptly describes the force of
her repressed masculine strivings.*

341     The following morning, when David comes home after having
        spent the night out, Alabama wonders why 'Men ... never
        seem to become the things they do, like women ...' She tries to
        tell herself that she doesn't care, but she does.

        'I can't stand this any longer,' she screamed at the
        dozing David. 'I don't want to sleep with the men or imitate
        the women, and I can't stand it.' (Ibid., p. 226)

        *When Alabama, Zelda's fictionalized characterization
        of herself, says she 'doesn't want to sleep with the men or
        imitate the women' and that she 'can't stand it,' what she is
        really saying is that she wants to be a man herself and 'can't
        stand' the tension her intense bisexual conflict arouses in her.
        At this point Alabama (Zelda) is on the verge of a
        schizophrenic collapse.*

342     On the 20th of May, 1932, Scott found a house on the
        outskirts of Baltimore, in Towson. It was called La Paix, and
        Zelda described it as 'a very feminine [house] – dowager
        grandmother,' adding that she had always chosen 'masculine
        houses with staring windows.' (Ibid., p. 257)

        *Scott's feminine nature found its counterpart in Zelda's
        masculinity, as is the case in all skewed or "neurotic"
        marriages. Scott picks out "a very feminine" house while*

*Zelda says she always preferred "masculine houses with staring windows."*

343   What Rennie had noticed was the growing discrepancy between the Fitzgeralds' ideas of the roles of husband and wife and the part they were individually prepared (or able) to play. Neither of them was at this point fulfilling his role to the satisfaction of his partner. Scott told Rennie: 'In the last analysis, she is a stronger person than I am. I have creative fire, but I am a weak individual. She knows this and really looks upon me as a woman. All our lives, since the days of our engagement, we have spent hunting for some man Zelda considers strong enough to lean upon. I am not. However, I am now so near the breaking point myself that she realizes she has me against the wall and that she can drive me no further.' (Ibid., p. 261)

*In the Fitzgeralds' marriage Scott essentially fulfilled the female role emotionally, while Zelda fulfilled the male one. Unfortunately, as is always the case in such marriages, neither party is sufficiently satisfied either emotionally or sexually by this state, and the stage is inevitably set either for divorce or for a mental breakdown in one or both partners. In the Fitzgeralds' case, the ultimate outcome of the severe bisexual conflict with which both were afflicted, was severe alcoholism, resulting in an early death on Scott's part and a complete schizophrenic collapse on Zelda's.*

344   Sara once warned them about their diving from the rocks high above the sea. 'One had to be a superb diver in order to make it during the day. There were notches cut in the rock at five feet, ten, up to thirty. Now, that's a high dive, a dangerous dive any time, but especially at night, one had to have a perfect sense of timing or one would have been smashed on the rocks below. Zelda would strip to her slip and very quietly ask Scott if he

cared for a swim. I remember one evening when I was with them that he was absolutely trembling when she challenged him, but he followed her. It was breathtaking. They took each dive, returning from the sea all shivering and white, until the last, the one at thirty feet. Scott hesitated and watched Zelda until she surfaced; I didn't think he could go through with it, but he did.' When Sara remonstrated with them, Zelda said very sweetly in her low, husky voice, 'But Sara – didn't you know, we don't believe in conservation.' And that was that! (Ibid., p. 124)

*This is a **chilling** account, both literally and figuratively, of the **length** to which a woman's intense penis envy and competitiveness with men can drive her. It demonstrates also Zelda's strong unconscious hostility, or "death wish," towards Scott, as either one or both of them could have been seriously injured or even killed by their derring-do, brought about by her direct challenge to his masculinity.*

345    What hopes the Fitzgeralds had invested in the riviera as a place which would revive their troubled spirits vanished, and they returned to Paris in October. It was on the automobile trip back to Paris along the Grande Corniche through the mountainous and steep roads of the south of France that Zelda grabbed the steering wheel of their car and tried to put them off the cliff. (Ibid., p. 156)

*Zelda has by this time lost control of her emotions, as this horrifying account of her attempted murder of Scott while concurrently trying to destroy herself so vividly illustrates.*

346    Inevitably the break came. During a luncheon party in April which the Kalmans, old friends of theirs visiting from St. Paul, attended, Zelda became afraid of missing her ballet

lesson and abruptly left the table to catch a taxi. Kalman, noticing how nervous she seemed, went with her. In the taxi, while Zelda changed into her practice clothes, he tried to persuade her to take a rest from the ballet. But she did not appear to hear him and mumbled something unintelligible. As the taxi paused at a crossing, Zelda ran from the car toward her studio. Kalman returned to Scott, told him what had happened, and suggested that there was something seriously wrong with Zelda.

Madame Egorova, too, had begun to notice a change in Zelda. One afternoon Zelda invited her to tea. They were alone in the apartment and it became clear to the older woman that there was something strange happening to Zelda – her gestures, her face, and even her voice seemed increasingly peculiar. When they had finished their tea, Madam Egorova sat down on the couch facing Zelda. Suddenly Zelda threw herself down on her knees at Egorova's feet. Trying to prevent the situation from going any further, Egorova rose calmly and told Zelda that it was late and that she had to go home, and quietly left the apartment.

On April 23, 1930, slightly more than a decade after their marriage, Zelda entered a hospital called Malmaison on the outskirts of Paris. She was in a state of extreme anxiety, and restlessly paced the room, saying: 'It's dreadful, it's horrible, what's to become of me, I must work and I won't be able to, I should die, but I must work. I'll never be cured. Let me leave. I must go see 'Madame' [Egorova], she has given me the greatest possible joy; it's like the rays of the sun shining on a piece of crystal, to a symphony of perfumes, the most perfect harmonies of the greatest musicians.' She was slightly intoxicated on her arrival and said that she found alcohol a necessary stimulant for her work. On the 2nd of May Zelda abruptly left the hospital against her physician's advice. (Ibid., p. 158)

*The "break" which "inevitably" came was Zelda's schizophrenic break, and, as is invariably the case, it was the result of intense bisexual conflict which could no longer be kept under repression and which finally broke through into partial awareness in the scene described here with Madame Egorova.*

*When Zelda threw herself at Egorova's feet, it was obvious to the latter that Zelda had passionate feelings for her and that she might momentarily lose all control and begin making sexual advances to her. To prevent this from happening, Egorova excused herself as gracefully as possible and quickly left Zelda's apartment.*

347     I spoke to twenty-four women who had been psychiatrically hospitalized at some time between 1950 and 1970. Twelve women clearly reported exhibiting opposite-sex traits such as anger, cursing, aggressiveness, sexual love of women, increased sexuality in general, and a refusal to perform domestic and emotional compassionate services. Four of these women also experienced 'visions.' —Women and Madness, Phyllis Chesler, Ph. D., Doubleday & Company, Inc., Garden City, New York, 1972, p. 164.

*Opposite-sex traits would have been operative in all 24 of the above-noted women, since bisexual conflict invariably forms the etiological core of all functional mental illness.*

348     Marsha: I was falling in love with a woman at the hospital – but that was considered 'sick.' They have these Saturday night dances you're supposed to go to, and you're not supposed to dance with another woman but only with a man. But you're not supposed to go to bed with him either. (Ibid., p. 170)

*Marsha's homosexuality, the repression of which has led to her mental illness and subsequent hospitalization,*

*finally begins to surface as she interacts with the other female
patients.*

349     <u>Lois</u>: One female therapist got scared when I became 'gay.' 'I
        can't treat homosexuals. There's nothing you can do with
        them.' She made it sound like terminal cancer ... One male
        therapist kept insisting I wasn't gay, but he told me it's
        something I'll outgrow ... He told me I'd end up alone and
        bitter in the gay scene, and <u>that</u> didn't appeal to me. It still
        doesn't ... Another woman therapist said, 'But men are so
        marvelous to sleep with! Lesbianism isn't necessary, it's
        absurd!'

        In a sense, being psychiatrically hospitalized helped
        me. I'd hit bottom. Now I could be a lesbian, that's not as bad
        as a crazy ... (Ibid., p. 193)

        *When Lois says "Now I could be a lesbian, that's not as
        bad as a crazy ..." she is in essence stating a very profound
        truth, namely, that schizophrenia is <u>the negation of</u>
        homosexuality, and that the cure for schizophrenia, therefore,
        is for the afflicted person, male or female, to come to terms
        emotionally with their homosexuality and consciously accept
        it. Then, if the person is sufficiently motivated, he or she will
        have the opportunity to grow into a more mature heterosexual
        orientation by means of psychotherapy or psycho-analysis.*

350     *Doris*: Were you sheltered?
        *Shirley*: No! Come on, girl. Well, number one, I was
        very confused and frightened about where I was coming from,
        actually.
        *Doris*: What do you mean by 'coming from'?
        *Shirley*: Well, I thought I was one of the sickest
        persons in the world. You know, I dreaded even thinking
        about the term 'lesbian' and I used to cope with the situation by
        telling myself that I was normal, you understand? And the

only thing that would take my normality away would be for me to have an actual gay experience. And I also used to tell myself that you're not gay if you never do it. So I didn't, 'cause I didn't want nothing to tread on my sanity. So I pretended to like boys and dresses and parties and all that bullshit.

*Doris*: So you were just fooling yourself?

*Shirley*: No, no, I wasn't fooling myself, I was trying to live with myself, and I went out with fellas and I let them fuck me. ...

*Doris* : Well, if you didn't want to be a girl why –

*Shirley*: That's what I'm saying. The more they did it, the worse I got, and the more I pretended to act normal, the crazier I got. And I mean I was going out of my mind. When my mother died I just stopped pretending to be something that I wasn't because it ain't done much straightness in the world and it put my mind at ease, you better believe it, and I regained my sanity which was slowly seeping away from me, from trying to be ungay and I am definitely gay. (Ibid., p. 201)

*This simple statement of Shirley's that "I regained my sanity which was slowly seeping away from me, from trying to be ungay and I am definitely gay" provides us with the definitive answer to the riddle which has plagued mankind since its beginning – namely, what causes a person to go mad?*

351         She let me just rot in the hospital that first time, she's a fuckin' whore, that's what I told her, that always gets to her. So she put me in the hospital again. She called her boyfriend over and he beat me up because I had disrespect for my mother. You son of a bitch, you try to put me in the hospital, I'll kill you. I tried to call my therapist but he punched me to the floor each time. They tied me down and put me in a straight jacket.

At the hospital – questions! 'What's the matter?' the psychiatrist wants to know. 'Wars stink. Prostitution stinks.

You stink.' 'I think we're gonna have to keep you,' he says. 'No foolin'! This time I had a beautiful woman doctor from Central America, and she really helped me get out ...

They gave a lot of psychological tests and, you know, I came out masculine. What does that mean? Like on one test they ask: do you want to be married and happy or rich and single? 'Oh, shit! Rich and single,' I said. (Ibid., p. 232)

*Every schizophrenic woman would demonstrate masculine qualities on psychological tests if she answered the questions honestly, just as would every schizophrenic man demonstrate feminine qualities on such tests.*

352          MY hands are not clean the bitten fingernails ingrained with dirt and my beard that began to grow when I was in Lawn Lodge grows more quickly now, yet no one, I think, suspects that I have a beard. I rub it off with a sandpaper mitt which my family sends me, and one of the perils of my life is to hide these mitts on my person without anyone knowing and to scrape my face with them each morning under the bedclothes.

I am vain. I am growing thin. I look at myself in the mirror in the corridor, at my ward skirt and ward sweater set, and my frizzy hair. I am twenty-eight; it is nearly eight years since I first came to Ward Four. Across the sea a king has died and a pall was thrown over the music and Carol cried out for the dirges to end their all-day flowing from the radio on its caged and locked shelf, and for <u>Some Enchanted Evening</u> to be played.    —<u>Faces in the Water</u>, Janet Frame, George Braziller (publisher) New York, 1962, p. 199.

*This patient is definitely a "bearded lady."*

353     I was more horrified to see that, at times, the nurses tried to provoke the patients into displays of violence. They did this with Helen who walked stiffly like a tin soldier, holding her

arms out as if to embrace anyone who came her way, and whispering, 'Love, Love,' in a manner that would have been banal in a Hollywood film but here seemed pitiful and real.

'Love me, Helen,' the nurse would call, and Helen smiling with anticipated joy, would advance carefully towards the nurse only to be turned aside with a scornful remark when her arms had almost encircled their longed-for objective of flesh. Her love changed to hate then; she would attack, and the nurse would blow her whistle bringing other nurses to her aid, and Helen would be put in a straight jacket and for the rest having been removed, to convey her anger and frustration.

And there was Milty, another favorite, a tall athletic woman with an engaging personality and a facility for finding cigarette butts and transforming them into smokeable cigarettes. She spent her day waltzing with one of the ghosts that are easy to conjure, when one is ill, held lovingly in her arms. And moving in dignity around the room – bestowing now always welcome blessings, turning a prophetic gaze upon the vision of squalor and agitation that surrounded her – a white-haired Christ walked up and down, confined and restless. She prayed. And she wept. And she flew to attack when they tried to restore to Milty the cigarette butt which Christ had snatched during her ministrations. (Ibid., p. 90)

*The only people Helen could embrace while walking around whispering about "love" were the other women patients on her ward. This activity allowed her partially to express her repressed homosexual feelings. And Milty, a "tall athletic woman," and the patient described as a "white-haired Christ," are both obviously very masculine females.*

354    I joined in the throwing of the food; Piona and Sheila, another ex-Borstal girl and I were accurate markswomen, breaking off precious breadcrumbs from our too-small slice of bread, and flicking them about the table, at the nurses and the other

patients. We would have aimed at the doctor too but he did not pass through the Lawn Lodge dayroom. We flicked; we banged our crockery on the table; we sang rude rhymes about 'I took my girl to the pictures and sat her in the stalls and every time the lights went out ...' (Ibid., p. 93)

*The activities described here are all of a masculine and "boyish" nature, yet performed by mentally ill females. The underlying opposite-sex nature of the schizophrenic person can invariably be observed if one looks carefully enough.*

355          BUT WHO AM I to say that Sister Bridge was in charge of Ward Two, when the real commanders were of course Mary-Margaret and Alice? Mary-Margaret had put herself in control of the pantry, like a general occupying enemy territory. She supervised the buttering of bread, the making of toast, the cutting and distribution of cake and the washing of the containers from the big kitchen. When these were washed after each meal Mary-Margaret used to open the kitchen door and with a lusty battle cry hurl the trays down the wooden steps to lie there higgledy-piggedly until they were collected by the kitchen van. No matter how many times Sister Bridge pointed out that the trays were being damaged and that complaints were being sent from the kitchen, Mary-Margaret refused to heed. Sister Bridge would shrug her shoulders and grin and say, 'Now Mary-Margaret we'll give you one more chance.'

          Mary-Margaret was a powerfully built straight-backed woman with snow-white hair which she usually decorated with a differently colored bandeau for each day of the week; these gave her a gypsy appearance. Her eyes, anyway, were those of a seer and one could be almost certain that whatever Mary-Margaret gazed at was something no one but herself could recognize and understand, as if, while the rest of us had studied only the primer of looking, Mary-Margaret had been a graduate for many years. (Ibid., p. 141)

*This description of Mary-Margaret is that of a very powerful, masculine and dominating personality.*

356     When she walked she moved her hands, trying to make elaborate sculptures of the intractable air, taking careful chicken steps and at times supporting herself by sliding her head along the wall. Forced to move from one side of a room to the other she panicked and clung to the wall until she was propelled by the scruff of her neck. Sometimes suddenly alone in the center of the room, she would overbalance and then laugh delightedly yet nervously, saying in a rush of breath, Oh dear, oh dear; and then she would turn to her brother who always followed her and whom she addressed formally as Mr. Frederick Barnes. She would curse him and add, 'Get out of here, Mr. Frederick Barnes.'

She called me Miss Istina Mavet. She would heave a great sigh, 'Oh I envy you Miss Istina Mavet!' Then she would put her hand up the leg of her striped pants and drawing forth, after a little manipulation, a lump of feces would exclaim, 'Look Miss Istina Mavet. Just look. I'm terrible, aren't I? I blame Mr. Frederick Barnes for this.' Her voice would deepen then and become tremendous and her face would flush purple. She would scream. Since her first operation she suffered from convulsions; often we saw her fall in a fit.

Although Brenda was more often confined in the dirty dayroom, as a special treat Sister Bridge would let her come to the clean dayroom to play the piano. She would sneak in, moving her hand along the wall, and approach the piano and, after lifting the lid of the stool the correct number of times in accord with her secret personal rhythm, she would sit down, shrugging her shoulders with pleasure, and begin to giggle in a deprecating way, blushing and staring at the piano as if it had begun to pay her compliments. It shone ebony; she could see her face in it, even the shadowy hint of her dark mustache. She would continue to giggle, clasping and unclasping her hands and adopting now postures of delight as if the piano were communicating good news to her; and then, in a flash, she would remember Mr. Frederick Barnes.

'Get out of here, Mr. Frederick Barnes,' she would rage, dropping her hands quickly to her lap as if she had been putting them to immodest use without knowing that she had been observed. 'Get out, Mr. Frederick Barnes.'

And turning to the patients who were now interested and waiting for her to play, for we liked her playing, she would excuse herself. 'It's Mr. Frederick Barnes. I hate him. I hate him, Ho Ho, Mr. Frederick Barnes. And I, of course, am Miss Brenda Barnes of Cliffhaven Mental Hospital.'

Then she would smile wistfully and break into a giggle and begin to play, gently and carefully, a few bars of what the patients called 'classical.' (Ibid., p. 148)

*Brenda Barnes' imaginary brother "Mr. Frederick Barnes" is in reality the "bearded" side of her "bearded lady" self. Or, to put it another way, he is the masculine side of her psyche that she has never consciously been able to come to grips with psychologically and thus assimilate into her total personality in a healthy and constructive manner. As a consequence, the severe bisexual conflict arising from this failure to integrate her masculine and feminine selves has driven her insane.*

357          The only survivor from the old refractory-ward fire was Big Betty who was rumored to have started the fire herself, perhaps intentionally, with a cigarette butt. This accusation returned from her remote conscience like a radar signal bounced from the moon. Big Betty was grandiose and uncompromising. She was over six feet tall, and bore with her

everywhere her two bags of treasure which included old magazines and two or three pairs of worn-out slippers. She refused to work at the Brick and her refusal was accepted. She preferred to stay in the clean dayroom, lying on her special sofa like Madame Recamier, her big feet stuck in the air like frog-men flippers. Her voice, not wishing to be outdone by size, emerged as a roar.

'Istina!' She used to bellow suddenly so that I leapt with fright.

'Now a young girl like you, now someone like you, I can understand someone like me, but someone like you ...' She would reflect a moment, rubbing her large purple nose, and then roar, 'What are you doing in this ward?' As if I had been accused of a grave crime I would try to find an excuse to offer the prosecuting Big Betty, but she had forgotten her own question and would boom, 'Istina, go and see to that poor soul over there!' (Ibid., p. 155)

*It would be difficult to find a more masculine, dominating personality than the one displayed here by Big Betty, unless it would be that of Mary-Margaret, as described previously in Quotation 355.*

358        I know. I had experienced the morbid curiosity. I once looked through at the men prowling unshaven in their tattered outlaw clothes, and I could not forget their hopelessness; it seemed deeper than that of the women, for all the masculine power and pride were lost and some of the men were weeping and in our civilization it seems that only a final terrible grief can reduce a man to tears. (Ibid., p. 170)

*The author makes note of a phenomenon invariably to be observed in mental institutions, which is that of the more submissive, apathetic appearance of the male patients as compared to the nosier, more boisterous and fractious behavior of their female counterparts. In short, male mental patients tend to exhibit more female, or feminine, behavior traits and the female patients more male, or masculine, behavior traits. This well-recognized phenomenon fits in perfectly with the fact that the genesis of schizophrenia lies in sex-role alienation in early childhood, which is then transformed into severe bisexual conflict and confusion by the hormonal changes accompanying the onset of puberty. And it is these hormonal changes which are directly responsible for triggering the classic symptoms of schizophrenia, such as audio and visual hallucinations, mania, depression and paranoid ideation. As stated previously, schizophrenia was at one time called dementia praecox (precocious dementia) due to the fact these classic symptoms first appear at puberty. From this fact one would think that the connection between sexuality and schizophrenia would be very obvious, but surprisingly, very few investigators have made it.*

359            Bertha's singing incensed Maudie who was God and did not think she should be thus addressed. Maudie was tall, well built, middle aged. Her hair was silver, her voice deep and powerful. She was God. She would stand in the dayroom pointing her finger menacingly at anyone who happened to annoy her.

'Down you go, Carol Page,' she commanded. 'Down you go. It is God speaking.'

'You're not God. You're a silly old woman,' Carol would taunt, at the same time turning to the other patients and half-stating, half-questioning, 'She's not God, is she?' ... Was Maudie God? Carol was never sure, for the minister in church had said that although God was in heaven he was also everywhere, spying on you to write your name in his book. Carol believed the minister. She always went up to him afterwards, to shake hands with him in the same way that she went to the lady visitors to get reassurance from them and tell them about her 'gagement ring' and her being 'jitimate.'

'Down you go!' Maudie shouted. 'Down you go, damn you.'

Then she would lift her ward skirt and dance a clean-dayroom version of the cancan; to her this seemed not inconsistent with the behavior of God. (Ibid., p. 209)

*Maudie thought she was God, the most powerful male figure imaginable. On the other hand, she thought nothing of lifting her skirt and dancing "a clean-dayroom version of the cancan." Thus did Maudie express her "bearded lady" self, or the severe bisexual conflict which had driven her insane.*

360 Because I am I, an odd piece of Egotism who could not make the riffle of living according to the precepts and standards society demands of itself, I find myself locked up with others of my kind in a 'hospital' for the insane. There is nothing wrong with me – except I was born at least two thousand years too late. Ladies of Amazonian proportions and Beserker propensities have passed quite out of vogue and have no place in this too damned civilized world. —These are My Sisters, a Journal From the Inside of Insanity, Lara Jefferson, Anchor Press/Doubleday, Garden City, New York, 1974, p. 11.

*When Lara Jefferson calls herself a lady of "Amazonian proportions and Beserker propensities" who is out of place "in this too damned civilized world," in essence what she is really saying is that she is a fiercely masculine and aggressive woman in a society which expects females to be feminine and submissive. She has good insight into this aspect of her personality but has dissociated from conscious awareness the fact that the type of woman she describes here would emotionally be a lover of other women, or homosexual.*

*It is the repression of these homosexual feelings and drives which has driven her insane.*

361        You might think the awful oaths and profanities she releases with such disruptive explosion would be shattered to splinters on hitting the ceiling. But there is nothing anemic about these curses. They are large and full-bodied and bounding with vigor, and much more capable of denting the ceiling than the ceiling is of denting them, and when they hit it, their direction is changed. ...

Never was there such a vocabulary! She could give a sailor lessons in the art of cursing. For her ability reaches far beyond Art. It is Genius!

She used to be a large woman, weighing more than two hundred pounds. Now she is shrunken to a fraction of that and her flesh hangs in loose folds about her tall frame. ...

... But I like Claw-Belly' – for she rose up and danced on the day I was put into a jacket. She danced to my singing – a wild, whirling dance – and she was stark naked. She got tied down for her compliment to my singing. It was not beautiful singing – and I was stark mad or I would not have sung in the bug-house. (Ibid., p. 31)

*"Claw-Belly" could give a sailor lessons in the art of cursing. This is but one more example of the extreme masculine, or mannish, behavior exhibited by female inmates of mental institutions. "Claw-Belly" also demonstrates homosexual exhibitionism when she dances naked in front of the other patients.*

362        At the head of the list is a middle-aged woman of stern virginal purity. I suppose she is still a virgin, but the sterness has grown and developed into something grim and terrible; and the 'purity' has been replaced by a maniacal obscenity which is revolting.

Now, in the middle years of her life she has left behind both natural modesty and her exalted idea of purity, since madness has claimed her – she has been swept far into unspeakable lewdness. She is so far gone into madness that she fashioned a set of male genitals out of a snuff box. She stands naked before all who may see her and gives voice to her madness by shrieking such foulness the very air around her is crawling and stinking with it. Until others who are mad also, and not easily shocked by such exhibitions, cannot endure the sight of her – who at one time in her life was modest to the point of prudery. (Ibid., p. 42)

*The "penis envy" which Sigmund Freud described as being at the core of every woman's <u>neurosis</u> is here carried to its <u>psychotic</u> extreme in an insane woman, demonstrating the fact that the greater the degree of unconscious penis envy, the greater the degree of the resultant mental illness.*

363      She is such a strange person, so poised, serene and soft spoken today as she moves in the 'hydro.' It is hard to connect with the same person who lay for weeks in a strait-jacket, raving her lungs out in the pain of her madness. It is hard to believe the soft voice in which she spoke to me this morning has another vocabulary filled with shrieking profanities and strident obscenities. (Ibid., p. 72)

*The patient described here has demonstrated her "lady" self while sedated in the "hydro" and her "bearded" self during those other times when she fills the air with "shrieking profanities and strident obscenities."*

364      The Medicine-maker was turned loose this morning and is sitting in the day-hall in brooding silence. It is the first time she has been out of a strait-jacket for weeks and weeks, but she walks steadily and does not seem weakened by the

long confinement. Long months inside have bleached the
swarthy texture of her skin to a soft glowing olive color.

She is such a handsome woman – with a compelling
fascination which cannot be called 'charm' in the accepted
sense of the word; nor beauty; nor any of the other adjectives
applicable to her.

She is in a class by herself. In all the world, I do not
suppose there is another creature like her. A close-knit,
powerful frame, whose contour is that of a woman, but there is
something beneath the smooth olive skin suggesting the
strength of a gladiator.

It lies along the smooth muscled fore-arm exposed in
the short sleeve of the dress she wears; and in the strong
tendons of her shapely hands, bleached by many long weeks in
the canvas sleeves of a strait-jacket. It is in the long sweep of
jaw bone and the strong teeth, whose shape and perfection is
suggestive of the teeth of a carnivorous animal; and when her
lips draw to a livid line around them the suggestion gives
place to – similarity. Above her indescribable eyes are two
swooping arches, penciled in one broad flowing line. Above
them her hair sweeps backward, so black and bristling it
crackles with electric vitality. (Ibid., p. 107)

*This is another excellent example of the "bearded
lady" features invariably to be found in every schizophrenic
person. Although this particular patient is a female,
underneath her femaleness one can sense "the strength of a
gladiator," as the author describes her.*

365           That made the Farm-woman thoroughly angry and she
came striding down the aisle like an avenging Fury. Her lips
were drawn in a snarl. There was a flush in her cheeks and a
glint in her eyes that boded no good to the other. When she
reached Claw-Belly's bed she stood and glared down upon her,
giving vent to a scalding stream of profanity more inclusive

and expressive than anything I had ever heard in my life, up to that time at least. (Ibid., p. 79)

*The "bearded" side of this schizophrenic woman's psyche is deftly revealed here by the author in her vivid description of the "Farm-woman."*

366      Even as I write this there is a stream of profanities and obscenities pouring out of the little sick girl's mouth – so vile, so foul, the very air is crawling and stinking. Her voice does not have the feminine sound of a girl's voice – it is heavy and throaty. There is a passion, a vitality – a madness in her speech that makes the words she uses seem pitifully inadequate to express her delusions.

She does not know death is upon her – nor would she care if she did know. Madness is upon her like travail upon a woman with child. It has come. It has claimed her. She can neither avoid it nor satisfy it. It is wasting all the life within her in a prodigal holocaust of raving; is preparing other victims for itself by consuming her here in the presence of all. Death is preferable. Thank God it is coming!

Even the doctor, who is armed with experience and wisdom – turned and fled from the sight of her – and his eyes held the stark look of human pain in them. He felt the grim helplessness, the painful inadequacy of his profession, which has only been able to provide a long name for her Madness. That was not an adequate armour this morning. (Ibid., p. 129)

*This unfortunate girl is dying from what used to be called, before the advent of the anti-psychotic drugs which can now prevent it, the "exhaust status" of catatonic schizophrenia. In this stage of mental illness the afflicted person becomes so exhausted from manic exertion that death ensues, as will be the outcome in this particular case.*

> *The clue to the intense bisexual conflict which has brought this young girl to such a tragic end is contained in the author's comment that "Her voice does not have the feminine sound of a girl's voice – it is heavy and throaty." What she is implying, perhaps without realizing it, is that the girl's voice has a definite <u>masculine</u> ring to it, befitting someone who could utter "a stream of profanities and obscenities" which are "so vile, so foul, the very air is crawling and stinking." This doomed patient is decidedly <u>un-feminine</u> in her demeanor, for the "bearded" part of her psyche, long repressed, has finally overwhelmed her.*

367     Bridal chamber – Bridal chamber – Bridal chamber! Well – Well – Well! So it is to be a 'bridle' next. I knew all along they had some such idea about me! Why already I've been fed more oats than old Beck and Kate have eaten all winter. Beck and Kate are two old mules and I've been enough like their papa, the jack-ass, to wear a horse jacket all spring. Bill Murray's horse jacket full of fleas and mange and itch! (Ibid., p. 141)

> *Here the author/patient unconsciously identifies as a male. She says she has "been enough like their papa, the jack-ass, to wear a horse jacket all spring."*

368     Well – that was that, William. We made it! Thank you! I have no idea what you have written the last few minutes – but I know I feel like Jacob of old who contended with the angel. I have an ankle out of joint and am so wringing wet with perspiration there is not a dry thread upon me. I am most grateful to you. The doctor can give my sick hypo to someone who did not have the good fortune to choose you for a delusion of grandeur – He can think what he likes of delusions of grandeur – but what you did for me, I could not do for myself. We made it! Whether the world ever knows it or not –

the writing you have been doing for the last half hour is an indication of greater genius than all your previous works put together!

Shakespeare, we got through that crisis – though it seemed for awhile it would happen and in spite of everything I was going to go off at the deep end – with a splash. When and if that happens there is only 'Three Building' left – and hopeless insanity. (Ibid., p. 195)

*Here the author/patient identifies herself both with Jacob and William Shakespeare, two strong male identifications.*

369     Only maniacs murder those whom they love. I don't have that on my conscience because some power prevented the blow from falling. Some power outside myself. I had picked up a hammer and aimed it with murderous intent and was filled with a fierce exultation because I felt as powerful as Sampson.

But a curious thing happened. Mid-way in its swing my arm was stopped as though another hand caught it; and I saw it descend to the table, gently; suspendedly, as though it were floating. I watched my fingers relax their murderous grasp on the weapon. Relax slowly, gently in an uncurling sort of a movement with no volition on my part.

It was the surprise at seeing this happen which brought me somewhat to my senses – and I turned and went from the presence of the loved one whom I had so nearly murdered. And though the rest of my body still felt a wild agitation – the hand which had held it was steady and poised and there was an odd tingling sensation extending to my shoulder. I make no attempt to explain it – that is just the way it happened. The next hour was a gethsemane I wish I could forget. It found me on my way to the court house to ask for a sanity hearing. They found me insane and sent me here under guard. Perhaps that would have been the end of the story if I could have stopped all thinking – but that is not such a simple matter. (Ibid., p. 201)

*Once again the author/patient identifies as a male, and a very powerful male at that – Sampson. Her bisexual conflict is so severe at this point that the inevitable madness which follows in its wake brings her perilously close to the act of murder.*

370          At home things really began to deteriorate. I seemed to be tired all the time and I'd sleep for hours without being refreshed by the rest. I became indifferent to Laurie and my sexual appetite vanished; on those rare occasions when we did have intercourse, neither of us was satisfied. I began to doubt my masculinity. There must be something wrong with a man who can't satisfy the woman he loves. Maybe I'm a homosexual. That thought terrified me. On the streets I began to fancy that other men were looking at me. I began to see homosexuals everywhere, and all of them were laughing at me. (A terrible kind of desexualization, a loss of masculine identity, seems often to accompany schizophrenia when it develops in men, and perhaps this accounts for their morbid anxiety over homosexuality.)  —In Search of Sanity, The Journal of a Schizophrenic, Gregory Stefan, University Books, Inc., New Hyde Park, New York, 1965, p. 19.

*Mr. Stefan's bisexual conflict has reached a critical phase, and his repressed homosexual drives are trying to gain access to conscious awareness in order to satisfying themselves. He has entered what is often referred to as the "homosexual panic" stage of a schizophrenic breakdown. His description of the "terrible kind of desexualization" or "loss of masculine identity" that takes place in schizophrenic men applies equally to schizophrenic women, who undergo "desexualization" and loss of feminine identity. And both sexes experience "morbid anxiety over homosexuality" as a direct consequence of the powerful homosexual drives which they have repressed and dissociated from conscious awareness.*

371    They're talking about me now. Everybody's talking about me. Later I apologized to Laurie, but I had hurt her deeply I knew, and all day she was very distant. We spent the day on the beach, sunbathing and swimming, but I was just going through the motions of enjoying myself. I felt exhausted and self-conscious and hypersensitive. Again I seemed to be losing my identity, feeling neither male nor female. That night, driving back to the city, I felt like the world was kicking me around. I felt like the world was full of lies and deceit and that nothing mattered anyway. My mind began chipping away at all belief and carrying me into the abyss of nihilism. I entertained thoughts of suicide. We got home late and went directly to bed. I was startled when a jet plane flew low overhead. Then I leaned back, thinking to myself. (Ibid., p. 46)

*It has been said that suicide is the most serious symptom of schizophrenia, and the time when a schizophrenic is most likely to choose suicide as a solution to the intense emotional pain generated by the bisexual conflict is when he or she is caught up in the profound turmoil of the "homosexual panic" stage of the illness.*

372    Laurie and I left early, about 10 o'clock. As we walked down East 86th Street, on the way to a movie, I was simultaneously buoyant and anxious, all the while twirling my umbrella and asking my wife, 'Who am I? Tell me who I am.' Two young men walked past us and I jabbed one in the behind with the umbrella. 'Ouch,' he screamed, 'Why did you do that?' I ignored him and kept on walking. 'Did you see what I did, honey?' I laughed. 'I jabbed that kid in the ass. How would you

interpret that? Maybe Gression will say that it was symbolic of a subconscious desire to have sex with the guy.' A Charlie Chaplin show was playing at the movie and I was eager to see it, but when we arrived I felt another panic attack coming on. I almost passed out. Laurie called a cab and we went back to the apartment. At home I kept telling her that I thought I was losing my mind. She assured me that I wasn't. 'What are you afraid of, honey?' she asked. 'I don't know,' I said. 'Everything – afraid of losing you, afraid of' … After a while, I calmed down and we went out and got some hamburgers. (Ibid., p. 36)

*When his wife asked him what he was so afraid of, the correct answer would be that he was terrified of his powerful homosexual drives which were trying to force their way into his conscious awareness from the depths of his unconscious mind, where they had long been repressed and held in a state of total frustration. This is a classic case of a man in the throes of "homosexual panic," which is a prominent feature of schizophrenic illness.*

373    July 25 – I have a hard time understanding why I waver, from day to day, and sometimes hour to hour, between a strong masculine identity and a self-conscious, insecure, frightened, almost feminine identity. I feel comfortable and happy in the strong masculine role, but it chips away so easily that I begin to see brittle feminine qualities in myself – hypersensitivity, indecision, insecurity. The roles, the moods, come and go without any relation to external events. Gression claims that all men are bisexual. Who the hell wants to be bisexual? I wish I could recapture my masculine identity and nail it down, but it's so elusive. (Ibid., p. 56)

*The author gives an excellent description here of what it feels like to be in the grip of the "bearded lady" disease – schizophrenia.*

374        Ed and I would play monopoly for hours together at night. His face flushed, he played the game with a vengeance, mercilessly, and I imagined he ran his ad agency the same way. As the game progressed, his face would get redder and redder, and then he would have to excuse himself and go into the bathroom. This happened frequently. Once I followed him to the bathroom and I found him sitting in a chair sobbing fitfully. I asked him what was wrong. 'It's the tension,' he said. 'This goddamn tension.'

We soon discovered that we were comrades in symptoms. We were suffering from all the same symptoms: the depression, the hypertension, the fears and hates, the doubts and anxieties. He, too, was doubting his masculinity and hating his wife and wanting to kill someone. He had precisely the same physical symptoms. (Ibid., p. 136)

*A great many homicides occur when a schizophrenic person's repressed homosexual tension builds up to such an intense pitch that something has to give, and often what gives is the schizophrenic's self-control. For one way to break the terrible schizophrenic tension, "This goddamn tension," is to embark upon a murderous rampage, or to "run amok," as this deadly phenomenon is sometimes referred to in other cultures.*

375        Sullivan's letter to Dorothy Blitzen shows his acceptance of his own lot in life, making it possible for him to deal gracefully with the marital problems of his friends. But earlier – in particular near the end of his years at Sheppard – he had a tragic awareness of his own situation. He had clear evidence from his patients – young males showing acute schizophrenic-like panic – that fear of so-called aberrant sexual cravings in the transition to adolescence was often a prelude to schizophrenic panic; and that early and skilled care within a therapeutic milieu could effect a social recovery, with the patient acquiring an ability to handle sexual needs without

interfering drastically with his self-esteem. By then, Sullivan was in the fourth decade of life, and he felt that his pattern of life was already determined; thus his discovery could help others more than it could effect any change in himself. In 1929, he reports on his conclusion from the Sheppard experience: 'In brief, if the general population were to pass through schizophrenic illnesses on their road to adulthood, then it would be the writer's duty, on the basis of his investigation, to urge that sexual experience be provided for all youths in the homosexual phase of personality genesis in order that they might not become hopelessly lost in the welter of dream – thinking and cosmic phantasy making up the mental illness.' His data and certain considerations which he spells out in the same article 'lend pragmatically sufficient justification for the doctrine of a 'normal' homosexual phase in the evolution at least of male personality.' [6]

Thus almost two decades before the first Kinsey report, in 1948, on the sexual behavior of the human male, Sullivan had arrived from his own data at one of the major findings of that report. He had located the lack of experience with a 'normal homosexual phase' in his own growing-up years, and hypothesized that this lack had occasioned his own encounter with schizophrenic episodes. Throughout the rest of his life, he had frequent encounters with that painful experience, as late as 1947, he confided in a woman colleague that he had had severe schizophrenic episodes early in life and that he still had them. [7] He told her that he liked to live alone and spend time away from people so that few people would realize that he had such episodes; in particular he was afraid that he would be put into an institution and that someone would 'tamper with his brain.' —Psychiatrist of America, The Life of Harry Stack Sullivan, Helen Swick Perry, The Belknap Press of Harvard University Press, Cambridge, MA, and London, 1982, p. 337.

*When Dr. Sullivan recommends that all male youths be provided sexual experience in the homosexual phase of personality development as a prophylactic measure to deter schizophrenic illness, he is but recommending a course of action which has long been practiced by the Keraki tribe of New Guinea and the Siwans of Africa, among others, according to Ford and Beach in their <u>Patterns of Sexual Behavior</u>. In these tribes all male youths undergo an initiation into manhood which consists of a period of time, usually about a year, wherein they engage in passive pederastic intercourse with older males. At the end of this period, these young men in turn take over the active pederastic role in intercourse with a new group of youths. When asked the purpose of this practice, the elders of the tribe reply that it makes the young men "strong."*

*With profound psychological intuition, these wise elders realize it is necessary for young males to come to terms with the feminine side of their nature before they can mature into truly adult masculine beings. By submitting themselves to passive anal intercourse, these youths are enabled to experience fully their feminine feelings. Thus by the end of their initiation period they are ready to relinquish their feminine strivings and accept with finality their adult masculine role.*

*In "modern" societies, where males are taught almost from infancy to repress and disavow their natural feminine feelings, which are an integral part of the bisexual heritage of all male mammals, the bisexual conflict which can result from this repression leads inevitably to schizophrenic illness, just as it does in females who have repressed their natural <u>masculine</u> feelings.*

376    At the time I didn't have any answer, not one single alternative to the circus. I guess it *was* the only gritty, real-life, grossly rapturous thing I could show my children, or safely

participate in myself. Now, however, I have an alternative –
and as Steve and I looped the loop on the cantilevered coastal
highway, we decided that the closest metaphor for our
communal experience was the circus. Life at the brink, and the
primal ooze – we had had all of that. Including the rankness.
And the magic. I think that's what e.e. cummings was getting
at when he wrote, 'Damn everything but the circus.' You
betcha.

But Corita Kent has already stolen that image for a
beautiful volume collecting her collages, so it was opted for.
Never mind – we sorted through all the circus images we
could think of, until we found one much more apt for us. By-
passing high-wire artists, trapeze artists, lions and tigers and
bears, even the Human Bullet, we settled happily on the
Bearded Lady. Yin and Yang in one gaudy and astonishing
package, the secret, lurking unity in every bi-polar self. The
androgyne. Our selves. The Devil. God. —The Bearded Lady,
Going On The Commune Trip and Beyond, Richard Atcheson, The John Day Company, New York, 1971, pp. 139–140.

*Unfortunately in schizophrenia, the Bearded Lady is
not "the secret, lurking unity in every bi-polar self," but the
secret, lurking dis-unity. The fortunate person whose Yin and
Yang are harmoniously united is that exceptional creature –
the mature individual. In the great majority of cases, however,
a person's Yin and Yang are conflicted, and this conflict,
depending upon its severity, always results in a greater or
lesser degree of mental illness.*

377            As the evening wore on, Tony behaved more and more
peculiarly. Despite Bernadette's enthusiasm for the House of
Plenty sexuality course, Tony had said next to nothing on the
subject, preferring to sit and apparently listen, brooding, But as
the conversation turned to more general subjects, he got up
and began to prowl the room, almost in parody of a jungle

animal. Nobody took much notice; we all assumed that he had been smoking some kind of powerful dope before he got there and was enjoying an interior trip he couldn't share. At one point he went over to Steve, and several times stroked his hair – but it was less a caress than a slap. Later he stalked me, like a cat, and looked in my eyes and said, 'I like you. You know, don't you? You know.'

I really didn't know, but it's always nice to be told I do, and I nodded at him and he nodded sagely back, and turned away to stalk somebody else. When Tony and Bernadette left, David said, 'Gee, Tony was really strange tonight. Wonder what he's been smoking.' And that's all that was said about it.

But later in the week I talked to David on the phone and he said things had been very bad with Tony and Bernadette. Apparently the sexuality rap at the House of Plenty had caused Tony to flip utterly. He was manic, as if stoned twenty-four hours a day, never sleeping, always grooving and freaking in this peculiar animalistic way. Little as she cared to, Bernadette took Tony to a straight psychiatrist who said he was schizoid, was in a profound homosexual panic, and ought to be sedated at once. Bernadette would have none of that. She got in touch with Julian Silverman, the Esalen-based shrink who runs the only Laing-oriented Blow-out Center in the country, in a wing of Agnews State Hospital near San Jose; Silverman agreed to accept Tony as a voluntary patient. Tony was rarely lucid during discussions leading to his arrival at Agnews, but he was able to agree to admittance and sign the right papers.

When I next saw Bernadette she was exhausted from dealing with Tony, sleeplessly, for four days, disturbed at what their families would conclude from all this, desperately eager that Tony be able to go through his psychosis quickly and come out, healed, on the other side. And she was fiercely angry with the House of Plenty, even if it *had* been a rap session only. Obviously, all this auto-erotic, plastic bottle stuff had got to Tony in secret places he didn't know about himself; his response had frightened him into the aforementioned homosexual panic. The House of Plenty people had asked Bernadette to bring Tony back to Oakland. They had seen this response occasionally in the past; perhaps they could help. But Bernadette was having none of that either: 'The bastards should have warned us that the rap was dangerous! It's all their fault.'

It wasn't, of course, but Bernadette was very tired and distressed, and at that moment I was not about to disagree with her.

The fault, if you want to call it that, <u>was</u> with the House of Plenty for assuming that everybody attending their basic sexuality seminar was sexually mature. The assumption would have seemed especially justified in Tony's case, on the evidence of his very considerable experience with Esalen and with group encounters of all kinds. But it seemed to us as laymen that the straight shrink's categorization of Tony's state as 'homosexual panic' was correct. The suggestion of sticking a plastic bottle up his ass may have triggered in Tony long suppressed homosexual fantasies. And to have these suggestions delivered – much as Bernadette transmitted them to us – in wholesome, straightforward circumstances, set Tony on a cosmic giggle that we also thought was funny, but threatened with him to last a lifetime. (Ibid., p. 194)

*Sigmund Freud once made the observation that what men repress, at the deepest level of their unconscious psyche, are their passive, anal erotic cravings. Certainly this case presents a classic example of a case of schizophrenia triggered by homosexual panic over exactly such cravings, cravings which had unexpectedly surfaced during a "basic sexuality seminar" in the House of Plenty.*

378        Nora felt that she was suited to all the roles in Oz's dream – the girl who gave the warning about the doped cigarette, the old woman who provided shelter; but also one of the low-rider orgiasts. 'I often feel like a boy,' she said, 'just as often as I feel like a girl. Sometimes I dream that I <u>am</u> a boy. A stud.' Steve conceded that he too would have been suitable for any role, except, perhaps, that of the old woman. (Ibid., p. 229)

*Nora definitely has a bisexual conflict, but it seems to be completely conscious, where she can deal with it. If it was unconscious, she would be schizophrenic.*

379        It was a dream that recurred often, especially when I was feverish, and it caused me the most frightful anguish. Later I always associated my unreal perceptions with the dream of the needle.

Here is the dream: A barn, brilliantly illuminated by electricity. The walls painted white, smooth – smooth and shining. In the immensity, a needle – fine, pointed, hard, glistening in the light. The needle in the emptiness filled me with excruciating terror. Then a haystack fills up the emptiness and engulfs the needle. The haystack, small at first, swells and swells and in the center, the needle, endowed with tremendous electrical force, communicates its charge to the hay. The electrical current, the invasion by the hay, and the blinding light combine to augment the fear to a paroxysm of terror and I wake up screaming, 'The needle, the needle!' — <u>Autobiography of a Schizophrenic Girl</u>, with Analytical Interpretation by Marguerite Sechehaye, New American Library, Grune and Stratton, Inc., 1951, p. 20.

*The needle in the dream seems to represent the penis this schizophrenic girl so desperately desires to have for herself, albeit unconsciously, while the haystack which*

*surrounds and engulfs the needle would appear to be the
pubic hair. Again, this is a case of Freudian "penis envy"
carried to the psychotic extreme.*

380     VERY SOON after the beginning of analysis I understood that
my fear was a cover for guilt, a guilt infinite and awful.
During the early sessions, masturbation and the hostility I
harbored toward everyone seemed to lie at the bottom. I
literally hated people, without knowing why. In dreams and
frequently in waking fantasies I constructed an electric
machine to blow up the earth and everyone with it. But what
was even worse with the machine I would rob all men of their
brains, thus creating robots obedient to my will alone. This
was my greatest, most terrible revenge.

Later, considering them appropriate, I no longer felt
guilty about these fantasies, nor did the guilt have an actual
object. It was too pervasive, too enormous, to be founded on
anything definite, and it demanded punishment. The
punishment was indeed horrible, sadistic – it consisted,
fittingly enough, of being guilty. For to feel oneself guilty is
the worst that can happen, it is the punishment of
punishments. Consequently, I could never be relieved of it
though I had been truly punished. Quite the reverse, I felt
more and more guilty, immeasurably guilty. Constantly, I
sought to discover what was punishing me so dreadfully, what
was making me so guilty. (Ibid., p. 35)

*The patient states she had constructed a machine
which would "rob all men of their brains, thus creating robots
obedient to my will alone." This fantasy demonstrates
enormous penis envy and hatred of men, on account of which
emotions she understandably feels tremendous guilt. Rather
than robbing men of their "brains," what she would really like
to do is rob them of their genitals – that is, castrate them.*

381       The next day a big woman came toward me from her cell and said with an excited laugh, 'Oh, this little one is nice,' giving me at the same time a smack on the cheek so violent that her fingers left a mark on the skin. Then she left. At the sight of my crimson cheek the nurse understood at once what had occurred. 'Oh, that's nothing,' she said, 'Miss Z smacks all the new arrivals. Otherwise she's not bad.' Despite her words, whenever I saw Miss Z I trembled lest she strike me again.

      But what terrified me most was something that took place a few days later. A female patient who had just been hospitalized for having shot another woman in a hotel, came over to my bed crying, 'This little girl is a darling,' and tickling me, she tried to lift my nightgown and to kiss me, until the nurse came to my relief and scolded her roundly for her perverse behavior. An awful fear and a loathing of her advances petrified me.

      Such experiences only added to my agitation and kept me constantly on edge in an attitude of desperate defense, defense against outside perils, defense against inner perils, steeled for the ever-present dangers that threatened me. (Ibid., p. 50)

*      The patient describes homosexual advances made to her in the hospital, advances which in reality are a source of unacknowledged sexual temptation to her. Her intense fear and loathing of these advances constitute a "reaction formation" to the unconscious sexual excitement they arouse in her. "Methinks the lady doth protest too much," as the old saying goes.*

382       The voices were screaming, crying out that I ought to throw myself in the river. But I resisted with all my strength as I ran to Mama. At last I reached there and threw myself into her arms, weeping and stammering, 'They made me eat, they

forced me to, and then the farmer's wife scolded me; I have nothing any more, I have no more apples; I'm going to die.'

Mama tried affectionately to calm me, but without success. 'Why,' She said, 'don't you take the apples I bring you?' 'I can't do that, Mama,' I answered. And while in my heart I was outraged that Mama too wanted to force me to eat, my eyes fell to her bosom, and when she insisted, 'But why don't you want the apples I buy you?' I knew what I was yearning for so desperately and I was able to bring out, 'Because the apples you buy are food for grown-ups and I wanted real apples, Mama's apples, like those,' and I pointed to Mama's breasts.

She got up at once, went to get a magnificent apple, cut a piece and gave it to me, saying, 'Now, Mama is going to feed her little Renee. It is time to drink the good milk from Mama's apples.' She put the piece in my mouth, and with my eyes closed, my head against her breast, I ate, or rather drank, my milk. A nameless felicity flowed into my heart. It was as though, suddenly, by magic, all my agony, the tempest which had shaken me a moment ago, had given place to a blissful calm; I thought of nothing, I discerned nothing, I reveled in my joy. I was fully content, with a passive contentment, the contentment of a tiny baby, quite unconscious, for I did not even know what caused it.

... A new day dawned. I was happy, but rather awkwardly happy, for I was frail as a chick just out of the egg. The nurse gave me the piece of apple cut by Mama which I 'drank,' leaning my cheek on a large apple that Mama gave me after holding it against her breast. For me, this apple was sacred, as Mama's bosom had been the day before. Later, she arrived and I ate or rather 'drank' my milk-apple lying against her breast in ineffable happiness.

During this second day, I realized that the voices had disappeared and particularly that I no longer risked being changed into a cat. I enjoyed everything I saw, everything I touched. For the first time I was in touch with reality. Mama too had changed in my eyes. Before she had appeared like an image, a statue that one likes to look at, though it remains artificial, unreal; but from this moment on she became alive, warm, animated, and I cherished her deeply. I had an intense desire to remain near her, against her, to preserve this marvelous contact.

But it was only an 'oral' contact, that is, it was only as 'Mama-nourishment' that I could have intimate contact with her; every other consideration but 'my apples' was indifferent and inimical to me. (Ibid., pp. 70-71)

*The patient's powerful homosexual yearning to suckle another woman's breast is able to find symbolic and partial fulfillment by using apples as a substitute for the longed-for breast.*

383     I was present when Mama first held a doll in her arms, a baby doll whom I named Ezekiel. She covered him, kissed him affectionately, put him to bed in his cradle. In the beginning it was enough for me to watch him avidly. All at once I experienced profound amazement that Ezekiel should receive Mama's love and affection without the occurrence of anything untoward. At any moment I expected Mama to cast Ezekiel off because I did not deserve to live. In my mind reigned utter confusion concerning Ezekiel and me. When Mama held him in her arms, I trembled lest she drop him precipitously in his cradle, and if she did, I had the uncanny impression that it was I who had been so treated.

Taking courage one day when Ezekiel was in Mama's arms, I pushed his head forward on her bosom to test whether I had the right to live. At this, Mama pressed him to her breast and let him nurse. This she did regularly several times a day so that I awaited the moment in fear of her forgetting. But Mama did not forget and I began to dare to live.

The self-destructive impulses decreased perceptibly, and instead of spending the day in bed with my head under the covers, I looked about me, interested in everything concerning Ezekiel. Then I, who had always refused food, even presumed to eat. A little later when I saw how Mama bathed and dressed Ezekiel, I consented with pleasure to being bathed and dressed myself and actually enjoyed it. In busying herself lovingly with Ezekiel it was as though Mama were bestowing on me the right to live. Slowly I came out of the lethargy and grew more and more interested in what Mama said and did to Ezekiel, an interest confined strictly, however, to feeding and cleanliness. I allowed myself to enjoy it a bit; even so, the dreadful crises of guilt persisted. (Ibid., pp. 80-81)

*The patient identifies completely with Ezekiel. Ezekiel is what she has always longed to be – a male. She is living out her heretofore repressed fantasy of being a boy and of having a mother who accepts her and loves her as such.*

384          'And that's the last oath I shall ever be able to swear,' she thought; 'once I set forth on English soil. And I shall never be able to crack a man over the head, or tell him he lies in his teeth, or draw my sword and run him through the body, or sit among my peers, or wear a coronet, or walk in procession, or sentence a man to death, or lead an army, or prance down Whitehall on a charger, or wear seventy-two different medals on my breast. All I can do, once I set foot on English soil, is to pour out tea, and ask my Lords how they like it. 'D'you take sugar? D'you take cream?' 'And mincing out the words, she was horrified to perceive how low an opinion she was forming of the other sex, the manly, to which it had once been her pride to belong. 'To fall from a mast-head,' she thought, 'because you see a woman's ankles; to dress up like a Guy Fawkes and parade the streets, so that women may praise you; to deny a woman teaching lest she may laugh at you; to be the

slave of the frailest chit in petticoats, and yet to go about as if you were the Lords of creation. – Heavens!' she thought, 'what fools they make of us – what fools we are!' And here it would seem from some ambiguity in her terms that she was censuring both sexes equally, as if she belonged to neither; and indeed, for the time being she seemed to vacillate; she was man; she was woman; she knew the secrets, shared the weaknesses of each. It was a most bewildering and whirligig state of mind to be in. The comfort of ignorance seemed utterly denied her. She was a feather blown on the gale. Thus it is no great wonder if, as she pitted one sex against the other, and found each alternately full of the most deplorable infirmities, and was not sure to which she belonged – it was no great wonder that she was about to cry out that she would return to Turkey and become a gipsy again when the anchor fell with a great splash into the sea; the sails came tumbling on deck, and she perceived (so sunk had she been in thought, that she had seen nothing for several days) that the ship was anchored off the coast of Italy. The Captain at once sent to ask the honour of her company ashore with him in the long boat.
——<u>Orlando,</u> Virginia Woolf, New American Library of World Literature, Inc., 1960, p. 103.

*No better description of the psychodynamics of the schizophrenic woman could be given than the one presented here by Virginia Woolf, herself an unfortunate victim of this malignant condition.*

*First, there is the great anger, contempt and envy directed towards men, exemplified by such fantasies as regretting the fact she would "never be able to crack a man over the head, or tell him he lies in his teeth, or draw my sword and run him through the body, or sit among my peers, or wear a coronet, or walk in procession, or sentence a man to death, or lead an army, or prance down Whitehall on a charger, or wear seventy-two different medals on my breast."*

*Secondly, there is her disdain for the feminine role, illustrated by her sarcastic references to pouring tea for the "Lords" and asking "D'you take sugar? D'you take cream?,", etc.*

*Thirdly, she demonstrates her severe bisexual conflict and confusion when she writes "that she was censuring both sexes equally, as if she belonged to neither; and indeed, for the time being she seemed to vacillate; she was man; she was woman; she knew the secrets, shared the weaknesses of each. It was a most bewildering and whirligig state of mind to be in. The comfort of ignorance seemed utterly denied her. She was a feather blown on the gale."*

*No better description of the typical "schizophrenic" state of mind could be given than the one above, and it is most appropriate that it was given by a woman who herself was severely afflicted by the "bearded lady" disease.*

*Supposedly* Orlando *was based on the life of Woolf's close friend, Vita Sackville-West, with whom she is reputed to have had a brief lesbian relationship, but in reality the book's protagonist, Orlando, is as much, if not more, a likeness of Virginia herself than it is of her friend Vita.*

385        But Orlando was a woman – Lord Palmerston had just proved it. And when we are writing the life of a woman, we may, it is agreed, waive our demand for action, and substitute love instead. Love, the poet has said, is woman's whole existence. And if we look for a moment at Orlando writing at her table, we must admit that never was there a woman more fitted for that calling. Surely, since she is a woman, and a beautiful woman, and a woman in the prime of life, she will soon give over this pretence of writing and thinking and begin to think, at least of a gamekeeper (and as long as she thinks of a man, nobody objects to a woman thinking). And then she will write him a little note (and as long as she writes little notes nobody objects to a woman writing either) and make an

assignation for Sunday dusk; and Sunday dusk will come; and the gamekeeper will whistle under the window – all of which is, of course, the very stuff of life and the only possible subject for fiction. Surely Orlando must have done one of these things? Alas – a thousand times, alas, Orlando did none of them. Must it then be admitted that Orlando was one of those monsters of iniquity who do not love? She was kind to dogs, faithful to friends, generosity itself to a dozen starving poets, had a passion for poetry. But love – as the male novelists define it – and who, after all, speaks with greater authority? – has nothing whatever to do with kindness, fidelity, generosity or poetry. Love is slipping off one's petticoat and – But we all know what love is. Did Orlando do that? Truth compels us to say no, she did not. If then, the subject of one's biography will neither love nor kill, but will only think and imagine, we may conclude that he or she is no better than a corpse and so leave her. (Ibid., p. 175)

*To understand this passage clearly, it is necessary to substitute the name "Virginia" for that of the androgynous "Orlando." This done, it becomes a highly revealing and accurate psychological self-portrait of the author, concluding with her chilling self-identification as a "corpse" – a fantasy which later became grim reality when she committed suicide.*

386        Women alone stir my imagination.   —Virginia Woolf

*Only a woman with a decidedly homosexual nature could, or would, ever make such a statement as this.*

387    <u>Joan</u>: When I was thirteen years old, I had a voice from God to help me govern my conduct. And the first time I was very fearful. And came this voice, about the hour of noon, in the summer-time, in my father's garden; I had not fasted on the eve preceding that day. I heard the voice on the right-hand

side, towards the church; and rarely do I hear it without a brightness. This brightness comes from the same side as the voice is heard. It is usually a great light. When I came to France, often I heard this voice. ... The voice was sent to me by God and, after I had thrice heard this voice, I knew that it was the voice of an angel. This voice has always guarded me well and I have always understood it clearly. —Joan of Arc, by Herself and Her Witnesses, Regine Pernoud, Stein and Day, New York, 1969, p. 30.

*Schizophrenia was originally called "dementia praecox," or precocious dementia, to mark the fact of its first appearance around the age of puberty. Joan of Arc's schizophrenia first began at the age of thirteen with the onset of both visual and auditory hallucinations – which she vividly describes here – both of which are classic symptoms of the disease.*

388          And the fact is that this conclusion convinced the King that she could perfectly well be allowed to take action and undertake that trial which, she declared, would be the 'sign' of her mission: the attempt to deliver Orleans. Another examination had, however, taken place, which was, as it were, a double-check to the first: the girl was calling herself Joan the Maid; but was she, or was she not, a virgin? If she was not then she was clearly guilty of a flagrant imposture; if she was, that might be proof that she had, as she claimed, indeed 'vowed her virginity to God,' virginity being the sign of one who dedicates himself or herself wholly to God.

          Jean Pasquerel: 'I have heard it said that Joan, when she came to the King, was examined by women to know how it was with her, whether she was a man or a woman and whether she was corrupt or virgin. She was found to be woman and virgin and maid. Those who visited her (person) were, as I have heard say, the lady de Gaucourt (Jeanne de

Preuilly) and the lady de Treves (Jeanne de Mortemer).' (Ibid., p. 58)

*From the very beginning of Joan's "mission" to "deliver Orleans" from the enemy, questions were raised as to "whether she was a man or a woman and whether she was corrupt or virgin." More so than with most schizophrenics, Joan's alienation from the normal sexual role her culture expected females to adhere to was so extreme that it was necessary to have her submit to a physical examination to determine her true gender. In short, although she claimed to be a female, her appearance, attitude and actions were all extremely masculine.*

389        What impression did this girl – whose company, given to her by the King, were obliged to obey her as they had to obey any other military commander – make on her soldiers? Several of them have told us.

Thiband d'Armagnac or de Termes, Knight, bailiff of Chartres: 'Apart from the matter of the war, she was simple and ignorant. But in the conduct and disposition of armies and in the matter of warfare, in drawing-up the army in battle (order) and heartening the soldiers, she behaved as if she had been the shrewdest captain in the world and had all her life been learning (the art of) war.' (Ibid., p. 62)

*It is quite extraordinary for a young girl, without prior experience of any kind, to rapidly and efficiently learn the arts of war. This can only be attributed to the early "masculinization" of her psyche, a direct product of her sex-role alienation as a child. Extreme sex-role alienation such as Joan experienced inevitably leads either to outright homosexuality or, if denied and repressed, to schizophrenia.*

390     Of more value to us are the details which Boulainvilliers gives on Joan's physical appearance; for despite the exaggerated tone of the whole letter, these may be more or less true since he did probably see Joan. 'This Maid,' he says, 'has a certain elegance. She has a virile bearing, speaks little, shows an admirable prudence in all her words. She has a pretty woman's voice, eats little, drinks very little wine; she enjoys riding a horse and takes pleasure in fine arms, greatly likes the company of noble fighting men, detests numerous assemblies and meetings, readily sheds copious tears, has a cheerful face; she bears the weight and burden of armour incredibly well, to such a point that she has remained fully armed during six days and nights.' (Ibid., p. 98)

        *The "bearded lady" aspect of Joan's personality is clearly shown by this passage, where her masculine attributes, such as her "virile bearing," her enjoyment of "riding a horse" and taking "pleasure in fine arms," the fact she "greatly likes the company of noble fighting men" and "bears the weight and burden of armour incredibly well," contrast markedly with her "pretty woman's voice" and her tendency to "readily shed copious tears."*

391             The regent Bedford, meanwhile, was taking advantage of the unhoped for respite. He was having Paris fortified and trying to diminish the prestige which the coronation had given Charles by discrediting (a foretaste of what was to be done at Rouen) Joan, who had accomplished that coronation. From Montereau he sent Charles a letter in the following terms:
        'We, John of Lancaster, regent of France and Duke of Bedford, make known to you Charles of Valois who call yourself Dauphin of Viennois and now without cause call yourself King because you have abusively made enterprise against the crown and lordship of the very high and excellent prince, my sovereign lord, Henry by the grace of God true,

natural and rightful King of France and England. ... You who cause to be abused the ignorant people and take to yourself the aid of people superstitious and reproved, as that of a woman disordered and defamed, being in man's clothes and of dissolute conduct ... who by force and power of arms have occupied in the country of Champagne and elsewhere cities, towns and castles belonging to my said lord the King ... summon and require you that ... taking pity of the poor Christian people ... choose in the country of Brie where you and we are, or in the Ile de France, some place in the fields, convenient and reasonable, or one day soon and fitting ... at which day and place, if you would appear there in person with the aforesaid defamed and apostate woman, we, at Our Lord's pleasure, will appear in person ...' (Ibid., p. 131)

*As can be seen from this passage, Joan's enemies had a very poor opinion of her, referring to her as "a woman disordered and defamed, being in man's clothes and of dissolute conduct... ."*

*It is interesting they called her a woman "disordered" and directly associated that condition with the fact she wore masculine attire. This shows psychological astuteness on the part of her enemies, as her schizophrenia – the cause of her being "disordered" – stemmed from the severe conflict between the masculine and feminine sides of her nature. Her enemies, obviously, were very aware of her masculine side, as it had caused them great injury and defeat during the war.*

392    The Burgundian chroniclers give a correct account of the facts touching the siege of Orleans, but do their best to run down Joan herself. We quote, as representative, Enguerrand de Monstrelet, a bastard of good family in the personal service of Phillipe the Good, Duke of Burgundy, from 1430:

'In the year (1429) came to King Charles of France at Chinon, where he dwelt a great part of the time, a Maid aged twenty years or thereabouts, named Joan, she being attired and dressed as a man and was born in a part between Burgundy and Lorraine, in a town called Domremy quite close to Vaucouleurs; the which Joan was long serving-maid in a hostelry and was bold in riding horses and taking them to water and also in other skills which young girls are not accustomed to do. She was put on the road and sent towards the King by a knight called messire Robert of Baudricourt, a captain of the King, at Vaucouleurs, which knight gave her horses and four or five companions. She said that she was a maid inspired by divine grace and that she was sent to the King to restore him to the possession of his kingdom... .' (Ibid., p. 102)

*The fact of Joan's alienation at an early age from the normal feminine sexual role of her culture is noted by the Burgundian chroniclers, who mention that she "was bold in riding horses and taking them to water and also in other skills which young girls are not accustomed to do."*

393    Before this retreat Joan hung up, as an ex-voto, a suit of armour taken from a prisoner she had captured before Paris.

Question: What arms did you offer in the church of Saint-Denis in France?
Joan: A white harness entire for gentleman-at arms with a sword which I won before the town of Paris.
Question: Why did you offer these arms?
Joan: It was in devoutness, as is the custom among men of war when they are wounded; and because I had been wounded before the town of Paris, I gave them to Saint-Denis because that is the (war)-cry of France. (Ibid., p. 138-139)

*In this passage Joan assumes a total masculine identification. When asked why she offered arms in the church* *of Saint-Denis, she answers that she did it "in devoutness, as is the custom among men of war when they are wounded..." obviously in her own mind she was definitely a <u>man</u> of war, which is the exact opposite of what the average female would consider herself to be. Joan's sex-role alienation is complete.*

394 The town gates were closed on his orders because the enemy was getting too close; Joan, as usual, was at the point where the danger was greatest; she had always been in the vanguard when it was a question of making an attack; and in the rearguard when a retreat had to be covered; her company had been thrown back upon Compiègne; and she happened to be one of the handful of combatants whom it was absolutely necessary to sacrifice if the town was to be saved.

    The Burgundian Georges Chastellain has left us a very lively account of Joan's capture: 'The French, with their Maid, were beginning to retreat very slowly, as finding no advantage over their enemies but rather perils and damage. Wherefore the Burgundians, seeing that and being flowing with blood, and not satisfied with having repulsed them in defence, since they could do them no more great harm than by pursuing them closely, struck among them valiantly both afoot and mounted, and did great damage among the French. Of which the Maid, passing the nature of women, took all the brunt, and took great pains to save her company, remaining behind as captain and bravest of her troop.' (Ibid., p. 151)

*In this account, Joan is described as an extraordinarily brave and valiant soldier, a leader in battle whose actions surpassed "the nature of women" to such an extent, in fact, that few men could equal her as a warrior.*

395 Of the time when she was a prisoner we have but little evidence. However, in the course of the Trial of Rehabilitation

a Burgundian knight gave evidence. This was Haimond de Macy who was in John of Luxembourg's service:

'I saw Joan for the first time when she was shut up in the castle of Beaurevoir for the Lord Count of Ligny (John of Luxembourg). I saw her several (many) times in prison and on several occasions conversed with her. I tried several times, playfully, to touch her breasts, trying to put my hand on her chest, which Joan would not suffer but repulsed me with all her strength. Joan was, indeed, of decent conduct (*honnête tenue*) both in speech and act.' (Ibid., p. 155)

*Joan was very intolerant of any kind of heterosexual contact, either before or after her imprisonment.*

396  La Fontaine: Since you have said that you would wear woman's clothes if you were allowed to go away, would that please God?

Joan: If permission were given me to withdraw in woman's clothes, immediately (thereafter) I should dress myself in man's clothes and do what is commanded me by God; and I have answered elsewhere that not for anything whatsoever would I take oath not to put on armour and not to wear man's clothes to do the Lord's commandment. (Ibid., p. 174)

*It would have been very difficult – if not impossible – for Joan to have justified her transvestism to herself without the aid of her schizophrenic delusion, which was that she had been chosen by God to become a fierce warrior as part of her "mission."*

397  La Fontaine: Why did you like to look at that ring when you were going to do some war-like deed?

Joan: That was for my pleasure and in honour of my father and mother; and I, having that ring in my hand and on my finger, I touched Saint Catherine who appeared to me visibly.

La Fontaine: In what part of this Saint Catherine did you touch her?

Joan: You will have nothing else on that.

La Fontaine: Did you kiss or embrace (accolé) Saints Catherine and Margaret?

Joan: I embraced both of them.

La Fontaine: Had they a pleasant odour?

Joan: It is good to know that they had a pleasant odour.

La Fontaine: When embracing them, did you feel any warmth or any other thing?

Joan: I could not embrace them without feeling and touching them.

La Fontaine: In what part did you embrace them, the upper or the lower?

Joan: It is more fitting to embrace them by the lower part than the higher. (Ibid, p. 177)

... To be glimpsed through these succeeding questions and answers are the principal accusations of which Joan was, if possible, to be convicted. There was the charge of witchcraft, to which we can refer those questions touching her standard and the story or it floating round the King's head; and those about her ring, with the suggestion that it had magical powers. Then there are the charges which, if proved, would convict Joan of impurity, of questionable intercourse with the beings whom, she claimed, appeared to her. And there are the questions relative to her deeds and prowess in war, with the possibility of convicting her of expressing hate or cruelty. Finally, there are the two charges which, cleverly confounded together, were, in the event, to enable the prosecution to convict her: wearing men's clothes; and the question of submission to the Church. It was on this point, and by making her male attire the symbol of her refusal to submit to the

Church, that they contrived to give an appearance of justification to the final sentence; for Joan's answers gave the prosecutors absolutely no foundation upon which to build up a case against her in the matter of her morals, and still less in the matter of witchcraft. (Ibid., p. 179)

*Joan's enemies intuituively realized that any woman who was as masculine in appearance and actions as she was would undoubtedly have strong homosexual tendencies, and La Fontaine, through his questions about her relations with her Saints – Catherine and Margaret – insinuates as much.*

398      On that day more than half the session was given up to this question of the oath, Joan remaining unshakable. After that Beaupère questioned her, notably about her voices.

Beaupère: Since what time have you neither eaten or drunk?

Joan: Since yesterday afternoon.

Beaupère: Since when have you heard your voice?

Joan: I heard it yesterday and to-day.

Beaupère: At what time did you hear it?

Joan: I heard it three times, one in the morning, one at the hour of vespers, and the third time when they were ringing the evening Ave Maria. And still have I heard it more often than I say.

Beaupère: What were you doing yesterday morning when the voice came to you?

Joan: I slept and the voice awoke me.

Beaupère: Did the voice wake you by touching your arm?

Joan: I was awoken by the voice without touch.

Beaupère: The voice, was it in your chamber?

Joan: Not that I know, but it was in the castle.

Beaupère: Did you thank this voice and do you go down on your knees?

Joan: I thanked it by rising and by sitting down on my bed and I clasped my hands and after that I asked it to come to my aid. The voice told me to answer boldly... (turning towards the bishop) you say that you are my judge. Consider well what you are about, for in truth I am sent from God, and you are putting yourself in great danger. (Ibid., p. 182)

*Even in the midst of describing her hallucinations to her enemies, Joan remains fiercely defiant and unrepentant, even to the point of telling her chief accuser, the Bishop Cauchon, that he is putting himself "in great danger" as the result of his actions towards her. This shows how far removed from reality Joan had become, due to her schizophrenia, for if anyone was "in great danger" it was she, as events were soon tragically to prove.*

399   Beaupère: How do you know how to make the distinction when you answer on certain points and others not?

Joan: On certain points I asked permission and received it. I would rather be torn apart by four horses than to have gone to France without God's permission.

Beaupère: Did he command you to wear man's clothes?

Joan: The clothes are a trifle, the very least of things. I did not put on man's clothes by the counsel of any man in the world and I did not put on the clothes and I did not do anything excepting by the commandment of God and the angels ...

Beaupère: Do you believe that you did right to put on man's clothes?

Joan: All that I have done, I have done by God's commandment and I believe that I did right, and I expect from it good warrant and good succour.

Beaupère: In the particular case of taking on man's clothes, do you think that you did right?

Joan: Of what I have done in the world I have done nothing but by God's commandment.

Beaupère: When you see this voice which comes to you, is there light?

Joan: There is much light everywhere, and that is very fitting. Not all light comes only for you. (Ibid., p.184)

*One of the main charges against Joan by her enemies was that she persisted in the wearing of men's clothing. The more she was questioned on this matter, the more fiercely did she defend herself. She justified her transvestism by claiming it was by "God's commandment" that she dressed in such a manner. Thus her schizophrenic delusion allowed her to rationalize her very masculine behavior, behavior that in her culture would otherwise have been abhorred and condemned when exhibited by any female.*

400    *Saturday, March 17th*

The interrogation for this day appears earlier in this chapter.

Finally, March 24th and 25th, Joan was again visited in her prison, still by only a restricted number of the assessors, but these included all the delegates from the University of Paris. More detailed answers were demanded of her in the matter of certain questions, notably that of wearing man's clothes which she still refused to change for female attire. It was on this occasion that she gave the answer which, for her, summed up the whole business: 'These clothes do not burden my soul and to wear them is not against the Church.' ...

That concluded the 'instruction' of the case, that is the preliminary examinations. (Ibid., p. 192)

*Joan explains that she is not psychologically troubled by her transvestism. "These clothes do not burden my soul," she says, "and to wear them is not against the Church." In truth, however, it is highly unlikely that the "Church" of that time would have looked favorably upon transvestism in any form, be it practiced by females or males.*

401    Better than anybody the usher Jean Massieu, charged with reading aloud the form of abjuration, could recall the scene: 'In what concerns the abjuration, when she was preached to by Master Guillaume Erard at Saint-Ouen, Erard held in his hand a *cédule* of abjuration and said to Joan: 'Thou shalt abjure and sign this *cédule*.' Then this *cédule* was handed to me that I might read it and I read it to Joan; and I well remember that in this *cédule* it was noted that in the future she would no longer carry arms nor wear man's clothes, nor shorn hair, and many other things which I no longer remember. And I know well that this *cédule* contained about eight lines and not more. (Ibid., p. 215)

*It is interesting that Jean Massieu states that he "well" remembers "that in this cédule it was noted that in the future she would no longer carry arms nor wear man's clothes, nor shorn hair, and many other things which I no longer remember." In other words, that which struck him as most memorable about the cédule was its reference to Joan's transvestism, or to all those attributes which, taken together, gave her the appearance of being a man rather than a woman.*

402    Now Cauchon, as an advocate experienced in dealing with the law, knew that, according to the rules of the Inquisition courts, none but those who, having recanted their heresy, had relapsed, could be condemned to suffer death by burning. And having succeeded in making the wearing of man's clothes (it is certain, from the evidence given by Jean Massieu, that the wearing of such clothes was expressly mentioned in the cédule) the symbol of Joan's failure to submit to the Church, he might be fairly sure that she would, without

much delay, show herself to have relapsed by retaining her male attire. Events were soon to prove him right. (Ibid., p. 218)

... Sunday, May 27th, Cauchon learned that Joan had resumed male attire. On the following day he went to the prison, accompanied by the vice-Inquisitor and several assessors. The following is from the official record:

'The Monday following, 28 of the month of May, on the day following Holy Trinity, we, judges aforesaid, went to the place of Joan's prison to see her state and disposition. Were present the lords and Masters Nicolas de Venderes, Thomas de Courcelles, Brother Isambart de la Pierre, Guillaume Haiton, Jacques Camus, Nicolas Bertin, Julien Floquet and John Gray.'

'Joan was dressed in a man's clothes, to wit tunic, hood and gippon (a short robe worn by men) and other man's clothes, attire which on our order she had formerly left off and had taken women's clothes: therefore did we question her to know when and for what cause she had again put on man's attire.'

Joan: I not long since resumed man's attire and left off woman's attire.

*Question*: Why have you assumed this male attire and who made you take it?

Joan: I have taken it of my own will. I have taken it because it is more licit and fitting to have man's clothes since I am with men than to have woman's clothes. I have resumed it because what had been promised me has not been observed, to wit that I should go to mass and should receive the Body of Christ and should be taken out of irons.

Pierre Cauchon: Have you not made abjuration and promised especially not to resume man's clothes?

Joan: I would rather die than remain in irons; but if it be permitted me to go to mass and I be taken out of irons and that I be put in a pleasant (gracieuse) prison, and that I have women, I will be good and will do what the Church wishes. (The item 'have women' is down in the French Minute but not in the official text of the proceedings.)

Cauchon: Since that Thursday, have you heard the voices of Saints Catherine and Margaret?

Joan: Yes.

Cauchon: What did they tell you?

Joan: God has sent to me by Saints Catherine and Margaret great pity for the mighty betrayal to which I consented in making abjuration and revocation to save my life, and that I was damning myself to save my life.

(Here the clerk has noted in the margin, *responsio mortifera*, mortal (fatal) answer.) (Ibid., p. 220)

*Bishop Cauchon, in his zeal to see Joan condemned to death, was psychologically astute enough to realize she would be unable to tolerate the wearing of female clothing and would soon "show herself to have relapsed by retaining her male attire." Unfortunately for her, "Events were soon to prove him right." Thus Joan's transvestism, one of the symptoms of her schizophrenic psychosis, whose compulsive hold on her she could not break, even though her very life depended upon her doing so, doomed her to die a horrible death by fire at the stake.*

403   The letter sums up the events following which 'This woman, who had called herself Joan the Maid, had, for two years and more, against divine law and her condition as of the feminine sex, worn male attire, a thing abominable to God, and in that state conveyed to our capital enemy, to whom and to those of his party, Churchmen, nobles and common people, she gave it often to be understood that she was sent by God. (Ibid., p. 237)

*Note is again made of Joan's insistence upon wearing male attire, which this particular correspondent proclaims is "against divine law and her condition as of the feminine sex" and "a thing abominable to God."*

404        In Paris itself the University did not fail to make known, with great ceremony, the outcome of the trial in which it had played a predominant role. The Journal d'un Bourgeois de Paris, written by a university man and therefore conveying university feeling exactly, has a long account of how. '... on the day of Saint-Martin-le-Bouillant (July 4th) a general procession was made to Saint-Martin-des-Champs and a brother of the Order of Saint Dominic, who was an Inquisitor and a Master of Theology, preached a sermon. In this he included a version of Joan the Maid's whole life; she had claimed to be the daughter of very poor folk; she had adopted man's attire when she was only fourteen and her father and mother would willingly have killed her then had they been able to do it without wounding their own conscience; and that was why she left them, accompanied by the hellish Enemy. Thereafter her life was one of fire and blood and the murder of Christians until she was burned at the stake.'

        The Journal records, before this, and in all the detail which the writer had been able to obtain, a life and trial of Joan in much the same spirit, adding an account of her execution which no doubt conveys more or less what was known in Paris and echoes the version put about by the university: 'When she saw that her punishment was certain she cried for mercy and orally abjured. Her clothes were taken from her and she was attired as a woman, but no sooner did she find herself in this attire than she fell again into error and asked for her man's clothes. She was therefore soon condemned to death by all the judges, and bound to a stake on the scaffold of plaster (cement) on which the fire was built. She perished soon, and her dress was all burned away, then the fire was drawn a little back that the people should not doubt. The people saw her stark naked with all the secrets which a woman can and should have. When this sight had lasted long enough, the executioner replaced great fire under that poor carrion which was soon charred and the bones reduced to ashes. Many people said there and elsewhere that she was a martyr and that she had sacrificed herself for her true prince. Others said that this was not so and that he who had so long protected her had done her ill. Thus spake the people, but whether she had done well or ill, she was burned that day.' (Ibid., p. 238)

*Joan herself reported during her trial that her voices and visions first appeared to her at the age of thirteen, and here we are informed by another source that she first adopted "man's attire" at the age of fourteen. Thus her hallucinations and her transvestism, following closely the one upon the other, were the first concrete signs of her schizophrenic psychosis, which clinically would be termed of the paranoid type. As is invariably the case, schizophrenic symptomatology springs from severe bisexual conflict whose roots lie in early sex-role alienation as a child. In Joan's case, the etiology of her schizophrenia is more glaringly apparent than it is in the "average" schizophrenic.*

*Thus we are presented with the tragic and heart-rending spectacle of a severely mentally-ill young girl, no more than 19 or 20 years of age at most, being tied to the stake and burned alive as the direct consequence of actions she had taken in pursuance of the tasks, and in obedience to the commands, levied upon her by her hallucinated "voices."*

*In life, her sex-role alienation had been so complete that her executioners deemed it necessary to draw back the fire momentarily to enable the witnesses to verify the fact that indeed she was a female and not the male she gave every evidence of being by dint of her outward appearance and war-like activities.*

405          It is not intended to go into details of the criticisms with which Freud's paper was received in psychiatric circles. But mention should be made of the review by Bleuler (1912), one of Freud's friendliest critics: 'This publication bears the hallmark of an important contribution by the very fact that it provides food for further thought, questioning and research,' though 'difficulties arise by trying to separate Schreber's illness from schizophrenia ... Paranoid and schizophrenic symptoms not only coexist in one patient, they also seem to merge and indeed appear to be two aspects of the same process.' —Memoirs of My Nervous Illness, Daniel Paul Schreber (Ibid., p. 371)

*When Sigmund Freud developed his brilliant theory of paranoia in the case of Daniel Paul Schreber, he had, without realizing it, also solved the mystery of schizophrenia and, consequently, of all functional mental illness. Freud stated in the Schreber case that paranoia invariably developed as the direct consequence of repressed homosexual cravings, whether in the male or the female, and irregardless of race, culture or social class. This finding is without doubt the most brilliant and important piece of insight ever uncovered by a psychological investigator, but unfortunately its discoverer immediately negated its overwhelming importance to the understanding of mental illness by stating that paranoia and schizophrenia were really two different diseases and therefore must have different etiologies. Of course he was completely mistaken in this assumption, as Professor Eugen Bleuler attempted to point out when he stated that "difficulties arise in trying to separate Schreber's illness from schizophrenia ... Paranoid and schizophrenic symptoms not only coexist in one patient, they also seem to merge and indeed appear to be two aspects of the same process." Bleuler was totally correct. Paranoia and schizophrenia are "two aspects of the same process" and therefore paranoia and schizophrenia would have a common etiology.*

*How ironic it is that in one stroke of genius Freud made a discovery of overwhelming importance and then immediately negated it by claiming that paranoia and schizophrenia were two different entities, thereby leading investigators who followed in his footsteps to deny that repressed homosexual drives, invariably the cause of paranoia, could also play such a key role in the etiology of what Freud incorrectly termed "that far more comprehensive disorder" of dementia praecox, or schizophrenia.*

406    It was Litzmann's impressive work, however, that enabled the psychiatrist Paul Mobius to construct (in 1906) the first longitudinal, developmental study of Robert Schumann's madness.

Mobius proposed the diagnosis *dementia praecox*, then considered to be a progressive mental disorder with a very poor prognosis. The diagnosis was changed to schizophrenia when in 1911 Eugen Bleuler included Schumann in his famous textbook about these illnesses. Bleuler's was the first modern (that is, twentieth century) effort at explaining schizophrenia in both psychological and physiological terms, and he felt that there were patients who did recover or who, like Schumann, staved off some of the more disabling symptoms through their creative activity. But this diagnosis had already been challenged (in 1906) by Hans Gruhle, a psychiatrist who reasoned that Schumann's madness had been a manic-depressive psychosis, complicated by terminal brain changes. —Schumann, the Inner Voices of a Musical Genius, Peter Ostwald, Northeastern University Press, Boston, 1985, p. xi.

*Here we see that Schumann was first diagnosed as*
*suffering from schizophrenia (dementia praecox), which at*
*that time was thought to be an incurable disease with*
*progressive deterioration, and then, when he exhibited the*
*ability to function creatively as a composer, the diagnosis was*
*changed to manic depression. Actually, manic depression and*
*schizophrenia are part of the same disease process, which*
*includes paranoia, hysteria, and the obsessive compulsive*
*syndrome as well.*

407          Sometimes Schumann's writing suggests that he may
have wanted to be both male and female, a desire that the
psychoanalyst Lawrence Kubie thought was fundamental to
much of human creativity.[39] For example, a poem written at
the end of 1828, when Schumann was eighteen years old, has
the flavor of a bi-sexual fantasy:

> And how wildly one youth loves the other
>     youth,
> And how he embraces him, and how they
>     weep together,
> That's how you are right now; once you
>     were my feminine beloved,
> Now you are my masculine beloved.
> And from the blossoms of your love
> Arises friendship, softly.

Several entries in Schumann's diary mention
homosexuality more explicitly (it was not a topic one could be
very open about; male homosexuality was illegal and was
punishable in many countries). For example, after a trip to a
tavern in Leipzig with his friend Johann Renz in March 1829,
he noted 'pederasty' in his diary. After returning to the tavern
the next day, he recorded a 'voluptuous night with Greek
dreams.'[41] (Ibid., p. 42)

*Schumann was afflicted with a very severe bisexual conflict which led, as it invariably does, to schizophrenic symptomatology. Here we see clear evidence of this conflict and of the sexual confusion engendered by it.*

408        Soon after making this entry, Schumann stopped practicing and plunged headlong into one of the wildest sprees recorded in the diary. Four times he called it 'the most debauched week of my life.' [51] On 9 February he wrote of 'madness' (Wahnsinn) and 'loss of consciousness.' He reeled from one tavern to the next, and went to innumerable parties, including a masked ball, where, according to Niecks, he dressed as a woman.[52] (Such behavior was not unusual among college students at the time, but it seems to have disturbed Schumann profoundly.) (Ibid., p. 61)

*Schumann's unconscious urges to be a female, which he attempted to repress, at times became so insistent that they overwhelmed his beleaguered ego and found temporary expression in transvestic and overtly homosexual behavior.*

409      Schumann's audiences were minuscule at first. They consisted mainly of Clara and a few intimate friends. But she, a musical genius in her own right, would gradually attract others to his music.
       Giddily he told her about his latest compositions:
       I've put on my frilly dress and composed 30 cute little things from which I've selected about twelve and called them 'Scenes from Childhood' [*Kinderszenen*]... They are like an echo to what you once wrote me, that I sometimes 'seem like a child' to you.[46] (Ibid., p. 140)

*As with all schizophrenics, Schumann experienced profound sex-role alienation in early childhood. When he writes that he "put on my frilly dress and composed 30 cute little things from which I've selected about twelve and called them 'Scenes from Childhood',"* he is demonstrating his early childhood identification with, and fixation upon, the feminine role.

410          Surely there was a biological determinant to Schumann's upsurge of creative energy as he approached the age of thirty. Even his erotic behavior up to that point had been somewhat immature; it consisted mainly of day dreaming, punctuated by an occasional affair with a woman or an unsatisfactory romance with a man. (Ibid., p. 156)

          *Again, mention is made of Schumann's bisexual conflict. His erotic life up to the age of thirty, we are told, consisted mainly of "day dreaming, punctuated by an occasional affair with a woman or an unsatisfactory romance with a man."*

411          An exotic poem, 'Lalla Rookh,' by Thomas Moore (1779-1852), struck Schumann as exactly suited to the sort of oratorio he had in mind. The central figure is the fairy ('Peri'), a fallen angel of ambiguous sex who has been expelled from Paradise and wants to get back in. To do so requires a special penance. First he/she travels to India and gathers up drops of blood spilled by a slain hero, but to no avail. Next he/she goes to Egypt and collects sighing last breaths from a maiden who is dying in the arms of her fatally ill lover, but even this precious commodity does not appease the gods. Finally he/she visits Syria and finds there a hardened sinner who miraculously begins to weep at the sight of a small child reciting its prayers. Peri catches the sinner's tears, and with this gift is readmitted to Paradise. ... No doubt the composer was excited by this material. He once confided to a friend that 'while writing <u>Paradise and the Peri</u> a voice occasionally whispered to me 'what you are doing is not done completely in

vain.' ' [73] And Clara thought she observed an almost pathological elation: 'He works on the [Peri] body and soul, with such a glowing heat that I sometimes fear it could do him some harm.' [74] (Ibid., p. 181-182)

*It appears Schumann identified strongly at an unconscious level with Peri, the "fallen angel of ambiguous sex," who was the protagonist of Thomas Moore's poem. In reality, all schizophrenics, including Schumann, are "fallen angels of ambiguous sex" and the "paradise" they have been expelled from is that normal state of human happiness, or satisfaction, which is denied them due to their severe bisexual conflict and consequent mental illness.*

412     It is difficult to define the personality disorder of a genius like Schumann according to concepts that have been developed for ordinary, more 'normal,' patients. He had what seems to have been a severely divided self, with conflicts centering around dependency versus independence, attachment versus separation, and femininity versus masculinity. (Ibid., p. 304)

*Although Schumann may have been a musical "genius," the "severely divided self" he suffered from is exactly the same as that which afflicts all schizophrenics, namely, the self which is divided between, and in conflict with, its masculine and feminine sides.*

413     A leading figure in German psychiatry at this time was Paul Mobius, M. D. (1853-1907). After listening to Schumann's music, he came to the conclusion that this must have been 'a very nervous man,' he also characterized the composer as extraordinarily 'passive' and 'feminine.'[16] It was Mobius's belief that Schumann had been 'mentally ill since his youth' and that the correct diagnosis was dementia praecox (called schizophrenia since 1911). (Ibid., p. 300)

*When Dr. Mobius called Schumann an extremely "passive" and "feminine" man, he was, perhaps without realizing it, calling attention to the composer's strongly homosexual nature. And it was this nature, in severe conflict with its heterosexual counterpart, which formed the etiological core of his schizophrenic symptomatology.*

414        To know that you have had cancer in your body and to know that it may return must be very horrible; but a cancer of the mind, a corruption of the spirit striking one at the age of thirteen and for the rest of one's life always working away somewhere, always in suspense, a Dionysian sword above one's head – this must be almost unendurable. So unendurable that in the end, when the voices of insanity spoke to her in 1941, she took the only remedy that remained, the cure of death. But her mind could make a scar that would serve, in some measure, to heal and to conceal her lasting wound. She did not, could not, admit all the memories of her madness. What she did recall were the physical symptoms; in her memoir of this period she hardly mentions the commotions of her mind and although we know that she had already heard what she was later to call 'those horrible voices,' she speaks of other symptoms, usually physiological symptoms. Her pulse raced – it raced so fast as to be almost unbearable. She became painfully excitable and nervous and then intolerably depressed. She became terrified of people, blushed scarlet if spoken to and was unable to face a stranger in the street. — Virginia Woolf, a Biography, Quentin Bell, Harcourt Brace Jovanovich, Inc., New York, 1972, p. 44.

*Virginia's "lasting wound" was, in reality, her life-long, deep inner anguish at not having been born a man, with everything that implies, both physically and mentally. The mental part she could, and did, compensate for, but the physical part was of course biologically unobtainable.*

*Her schizophrenic symptoms, as was the case with Joan of Arc, first appeared at the age of thirteen. They consisted primarily of audio hallucinations – "those horrible voices" – but later visual hallucinations occurred as well. As Quentin Bell so movingly relates, Virginia was assailed throughout her life by schizophrenic symptomatology, including manic depression, and finally, to escape its ravages, she weighted the pockets of her coat with heavy stones and walked into the river.*

415   Virginia was in fact in love with her. She was the first woman – and in those early years Virginia fled altogether from anything male – the first to capture her heart, to make it beat faster, indeed to make it almost stand still as, her hand gripping the handle of the water-jug in the top room at Hyde Park Gate, she exclaimed to herself: 'Madge is here; at this moment she is actually under this roof.' Virginia once declared that she had never felt a more poignant emotion for anyone than she did at that moment for Madge. Certainly it was a very pure and very intense passion – pure in almost every sense of the word; Virginia at sixteen, for all George's kissings and fumblings, was by modern standards almost unbelievably ignorant. It was pure also in its sincerity, in its lack of jealous feeling. It was the passion of a girl in a junior form for a dashing senior, not a passion based upon intimacy.

The friendship with Emma and the passion for Madge were valuable; they provided some measure of relief in the domestic storms of the period, those afflictions to which we must now return. (Ibid., p. 60)

*Virginia's powerful homosexual nature is vividly described in this passage. At the age of sixteen, when most "normal" girls have begun to have crushes on boys, she is experiencing an intense homosexual passion for Madge.*

416          Virginia's numerous letters to Violet have been
preserved and from this it is clear to the modern reader,
though it was not at all clear to Virginia, that she was in love
and that her love was returned. For they are passionate letters,
enchanting, amusing, embarrassing letters full of private jokes
and endearments, letters in which Virginia invents nicknames
for herself, imagines herself as some shy half-wild animal, a
pet to be fondled and cherished; and from which one tries to
conjure up a picture of the recipient.

          ... Like Madge Vaughan, Violet Dickinson fulfilled a
need. She provided sympathy and stability at a time when it
was badly needed. I do not think that she made any very great
contribution to Virginia's intellectual development. Virginia
did indeed send her manuscripts for criticism (she also wrote a
kind of joke biography of her friend) but I doubt whether
Violet's criticism as distinct from her encouragement was very
important to her. Her gifts were chiefly moral and, when other
and more remarkable people came into Virginia's life, passion
slowly faded into kindness. One must think of this friendship
as an affair of the heart, where I think that in fact it remained;
while the affair was at its height, that is to say from about
1902 to 1907, it was intense. (Ibid., p. 83)

          *Again, we see evidence of Virginia's strongly
homosexual nature in her relationship with Violet Dickinson.
As Quentin Bell writes, this was definitely "an affair of the
heart" which lasted from "about 1902 to 1907," was "intense,"
and the "passion slowly faded into kindness."*

417          In the breakdown that followed she entered into a
period of nightmare in which the symptoms of the preceding
months attained frantic intensity. Her mistrust of Vanessa, her
grief for her father became maniacal, her nurses – she had
three – became fiends. She heard voices urging her to acts of
folly; she believed that they came from overeating and that she

must starve herself. In this emergency the main burden fell upon Vanessa; but Vanessa was enormously helped by Violet Dickinson. She took Virginia to her house at Burnham Wood and it was there that she made her first attempt to commit suicide. She threw herself from a window, which, however, was not high enough from the ground to cause her serious harm. It was here too that she lay in bed, listening to the birds singing in Greek and imagining that King Edward VII lurked in the azaleas using the foulest possible language.

All that summer she was mad. It was not until early September that she was able to leave Burnham Wood, thin and shaken, but sane enough to be able to live at peace with Vanessa. (Ibid., p. 89)

*There was always an intense homosexual bond between Virginia and her sister Vanessa, as there also was between Virginia and Violet Dickinson. Her "mistrust" of Vanessa was a paranoid defense mechanism utilized by her unconscious to shield her from the inadmissable realization that she was homosexually attracted to her sister. And we have already been informed by Quentin Bell that Virginia had "passionate" feelings for Violet Dickinson. This being the case, having Violet take care of her during this spell of madness could only have aggravated Virginia's illness, in light of the fact that her paranoid schizophrenic symptoms were the direct consequence of her repression and disavowal of these "passionate," or erotic, homosexual feelings directed towards both Violet and Vanessa.*

418   Two of them, Sydney-Turner and possibly R. G. Hawtrey, came to stay in Cornwall with the Stephen children that summer and Virginia observed them with amazement. They were, she declared:

... a great trial; they sit silent, absolutely silent, all the time. Occasionally they creep to a corner and chuckle over a latin joke. Perhaps they are falling in love with Nessa; who knows? It would be a silent and very learned process. However I don't think they are robust enough to feel very much. Oh women are my line and not these inanimate creatures. The worst of it is that they have not the energy to go ... . (Ibid., p. 97)

*Only a woman of decidedly homosexual temperament could make such a statement as: "Oh women are my line and not these inanimate creatures." The "inanimate creatures" she is specifically referring to here are two male acquaintances, but from Virginia's point of view they could personify the entire male sex, of which she was not very fond. That simple declaration, "Oh women are my line ...," deftly sums up Virginia's psychosexual bent, or sexual orientation, as it is currently referred to. Considering the intensity of her homosexual feelings, the only alternatives open to Virginia were either to become openly and actively a homosexual woman, with all that entailed both emotionally and physically, or else to become insane, or schizophrenic, as the result of repressing these feelings. Virginia, as we see here, took the latter course.*

419          On the morning of 10 February 1910, Virginia, with five companions, drove to Paddington Station and took a train to Weymouth. She wore a turban, a fine gold chain hanging to her waist and an embroidered caftan. Her face was black. She sported a very handsome moustache and beard. Of the other members of the party three – Duncan Grant, Anthony Buxton and Guy Ridley – were disguised in much the same way. Adrian was there, wearing a beard and an ill-fitting bowler hat so that he looked, as he himself put it 'like a seedy commercial traveller,' while the sixth member (and leader) of the party, Horace Cole, was convincingly attired as an official of the Foreign Office.

The object of their excursion was to hoodwink the British Navy, to penetrate its security and to enjoy a conducted tour of the flagship of the Home Fleet, the most formidable, the most modern and the most secret man o' war then afloat, H.M.S. <u>Dreadnought</u>. (Ibid., p. 157)

*This display of transvestic behavior by Virginia fits in harmoniously with her masculine, homosexual nature. We have seen similar behavior in two other previously described schizophrenics, Zelda Fitzgerald and Joan of Arc.*

420    It was not until the end of February that Leonard was allowed to send Virginia a studiously boring letter and when at length she was released, Vanessa dismissed him with gentle but firm benevolence to Somerset; here he received a letter from Virginia in which she declared:

'I shall tell you wonderful stories of the lunatics. Bye the bye, they've elected me King. There can be no doubt about it. I summoned a conclave, & made a proclamation about Christianity. I had other adventures, & some disasters, the fruit of a too passionate & enquiring disposition. I avoided both love & hatred. I now feel very clear, calm, and move slowly, like one of the great big animals at the zoo.' (Ibid., p. 182)

*One of Virginia's delusions when she was severely mentally ill was that she had been elected "King" by a "conclave." Since being a King is commonly considered to be a position of extreme masculine power, for a woman to have a delusion that she is one demonstrates powerful unconscious wishes to be a man, and a very potent man at that. Again, this is an example of Freud's neurotic penis envy in the female carried to its psychotic extreme.*

421    It is a proof of their deep and unvarying affection that it was not dependent upon the intenser joys of physical love. Even

before her marriage, they must have suspected that Virginia would not be physically responsive, but probably they hoped that Leonard, whose passionate nature was never in question, could effect a change. A letter written from Saragossa to Ka Cox shows clearly enough that, if this hope was entertained, it was also disappointed.

'Why do you think people make such a fuss about marriage & copulation? Why do some of our friends change upon losing chastity? Possibly my great age makes it less of a catastrophe; but certainly I find the climax immensely exaggerated. Except for a sustained good humour (Leonard shan't see this) due to the fact that every twinge of anger is at once visited upon my husband, I might still be Miss S.'

Thus, with placid conversational ease, Virginia alludes to her frigidity. It was, nevertheless, a cause of worry to both of them, and when they were back in England they sought Vanessa's advice.

'They seemed very happy, but are evidently both a little exercised in their minds on the subject of the Goat's coldness. I think I perhaps annoyed her but may have consoled him by saying that I thought she never had understood or sympathized with sexual passion in men. Apparently she still gets no pleasure at all from the act, which I think is curious. They were very anxious to know when I first had an orgasm. I couldn't remember. Do you? But no doubt I sympathized with such things if I didn't have them from the time I was 2. ... Of the two women who knew her best, one, as we have seen, said that she had no understanding of sexual passion in men, the other – Vita Sackville-West – was to note many years later that 'She dislikes the possessiveness and love of domination in men. In fact she dislikes the quality of masculinity.' (Ibid., Vol. II, p. 56)

*We learn from this quotation that Virginia was frigid in her marriage – "Apparently she still gets no pleasure at all from the act." – that "she never had understood or sympathized with sexual passion in men," and finally, that "She dislikes the possessiveness and love of domination in men. In fact she dislikes the quality of masculinity."*

*The psychological profile presented here is that of a woman with very pronounced homosexual tendencies, who, if she were at peace with, and accepting of, her true feelings, would be a practicing lesbian. The fact she was not, and that later she lived with a man in an asexual marriage, proved to be her undoing, for this physical and emotional denial of her strongly homosexual nature was the immediate and direct cause of her schizophrenic illness and, thus, eventually of her suicide.*

422     All of which might be a form of bravado and sisterly one-upmanship. Finally, considering the case for – what is it, the prosecution? – take the evidence of Vita's monument, Orlando, of all Virginia's novels the one that comes nearest to sexual, or rather to homosexual, feeling; for, while the hero/heroine undergoes a bodily transformation, being at first a splendid youth and then a beautiful lady, the psychological metamorphosis is far less complete. From the first the youth is a little uncertain of his sex; when he puts on petticoats he becomes, not simply a woman, but a man who enjoys being a woman. Orlando is also Virginia's most idealized creation; he/she is modelled near to the heart's desire (and not only to the heart) – near, in fact, to the glamorous creations of the novelette. Compare Virginia's treatment of him/her to the cool ironies of Mrs. Dalloway or to the floral metamorphosis of Jinny in The Waves – a bouquet on a gilded chair – or the discreet glimpses of Jacob's loves. (Ibid., Vol. II, p. 118)

*Supposedly Virginia Woolf's androgynous novel Orlando was formed around the character of her friend, and reputedly for a brief time her lover, Vita Sackville-West.*

*However true this may be, the novel also represents a starkly revealing autobiographical account of Virginia's own severely conflicted bisexual nature, even though that may have been the furthest thing from her conscious mind while she was composing the story.*

423        Then, early in September, Maynard and Lydia Keynes gave a party at Tilton. Jack (later Sir John) Sheppard enacted the part of an Italian *prima donna*, words and music being supplied by a gramophone. Someone had brought a newspaper cutting with them; it reproduced the photograph of a pretty young woman who had become a man, and this for the rest of the evening became Virginia's main topic of conversation.
       Never had she worked so fast. She threw in everything that so beautifully, as it seemed so inevitably, lay to hand. In that autumn, 'that singularly happy autumn,' Orlando shoved everything aside. (Ibid., Vol. II, p. 132)

*Here we see that the impetus for writing Orlando originated when Virginia first read a newspaper article about a young lady who transformed herself into a male. This idea so intrigued her that she went to work immediately writing her new novel based upon this incident. As Quentin Bell describes it: "Never had she worked so fast." The concept of being able to change from a female into a male had struck a very responsive chord in Virginia's tortured bisexual psyche.*

424   It was finished by the middle of May and in October the book was published under the title A Room of One's Own. It is, I think, the easiest of Virginia's books, by which I mean that it puts no great burden on the sensibilities. The whole work is held together, not as in her other works by a thread of feeling, but by a thread of argument – a simple well-stated argument: the disabilities of women are social and economic; the woman writer can only survive despite great difficulties, and despite

the prejudice and the economic selfishness of men; and the key to emancipation is to be found in the door of a room which a woman may call her own and which she can inhabit with the same freedom and independence as her brothers. The lack of this economic freedom breeds resentment, the noisy assertive resentment of the male, who insists on claiming his superiority, and the shrill nagging resentment of the female who clamours for her rights. Both produce bad literature, for literature – fiction, that is – demands a comprehensive sympathy which transcends and comprehends the feelings of both sexes. The great artist is Androgynous.

This argument is developed easily and conversationally, striking home in some memorable passages but always lightly and amusingly expressed. It is that rare thing – a lively but good-tempered polemic, and a book which, like Orlando, is of particular interest to the student of her life. (Ibid., Vol. II, p. 144)

*Virginia's argument, that the great artist always is androgynous, certainly correlates with her own self-perception and experience. However, Virginia was not so much androgynous as she was masculine and homosexual – this to a much greater degree than she was feminine and heterosexual. If she had acted on her true feelings, rather than repressing them, she would have lived her life as a lesbian and, consequently, been able to avoid the life-long ravages of her schizophrenic illness.*

425   To me the wonderful thing is not that she was the object of criticism, but that those criticisms were for the most part so mild and so limited. For her manner of writing was not one to arouse the enthusiasm of young people in the 'thirties. To many she must have appeared as an angular, remote, odd, perhaps rather intimidating figure, a fragile middle-aged poetess, a sexless Sappho and, as the crisis of the decade drew

to its terrible conclusion, oddly irrelevant – a distressed gentlewoman caught in a tempest and making little effort either to fight against it or to sail before it. She made far less of an attempt than did Forster to contribute something to the debates of the time, or rather, when she did, it was so idiosyncratic a contribution that it could serve no useful purpose. (Ibid., Vol. II, p. 185)

*Quentin Bell refers here to Virginia as a "sexless Sappho" or as a homosexual woman who denies her sexuality. It is a very astute and accurate description.*

426    As the reactionaries went from strength to strength those who opposed them had to consider whether force should be countered by force. Virginia hated violence – she associated it with masculine assertiveness. But were we then to scuttle like frightened spinsters before the Fascist thugs? (Ibid., Vol. II, p. 186)

*Quentin Bell remarks that Virginia "hated violence" because "she associated it with masculine assertiveness." What this attitude signifies in reality is that she hated men – perhaps not homosexual men, but certainly "assertive," heterosexual men. As an unacknowledged lesbian, this attitude is understandable, for it undoubtedly would be difficult to find many lesbians who are fond of assertive, masculine, heterosexual men. This fact would account for the preponderance of homosexual men in the "Bloomsbury" group, which Virginia was actively involved in.*

427    She was frankly amazed, neither agreed nor disagreed, but thought it a very strange explanation. To her, I think, it appeared that the horrible side of the universe, the forces of madness, which were never far from her consciousness, had

got the upper hand again. This to her was something largely independent of the political mechanics of the world. ...

Thus she tended, unlike Leonard, to be an out-and-out pacifist; she never made this clear in terms of policy, but it was her instinctive reaction, the feminine as opposed to the masculine – 'the beastly masculine' – reaction. (Ibid., Vol. II, p. 187)

*Again, we see more evidence of Virginia's deep hatred of men and of their masculinity – "the beastly masculine." Virginia Woolf was afflicted with a very severe case of Freudian "penis envy," a complex which played an integral part in the etiology of her mental illness, as it invariably does in all cases of functional mental illness among females.*

428    Under the circumstances, work and society might both be used as opiates, and so she saw a great many people and returned to <u>Three Guineas</u>. Whatever else may be said for or against that work it was certainly therapeutic; she had always to be writing something; but <u>this</u> writing induced none of those aesthetic miseries which always accompanied her novels. It enabled her to let off steam, to hit back at what seemed to her the tyrannous hypocrisy of men. (Ibid., Vol. II, p. 197)

*Due to her intense penis envy and homosexual proclivities, Virginia Woolf disliked everything about men, including their so-called "tyrannous hypocrisy."*

429    Virginia Woolf's interest in the accepted versus the real differences between the sexes was aroused when she was quite young, for she perceived and resented the fact that her father, Leslie Stephen, expected more of his sons than of his daughters.[4] Moreover, she became increasingly aware of the limitations which society placed upon the freedom of women. Her brother Thoby served as a model for Jacob Flanders in her

third novel, <u>Jacob's Room</u>. Jacob's life of intellectual contacts, friendships, sexual experiences, and travels is contrasted with his sweetheart's dull life of tea and supper parties. —<u>Virginia Woolf and the Androgynous Vision</u>, Nancy Topping Bazin, Rutgers University Press, New Brunswick, New Jersey, 1973, p. 4.

*Virginia's intense penis-envy arose, in part, from her jealousy of her brother Thoby. She concluded from the manner in which she was raised that males are treated more favorably than are females, and she deeply resented it. Unfortunately for her there was no way she could become a male physiologically, but she could, and did, become one emotionally and intellectually.*

430    As a female, she believed that her vision, though ideally bisexual, should on the whole be distinctly feminine, that is, 'woman-manly' as opposed to 'man-womanly.' (Ibid., p. 5)

*Although Virginia Woolf professed that her bisexual "vision" should be "woman-manly" rather than "man-womanly," in actuality it was her repression of the extremely powerful "man-womanly" side of herself that led directly to the development of her schizophrenic symptomatology.*

431    In her fourth novel, she suggests the lesbian's experience by describing Mrs. Dalloway's sexual response to Sally Seton (p. 36).
            Virginia Woolf's efforts to understand and harmonize the feminine and masculine aspects of her own nature were further complicated by the mental illness from which she suffered. (Ibid., p. 5)

*Virginia's "efforts to understand and harmonize the feminine and masculine aspects of her own nature" were not "further complicated by the mental illness from which she suffered," as Nancy Bazin states; rather her mental illness was the direct product of the severe bisexual conflict engendered by her failure to "understand and harmonize" these opposing instinctual drives.*

432     Virginia Woolf's very lifelike portraits of her parents in To the Lighthouse reveal to what extent her concepts of the masculine and feminine ways of knowing were influenced by her observations of her parents and to what extent her inability to harmonize the two in any lasting way was related to her manic-depression. (Ibid., p. 10)

*Nancy Bazin makes a very astute observation here when she suggests that Virginia's "inability to harmonize" her masculine and feminine sides "in any lasting way was related to her manic-depression," for bisexual conflict is the pathogen at the core of all functional mental illness, "manic-depression" being but one of the many manifestations of disturbed emotional functioning.*

433     The duality inherent in Virginia Woolf's illness, her parents' personalities, her own view of life, and her aesthetics may be further illuminated by John Custance's description of his feelings as a manic-depressive. Considering differences in personalities and the limited information we have about Virginia Woolf's experience while ill, [32] we cannot say that her manic-depression was exactly like his. Yet his vision of the world in terms of the masculine and the feminine, his association of the masculine with depression, the feminine with mania, and his feeling that what was wrong with individuals and societies was that they weren't androgynous because they were not feminine enough [33] suggest some basic similarity in the way their minds worked. (Ibid., p. 17)

*John Custance's manic-depression – a part of his schizophrenic symptomatology just as it was a part of Virginia Woolf's – likewise had the same etiology, namely, severe bisexual conflict. Nancy Bazin is an extremely intuitive psychologist for having recognized the emotional similarity between Woolf and Custance.*

434     The intensity of her quest for the androgynous ideal, reflected in her diary, her essays, and her novels, may be better appreciated when we realize that in her mind it meant the difference between sanity and insanity.

     ... Worse yet, looking behind the fear of attacks of manic-depression was the greater fear of incurable insanity; for if a manic-depressive is not permanently cured, with age the attacks often became more and more schizophrenic in nature.[37] During the last two attacks of hypomania described by Custance in <u>Wisdom, Madness and Folly</u>, he claimed that he had slipped over the line into schizophrenia (pp. 135, 138). A comparison of this first book with his second suggests the difference between the manic-depressive and the schizophrenic cited by White in <u>The Abnormal Personality</u>: to an observer, the manic-depressive appears abnormally speeded up or slowed down 'and thus seriously disorganized but not unintelligible or queer'; however, the schizophrenic seems 'crazy' (pp. 520-521). Moreover, the schizophrenic's chances for periodic or permanent recovery are much less than the manic-depressive's. For instance, a schizophrenic may have to live forty to fifty years in a mental institution.[38] This illuminates Virginia Woolf's explanatory suicide note, in which she expressed her belief that she was going mad again and that this time she would not recover.[39] (Ibid., p. 19-20)

*Manic-depression is part of the schizophrenic process. Every schizophrenic person exhibits at one time or another so-called "manic-depressive" behavior. In fact the symptoms of*

> *manic-depression and schizophrenia are so closely interwoven that the psychiatric profession has invented a new word – "schizo-affective" – to document this fact.*

435    Rachel's situation is similar; by tradition, she is expected to play a submissive role in her relationship with Terence. Moreover, Antigone both boasts of her choice (death rather than submission) and complains that her 'doom' is 'unjust.' [11] Virginia Woolf's attitude towards Rachel's death reflects Antigone's. ...

     After this symbolic descent into the womb, Rachel is closer to having solved the problem of her sexual identity; therefore, in her hallucination she sees herself as feminine instead of masculine. Yet her shadow-self is still 'deformed'; for, although she has matured, she is still afraid. She cannot attain wholeness via her love for Terence, despite her androgynous vision, for she still rejects for herself the sexual role of the woman. Hence, immobilized by fear in the dream, she is immobilized by death at the end of the novel. Indeed, to die rather than to establish a relationship may be seen either as courageous or as cowardly. Whereas, in one sense, it preserves the integrity of Rachel's spiritual self, in another sense, it denies the realization of her sexual self. (Ibid., pp. 66-67)

> *To understand this quotation fully, it is necessary to substitute Virginia Woolf's name for that of "Rachel" and Leonard Woolf's, Virginia's husband, for that of "Terence." Virginia felt that she too was expected "by tradition" to "play a submissive role in her relationship" with Leonard. But, like Antigone, she would rather die than submit, and eventually she did die by her own hand. Virginia is really speaking of herself when she says of Rachel that "although she has matured, she is still afraid. She cannot attain wholeness via her love for Terence, despite her androgynous vision, for she still rejects for herself the sexual role of the woman."*

*Throughout her long marriage to Leonard, Virginia likewise*
*rejected the "sexual role of the woman," for, as we have*
*previously been informed, she was completely frigid in her*
*sexual relations with him, ceasing them altogether not long*
*after they were married. Thus, as Rachel was "immobilized by*
*death at the end of the novel," so too was Virginia as the result*
*of her similar Antigone-like choice of "death rather than*
*submission" to the male. Like Rachel, Virginia chose death*
*rather than establish a sexual relationship with a man, thus*
*preserving the integrity of her "spiritual self," as Rachel had,*
*while denying "the realization of her sexual self." In truth,*
*Virginia could only have fully realized her sexual self in a*
*homosexual union, but she chose death over this, too, for to*
*her it was an intolerable alternative.*

436     In fact, like Septimus, Clarissa feels attracted to persons of her
        own sex. Clarissa admits to herself that 'she could not resist
        sometimes yielding to the charm of a woman.'
                She did undoubtedly then feel what men felt. Only for
        a moment; but it was enough. It was a sudden revelation, a
        tingle like a blush which one tried to check and then, as it
        spread, one yielded to its expansion, and rushed to the farthest
        verge and there quivered and felt the world come closer,
        swollen with some astonishing significance, some pressure of
        rapture, which split its thin skin and gushed and poured with
        an extraordinary alleviation over the cracks and sores. ... But
        the close withdrew; the hard softened. It was over – the
        moment. (Ibid., p. 36)

        *Virginia again makes use of her main character to*
        *express her own homosexual feelings, for Virginia, like*
        *Clarissa, "could not resist sometimes yielding to the charm of*
        *a woman." Also, like Clarissa and Septimus, Virginia "feels*
        *attracted to persons of her own sex." And then there is her*
        *(Clarissa's) admission that she "did undoubtedly then feel*

*what men felt." Although it was "Only for a moment," she writes, "it was enough." The vivid words Virginia uses to describe her (Clarissa's) masculine feelings, such as "tingle," "blush," "quivered," "swollen," "pressure of rapture," "gushed and poured," "the hard softened," all might be allusions to sexual excitement in the male, culminating in orgasm.*

437     Virginia Woolf goes on to describe Clarissa's attraction to Sally Seton (pp. 37-40). This explains why she does not seem to need Richard physically; however, emotionally she depends upon his support. (Ibid., p. 117)

     *Because Virginia Woolf was homosexually attracted to Vita-Sackville-West, among others, and so did not need her husband, Leonard, sexually, yet she depended heavily upon him for emotional support, and thus could easily imagine how a relationship between Clarissa and Richard might follow exactly the same pattern.*

438     This time, however, being older, Bernard notices a change in his outlook which leads him to wonder: 'Was this, then, this streaming away mixed with Susan, Jinny, Neville, Rhoda, Louis, a sort of death? A new assembly of elements? Some hint of what was to come?' (p. 198) Nor is he sure now whether he is 'man or woman, Bernard or Neville, Louis, Susan, Jinny, or Rhoda – so strange is the contact of one with another' (p. 199). Indeed, he no longer knows whether he is 'all of them' or 'one and distinct' (p. 205). Involved in his attitude is a preparation for death, for the moment when he will become one not just with 'all of them' but with the all. (Ibid., p. 154)

     *Virginia is describing here, undoubtedly from personal experience, the overwhelming confusion as to one's sexual identity which is the distinguishing characteristic of the schizophrenic breakdown.*

439          A young girl, vaguely familiar to me, huddled against the wall, her legs pulled under her, and only one breast was nippled. The other had been chewed off. And then I remembered. Her eyes were still dead, and the only sustained activity was the constant chattering of her teeth.
          Women who thought they were men masturbated invisible penises with swaggering pride.
          Women who dreamed that they had given birth to the Messiah watched constantly for His return.
          Women, freaks in their baldness, talked of their breathtaking beauty and sexual prowess.
          Women with menstrual blood streaming down their legs giggled and pranced, ignoring the reality of madness. — Will There Really Be a Morning?, Frances Farmer (an autobiography), G. P. Putnam's Sons, New York, 1972, p. 219.

          *The "women who thought they were men" and "masturbated invisible penises with swaggering pride" provide further clinical evidence of how neurotic Freudian "penis envy" can be carried to a psychotic extreme, wherein the unconscious wish to be a man becomes so powerful it overwhelms the repressing ego and assumes its own reality.*

440          During the next three and a half years I subsisted in a neuter exile, but for the first time in my life I was unencumbered. I was responsible only to myself. (Ibid., p. 238)

          *Frances Farmer's reference to a "neuter exile" accurately describes her schizophrenic "bearded lady" status as neither man nor woman, but an equal mixture of both.*

441        I felt it necessary to purge myself in the confessional, but we started off on the wrong foot – he thought I was a man. I have a deep, theatrical voice, my so-called trademark, but to the father, I was someone in the confessional making fun. We finally settle down, and I think I sent him into shock with my confessions. (Ibid., p. 308)

*Undoubtedly it was more than her deep voice that convinced the priest in the confessional that he was talking with a man, for Frances Farmer's strong masculine presence would have made itself felt in other subtle ways also, such as by her attitude, vocabulary, and expressed interests, etc.*

442   She went back often again, hearing grandfather's familiar voice saying, 'Second in the class is not enough; you must be the first.' 'If you are hurt, never cry, but laugh. You must never let them know that they are hurting you.' It was all directed against the smiling sharers of the secret joke. Pride must be the ability to die in agony as if you did it every day, gracefully. Even his pride in her was anger. 'You're smart – you'll show them all!' He had sharpened her word-wit on his own, cheered the cutting edge of it, called women cows and brood-bitches, and slapped her half-roughly because she would grow up wasted, a woman. She would have to take on the whole world of fools and ingrates, and, even though she was a woman, win his battle: the ancient, mystical battle between a crippled immigrant and a long-dead Latvian Count. —I Never Promised You A Rose Garden, Hannah Green, A Signet Book, New American Library (Holt, Rinehart and Winston, Inc.) New York, 1964, p. 96.

*Deborah's highly neurotic grandfather impressed upon his granddaughter that the only way she could win his love and admiration was by denying her femininity and becoming the aggressive, successful masculine figure he himself would like to have become, rather than the embittered, misogynistic failure he became. Unfortunately for her emotional well-being, his granddaughter attempted to become a "manly" woman, the only type her grandfather could love and admire, and in the process metamorphosed into a "bearded lady" – one who is afflicted by schizophrenia.*

443        Then she was standing above herself, dressed in her Yri rank and name, kicking the herself that was on the floor, kicking her low in the stomach and in the tumorous place that gave like a rotten melon. When the ceremonial creak of leavetaking sounded, the sky was burdening itself with darkness outside the barred window. She looked out, finding herself erect and in front of the window and saying quietly, 'Let me die, all of you.' (Ibid., p. 101)

*The "tumorous place" that was "low in the stomach" and that "gave like a rotten melon" was Deborah's genital area, from which a tumor had been removed when she was a child. Because she had repudiated her femininity so completely, in her schizophrenic mind her female genitals represented nothing more than "rotten melon".*

444        He was not hurt in the flight nor in the fall, but he was nearly run over in the stampede of staff that rushed back to subdue the source of his propulsion. The patients followed to watch and heckle. Miss Coral stood at the open door. Her tiny being was like electricity. *That hair has been burned white,* Deborah said quietly in Yri. The three men who went to move Miss Coral were pitiful against the sharp motions of her fighting body; she literally shook them off, her blank and expressionless face staring straight ahead. When more attendants leaped into the melee there was less for her to do, and she stood still because they were working against one another. Helene, sensing a challenge to her reign as at least the

most feared on the ward, ran into the deserted upper hall, removed the hasps from the hinges of the nursing-station door, tore the door off with its own weight and hers, flung it into the hall, and followed it with everything that came to hand. Sylvia, planted like a poorly made statue against the wall, found that she could not bear the tension of Helene's violence and suddenly exploded, diving at Helene in the broken ruins of the door, trays, medicine, cutlery, and towels. Someone rang the emergency bell, and it took twelve extra people to still the riot and put Helene and Sylvia in pack. Apparently the orders for Miss Coral had been forgotten by the ward administrator, because the door was simply closed after her and that was that. (Ibid., pp. 114-115)

*This quotation provides a vivid example of the extraordinary masculine force and activity exhibited by a group of schizophrenic women on a hospital ward. From examples such as this observers have concluded that schizophrenic women display more aggressive and disruptive behavior in the institutional setting than do schizophrenic men, who tend, generally, to be more passive and apathetic, thus further confirming the "bearded lady" dynamics of schizophrenia.*

445  Overheard, in the dimension of Yr, Lactamaeon, tauntingly beautiful, was free in his open sky, enjoying the shape of a great bird. She had once been able to soar with him in that great sweep. *What do you see?* she called to him in Yri.

*The cliffs and canyons of the world; the moon and the sun in the same bowl*, he answered.

*Take me with you!*

*Just a moment!* The Censor intervened with his rasp voice. Deborah never actually saw the Censor because he was not of either world, but had a part in both.

*Yes. ... wait.* Idat, the Dissemblor, unmale, unfemale, joined him. While they discussed the matter elaborately, parodying the now familiar psychiatric manners and terms, Lactamaeon found a chasm, dove into it with a high eagle-scream of triumph, and was gone. (Ibid., p. 125)

*Deborah had once identified with Lactamaeon as a great male bird, soaring alongside him through the skies. And "Idat, the Dissembler, unmale, unfemale," who met with the Censor to discuss Deborah's desire to rejoin Lactamaeon, symbolizes her own state of severe bisexual confusion and conflict.*

446     'During the war ...' she said, 'I was a Japanese.'

'An actual Japanese?'

'I was disguised as an American, but I was really not an American.'

'Why?'

'Because I was the Enemy.'

It seemed to Deborah an ultimate secret, and Dr. Fried was forced to ask her to speak louder time and time again. She began to explain that because she could go into Yr or rise out of its incredible distances without visibly changing, Yr had given her, as a gift for her ninth birthday, the power to transmute herself in form. For a year or so she had been a wild horse or a great bronze-feathered bird. She quoted to Dr. Fried the Yr incantation which had once freed the bird-self from the illusion of the ugly and hated girl:

'e, quio quio quaru ar Yr aedat

temoluqu' braown elepr' kyryr ... '

(Brushwinged, I soar above the canyons of your sleep singing...)

... On a certain night before falling asleep, Deborah had been reborn as a captured Japanese soldier. From behind the mask of an American-Jewish girl with a past of an

American suburb and city, the elliptical eyes of the Enemy looked for the day of his unmasking. The tumor's impossible, insistent anguish was his war wound, and his mind, versed in a strange language, rang with dream of escape. He did not hate his captors – he never wished that they would lose the war, but the world now offered meaning to the irreconcilable oppositions in Deborah, the ruination of her secret and female parts, the bitter secrecy of her wound, and the hidden language. Captivity and secrecy and the glory and misery of Yr's declaration <u>You are not of them</u> were somehow justified. [Note: Deborah had undergone an operation for removal of an urethral tumor when she was a young girl.] (Ibid., pp. 130-131)

*The gift Deborah was given by Yr on her ninth birthday, "the power to transmute herself in form," enabled her to fulfill her deepest need, namely, that of freeing herself "from the illusion of the ugly and hated girl" through a series of transformations, first as a wild horse and then as a "great bronze-feathered bird," until finally she emerged as a Japanese soldier, albeit a genitally-wounded one but nevertheless the male she had so desperately wanted to be for such a long time.*

*Obviously her operation for the removal of an urethral tumor when she was very young had traumatized her to such an extent that she felt her female genitals had been ruined, thus making it more difficult for her to identify herself as a female. This, along with her neurotic grandfather's harsh denigration of womanhood, were two powerful elements in shaping her negative attitude towards her femininity.*

447      It was the second spring that she was gone, and how much closer was she to the modest, obedient, womanly being that his heart cried out to have as a daughter? No closer. There had been no improvement at all. (Ibid., p. 149)

*Deborah admits that after two years in the mental hospital she is still, in essence, the <u>un</u>womanly, <u>im</u>modest and <u>dis</u>obedient daughter whom her father found so objectionable. She is still, in other words, clinging to her unconscious identification as a male.*

448        They spent the time cutting ways to the old secrets and seeing facets of them that needed the new hunger for life to come real. Deborah saw that she had taken the part of the enemy Japanese as an answer to the hate of the ones at the summer camp, his foreignness and violence being an embodiment of anger. A part of the same insight opened on to the subject of martyrdom – that being martyred had something to do with Christ, the pride and terror of every Jew.

'Anger and martyrdom,' she said, 'that's what being a Japanese soldier was, and I gave the doctors the 'good soldier' that they wanted. Anger and martyrdom. ... It sounds like something more ...like the description of something I know ...'

'What more?' Furii asked. 'It must have had many walls to have supported itself for all these years.'

'It's a description of ... why ... why, it's <u>grandfather</u>!' Deborah cried, having unearthed the familiar tyrannical Latvian to whom she had given such an unrecognizable mask. It was a description of him and it fitted him better than height or weight or number of teeth. 'The secret soldier that I was is a <u>mutu</u> – what Yr calls a kind of hiding image of my kinship with him.'

'Coming to see this ... does it hurt so much?'

'A good hurt,' Deborah said.

'The symptoms and the sickness and the secrets have many reasons for being. The parts and facets sustain one another, locking in and strengthening one another. If it were not so, we could give you a nice shot of this or that drug or a quick hypnosis and say 'Craziness, begone!' and it would be an easy job. But these symptoms are built of many needs and serve many purposes, and that is why getting them away makes so much suffering.' (Ibid., pp. 194-195)

*Deborah is discovering through her psychotherapy that part of her motivation for wishing to be a man arose from her strong unconscious identification with her grandfather, the "familiar tyrannical Latvian to whom she had given such an unrecognizable mask" – the mask of the Japanese soldier she had become.*

449     They stayed for a while and Deborah was introduced to some of the male patients, wondering as she heard their names what could possibly make <u>men</u> sick. When the two girls left, they walked toward A ward, which was open and where there was a coffeepot for both patients and staff. (Ibid., p. 201)

*As a female who wanted so badly to be a male, it was very difficult for Deborah to understand how someone who actually <u>was</u> a male could be anything but happy and healthy.*

450     *Am I not beautiful in this tree?* the goddess asked. Questions had a particularly poignant quality in Yri because they used a familiar form and because they gave hint of the quick and ephemeral quality of asking anything. Idat was the Dissembler and her answers were always difficult. *I think I shall be a woman always*, she said now. *You can have something on which to model yourself.* (Ibid., p. 206)

*Deborah is finally beginning to accept the fact she is a female, and will use the beautiful goddess in the tree as her role model. Idat, the Dissembler, who is a "bearded lady," both male and female, has represented Deborah's schizophrenic self, so when Idat (Deborah) says "I think I shall be a woman always," it means she can now emerge from her schizophrenic state and become an emotionally healthy person.*

451        The pain of looking at him escaped in a laugh. 'Oh, I know – that must have been big, dumb old Lucy Martenson. She gets even with everybody by playing Tarzan out the front windows of the D ward and scaring the visitors to death.' (Ibid., p. 211)

          *In order for "big, dumb old Lucy Martenson" to regain her sanity, i.e., emerge from her schizophrenia, it would be necessary for her to accept the fact, both emotionally and intellectually, that she is "Jane" rather than "Tarzan" – or a female rather than a male.*

452       Dead pale, cold-handed, in a lilac flowered dress that ill suited the lithe tiger wearing it, Helene came to B ward. Her 'normal' smile seemed wired, like a booby trap. (Ibid., p. 222)

          *Even a fellow-patient can sense that a feminine-style dress somehow looks very inappropriate on Helene, for the description of her as a "lithe tiger" conveys a strong feeling of masculine power and ferociousness rather than one of feminine softness and gentleness, which would be more appropriate for a person wearing such attire.*

453       'It's nice to walk with Lactamaeon when he is in a good mood. After the sewing class, where I don't belong, or the church choir where I am a stranger, it's good to walk home with someone who can laugh and be silly or turn beautiful and make you cry, looking at the stars while he recites.'
          'You know, don't you, now, that you made him up out of yourself – that you created him out of your own humor and your own beauty?' Furii said gently.

'Yes – I know now.' It was an admission that gave much pain. (Ibid., p. 228)

*Lactamaeon was Deborah's alter ego, the male she would like to have been. Recognizing this truth, discovered during psychotherapy, gave her "much pain."*

454    There is no point in discussing the differential diagnosis in relation to the other psychoses which are still being designated as paranoia since all the known paranoid forms belong with our concept of schizophrenia. —<u>Dementia Praecox or the Group of Schizophrenias</u>, Eugen Bleuler (Ibid., p. 317)

*Dr. Bleuler again emphasizes the fact that paranoia is an integral part of the schizophrenic process. Unfortunately, Dr. Sigmund Freud, in his analysis of the case of Daniel Paul Schreber, came to the erroneous conclusion that paranoia and schizophrenia are separate psychopathological processes with dissimilar etiologies. Unbeknownst to Freud, by correctly identifying Schreber's severe bisexual conflict as the prime pathogen in his paranoia, and then by extending this discovery to apply invariably to <u>every</u> case of paranoia, Freud had in reality discovered the cause of schizophrenia, since paranoia and schizophrenia are one and the same "disease".*

455    Very frequently the patients employ the various symbols interchangeably. One of our paranoids spontaneously changed the 'fiery lance' in her body to 'many fiery needles' while she was being questioned about her body hallucinations. Then the 'lance' became a 'thick thing' that was thrust into her chest and lower abdomen, whereby she exhibited a great deal of affect in relation to her lower abdomen but none to that of the chest. The 'needle,' too, is frequently used in the same sense. The symbolic significance of the needle was particularly apparent

in the case of a young catatonic woman who blushed whenever she saw a needle. (Ibid., p. 413)

*The "fiery lance" which Dr. Bleuler's paranoid patient believed she had in her body symbolized the penis she unconsciously wishes for, the penis which would make her the man she has always wanted to be. As Dr. Bleuler notes, the symbol of the "needle" is "frequently used" by schizophrenics to represent the male phallus.*

456    A woman patient complained about our 'hay-snout-beds' (hay is vulgarly used for 'pubic'); there were a number of men who left 'their hay-snouts in her bed' (the expression on her face showed unmistakable sexual excitement). (Ibid., p. 415)

*In quotation 379, we note that the needle in the haystack symbolizes the penis surrounded by pubic hair. Likewise, in this quotation and in the one above, "needle" and "hay" represent penis and pubic hair.*

457    She is not a large woman, but I was just a child then, when she smiled at me and said, 'You were a little mistake,' and I knew I was supposed to smile back at her, but I didn't feel like smiling. I wanted to run away and hide, to curl up in some cozy dream corner where there were no spiders, no wolves masquerading as Grandma and no mothers who smiled enormously and showed their large front teeth and pink gums and said, 'Mistake!'
       'Of course, we loved you after you were born,' she always added each time she said, 'You were a little mistake.' But I knew that loving me was something she had no choice about. She had to love me because I was her child, just as I had to love her because she was my mother. I had to, even though sometimes she frightened me.

'And if we *had* wanted a third child, we would certainly have wanted a boy, not another girl. We had your name all picked out: Ralph Stuart Wolfe, Stuart, after your real uncle; Ralph, for Daddy's good friend, Uncle Ralph. We never even thought about what we'd name a girl. Everyone was so sure we'd have a boy ... and then *you* came along.'

That then was my original sin, being born at all. I never even got a chance at the apple. My doom, like the afterbirth, followed me into the world. —Aftershock (The Story of a Psychotic Episode), Ellen Wolfe, G. P. Putnam's Sons, New York, 1969, pp. 143-144.

*Ellen's "original sin" was being born a girl rather than a boy, at least in the eyes of her neurotic parents. Thus, from an early age, in a vain attempt to win their approval and love, she alienated herself from her natural sexual and emotional role as a female and instead developed a decidedly masculine personality, thereby setting the stage for the development of the severe bisexual conflict which eventually precipitated a schizophrenic psychosis.*

458    In the taxi we rode in silence. Once David said, 'If I could, I would change places with you. Gladly. You know that, don't you?'

'I suppose,' I said. I guess he expected me to smile bravely at him, but I didn't. Words. What did they mean? Nothing at all. He knew he could not change places with me. I hated him, he was male, exempt forever from this kind of misery.

What else did I remember?

Some preparations – I suppose the nurse shaved me.

And pain.

Rather less than I had expected. It was no worse than mild labor pains or bad menstrual cramps. (Ibid., p. 157)

*Ellen says of her husband that "I hated him, he was male, exempt forever from this kind of misery." What she really means is that it is "misery" to be a female and that she hates her husband for being what she would like to be but isn't – a man. In Freudian terminology, Ellen is afflicted with a severe case of "penis envy."*

459         If we summarize our impressions of the attitudes of these mothers toward their own parents, we may say that as a group they reported that they loved their fathers or felt that they had some love from them. But, on the whole, the fathers were weak, sometimes brutal, absent, and in one way or another quite inadequate and unreliable. Frequently also there was some feeling that the fathers were either somewhat abnormal heterosexually or were regarded as possibly homosexual. On the other hand, these mothers of schizophrenics nearly uniformly report their respect for their mothers. Almost without exception, they give the impression that they are saying not only that they respect their particular mothers but that through their mothers they have come to idealize motherhood – they believe in the divinity of maternity. This is not an uncommon idea in our culture, but one feels that these women are more desperately devoted to it than are the run of people. The maternal grandmothers of the patients are usually reported to have ruled their homes either directly or, more commonly, through tears and suffering. Mothers of the patients have learned this technique from these grandmothers and with very few exceptions dominate, in one way or another, the family situation, including the husband. Usually they employ the hurt techniques to make others feel guilty; much more rarely they are arbitrarily and angrily in charge. As for the relation to the children, these mothers, in addition to reporting them as model children, also most frequently remark that as little children the patients worshipped their mothers; they frequently comment that they

still do. —Psychotherapeutic Intervention in Schizophrenia, Lewis B. Hill, M. D. (Ibid., pp. 112-113)

*Dr. Hill comments on the well-known fact that the mothers of schizophrenics tend, in almost every case, to be the dominant spouse in the marriage, or the one who, as the old saying goes, "wear the pants" in the family. In short, in these schizophrenogenic families there has been a sex-role reversal in the parental configuration which leads to sex-role alienation and confusion in the children who, as a consequence, are inclined to the development of schizophrenic symptomatology.*

460        It would seem that the schizophrenic patient is often of the third generation of abnormal persons of whom we can gain some information. The preceding two generations of mothers appear to have been obsessive, schizoid women who did not adjust well to men. There is some evidence that they were, in a sense, immature and that within the obsessive character structure could be found hysterical difficulties. It is to be noted, also, that there are two preceding generations of men who are not masters, or equals, in their own marriages and homes, or psychosexually very successful, and who are often described as immature, alcoholic, and passive, or hard-working, self-centered, and detached from the family. We do not know what sort of mothers and fathers these fathers of schizophrenics may have had, but it could be presumed that the fact that they let themselves be married to mothers of schizophrenics implies something concerning their own mothers.

        Loosely, the pattern which emerges is that of two generations of female ancestors who were aggressive, even if in a weak-mannered and tearful way, and two generations of male ancestors who were effeminate, even if the effeminacy was disguised by obsessive or psychopathic tendencies. It might be expected, or at least we would not be surprised to find, that the child of such ancestry would have difficulties centering around the problems of active aggressiveness and passive submissiveness. If the child is unstable in its balance of activity and passivity, the likelihood is that, under the guidance of the sort of mother who gets herself called 'schizophrenogenic,' the passive behavior will emerge as the overt character of the child, whereas the active behavior will be noted only in the form of negativism, of stubbornness, of retentiveness, and so forth. (Ibid., pp. 134-135)

*Dr. Hill again emphasizes the fact that the mothers of schizophrenics tend to be domineering and aggressive in contrast to the fathers who are usually passive and apathetic, except in those instances of reaction formation where the fathers tend to be overly dominant and aggressive to compensate for their unconscious effeminate tendencies. It is important to remember that the dominant mother – passive father parental configuration is responsible not only for producing schizophrenic children but also homosexual ones, thus giving validity to the formula that schizophrenia is, in essence, the negation of homosexuality.*

461        Though simple and hebephrenic schizophrenic reactions become visible during early and middle adolescence, the characteristic reaction is that of an acute catatonic episode. Catatonic reactions are by far the most frequent schizophrenic disorganizations seen during this period and, side by side with the acute conversion reactions, constitute the bulk of emergency psychiatric difficulties during adolescence. Catatonic episodes can develop in a matter of hours and express themselves in great motor inhibition or overactivity, highly overactive and paranoid thought and speech patterns, totally inhibiting panic or desperate grandiosity. Fears centering around homosexuality, sexual inadequacy, or sexual

guilt, together with a remarkable concern with philosophic and religious issues of a grandiose nature, almost universally accompany such reactions. Characteristically, catatonic patients have the ambivalent wish to change themselves or feel that they have been transformed into another sex. They wish to change the world immediately, to purify it and bring news to everyone else that has been given them in a revelation. Quite often such wishes are put into action in totally inappropriate and aggressive ways that are disturbing to the people in the patients' environments. —[Sydney L. Werkman] <u>American Handbook of Psychiatry</u>, Vol. II, edited by Gerald Caplan, Basic Books, Inc., New York, 2$^{nd}$ ed., 1974, p. 230.

*The genesis of schizophrenia lies in sex-role alienation in early childhood. This in turn leads to the development of severe bisexual conflict and confusion in the sex-role alienated child, culminating in the initial appearance of frankly psychotic symptomatology at the onset of puberty, the time when the major hormonal sexual changes take place within the individual. In this quotation, Sidney L. Werkman described the various ways in which schizophrenia manifests itself in the adolescent male and female.*

462   Perhaps the most frequent and highly charged dilemma encountered among psychotics is between gender identities, i.e., whether to become or remain a man or woman.

A woman patient's childhood had been marked by total rejection by her parents, who openly preferred her brother. As a result, she struggled throughout her life among conflicting unconscious drives to possess her brother, to kill him, to supplant him in her father's love by becoming a big blond boy like her brother; yet, she never totally abandoned all feminine goals or identifications. She struggled over whether to grow older or younger, whether to be boy or girl, or both. With each birthday, this struggle became sharper, and she became more depressed.

She was still able to function when she unconsciously sought a solution to her unresolved conflict through a surrogate relationship, namely, through marriage to a man who had been her brother's best friend. In addition, her new husband's father was a close friend of her own father; and prior to the marriage, he had always shown the patient far more affection than had her own father. But immediately after the marriage, the new father-figure turned away from her. With this repetition of her childhood pain and loss, she became bewildered and unhappy. Her husband's complete recovery from a dangerous illness came soon afterwards, and turned out to be a psychological catastrophe for her, by reactivating her buried death-wishes toward her brother and her need to replace him.

Thereupon, from having been freely active, she became anxiety-ridden and severely agoraphobic, so that she could hardly bring herself to move more than a few blocks from her home. With the passing years, and further deterioration of the marriage, she superimposed on this terror an equally violent claustrophobia. At this point, she was trapped between two terrors, so that she sometimes stood on the threshold of her home for hours, equally terrified to go in or go out, to be among people or to be alone, to move or to remain motionless. Here, then, was a juxtaposition of irreconcilable drives and irreconcilable defenses. This brought on the imminent threat of full-blown psychotic disorganization, which, fortunately, led her into intensive treatment just in time to save her. [Lawrence S. Kubie] (Ibid., Vol. III, p. 14)

*The patient described in this quotation was driven to the very brink of a schizophrenic breakdown by her severe bisexual conflict. Fortunately she was able to receive capable help before this happened.*

463        Furthermore, regression can mean many things. It can mean an abandonment of adult life itself, with the unconscious implication that 'If I go back to the beginning, I can start over and grow up different.' It can be and often is linked to difficulties about gender identity and to the desire to change sides, to be the other sex, or both, or neither, which the psychotic patient so frequently expresses in many, varied, and transparent forms. It is not surprising, then, that one of the forms which the regressive movement can take is a suicide effort, which is not in reality an effort to die but rather to be reborn. [Lawrence S. Kubie] (Ibid., Vol. III, p. 14)

*Schizophrenics commit suicide when they can no longer tolerate the severe emotional and sexual frustration created by their basic sex-role alienation and resultant bisexual conflict.*

464    Somatic pathology is universal and so is psychopathology, and what is more, psychopathology appears in basically identical clinical forms, wherever it occurs in the world. According to Forster: [44]

Psychiatric syndromes or reactions, by and large, are similar in all races throughout the world. The mental reactions seen in our African patients can be diagnosed according to Western textbook standards. The basic illness and reaction types are the same. Environmental, constitutional, and tribal cultural background merely modify the symptom constellation. Basically the disorders of thinking, feeling, willing, and knowing are the same. And Edgerton [42] writes:

It is remarkable how alike the African conceptions of psychosis are to the Western-European psychoses. The Africans of the four tribes do not regard a single behavior as psychotic which could not be so regarded in the West. That is, they do not produce symptoms which are understandable as psychotic only within the context of their own culture. What is psychotic for them would be psychotic for us. [Johannes M. Meth] (Ibid., Vol. III, p. 723)

*Schizophrenia is found in every race and culture due to the fact that all human beings are susceptible to the development of bisexual conflict and consequently to the ravages of the mental illness which invariably follows in its wake. And, as this quotation illustrates, mental illness everywhere expresses itself in identical symptomatology.*

465    I have often marveled about the frequency with which psychotic episodes in Latin-Americans begin with a homosexual panic, until I understood that the word *maricon* (homosexual) is the most derogatory term, used constantly in Spanish-America. Contempt and self-contempt has no parallel or equally meaningful word in Spanish. [Johannes M. Meth] (Ibid., Vol. III, p. 729)

*"Homosexual panic" is an integral part of every psychosis, since a psychosis is actually nature's way of trying to effect the release of powerful homosexual longings and drives which have long been repressed by the schizophrenic's ego, resulting in the total frustration of any kind of sexual release, homosexual or heterosexual.*

466    The origin of the word 'koro' is not clear. It may stem from the Malayan word 'kuru,' shake; the Javanese word 'keruk,' shrink; or according to Yap,[153] from the Javanese word for tortoise. The Chinese and Southeast Asians call the glans penis tortoise.
       The Chinese name for the syndrome is 'shook yong.' It has been known in China for centuries. One of their emperors

died supposedly of shook yong. The Chinese author Pao described it in 1834. He claimed that it is precipitated by exposure to cold or by the ingestion of cold or raw food. It starts out with abdominal pain, spasms, and cyanosis of the limbs, retraction of the penis and scrotum into the abdomen; then, there is trismus, and finally death. It is a serious emergency. According to Chinese folk medicine, it is related to the middle female meridian which is supposedly governed by the liver – the organ most susceptible to worry, fear, and anger. One of the triggering causes is believed to be excessive intercourse or improper sexual relations.

The symptoms usually start without warning. The patient, usually between thirty and forty years of age, is suddenly worried that his penis will disappear into his abdomen and that he will die. To prevent this from happening, the patient has to grip his penis firmly; when he becomes tired, his wife, relatives, or friends help him. The Chinese constructed a special wooden clasp for this purpose. At times, fellatio, practiced immediately by the patient's wife, can stop the phobia, otherwise it can last for days, or even weeks. Linton [97] describes a female equivalent of koro in Borneo where the patient is afraid that her breasts are shrinking as well as her labia, which would lead to the disappearance of important female characteristics.

The Chinese believe that shook yong is caused by an imbalance of yin and yan. The prevalence of the female factor yin must be counteracted by the administration of a drug which increases yan, for example, powdered rhinoceros horn. [Johannes M. Meth] (Ibid., Vol. III, p. 730)

*The Chinese were correct in believing that "koro," wherein the afflicted male believes his penis is either disappearing or being retracted into his abdomen, is the result of an imbalance of the yin and the yan, or of the male and the female elements within each individual. To be more precise, "koro" describes a condition that in Western society would be labeled as an attack of acute "homosexual panic" immediately preceding a paranoid schizophrenic break with reality. As Freud's famous paranoid, Daniel Paul Schreber, states in his memoirs, "This process of unmanning consisted in the (external) male genitals (scrotum and penis) being retracted into the body and the internal sexual organs being at the same time transformed into the corresponding female sexual organs, a process which might have been completed in a sleep lasting hundreds of years, because the skeleton (pelvis, etc.) had also to be changed." (Memoirs of My Nervous Illness, Daniel Paul Schreber, Ibid., p. 73.)*

467        Among the Siwans of Africa, for example, all men and boys engage in anal intercourse. They adopt the feminine role only in strictly sexual situations and males are singled out as peculiar if they do not indulge in these homosexual activities.[4] Prominent Siwan men lend their sons to each other, and they talk about their masculine love affairs as openly as they discuss their love of women. Both married and unmarried males are expected to have both homosexual and heterosexual affairs. Among many of the aborigines of Australia this type of coitus is a recognized custom between unmarried men and uninitiated boys. Strehlow writes of the Aranda as follows: ... 'Pederasty is a recognized custom. ... Commonly a man, who is fully initiated but not yet married, takes a boy ten or twelve years old, who lives with him as a wife for several years, until the older man marries. The boy is neither circumsized nor subincised, though he may have ceased to be regarded as a boy and is considered a young man. The boy must belong to the proper marriage class from which the man might take a wife.' (Strehlow, 1915, p. 98)

           Keraki bachelors of New Guinea universally practice sodomy, and in the course of his puberty rites each boy is initiated into anal intercourse by the older males. After his first year of playing the passive role he spends the rest of his bachelorhood sodomizing the newly initiated. This practice is believed by the natives to be necessary for the growing boy. They are convinced that boys can become pregnant as a result of sodomy, and a lime-eating ceremony is performed periodically to prevent such conception. Though fully sanctioned by the males, these initiatory practices are supposed to be kept secret from the women. The Kiwai have a similar custom; sodomy is practiced in connection with initiation to make young men strong. —Patterns of Sexual Behavior, Clellan S. Ford, Ph. D. and Frank A. Beach, Ph. D, Harper & Brothers, Publishers, and Paul B. Hoeber, Inc. Medical Books, 1951, pp. 131-132.

*It is interesting to note how psychologically astute so-called "primitive" cultures are, or were, in recognizing the paramount importance of having young males experience the feminine side of their nature, both emotionally and physically, through the medium of passive anal intercourse with older members of their tribe. Rather than being taught to repress their natural feminine feelings, as happens in so-called "civilized" societies, these young men are provided the opportunity to "work through" these feelings, thereby enabling them to mature into strong, well-adjusted, heterosexual men. In stark contrast, males who have been discouraged from experiencing these natural, opposite-sex feelings and consequently have repressed them, are doomed to suffer life-long neuroses, and even psychoses, as a direct result.*

468        G. V. Hamilton also observed homosexual relations between male monkeys. He reports the occurrence of anal intercourse and so far as one can tell, the details are similar to those listed by Kempf. Hamilton describes a homosexual friendship between an adult and an immature male macaque which was accompanied by frequent sodomy, mutual

embracing, and social protection of the young animal by his full-grown partner. When the pair was separated the adult male mated readily with available females; and when the smaller male was reintroduced into the enclosure, the homosexual partnership was resumed, although heterosexual coitus on the part of the grown animal was not appreciably reduced.

Carpenter reports the occurrence of homosexual mounting by free-living male macaques, but Kempf and Hamilton are the only writers who have observed complete anal intercourse between males. (Ibid., p. 135)

*Quotations 468 through 474 – Each quotation within this group provides clear and convincing evidence that homosexual behavior is an innate characteristic of all mammals, including man. Man, alone, however, possesses the requisite mental capability to be able to repress, when motivated accordingly, this particular facet of his mammalian heritage. Unfortunately for him, this unique ability to repress his feelings also makes him the only mammal susceptible to mental illness, or schizophrenia, the etiology of which lies in the severe bisexual conflict which is the direct product of this repression.*

469        Inversion of the sexual role is common among animals of several species other than <u>Homo sapiens,</u> and it is particularly frequent in infra human primates. (Ibid., p. 134)

470        Hamilton records a single instance of homosexual relations in female monkeys which he believes involved 'true desire'. This was a case in which a mother and her grown daughter had been separated for some time and were then reunited. The two animals rushed together and the younger individual promptly assumed the presentation posture. Her mother immediately mounted with vigorous copulatory

thrusts, making the lip-smacking sounds that accompany normal coitus. (Ibid., p. 138)

471        There are, however, rare instances in which male animals of certain lower mammalian species have been known to display mating behavior like that of the receptive female. Two observers (C. P. Stone and F. A. Beach) have independently discovered a few male rats that reacted to the sexual advances of other males with the display of coital reactions typical of the estrous female. When this occurs other males become much more active in their pursuit of the temporarily reversed individual. Two comments are pertinent at this point. First, male rats that are given a choice of mating with females or with 'reversed' males usually select the feminine partner. Second, those few masculine individuals that occasionally exhibit feminine copulatory reactions are not 'feminized' in the usual sense of the term. They inevitably prove to be vigorous copulators when placed with a receptive female. As a matter of fact, males of this type may respond in feminine fashion to the advances of another male and then within a few seconds switch to the masculine pattern and copulate with the female. The adjective 'bisexual' has been applied to behavior of this type, but the data actually demonstrate reversible inversion of the usual sexual role. Kinsey, Pomeroy, and Martin correctly point out that 'inversion of sexual behavior' would be a more accurate description of the phenomenon.

The physiological basis for inversion of mating reactions in males of lower mammalian species is not completely understood but it does not appear to involve hormonal abnormalities. One male rat showing this form of sexual activity was castrated and the feminine responses disappeared within a few days after operation. Masculine coital performance declined gradually, and after it had reached a base level a male hormone was administered by daily injections. The effect of the androgen treatment was to restore

<u>both</u> male and female mating patterns. Subsequent administration of ovarian hormones evoked some feminine behavior, but the responses were less intense than those appearing under the influence of the male hormone. These findings suggest that the original capacity for both masculine and feminine behavior depends upon hormonal secretions from the testis. Apparently ovarian hormones are not essential to female behavior in such instances. This interpretation is supported by the fact that both types of reaction reappeared when androgen was administered. The injection of female hormones will evoke the receptive response but they are less effective than androgen. (Ibid., pp. 140-141)

472    According to Zuckerman, homosexual behavior frequently occurs in the baboon family group. All the members may be involved. The responses include mutual grooming, genital examination, and sexual mounting. Adult males of this species living in the native state sometimes present sexually to one another and mounting may follow.

Bachelor baboons who have restricted opportunities for contact with females sometimes strike up homosexual friendships, and for a time a masculine pair remains constantly together. Immature males often join full-grown bachelors and engage in sexual activity. Prepuberal and adolescent males show a wide range of sex responses. They display the feminine sexual presentation, masturbate, and mount one another. They also mount and are mounted by adult members of their own sex. And they engage in manual, oral, and olfactory genital examination with other males of their own age. (Ibid., p. 135)

473    The cross-cultural and cross-species comparisons presented in this chapter combine to suggest that a biological tendency for inversion of sexual behavior is inherent in most if not all mammals including the human species. At the same

time we have seen that homosexual behavior is never the predominant type of sexual activity for adults in any society or in any animal species.

... The basic mammalian capacity for sexual inversion tends to be obscured in societies like our own which forbid such behavior and classify it as unnatural. Among these peoples social forces that impinge upon the developing personality from earliest childhood tend to inhibit and discourage homosexual arousal and behavior, and to condition the individual exclusively to heterosexual stimuli. Even in societies which severely restrict homosexual tendencies, however, some individuals do exhibit homosexual behavior. In our own society, for example, homosexual behavior is more common than the cultural ideals and rules seem to indicate. (Ibid., p. 143)

474    *Females.* Mounting of one female by another is not confined to the primates. It is, in fact, common among many subprimate mammals including lions, domestic cats, dogs, sheep, cattle, horses, pigs, rabbits, guinea pigs, hamsters, rats, and mice. There are several indications that the appearance of malelike behavior in females is closely related to a condition of sexual arousal. For example, female rabbits normally do not ovulate unless they have copulated with a buck. But when one estrous doe mounts another and executes vigorous copulatory thrusts, the *mounting animal* may ovulate afterward. Furthermore, this type of behavior is, for many species, closely associated with estrus, the time at which the female is sexually receptive.

Stock breeders have long been aware of this fact and have taken the occurrence of masculine behavior as a reliable sign of receptivity on the part of the female showing the temporary sexual inversion. Sows that are ready to breed are often said to 'go boaring,' mares in heat are said to 'horse,' and cows to 'bull.' Laboratory investigations of female guinea pigs demonstrate that mounting behavior shown towards other females is a regular precursor or accompaniment of the estrous condition.

... It is difficult to decide whether behavior of this type indicates sexual attraction exerted by one female toward another, or if it represents the expression of a high level of arousal in the mounting individual, the sex of the mounted animal being of little importance. Arguments in favor of the latter hypothesis can be adduced from the fact that for most species masculine responses most often occur when a female is in heat and, furthermore, that under such conditions the female will mount males as well as females. For some lower mammals, however, the sexual condition of the stimulus female is important. Female rats, for example, are most likely to display mounting reactions in response to another female that is in estrus. Apparently, in this case the stimuli presented by a receptive female are maximally effective in eliciting masculine reactions on the part of a second individual regardless of whether the latter is a male or female.

The female mammal that is mounted by another member of her own sex usually responds as she would to a male, displaying the signs of sexual excitement. It is important to note that in the species mentioned here inversion of mating behavior is not aberrant; instead it constitutes one aspect of the female's normal sexual repertoire. Feminine and masculine reactions may and often do occur in the same female in rapid succession. (Ibid., pp. 141-142)

475            I am indebted to Dr. Will Elgin, of the Sheppard and Enoch Pratt Hospital, for another repeated observation which, because it is characteristic, needs reporting. For many years Dr. Elgin, in the process of admitting patients, observed the enactment of a scene which assumed diagnostic significance. His office arrangement permitted relatives a choice of three seats, one opposite his desk, one at the end of it quite near

him, and one several feet away. He observed that when the mother and father of the patient appeared together to arrange admission, there occurred something of significance. If mother sat in one of the two chairs at his desk, and father sat off in a corner, it usually followed that mother took over the discussion, did the talking, made the arrangements, and even read the fine print on the contract. Father, meanwhile, looked unhappy and was silent save for an occasional abortive effort to modify certain of the mother's statements. When this was the course of the admission interview, he came to know that the odds were that the patient would be schizophrenic. There is an interesting addendum. In a later interview father, appearing alone, was often very aggressive in his criticism and his demands and accusations. However, it could often be demonstrated that his belligerence was that of a very unwilling agent of his wife. —Psychotherapeutic Intervention in Schizophrenia, Lewis B. Hill, M. D., Ibid., p. 106.

*In this simple scene in a doctor's office can be found all the elements which conspire to produce the mental disability we call "schizophrenia." First and foremost, the parents of a schizophrenic always evidence a greater or lesser degree of sex-role alienation in their behavior. We see evidence of that in this particular instance when the mother of the schizophrenic is described as always being forceful, aggressive and domineering in contrast to the father who is passive, submissive and often "a very unwilling agent of his wife." The child of such a couple grows up to become even more sex-role alienated than his parents are and consequently evolves either as an overt homosexual or else, in an attempt to defend himself against his strong homosexual tendencies, develops schizophrenia. This formula applies equally to the female children of sex-role alienated parents.*

476      Jeanette was of seemly converse so far as a girl of her
         condition can be, for her parents were not very rich. And in
         her youth and until the time when she left her father's house,
         she went to the fields to plow and sometimes guarded the
         animals in the fields, and did women's work, spinning and the
         rest. Jeanette would go often and of her own will to the church
         and to the hermitage of Notre Dame de Bermont near to the
         town of Domremy, when her parents thought she was
         ploughing or working elsewhere in the fields. —Joan of Arc,
         By Herself and Her Witnesses, Régine Pernoud, Stein and Day
         Publishers, New York, 1969, Ibid., p. 16.

         *"And in her youth," states Jean Moreau, a farmer,*
         *during Joan's trial, "and until the time when she left her*
         *father's house, she went to the fields to plough and sometimes*
         *guarded the animals in the fields, and did women's work,*
         *spinning and the rest." We notice here that Moreau does not*
         *put ploughing the fields and guarding the animals in the same*
         *category of "women's work" in which he puts "spinning and*
         *the rest." Thus it could reasonably be assumed that he thought*
         *of the former occupations as more man's than woman's work,*
         *an assumption that would be valid even in today's society.*
         *However that may be, it is an indisputable fact that Joan*
         *experienced a marked degree of sex-role alienation as a child,*
         *an alienation which set the stage for the development of severe*
         *bisexual conflict and confusion at puberty.*
         *As is invariably the case in all instances of marked*
         *sex-role alienation, Joan was faced with the choice of either*
         *becoming homosexual or schizophrenic. Homosexuality in her*
         *time was considered a mortal sin by the religious authorities*
         *and a capital offense by the civil ones, so Joan, a devout*
         *Catholic, had but one choice available to her, albeit an*
         *unconscious one, and that was to repress her homosexual*
         *nature, thereby precipitating a paranoid psychosis, a*

*psychosis which launched her on her road to fame and to an early, tragic death.*

*As can be seen from her brief but furious career, however, her psychosis did allow her to display and use her masculine powers in a manner which was ego-syntonic, thereby absolving her from any conflict or guilt about them. Actually a psychosis is nature's method of providing the afflicted individual the opportunity to ventilate, or abreact, opposite-sex feelings and drives which are ego-dystonic and which consequently have been deeply repressed. In this particular case, the psychosis allowed Joan the freedom to behave like a man, dress like a man and think like a man, yet her transvestism met with the whole-hearted approval of her immediate peers. This would have been impossible for her to accomplish without the development of a psychosis.*

477         Another patient was a schizophrenic adolescent who had received intensive shock therapy at another institution during the course of which he suddenly developed a high-pitched voice. The psychiatrist was uncertain whether he was trying to mimic a girl or a child. When the patient was told that it seemed as if he wanted to be a child, he replied, 'I don't want to be any older. I want to play children's games.' When asked if he saw no fun in being older, he answered, 'Yes, but that has to do with sex. Sex is ugly. Sex has a lot to do with growing up. I don't want to commit myself to sex. The real trouble started when I dyed my hair when my mother wasn't there. I began putting on women's clothes ...' and so on. — Homosexuality, A Psychoanalytical Study of Male Homosexuals, Irving Bieber et al., Vintage Books, Random House, New York, 1962, p. 212.

*It is very obvious that this schizophrenic youth has a very severe bisexual conflict, the cause of his mental illness. His early sex-role alienation became manifest when he started dyeing his hair and "putting on women's clothes" when still a child.*

478     Patient No. 240

This patient entered analytic therapy at the age of seventeen, following an acute schizophrenic reaction characterized by paralyzing anxiety, confusion, withdrawal, and inability to continue either at school or on the job. He was preoccupied with fears of sexual inadequacy and fears of being homosexual. The manifest content of his dreams was homosexual and he responded with fear and rage when in the presence of homosexuals. He was obsessed with a need to have a heterosexual experience and ruminated continually over his past sexual failures. (Ibid., p. 263)

*This young man is suffering from the "bearded lady" disease. He has become schizophrenic as the result of repressing his strongly homosexual nature, the product of the sex-role alienation he experienced as a child.*

479     Patient No. 211

This patient, a twenty-eight-year-old male, diagnosed as schizophrenic, entered psychoanalysis following the onset of an acute panic. Included among his symptoms were fears of homosexuality, anxiety in the presence of homosexuals, and conscious homosexual impulses. In addition, there was homosexuality in the manifest content of his dreams.

The relationship between the parents was described by the psychoanalysts as poor. There were frequent arguments and no open demonstrations of affection. The mother was the dominant member in the marriage, regarded the father as inferior, and was openly contemptuous of him.

*Again, we note how schizophrenia invariably develops as a defense against powerful, unacknowledged homosexual strivings.*

480        The patient, an only child, had the same close-binding relatedness to the mother as did the other members of this group of patients. The mother was very affectionate to him, expressing it through frequent kissing and hugging. But her ambivalence was revealed by her alternating between acceptance and admiration, and contempt and humiliation. She demanded the patient's complete attention and intruded on his free time. She discouraged masculine activities and encouraged feminine activities. She was described as puritanical and sexually frigid. On the other hand, she was very seductive, and undressed frequently in front of the patient. She stimulated him genitally when she bathed him; she slept with him and would use the bathroom while he was present. In addition, she interfered with his adolescent sexual activity by belittling his girl friends and demonstrating her jealousy of them. (Ibid., p. 270)

*This patient is a product of the typical "schizophrenogenic" family, wherein the mother is dominant, the father subordinate and the children, as a consequence, become very unsure of their own sexual identity, with homosexual concerns playing a determining role in their lives. The stage is thus set for the development of schizophrenia, as we see in this case, when one of the children of such a family attempts to deny or repress his (or her) homosexual strivings.*

*The description of the mother of the patient reported upon here is that of the "CBI" mother, the initials standing for "Close-Binding-Intimate." This is the mother whose children tend to grow up to become either homosexual or schizophrenic, the schizophrenia developing, as stated above, as the result of the repression of their homosexuality.*

481            Our study has helped us refine and extend certain concepts relevant to the etiology of male homosexuality. Certainly, the role of the parents emerged with great clarity in many detailed aspects. Severe psychopathology in the H-parent-child relationship was ubiquitous, and similar psychodynamics, attitudes, and behavioral constellations prevailed throughout most of the families of the homosexuals – which differed significantly from the C-sample. Among the H-patients who lived with a set of natural parents up to adulthood – and this was so for the entire H-sample except for fourteen cases – neither parent had a relationship with the H-son one could reasonably construe as 'normal.' The triangular systems were characterized by disturbed and psychopathic interactions; all H-parents apparently had severe emotional problems. Unconscious mechanisms operating in the selection of mates may bring together this combination of parents. When, through unconscious determinants, or by chance, two such individuals marry, they tend to elicit and reinforce in each other those potentials which increase the likelihood that a homosexual son will result from the union. The homosexual son becomes entrapped in the parental conflict in a role determined by the parents' unresolved problems and transferences.

Each parent had a specific type of relationship with the homosexual son which generally did not occur with other siblings. <u>The H-son emerged as the interactional focal point upon whom the most profound parental psychopathology was concentrated</u>. Hypotheses for the choice of this particular child as 'victim' are offered later in this discussion. (Ibid., p. 310)

*In the above quotation, if S-son (schizophrenic son) is substituted for H-son (homosexual son), the family dynamics <u>still</u> fit perfectly, thus proving that schizophrenia is a <u>defense against</u> homosexuality.*

*The H-parents described in this quotation produce not only H-sons but also H-daughters. Furthermore, the same parental psychopathology which is responsible for producing homosexual children is also responsible for producing schizophrenic children, since schizophrenia and homosexuality are inseparably connected through the mechanism of repression – the repression of the homosexuality leading directly to the development of the schizophrenia. Schizophrenia is the negation of homosexuality. The parental psychopathology is determined when a passive, effeminate-type man marries a dominant, masculine-type woman. This sex-role reversal by the mother and father causes severe gender confusion and conflict in their children, who become unsure of their own sexual orientation, or identity. Some of these children become homosexual; others, as the result of repressing their homosexuality, develop schizophrenia.*

482    On the night of the San Francisco killing, [Name Deleted] said he was 'so high' that he continued to feel the effects of the drugs for several days.

His roommate, [Name Deleted], was sitting across a table talking about vacation plans.

'I suddenly got this wild urge to kiss him, passionately, on the mouth,' [N.D.] said. 'I leaped over the table and did it, kissed him, and he reacted with shock and horror.'

'I started hitting him. And then I realized he was not a human being but an Android and then I heard the voice commanding that I kill him and then kill myself,' [N.D.] recalled. — "Killer on LSD 'Heard the Lord'," Paul Avery, San Francisco Chronicle (date and page not noted).

*This is a classic example of a man "running amok" to defend himself against powerful homosexual urges which, hitherto repressed, had suddenly, due to the disinhibiting effect of drugs and the close proximity of a man who elicited his lust, broken through into conscious awareness. In a desperate attempt to disavow these, to him, terrifying homosexual feelings, he developed a classic paranoid schizophrenic delusion wherein the object of his desire became a non-human who deserved to be killed. Tragically acting out his paranoia, he violently removed the object of homosexual temptation from his immediate environment, thus diminishing somewhat the intensity of the conflict over his inadmissable urges.*

483        [Name Deleted], the 29-year-old woman accused of attacking a fellow employee in a Sausalito shop with a samurai sword, yesterday was declared legally sane enough to stand trial.

Judge Samuel W. Gardiner of Marin Superior Court made the finding after reviewing reports by two psychiatrists, both of whom said [N.D.], although psychotic, is sane enough to cooperate with an attorney and understands the charges against her.

[N.D.], who affects men's clothing along with a shaved head, is charged in connection with the stabbing of Norman Williams, 20, shop steward at Heath Ceramics where [N.D.] was a glazer.

She reportedly went straight to Williams after arriving at work on Aug. 4 and stabbed him from behind. — "Samurai Woman Sane Enough to be Tried," San Francisco Chronicle (date and page not noted).

*This woman has developed a schizophrenic psychosis as the result of her marked sex-role alienation and consequent severe bisexual conflict and confusion.*

484        Showing the Middlemists the bathtub where the Birdman used to take his weekly bath, Heaney said: 'Stroud was brilliant but psychotic, and because he was considered a

suicide risk I used to have to watch him shave. What was different was that he'd shave all the hair on his body. I was only 21 at the time and he'd look at me pretty close. I considered him a dirty old man.' San Francisco Chronicle (date and page not noted).

*Stroud, the "Birdman of Alcatraz," would shave off all the hair on his body because unconsciously he wanted to be a woman. His denial of his opposite-sex, or homosexual, cravings caused him to become insane. These tendencies, however, were very obvious to the young guard who stated that Stroud would "look at me pretty close. I considered him a dirty old man."*

485         [Name Deleted] was in a 'homosexual panic' before killing a Mill Valley teenager, Daniel Shallock and the boy's parents last March, a psychiatrist testified in San Rafael yesterday.

Dr. Joseph F. Gutstadt told the murder jury that the 22-year-old former lifeguard had suffered from chronic pain in his urethra, which he said is produced in some men when they refuse to accept and deal with their homosexual tendencies.

The doctor said that while [N.D.] had never had a homosexual experience he was aware of his tendencies and unable to accept them, often saying his uneasiness was caused by others.

Shallock, 19, and his parents, Melvin and Ruth Shallock, were killed by shotgun blasts admittedly fired by [N.D.] when he broke into their Mill Valley home at 3 a.m. on March 16 and then set fire to it.

Gutstadt testified that [N.D.], a psychology major at Marin Community College, went to the mental health clinic at Marin General Hospital last December for treatment of a constant pain in his penis that was so bad the youth threatened to kill himself.

The psychiatrist testified that during therapy it appeared [N.D.'s] problem stemmed from a basketball game in which, [N.D.] claimed, Shallock hit him in the genitals. Gutstadt said it was unclear whether the action was deliberate or accidental.

[N.D.] concluded that 'this had caused him to be sterile and to lose his ability to function sexually,' Gutstadt told the jury.

'He thought that Danny could just drive by his home and look toward the house and cause him to have the pain,' he testified. '... He thought Danny could cause the pain by just dialing his phone and hanging up even before the telephone rang.'

... At the hospital's Community Health Facility, [N.D.] was diagnosed as in a 'paranoid schizophrenic state,' but after some days of treatment he was released because the medical staff felt he was 'well on his way to recovery,' he testified. The psychiatrist described [N.D.'s] groin pains as 'classical symptoms of homosexual panic.' — "Doctor Tells of [N.D.] Pain," San Francisco Chronicle (date and page not noted).

*Again we see an example of how intense homosexual love for another, when denied and repressed, can change into a paranoid schizophrenic rage so murderous that it results in the physical destruction of the tempting object and his (or her) removal from the immediate environment, thereby temporarily diminishing the severity of the psychotic's bisexual conflict. This is the operative psychodynamic mechanism in every case of "running amok," irregardless of the culture or the country wherein it occurs.*

486        A British businessman made a citizen's arrest on a London sidewalk yesterday, nabbing an American spinster hunted by Scotland Yard for questioning in the shooting death of one of her friends.

[Name Deleted], 55, a native of Kansas City, Mo., was spotted on Kensington High street by James Hazan, who saw her hailing a taxi.

...[N.D.], a $16,000-a-year secretary at the U.S. Navy office in London, had been sought by police since the Sunday night slaying of Margaret Philbin, 45, who died of a head wound a few hours after being shot at a London bus stop.

...Police said [N.D.] became disturbed after a hysterectomy operation four years ago, apparently believing it led to a loss of her femininity. They said she apparently blamed the murder victim, Philbin, a friend of 25 years, as well as doctors and other friends for talking her into having the operation.

Queen Elizabeth II's gynecologist was one of 30 persons she named in a rambling letter found in the apartment of the murder victim. —"Businessman Spots A Murder Suspect," Associated Press, San Francisco Chronicle, Nov. 9, 1978 (page not noted).

*The murderous "spinster" in this case had become insane as the result of repressing her homosexual feelings for her "friend of 25 years," now the victim of the killer's paranoid delusions. She blamed the victim, among others, for having persuaded her to have a hysterectomy, whose effect was to make her feel she had sustained "a loss of her femininity." Actually, the "loss of her femininity" was the direct outgrowth of her growing homosexual feelings for the victim, her "friend of 25 years." Being unable to tolerate these unacceptable feelings, she repressed them and consequently developed a classic case of paranoid schizophrenia, the direct result of which was to bring about the destruction of the object of homosexual temptation, thus temporarily alleviating the murderer's severe bisexual conflict. (We have seen this same mechanism at work in previous cases of "running amok.")*

487     Police yesterday ruled the death of exotic dancer Carol Cybolski, who was bitten to death at home by a four-foot rattlesnake used in her act, a suicide.

The 37-year-old divorcee had grown despondent after the night club at which she was working was raided and most of the dancers arrested, police said. She later quit, telling the club's manager she was interested in finding a more respectable line of work.

Mrs. Cybolski, who appeared on stage with the rattlesnake, water moccasin and tarantula as 'Jessie James and her Killers,' was found in her apartment last week and taken to a hospital where she died.

Police said some letters about her possible death were found in the apartment. —"Dancer's Suicide by Rattlesnake," Associated Press, San Francisco Chronicle, Dec. 19, 1974, p. 6.

*It is interesting to note that this suicidal dancer referred to herself on stage as "Jesse James and her Killers." The fact she chose a man's name, that of a notorious outlaw, and worked with snakes – phallic symbols of power and danger – is compelling evidence that she was afflicted with a severe bisexual conflict. Furthermore, the fact she committed suicide, an act which understandably has been called the most serious symptom of schizophrenia, demonstrates the intensity of her bisexual conflict and also the invariable and paramount role this conflict plays in the etiology of schizophrenic symptomatology.*

488     The history of castrant sects goes back to very early times. It reached its height in rites connected with the worship of the great mother goddess in ancient Syria during which young celebrants, duly fortified by drugs and roused to religious frenzy stepped forth to the altar and in the presence of all cut off their organs and flung them at the foot of the idol.

—<u>Sex and the Supernatural</u>, Benjamin Walker, Harper & Row Publishers, New York, Evanston, IL, San Francisco, CA, and London, 1970, p. 84.

*The members of the "castrant sects" mentioned here, accomplished in reality what all schizophrenic males do psychologically, namely, castrate themselves in order to appease the envious, dominant, all-powerful mother, the so-called "schizophrenogenic" mother who does not wish to be, nor will tolerate being, challenged by any potent male, sons and husbands included. In fact, so intense is the prohibition by the schizophrenogenic mother of any masculine behavior on the part of the son (who will eventually develop schizophrenia), that this son will sometimes literally castrate himself, in the manner of the youths in the "castrant sects." It should be emphasized that the members of these sects were obviously insane themselves, witness to the fact that the madness resulting from severe bisexual conflict which we now call "schizophrenia" has plagued mankind since the beginning of recorded history.*

489         Taoism teaches that the great unitive principle of the universe is revealed in two forms of energy known as yang and yin which are immanent in all things, so that each thing as we experience it partakes of the nature of these two forces to a greater or lesser degree. In general yang is said to be active, masculine, positive, light; and the yin passive, feminine, negative, dark.

In the human species the male is yang and the female yin. But there is also a yang-yin pattern within each individual. Thus a man is yang, having a woman as his yin; but within himself his head is yang and his heart yin, and several other dualities besides these exist within each person. Such variations in gender provide the opposite stresses required to give things identity, vitality, and existence. They also provide the nuclear opposites for the operation of sexual magic. The yang-yin idea is symbolically expressed in a famous diagram of the circle of t'ai-chi bisected by a sigmoid line, which shows the two black and white forces locked in an embrace of opposites. (Ibid., p. 93)

*It is necessary to study the teachings of Taoism to understand the mysteries of schizophrenia, for it is in the clash of an individual's yin and yang, rather than in their harmony, that the etiology of schizophrenia is inevitably to be found.*

490     Elements of the first may be discerned in Plato's Symposium where it is said that in the beginning male and female were halves of a primordial androgyne (man-woman) which had existed in united form and afterwards divided. The notion of such a 'splitting' underlies the meaning of the word sex, for sex simply means 'division'.

A similar idea appears in one interpretation of the Garden of Eden story, in which Adam is described as an hermaphrodite being a single whole comprising both male and female. Eve was created from his flesh. Like Platonic man, Edenic man 'split' to form his helpmeet. Variations of this legend occur in Hinduism and several other mythologies of the world. (Ibid., p. 21)

*The fact that man is innately a bisexual creature is a concept that has been recognized since the early days of mankind, as this quotation illustrates.*

491     Two souls, alas, are housed within my breast!    —
Goethe.

*The "two souls" Goethe is speaking of here are his yin and yang, or masculine and feminine selves, which he intuitively realizes can cause one intense pain and grief – thus his use of the word "alas" – when they are antagonistic to each other, which obviously his were when he penned this famous phrase. Invariably the "two souls" which are "housed within" every schizophrenic's "breast" are locked in bitter conflict, the one attempting to deny and repress the other out of fear and loathing of the other's terrifying power and irresistible attractiveness.*

492      Then, his mind stole his future. Over the course of several years, he began having delusions. Doctors would later diagnose him as schizophrenic. He lost interest in his high school teaching job and quit. He became paranoid and argumentative.

His parents took him in, but he no longer trusted them. He claimed they had stolen him from his true parents: Marilyn Monroe and Jack Lemmon.

Because he refused to see a psychiatrist, mental health officials said they could do nothing for him.

Cowart, 42, is now on medication and living in a group home. As he describes it: 'One day I was minding my own business and the police hassled me and turned me over to a mental hospital.'

Cowart had been walking by an elementary school in Vallejo. His mother says police picked him up because he was wearing a dress. He agreed to be treated for his mental illness, because, he says, he was afraid to fight the system.

Meanwhile, his parents deposited a Social Security check in his bank account each month and struggled to keep track of him through bank statements that showed which automatic bank teller machines he used.

'When we didn't hear from him for a while,' his mother said, 'we were afraid he had ... you know ... that he was dead.'

Then he would call to ask for money. One day, his parents arranged to meet him in Oakland. His mother remembers noticing from a distance, with a touch of hope, that his beard was gone. When he got closer, 'I burst into tears,' she said.

Her son was wearing a flower-print dress, high heels, lipstick, makeup and jewelry.

'Jim,' his mother said.

'Jamie, please,' her son corrected.

He doesn't seem to remember that.

Sometimes, when he hadn't called for a while, they looked for him, often finding him at a Berkeley BART station, shouting at passers-by. 'I'm politically outspoken,' he admitted with a shy smile.

Now, he spends most days watching television. Sometimes he goes for walks. His parents pick him up Friday afternoons for weekends at home. —"A Son's Tragic Slide," Tony Bizjak, (staff writer), San Francisco Chronicle, March 15, 1989, p. B6.

*The man described in this newspaper story is suffering from a classic case of schizophrenia as the direct consequence of his severe bisexual conflict and confusion. One slightly humorous, yet ironic, note in an otherwise tragic tale is provided by the incident where his mother spots him from a distance and observes "with a touch of hope" that her son has shaved off his beard (which is actually a prominent secondary sexual characteristic of the male primate) only to discover on closer inspection that not only has he shaved off his beard but that he is now dressed completely in female attire. Here we have a mother who subtly discourages her son's striving for masculinity, symbolized by his growing of a beard, and then professes to be horrified when he rejects his maleness and adopts a feminine persona. The discouragement of a son's masculinity, or of a daughter's femininity, is the single most pathogenic trait of the so-called "schizophrenogenic" mother, for it is the one which is directly responsible for the development in the child of severe bisexual conflict and consequent sexual-identity confusion.*

493          Theresa, a 23-year-old mother of a newborn and a toddler, was the first of the 21 residents to go. She became incoherent at 2 a.m. on a Wednesday. She said she was scared to sleep for fear she wouldn't wake. Two shelter workers listened to her cries. Throughout the night, she talked. At times, her plaints were pitiful. 'I didn't hurt anyone,' she said. 'Why do I feel like this?'

At one point, she opened a safety pin and began to stick it into her hand. A counselor gently took the pin away.

By morning, she was calm and more coherent. Counselors decided to escort her to a local hospital. Emergency room attendants checked her physical signs and recommended that she seek psychiatric care. The next day, a psychiatrist prescribed an antidepressant and suggested that she be placed in a psychiatric facility.

She was allowed to return to the shelter for another night. That evening, as others settled down with their children, Theresa became incoherent again. She talked in a man's voice, then a child's voice, holding her 5-month-old son in her arms.

The counselors decided that Theresa needed immediate psychiatric help. Twice during the night, they took her to the hospital, where she was given emergency treatment with pamelor, an antidepressant. Doctors there spoke to Theresa but decided she was not in imminent danger and sent her back to Greentree.

In the morning, Greentree counselors took Theresa to another hospital, where she was admitted to the psychiatric ward. —"No Home and Not Much Hope," Chris Spolar (staff writer), The Washington Post National Weekly Edition, March 27 - April 2, 1989, p. 6.

*Theresa's bisexual conflict, the cause of her schizophrenic break with reality, is hinted at in this account when she is described as talking "in a man's voice," as well as that of a child's. The fact she would speak like a man shows definite evidence of sexual-identity confusion.*

494          (4) It is impossible to avoid asking, in view of the close connection between the two disorders, how far this conception of paranoia will affect our conception of dementia praecox. I am of opinion that Kraepelin was entirely justified in taking the step of separating off a large part of what had hitherto been called paranoia and merging it, together with catatonia and certain other forms of disease, into a new clinical unit – though 'dementia praecox' was a particularly unhappy name to choose for it. The designation chosen by Bleuler for the same group of forms – 'schizophrenia' – is also open to the objection that the name appears appropriate only so long as we forget it's literal meaning.[2] [i.e. 'split mind'] For otherwise it prejudices the issue, since it is based on a characteristic of the disease which is theoretically postulated – a characteristic, moreover, which does not belong exclusively to that disease, and which, in the light of other considerations, cannot be regarded as the essential one. However, it is not on the whole of very great importance what names we give to clinical pictures. What seems to me more essential is that paranoia should be maintained as an independent clinical type, however frequently the picture it offers may be complicated by the presence of schizophrenic features. For, from the standpoint of the libido theory, while it would resemble dementia praecox in so far as the repression proper would in both disorders have the same principal feature – detachment of the libido, together with its regression on to the ego – it would be distinguished from dementia praecox by having its dispositional fixation differently located and by having a different mechanism for the return of the repressed (that is, for

the formation of symptoms). It would seem to me the most convenient plan to give dementia praecox the name of *paraphrenia*. This term has no special connotation, and it would serve to indicate a relationship with paranoia (a name which cannot be changed) and would further recall hebephrenia, an entity which is now merged in dementia praecox. It is true that the name has already been proposed for other purposes; but this need not concern us, since the alternative applications have not passed into general use.

The prognosis is on the whole more unfavourable than in paranoia. The victory lies with repression and not, as in the former, with reconstruction. The regression extends not merely to narcissism (manifesting itself in the shape of megalomania) but to a complete abandonment of object-love and a return to infantile auto-erotism. The dispositional fixation must therefore be situated further back than in paranoia, and must lie somewhere at the beginning of the course of development from auto-eroticism to object-love. Moreover, it is not at all likely that homosexual impulsions, which are so frequently – perhaps invariably – to be found in paranoia, play an equally important part in the aetiology of that far more comprehensive disorder, dementia praecox. — Psycho-Analytic Notes on an Autobiographical Account of a Case of Paranoia (Dementia Paranoides) (1911), Sigmund Freud, Ibid., pp. 75-77.

*In his analysis of the Schreber case, from which this quotation is taken, Freud concluded that repressed homosexuality is the primary pathogenic factor leading to the development of paranoia. He felt strongly, however, that paranoia and schizophrenia, while closely related, were nevertheless separate disorders and consequently that "paranoia should be maintained as an independent clinical type, however frequently the picture it offers may be complicated by the presence of schizophrenic features."*

*Furthermore, he believed that "it is not at all likely that homosexual impulsions, which are so frequently – perhaps invariably – to be found in paranoia, play an equally important part in the aetiology of that far more comprehensive disorder, dementia praecox."*

*Of course we now know that paranoia and schizophrenia are one and the same disorder, and that if repressed homosexuality plays the major etiological role in the development of paranoia, which it does, then it must also play the same key etiological role in the development of schizophrenia. It would be accurate to state that paranoia is the one stage in the course of schizophrenic development wherein the etiology of the disorder – repressed "homosexual impulsions" – becomes most apparent, as is strikingly illustrated by the case of Daniel Paul Schreber, which Freud is referring to in this quotation.*

495          There was admitted to the hospital some years ago a gentleman fifty-one years of age, in the throes of a very severe acute schizophrenic panic.

          … On admission he was found to be in very fair physical condition, somewhat arteriosclerotic. He was at times blocked in his speech, being seemingly unable to express himself. He asked how his sexual energies could be controlled, and inquired as to the advisability of castration, and so on. That night, he became much disturbed, much excited, noisy, and at times actively antagonistic. The next morning, he was quieter but seemed rather disoriented and actively hallucinated. He appealed to various staff physicians to be operated upon for the control of his 'sex energies,' made many references to his 'bestial nature.' His excitement was continuous, greater at night, and he progressed into a state of physical exhaustion. He said, 'My passions run toward the organs of reproduction,' and recounted how since childhood he had experienced a recurring dream, perhaps once or twice a month, in which he sees a beautiful stallion. In the dream he glories in its grace of form, its motion, gallops and rhythm. It is his desire to ride the horse or drive it. Then his 'feelings become base,' he gives way to a desire to finger the sexual organs of the horse, at which junction he has pollution. Not only does he dream of horses, but his thoughts during the daytime continually revert to them. His life has been one of struggle to overcome this tendency. The greater the effort he has made, the greater in his desire and thought about horses. He says that he is beastly, morbid, and inhuman in these desires. It has been largely because of constant thoughts of a horse that he has felt himself unable to marry. People now believe him to be a prostitute or that he maintains a house of prostitution. While describing his difficulties, he is very tense. He believes that he is under a spell, that he is hypnotized – perhaps by the physician who was called early in the acute illness. [18] His productivity was shortly greatly reduced by incoherence, perseveration, and blushing. He insisted on going nude to 'purge myself of sin,' was destructive, resistive, but also most affectionate to attendants. His feeding was a great problem; artificial feedings were regurgitated.

By the thirteenth day under care, the patient's physical condition was grave, our therapeutic armamentarium seemed exhausted, and I had recourse for the first time to ethyl alcohol as a chemotherapeutic agent for the relief of a schizophrenic impasse. It seemed that the patient was shortly to die of exhaustion unless we could interfere with the violent conflict-situation including his highly organized ideals and the sexual cravings.

The results quite justified my optimism. Improvement became apparent almost at once and he went on to discharge as 'recovered' about four months subsequent to admission. It developed, incidentally, that the 'hypnotic spell' which he believed to have initiated his illness had been cast upon him by an attractive and persuasive book canvasser. He has been occupied successfully with his former duties for some several years past. —Personal Psychopathology (Early Formulations), Harry Stack Sullivan, M. D., Ibid., pp. 296-299.

*The "very severe acute schizophrenic panic" that this patient was admitted to the hospital for could just as well have been described by Dr. Sullivan as an "acute homosexual panic," for that is what it was. His love for the male sexual organ, as evidenced by his obsession with the penis of his hallucinated stallion, as well as his thinly disguised wish to be castrated, confirm the fact that he is afflicted with severe bisexual conflict stemming from a deep-seated alienation from his normal masculine sexual role. His paranoid belief that people are now referring to him as a "prostitute," i.e., as a woman, illustrate his unconscious wish to be of the opposite sex.*

*This patient could have died as the result of his extreme state of exhaustion brought on by the continuing frustration of his intense repressed homosexual cravings – a condition that formerly (before the advent of anti-psychotic drugs developed in the 1950's provided the means by which to bring it under control) was referred to as the "exhaust status" of catatonic schizophrenia. Fortunately for this particular patient, Dr. Sullivan's rather unorthodox use of "ethyl alcohol as a chemotherapeutic agent" saved him from a fatal outcome by sufficiently dissipating the lethal intensity of his irreconcilable bisexual conflict.*

*The "hypnotic spell" placed upon the patient by the "attractive and persuasive book canvasser," which he believed had precipitated his schizophrenic illness, was in reality an intense homosexual "crush" which he had unconsciously experienced when he was in this person's presence. Thus, he was very intuitive in connecting his illness with this particular individual, since his homosexual panic and the ensuing schizophrenic breakdown were the direct result of his disavowal and frantic flight from his inadmissable homosexual craving directed towards this man.*

*Finally, the use of ethyl alcohol by Dr. Sullivan as a "chemotherapeutic agent" to save his patient from becoming fatally exhausted while in the throes of catatonic schizophrenia is exactly the same agent used by alcoholics, albeit unknowingly, to "interfere with" their own "violent conflict-situation" encompassing "highly organized ideals" and "sexual cravings," which, as in the case of Dr. Sullivan's patient, invariably involves a desperate attempt by the alcoholic's ego to erect a defensive barrier against severe bisexual conflict with accompanying homosexual concerns.*

496    The onset of the psychosis, as we reported it, was as follows: 'I had been very tired after that night, but got pretty rosy and didn't have enough sense to go home to bed when I got off duty. I went to the old place and drank some more with some former cronies. You remember, I had been called as a witness in an inquiry into drinking at that place, before my transfer. I had talked to some of my friends, there, about the drinking of that night before. Then I went home and slept for hours. I awoke after a dream; never had such a dream – never thought of such a thing before, in my life; I dreamt that X (the landlady's eldest son) and I had a sexual affair.' So far as I could discover, this is the only time that a frank homosexual content had made its appearance in the patient's consciousness, in many years past. The close friendship, alcoholic indulgences, and intimate and entirely 'ethical' association with very loose women had apparently served for release from a dangerous accumulation of desire connected with the dissociated tendencies. (Ibid., p. 303-304)

*As invariably happens, the patient's psychosis was triggered by the eruption into conscious awareness of previously deeply-repressed homosexual cravings, or, in Dr.*

*Sullivan's words, "from a dangerous accumulation of desire connected with the dissociated tendencies." A psychosis is nature's way of providing an outlet for this "dangerous accumulation of desire."*

497    743 – In regard to the management of patients we found in St. Eliz. Hospital that confused males who are fearful of their inability to control their cravings to submit themselves to homosexual seductions are partly relieved by being attended or supervised by a female. The more maternal she is in her personal attributes the more successful her influence. The narcissistic or homosexual type of female nurse is of little value in such cases. The patient apparently does not feel confidence in her presence because he cannot trust her sympathy. ... Similarly, the female patient who is in a panic because of fear of homosexual assault will attack (defensive) female physicians and nurses when they approach her, but will show signs of relief when attended by a male physician. — Psychopathology, Edward J. Kempf, M. D., Ibid., p. 743.

*The primary etiological role of repressed homosexual cravings in the development of mental illness is illustrated very clearly in this description by Dr. Kempf of schizophrenic patients in "St. Eliz." Hospital.*

498    When, in the prepsychotic phase, the ego loses its power to master certain conflicts by reality means and therefore contact with reality has to be relinquished, an attempt at restitution sets in. This restitutional attempt deals with the same conflict and solves it by unrealistic means.
    Let me cite two short examples:
    (1) In the last phase of the prepsychotic period the conflict of the male patient revolves around the wish to be a woman in relation to a father-figure. After contact with reality is severed, one result of the restitutional attempt may be that

the unconscious wish to be a woman no longer constitutes a part of the unconscious but becomes, through projection, a part of the delusional outer world in the following way: the patient believes himself persecuted by a father-figure who wants to use him (the patient) as a woman or to make a woman out of him.

(2) The restitutional attempt may also take another way of resolving the conflict. The feminine part is still projected but this time to a mother-figure. The patient has lost his unconscious feminine part and in his delusion is in love with a mother-figure who represents his own projected femininity. We shall return to a discussion of this mechanism presently. —The Importance of the Non-Psychotic Part of the Personality in Schizophrenia, M. Katan, M. D., International Journal of Psycho-Analysis, No. 35, 1954, pp. 119-120.

*The conflict that leads to psychosis in the male, states Dr. Katan, "revolves around the wish to be a woman in relation to a father-figure." This is confirmed by the material produced by Daniel Paul Schreber in his Memoirs of My Nervous Illness, the famous autobiography on which Sigmund Freud based his theory of paranoia, and which is generally known today as "The Schreber Case." It would have been helpful here if Dr. Katan had broadened his statement to include female psychotics as well, by stating that the conflict that leads to psychosis in the female revolves around the wish to be a man in relation to a mother-figure.*

*Freud was the first to make note of the fact that the so-called Oedipus complex was divided into two parts, the positive and the negative. In the positive Oedipus complex, the child identifies and competes with the parent of the same sex for the love of the parent of the opposite sex, thus establishing a heterosexual orientation for itself. In the negative Oedipus complex, however, the child identifies and competes with the parent of the opposite sex for the love of the parent of the*

*same sex, thus establishing a* <u>homosexual</u> *orientation for itself.*
*This homosexual orientation will result in the child either*
*becoming overtly homosexual at puberty, or (as the*
*consequence of repressing its homosexual orientation)*
*neurotic or psychotic – the severity of the ensuing mental*
*illness depending upon the relative strength or weakness of the*
*repressed homosexual drive.*

499     Recognizing the important role which homosexuality plays in
        the schizophrenic psychosis, let us focus our attention
        temporarily upon the homosexual perversion. This perversion
        may be strongly rooted in pre-oedipal developments.
        Constitutional and environmental factors in the pre-oedipal
        phase may already be so strong that eventually the
        homosexual perversion cannot be avoided. Nevertheless, pre-
        oedipal developments must still pass through the oedipal
        phase. (Ibid., p. 120)

        *Dr. Katan emphasizes "the important role which*
        *homosexuality plays in the schizophrenic psychosis."*

500     When the Oedipus complex is lost, only pre-oedipal fixations
        remain. In this pre-psychotic stage the homosexual urge
        predominates. Because of the loss of the Oedipus complex, the
        structure of the homosexual urge in the pre-psychotic stage
        differs from the structure of homosexuality in the perversion
        or in the neurosis.
        To stress this difference, I shall repeat the sequence of
        events. Through the loss of the Oedipus complex, the
        homosexual urge has now a pre-oedipal character. The pre-
        psychotic schizophrenic male patient wants to be a woman.
        This wish has its origin wholly in the constitutional wish to be
        a woman and does not arise from attempts to ward off oedipal
        demands. In the woman, the wish to be a man predominates.
        Here again this desire for masculinity does not stem from the

positive female Oedipus complex but is directly derived from the constitutional factor of masculinity.

Thus we meet the problem of bisexuality. Of course, this problem also is present in the common neurosis. Yet in the neurosis the problem of bisexuality is dealt with on an oedipal level and does not endanger the ties with reality.

In schizophrenia, on the other hand, attempts to solve the bisexual problem and still remain in contact with reality fail. Therefore, in its deepest nature, schizophrenia arises from a bisexual conflict, and this bisexual conflict eventually leads to a state where the heterosexual factor is relinquished. (Ibid., p. 121)

*The genesis of schizophrenia lies in sex-role alienation in early childhood. With the advent of the powerful hormonal changes occurring at the time of puberty, this sex-role alienation is transformed into a state of severe bisexual conflict and confusion, the requisite pathogen for the development of functional mental illness, the most severe manifestation of which has been labelled "schizophrenia." Or, as Dr. Katan explains it, "in its deepest nature, schizophrenia arises from a bisexual conflict, and this bisexual conflict eventually leads to a state where the heterosexual factor is relinquished."*

501 Let us take as an example the catatonic patient who lies curled up in a foetal position. This behavior points to a pre-psychotic ego defence of a flight back to the womb in order to ward off the genital homosexual danger. Such an ego defence is not possible in the sphere of reality. Therefore, although the pre-psychotic ego makes use of regression, an observer would not be aware of the presence of this regressive material if it were not revealed by the psychotic catatonic symptoms, the latter being a delusional expression by means of the body.

Within the frame of ego regression, the very early pre-oedipal relationship to the mother constitutes a special problem. For instance, there are analysts who think that the homosexual conflict as I have described it, is not something fundamental to the development of schizophrenia but represents only a later phase of a development which began with the early oral attachment to the mother. In my opinion, clinical material leaves no doubt as to the overwhelming importance of the homosexual conflict. (Ibid., p. 125)

*Dr. Katan strongly disagrees with those investigators who do not think the homosexual conflict is "fundamental to the development of schizophrenia but represents only a later phase of a development which began with the early oral attachment to the mother." In Dr. Katan's opinion, "clinical material leaves no doubt as to the overwhelming importance of the homosexual conflict."*

502    I have already explained why I think that the passive feminine urge of the pre-psychotic phase (in the man) is a constitutional one. It is thus my impression that if the early attachments to the mother are expressed at all, they are channelled into the all-prevailing homosexual conflict. Some male schizophrenic patients, for example, will insist that the female head nurse is a man in disguise. (Ibid., p. 125)

*The male schizophrenic patients who "insist that the female head nurse is a man in disguise" are obviously showing clear evidence of severe sexual confusion due to their bisexual conflict. However, they may also be demonstrating an intuitive understanding of any masculine qualities exhibited, either emotionally or physically, by the head nurse.*

503    His [Schreber's] excitement, which had its origin in the non-psychotic part of the personality, took a different course from

that in the pre-psychotic period prior to the psychosis. In the pre-psychotic period the excitement led to genital emissions; a few weeks later, in the psychosis, before a situation leading to excitement could arise, the energy of the homosexual urge was withdrawn and then used to form the hallucination. Thus the hallucination is formed in anticipation of a danger. The energy of the homosexual urge evaporates in forming the hallucination. <u>The hallucination is therefore a discharge phenomenon which serves to prevent the development of danger</u>. Of course, when the homosexual urge acquires energy again, then the danger returns.

... Through the hallucination the energy of the dangerous urge which would destroy contact with reality is discharged, and this fact leads to the conclusion that the hallucination serves to maintain contact with reality in the non-psychotic layer. This goal of maintaining contact with reality can be achieved only by abandoning it for a short while through the formation of a psychotic symptom (the hallucination). It is like avoiding a major evil by accepting a minor one. (Ibid., p. 126)

*When the schizophrenic's bisexual conflict becomes overwhelming, the repressed homosexual excitement discharges itself through the medium of the psychotic hallucination rather than through the medium of genital orgasm, as would be the case under normal circumstances where there was no repression of the homosexual lust by the ego. Thus the psychotic hallucination is actually a "hysterical conversion" mechanism utilized by the organism for the discharge of sexual tension which has been blocked by repression from its normal route of genital orgasmic discharge.*

504        As far as the cause of schizophrenia is concerned, two factors come at once to the fore: constitutional and

psychogenic. In view of the changes taking place in the constitutional bisexuality, namely, the disappearance of heterosexuality and the predominance in the pre-psychotic development, of an urge towards femininity in the man (and towards masculinity in the woman), one is inclined to add a third factor, an acquired organic one, which is probably of endocrinological nature. (Ibid., p. 128)

*The person who eventually develops schizophrenia will invariably have shown opposite-sex tendencies to a greater degree than average during his or her "pre-psychotic" phase. In part, these opposite-sex feelings are based on man's innate bisexual constitution, one which he shares with all other mammals. However, the deciding factor in these cases is always the psychogenic one, wherein the parent(s), or parent-surrogate(s), subtly (or not so subtly) encourage the child to cultivate and express his or her normal quota of opposite-sex feelings, but to such a degree that they eventually become more powerful and demanding than the same-sex feelings. The development of severe bisexual conflict in a child raised under such conditions is inevitable, resulting in a person destined to become either overtly homosexual or else severely neurotic or schizophrenic as a consequence of repressing their hom-sexuality.*

505    Diagnosis
        About one-half the patients were diagnosed as suffering from 'schizophrenia.' With two exceptions, the remainder of the patients were considered to be 'schizoid' or 'schizophrenic personalities.' Many of the patients who were not diagnosed as overtly schizophrenic had schizophrenic Rorschach protocols, as had the boys in the total sample who had strongly identified themselves with girls. — Homosexuality, A Psychoanalytical Study of Male Homosexuals, Irving Bieber, et al. (Ibid., p. 208)

*The male patients in the sample who had "strongly identified themselves with girls" had "schizophrenic Rorschach protocols," even though they had not yet been diagnosed as "overtly schizophrenic." Likewise it would be correct to surmise that any female patients in such a sample who had "strongly identified themselves" with boys would also have "schizophrenic Rorschach protocols," whether or not they had yet been diagnosed as "overtly schizophrenic," for the pathogenic factor in the genesis of schizophrenia is invariably that of sex-role alienation in early childhood.*

506         Except in shapes of horror, women never appeared in my depressive phantasies. I was dominated by a sense of repulsion to women and all forms of sensuality, bound up with my sense of sin. It was as though the whole tide of Eros in my being was at the lowest ebb. This is a regular feature of my depressive periods; even in minor attacks I cannot even trouble to notice a pretty girl. At the same time I am practically impotent, and if I attempt sexual relations premature ejaculation makes them virtually impossible. Precisely the opposite conditions prevail in manic periods.

        Everything, in fact, seems to suggest that the opposed states of manic-depression are closely related with or possibly caused by some fundamental opposition or process connected with sex. —Wisdom, Madness and Folly, (The Philosophy of a Lunatic), John Custance (Ibid., p. 80)

*John Custance's strongly homosexual nature is demonstrated by his feelings of loathing and repulsion towards women. When he says that manic-depression, actually a symptom of schizophrenia, is "possibly caused by some fundamental opposition or process connected with sex," he shows great insight, for the "fundamental opposition" he speaks of is in reality the irreconcilable conflict between his homosexual and heterosexual selves, the same conflict which is the primary etiological pathogen in all functional mental illness.*

507     ... and so with the unintelligible, confused behavior of a dissociated personality, who spends weeks in religious incantations and prophetic exhortations and finally eats the plants on the ward, 'root and all,' and then tries to perform fellatio and be 'crucified,' we must recognize that the psychosis has been largely a struggle with uncontrollable oral homosexual cravings, which finally dominated the ego and obtained <u>free</u> control, after perhaps years of repression and certainly months of suppression of the cravings. — <u>Psychopathology</u>, Edward J. Kempf, M. D. (Ibid., p. 14)

*A psychosis is nature's way of trying to heal, as this case so clearly shows. After years of repression, this man's powerful homosexual cravings have finally broken through the defenses erected by the ego and emerged into conscious awareness, where they now have the opportunity to satisfy themselves. This patient, with the proper psychotherapy, will gain insight into the fact that his mental illness resulted from the denial and consequent repression of these "perverse" cravings, and that the path to mental health now lies in coming to terms with these intolerable feelings. This can be accomplished either by utilizing conscious masturbatory fantasies to discharge the sexual excitement engendered by these cravings, or else by satisfying them in actual homosexual activity.*

508     Christ and the Virgin Mary were also represented by her family. She herself was Jehovah. She was not God but God's disciple, she sat at his right. The King of Glory was Mr. H. When she talked about the latter (and often quite profanely) she always mixed in a deluge of biblical phrases. Since she has ceased loving him, her husband had appeared to her in the

most varied forms, but he always had black hair (as he actually did). —<u>Dementia Praecox or the Group of Schizo-phrenias</u>, Eugen Bleuler (Ibid., p. 419)

*This schizophrenic woman totally identifies herself as a man – Jehovah. In this she is no different from any other schizophrenic woman, all of whom, due to sex-role alienation beginning in early childhood, have developed very strong, unconscious masculine identifications.*

509     In some ways, sketching in these details of Schumann's early career amounts to saying that he was dramatizing himself in a rather adolescent way as the mad genius in the making. Apprenticing himself for the role, he began to hear noises in his head. Then the voices began to address him. He personified two of these and gave them proper names. On once engaging in self-recrimination, 'My genius, are you going to abandon me?' he was answered by the arrival of a disembodied voice, 'Florestan,' who over the years became the confident, extrovert and manly alter ego. Schumann liked to see 'Florestan the Improviser' as his 'bosom friend ... my own ego.'

    The other voice that haunted him came slightly later, and was to be christened 'Eusebius.' This was Schumann's more sensitive, withdrawn, passive, feminine part. Of course, the advent of these figures reflected fashionable Romantic thinking about <u>Doppelgänger</u>, derived from Jean Paul. But, once they appeared, the solitary Schumann was often to be found talking to his selves. —<u>A Social History of Madness</u>, Roy Porter, E. P. Dutton, New York, 1989, pp. 67-68.

*Schumann's bisexual conflict, the cause of his schizophrenia, is symbolized by the division between his masculine self, Florestan, and his feminine self, Eusebius.*

510        The key to understanding this neurosis lay in
Haitzmann's attitude towards the Devil. For Freud,
Haitzmann's Devil was a father-substitute. Haitzmann's
unconscious had fantasized the notion of the pact with the
Devil; doing so had been for him the only legitimate means of
expressing what must have been his profound passive-
homosexual longings for his own father. The death of the
father had caused Haitzmann's melancholy and inability to
work. Haitzmann's compact with the Devil offered him an
outlet, a kind of marriage with his father. It was for nine years
because (if one read 'years' as a screen for 'months') that was
how long it would take for his father's baby to gestate in him.

Supporting these ambivalences, Haitzmann's portrayals
of the Devil had shown him with prominent female secondary
sexual characteristics – in particular, large breasts. Freud
claimed that this was most 'unusual' in representations of the
Devil, and hence a psychologically significant way of
representing Satan. It probably meant a 'projection' of
Haitzmann's own feelings of femininity. (Ibid., pp. 86-87)

*Haitzmann's "profound passive-homosexual longings
for his own father," which Freud correctly believed was the
cause of his "melancholy and inability to work," had their
origin in Haitzmann's negative Oedipus complex. In this
complex, which Freud originally gained insight into as the
result of his own self-analysis, the son assumes a passive,
feminine attitude towards the father and a hostile, competitive
attitude towards the mother. In the female, the negative
Oedipus complex occurs when the daughter assumes a
masculine, protective attitude towards the mother and a
hostile, competitive attitude towards the father. This particular
complex invariably leads to the growth of a strong element of
homosexuality in both the son and the daughter, and is
directly responsible for the development of the functional
mental illness which inevitably arises when puberty is reached*

*and the individual attempts the overwhelming task of resolving the severe bisexual conflict and confusion generated by the powerful homosexual tendencies, which the negative Oedipus complex has given birth to.*

511      Cowper's immensely sad existence was stained with mental disturbance of the melancholy kind (as he put it, the thread of his life had a sable strand woven into it). He suffered five distinct severe breakdowns, during some of which he tried to take his own life. The first came in his early twenties; the last set in when he was sixty-three and dogged him to the end of his days. And even in between these episodes, the black mark of despair was rarely far away, sometimes kept at bay only by enforced sociability, application and activity (for Cowper, writing verse was quintessentially occupational therapy, to stave off idleness which led to melancholy).

... Attempts have been made from various twentieth-century viewpoints to diagnose Cowper's condition. James Hendrie Lloyd resolved the whole problem in a few words. 'The case is probably best described as a form of circular insanity, with alternating phases of profound depression and mild hypomanic reaction, but without distinct intervals of complete sanity ... It was a constitutional psychosis.' Good to know. R. R. Madden thought that the answer lay in the guts. He speculated in particular that Cowper may have suffered from some organic disease, akin to Dyspepsia – why else would Cowper have complained so much about his digestion? If only some doctor had put Cowper's stomach to rights, thought Madden, he would have been spared the agonies of the soul.

Others have puzzled whether some embarrassing physical defect perhaps created that shyness and solitariness which so plagued Cowper and made him feel like a lone tree on a hill. Early in the nineteenth century the diarist Charles Greville obliquely recorded that Cowper had apparently been a 'hermaphrodite' (but what exactly did that term mean to Greville?). And it is well known that Dr. William Heberden reported a case of a man who castrated himself, the facts of which fit Cowper. The hypothetical presence of some abnormality of the sexual organs (possibly self-inflicted) could perhaps account for the fact that on one occasion when Cowper became engaged to be married, he rapidly plunged into another of his insane episodes, and the engagement was called off. But this seems destined to remain no more than speculation. (Ibid., pp. 93-94)

*Cowper was undoubtedly afflicted with schizophrenia, the "bearded lady" disease. If in fact he had once attempted to castrate himself, this would demonstrate in striking fashion how intensely he loathed his masculine sexuality and how much he would have preferred to be like a woman. Cowper was certainly a hermaphrodite emotionally and perhaps also physically, the latter depending upon the extent of his genital self-mutilation.*

512        The Freudian might also suggest that we have here a case of that dialectic between paranoia and homosexuality which Freud outlined in the case of Daniel Schreber. Perceval perhaps affords us some positive evidence of unconscious homosexual urges. He recalls a dream set in Portugal in which he had robbed a monastery, assassinated a vicar and in the company of monks had become the 'enjoyer of their unnatural lusts.' Of this dream he himself offers no interpretation. He openly admired the male form and frequently wrestled with young men in the asylum. Perceval's text may inadvertently reveal such desires, but there is no sign that he was conscious of any. Full of confessions, excuses, self-vindications and rationalizations, and saturated with a sense of guilt, menace and punishment, the Narrative affords abundant evidence of a raging world of unconscious desire beyond the conscious

candour of his own professions of innocence. (Ibid., pp. 173-174)

*The "raging world of unconscious desire" attributed to Perceval was in reality a raging world of unconscious homosexual desire, as this quotation makes abundantly clear. Drs. Ida Macalpine and Richard A. Hunter once said of Daniel Paul Schreber (the subject of Sigmund Freud's famous study on the etiological relationship of repressed homosexuality to paranoia) that "Schreber's name is legion." Perceval is a member of this "legion," which includes all schizophrenics, those unfortunate people who have become mentally ill as the direct result of a "raging world of unconscious [homosexual] desire" within their psyches.*

513 If this much can be established without difficulty of healthy persons, and if we take into account what has already been said [p. 50] about the fuller development in neurotics of the normal genus of perversion, we shall expect to find in these latter too a fairly strong homosexual predisposition. It must, indeed, be so; for I have never yet come through a single psycho-analysis of a man or a woman without having to take into account a very considerable current of homosexuality. When, in a hysterical woman or girl, the sexual libido which is directed towards men has been energetically suppressed, it will regularly be found that the libido which is directed towards women has become vicariously reinforced and even to some extent conscious.

I shall not in this place go any further into this important subject, which is especially indispensable to an understanding of hysteria in men, because Dora's analysis came to an end before it could throw any light on this side of her mental life. —The Standard Edition of The Complete Psychological Works of Sigmund Freud, Vol. VII, The

Hogarth Press and the Institute of Psycho-Analysis, London, 1953, p. 60.

*If Freud admits to having discovered "a very considerable current of homosexuality" in every "neurotic" patient, male or female, that he psycho-analyzed, it seems he should have had no difficulty in theoretically extending this finding to the more seriously mentally ill – the psychotics. He was able to do this only in the case of paranoia, but failed to apply it to "that far more comprehensive disorder of dementia praecox," which is now called "schizophrenia." This was Freud's great failure as a theoretician and clinician – the fact that he was unable to recognize that repressed homosexuality is the basic etiological factor in all functional mental illness, from slight hysteria up to and including the most malignant forms of schizophrenia.*

514          This condensed report has to do with a young man who, somewhat late in his intensive treatment, which had been instituted because of an acute catatonic episode, awoke from sleep one night in panic about a dream. In this dream he encountered a jungle feline which lived in a 'pit.' He described this beast in all its horrible and terrible characteristics. According to his spontaneous account, this jungle feline was representative of a penis, and the pit represented a vagina. These two lines of associations were jumbled together, so that he said that the jungle feline was himself, it was his penis, it was his mother, and her penis, her vagina, it was full of all the penes in the world, and it sought to devour all of them. He further stated that it was filthy, fecal, putrid, stinking, bloody, *and fascinating.* In the fury of his revulsion (note the juxtaposition of *fascination* and *revulsion*) the patient asserted among other things that he hated his penis; he wanted to cut it off and be free forever from the jungle feline.

Being translated by the therapist, this impassioned outflow of words conveyed to him the idea that the patient felt that this penis of his, his sexuality, his very being and sanity, were all given to him in the process of birth. Thereby his mother had lost her penis. He saw himself as bound to his mother because his penis, his sexuality, his personality, and his sanity were all on loan from her. He visualized his mother's destructiveness if he were to permit anyone else to share in what he felt belonged to her. In the fury and terror of these associations, he actually perceived the doctor's office as literally filled with these jungle felines. The only solution he could devise to his state of panic was to cut off his penis. Unsaid, but inferred, was the thought that he could then return to his mother and be free both of her mortgage upon him and of her revenge. He could be again in peaceful symbiosis with her. It is worth noting that, although it also was not said, other productions of the patient on other occasions indicated that, having by this desperate self-mutilation freed himself from his mother, the patient would be able to enjoy real relationships, including the sexual, with other persons. For all its concreteness, his expression 'to cut off his penis' does not imply, in his magical thinking, that he will then be without one. However, in a situation such as this, there is a practical danger that the patient may mutilate himself.

What the therapist said to the patient at this time was stated quietly, firmly, and definitely. It was, 'I do not believe you hate your penis. You like it. You need not cut it off.' This brought this interview to a close. Of course, there was much later reference to this dream as treatment progressed toward the patient's freedom, confidence, and courage to live in the real world. —Psychotherapeutic Intervention in Schizophrenia, Lewis B. Hill, M. D., (Ibid., p. 209-211)

*The only way a son can be in "peaceful symbiosis" with his mother is by psychologically castrating himself. In a few instances, this self-castration is carried out both psychologically __and__ physiologically, the latter being a danger which must always be taken into account by whomever is treating a male schizophrenic patient, as Dr. Hill points out in this passage.*

515        Swedenborg indicates the possibility of spirits acting through the subject (AC5990), which is to possess him. This I have occasionally seen. For instance the man who thought he was Christ within a woman sometimes spoke through her, at which time her voice was unnaturally rough and deep. She also had trouble with him dressing at the same time she was because she would be caught in the incongruities of doing two different acts at once. —The Presence of Spirits In Madness, Wilson Van Dusen, The Swedenborg Foundation, Inc., New York, 4th ed., 1983, p. 24.

*This patient is afflicted with schizophrenia, the "bearded lady" disease, for he believes he is "Christ within a woman."*

516    One of my female patients was found going out the hospital gate arguing loudly with her male voice that she didn't want to leave, but he was insisting. Like many this particular hallucination claimed to be Jesus Christ. But his bragging and argumentativeness rather gave him away as of the lower order. (Ibid., p.12)

*This patient projects her own unconscious masculine identification onto the hallucinated figure of Jesus Christ, thus diminishing the intensity of her severe bisexual conflict. She, also, is a victim of the "bearded lady" disease.*

517    Though the patient was a high-school educated gas-pipe fitter, his female vision showed a knowledge of religion and myth far beyond the patient's comprehension. (Ibid., p. 13)

*This is yet another example of how bisexual conflict and confusion form the etiological core of schizophrenia.*

518    "I'm thinking I'm living through life as it's happening in the holy Bible," she recalled. "Jesus is sitting right next to me. The president on TV knows who I am." Later, her hallucinations would recur along two threads: she was a prophet doing battle with Satan, or she was in communication with NASA." ... "At 28, disowned by her family and desperate for a new start, she lied about her medical history and enlisted in the Army." —"Our Towns," David M. Halbfinger, The New York Times, March 24, 2002, p. 32.

*This woman, suffering from paranoid schizophrenia, is here displaying her severe bisexual conflict and gender confusion when she hallucinates being a "prophet doing battle with Satan" and also being in contact with NASA.*

*In 99 out of 100 cases, prophets are invariably thought of as being male figures, and it would also be quite unlikely that an ordinary female like herself would be in touch with NASA unless, of course, she thought she was an astronaut undergoing training, or applying to be one. Both of these themes in her recurring schizophrenic hallucinations point to megalomanic, grandiose estimates of herself as being a male figure of great influence and power in worldly affairs. And the fact she enlisted in the Army further points to a masculine identification, for down through history, until very recent times, the armies of all nations have been overwhelmingly male-oriented.*

*This woman is obviously afflicted with schizophrenia, the bearded lady disease.*

519          But his doubts about their two-month experiment in communal living in the Provencal town of Arles were confirmed the next night, when Van Gogh, distraught over Gaugin's impending departure, ran after him in the street hurling wild accusations.  Gaugin turned to confront him, whereupon Van Gogh returned to the house they shared. There he used a  razor to cut off part of his left ear, which he carefully wrapped and presented to a young woman at the local brothel.  Van Gogh was hospitalized, and Gaugin left for Paris the next day.  But after Van Gogh's discharge from the hospital, he begged Gaugin in a letter not to speak ill of "our poor little yellow house."  Some dreams die hard.  —"Strange Bedfellows," Joseph Harris, The Smithsonian Magazine, December 2001.

*This famous episode in the lives of these two artists is very telling, in that it demonstrates the very powerful feelings of love Van Gogh had for Gaugin.  Van Gogh's "distraught" actions were similar to what a jilted woman might do and feel if her lover planned to leave her.  "Some dreams die hard," Mr. Harris comments.  And truly, Van Gogh's dreams were to have Gaugin live happily ever after with him in "our poor little yellow house."*

*Van Gogh's lifelong schizophrenia had its roots, as is always the case, in the severe bisexual conflict and confusion which he was never able to resolve satisfactorily.  The extreme mental anguish resulting from this conflict is what finally drove him to suicide.*

520          He was 5-foot-1 and talked to himself more than to anyone else.  He grew up in an asylum for "feeble-minded" children but wrote, and lavishly illustrated, a fantasy novel more than 15,000 pages long.  He died in obscurity in Chicago; today he is one of the stars in an international constellation of outsider artists. ...

While many of Darger's scenes are pastoral idylls, others show children being throttled, eviscerated and crucified en masse by their enemies. The fact that the victims are often nude girls, some with male genitals, only adds to the impression that "The Story of the Vivian Girls" is the record of an unhinged psyche suddenly laid bare. —"Visions of Childhood Showing Purity and Evil," Holland Cotter, <u>The New York Times</u>, April 19, 2002, p. B36

*The American artist Henry Darger (1892-1973), now considered one of the most famous of a group of artists known as "outsider artists," was afflicted by schizophrenia throughout his life. And as is invariably the case, the factor of severe bisexual conflict and confusion formed the pathogenic core of his illness. This is best exemplified by the scenes in some of his drawings where "the victims are often nude girls, some with male genitals," which "only adds to the impression that 'The Story of the Vivian Girls' is the record of an unhinged psyche suddenly laid bare." Exactly: Unconsciously Darger identified as one of the Vivian girls, albeit a girl possessing a penis, and his lifelong schizophrenia stemmed from this conflict between his unconscious female identification and his conscious male (penis) one. Finally, the fact Darger was only five-foot-one would make it easier for his unconscious psyche to identify as a female rather than as a male. Darger was truly a bearded lady.*

521　... The first clue as to this came in a dream in which she and another person were in a house. The other person seemed to be a part of herself and at the same time seemed to be a man. She was afraid someone would see the man so she jumped into bed and pulled the sheet over her head but then said, as if speaking to the man who was a part of herself, 'What does it matter if they do see you? Why try to conceal it any longer?'

This dream foreshadowed an increasing realization of the resentment she felt at her own femaleness and the envy she felt toward men. She recognizes (in the dream) that she thinks of herself as part man, part woman – but tries to conceal the 'man' part. In fact, it could be said that her entire life centered about the wish to become a boy like her brothers and the feeling of guilt implicit in the idea of becoming a boy by robbing them of their masculinity. It proved to be the unconscious motive back of her repeated submission to surgeons. One day while in church to which she had gone compulsively as a part of her atonement ritual, it suddenly came to her that perhaps she wanted to suffer like Jesus as she had obviously been doing for a long time, even to the point of having the same pain in her side that Jesus had, for the following reasons: Jesus was a man; hence, by being Jesus, even though one suffers, one can be a man.

Such an 'irreligious thought,' as she termed it, disturbed her very much, but later she returned to a realization that it was the basis of much of her religious fervor. It explained her wish to believe in miracles, her faithfulness to her devotions, her feeling that some day she would get her reward and that God would answer her prayers. She felt that perhaps if she suffered greatly she might be granted the privilege of becoming a man. This began to appear very clearly in her analysis. She kept complaining that she was getting nowhere. It was not clear what she wanted of the analysis but she evidently expected something wonderful to happen. She expected the analysis to gratify her lifelong quest for masculinity. To this end she assured the analyst of her belief in miracles and implied that she expected a miracle to happen in her analysis. In every way she showed that unconsciously she was taking the position that if the analysis would make her into a man it was worth the suffering it cost her. —Man Against Himself, Karl Menninger, M. D., (Ibid., pp. 135-136)

*This case illustrates how deep-seated and intense can be the wish to be of the opposite sex, and how this wish, when repressed and unconscious, can lead to the development not only of the severe psychopathology which is to be found in schizophrenia but also to the growth of florid psychosomatic symptomatology, as demonstrated by the patient's voluntary submission to unnecessary and potentially harmful medical treatment.*

522     Another case will bring out more of the motives. A thirty-year-old naval officer, married, was brought to the hospital with a history of having mistreated himself and of having contemplated suicide. He was quiet, neat, mildly depressed.

The history was that his father had been very religious but very difficult to get along with and had deserted the family while the patient was yet small. The mother had been obliged to work very hard to support them. The boy himself had to go to work at an early age but in spite of this obtained a fair education intermittently. He had joined the navy and worked himself up to petty-officer rank. A year before admission he noted that he worried about his work and asked his friends if they noticed that he was not doing so well. He became increasingly depressed.

Then he began to notice strange noises, thought he heard his shipmates talking about him and accusing him of perverted practices (i.e., of being homosexual). (Individuals with such fears and hallucinations rarely <u>are</u> homosexual overtly, but react with terror to the thought that they might be – just as 'normal' persons do, but in greater degree.) Finally he went to the bathroom and with a safety razor amputated his penis.

When questioned about it the patient said he has been confused and hadn't known what he was doing. He seemed however, to show little concern or regret. Later he jumped overboard but climbed back aboard the ship on the anchor chain. He admitted, however, that the thought of drowning had always fascinated him.

The examination showed that he still suffered from auditory hallucinations with voices telling him to do odd things and commenting on what he did. Concerning the charge of homosexuality he was quite perplexed because he had never indulged in it but began his heterosexual life very early. Except for the mutilation his physical condition was excellent and his intelligence above average.

Later the patient announced that he was 'ready for the supreme sacrifice' (suicide) and wrote a note saying, 'I am a pervert and will pay the penalty.' He became increasingly restless and disturbed and exhibited impulses to fight with patients and attendants.

... There is, however, another element which we must not lose sight of. A man who feels guilty about his sex organs because of conscious or unconscious homosexual impulses, accomplishes two purposes when he cuts off his genitals. He punishes himself, but at the same time he converts himself by this deprival into a passive, penis-less individual, anatomically comparable with the female. By this anatomical identification, he comes closer to the homosexuality about which he feels guilty than he was before the act. He feels guilty about his homosexual wishes and by castrating himself appears to atone for and relinquish them, but in reality only changes himself so as to be incapable of the active role and even more disposed to the passive role. [35] (Ibid., pp. 236-237)

*Because he lacked a close male role model early in life, the father having deserted the family, the patient unconsciously identified himself more as female like his mother than as a normal male. The sex-role alienation which resulted from this primary female identification subsequently led to such a severe bisexual conflict that it drove the patient mad, or schizophrenic, and in the midst of this madness he amputated his penis, thereby gratifying his powerful, unconscious homosexual desire to be a female.*

523          Most schizophrenics have a homosexual bent or conflict. This was fully confirmed by the histories and psychological tests of our two groups of patients: 27 of the 30 in each group revealed homosexual tendencies. But there was a sharp contrast in expression of the tendency. In the 27 Irish patients the homosexuality was latent but repressed, whereas 20 of the 27 Italians had become overt homosexuals. The underlying factors in both cases are clear. The Italians had rejected a male role out of hostility to their overbearing fathers and elder brothers. Italian men, no less than Irish men, take pride in masculinity; indeed, they are, if anything, more masculine in behavior. But they are also readier to act on sexual impulses, and when they lose their sense of sexual identification in schizophrenic illness, they do not shrink from overt homosexual behavior. Irish men, on the other hand, flee from their identity as males through fear of the mother rather than hostility to the father. All of our Irish schizophrenic patients were either pallidly asexual or latently homosexual. Most of them avoided females. Their homosexuality was repressed because sexuality in general is inhibited in the Irish culture. But it emerged in their fantasies. Indeed, some misidentified themselves as women: one patient had the delusion that the front of his body was covered by an 'apron which bled periodically.'   —"Schizophrenia and Culture," Marvin K. Opler (publication not recorded), August 1957, p. 120.

*All schizophrenics "have a homosexual bent or conflict," not just "most," for without the severe bisexual conflict there would be no schizophrenia.*

*The Italian male schizophrenics mentioned here who "do not shrink from overt homosexual behavior" have a much greater chance of recovery from their illness than do the more sexually repressed and inhibited Irish males, for schizophrenia can only be "cured" by the process of allowing the unconscious homosexual cravings to become conscious so that they can then either be satisfied orgasmically or else sublimated, that is, their sexual energy utilized in other, non-sexual endeavors.*

524        Frazier, an auto mechanic who appeared in the courtroom one day with the left side of his head, beard and eyebrows shaved, pleaded not guilty by reason of insanity. — "Woman Painfully Recalls Family's Brutal Murder," Dawn Garcia (staff writer), San Francisco Chronicle, October 20, 1990.

*Frazier is a classic example of the "bearded lady" disease – schizophrenia. He is half man – half woman, one side of his head shaved, or female – the other hairy, or male. His outward appearance reflects the state of his inner psyche, which is one of intense bisexual conflict and confusion.*

525        He had been a girl
It had been a trick, a deception.
He bounced back, righted himself.
He assumed his rightful place in the company of men.
He went further, he became a super-boy.
Secretly, he believed in his invulnerable and unique intelligence.
In psychotic transformation he became a super-man.
He assumed his rightful place in the company of the gods.
It had been his secret, mythic life all along.

But he was even more special than the gods – he was a mortal who accomplished it on his own.

Born somewhat late in his parents' lives, he was their only child. His father, known for his heavy drinking and occasional episodes of abuse, maintained an emotional distance from his son. On the other hand, Donald was very close to his mother and was clearly a treasure in her life. They communed with each other about their experience of God and she did her best to protect him. But all the evidence indicates that she was bringing him up as a girl! A photograph of him at the age of six shows him with long curly hair, which hung below his shoulders. He is demurely sitting in his parents' garden in a white sunsuit and gives the unmistakable appearance of being a little girl. His mother had longed for a daughter, and on her insistence his hair was not cut until shortly after his seventh birthday. A picture from that time shows his remarkable change into a little boy, holding his sailboat. Within a year came the first reports of the bravery that was to become the signature of his character. —The Seduction of Madness, Edward M. Podvoll, M. D., Harper Collins (Publishers), New York, 1990, p. 109.

*Due to his faulty upbringing, Donald was destined to become either a homosexual or a schizophrenic. He rejected his homosexuality and consequently became schizophrenic, thus validating the concept that schizophrenia is the negation of homosexuality. The classic parental configuration of an emotionally distant father and of a close, binding, intimate (CBI) mother invariably produces a son with strong homosexual tendencies. These can either be acted upon or else repressed. If repressed, the outcome for the son will be the development of a neurosis or a psychosis, the strength of the repressed homosexual drive determining the severity of the ensuing mental illness.*

526     ... They both reported finding Bretnall dead when they entered the house; she was disemboweled and her eyes were gouged out.

[Name Deleted] was found next to the mutilated Bretnall stabbing herself in the neck while reportedly saying, 'I am the devil. I was making love to her. I killed her.'

... Those who knew [N.D.] said that for months before the slaying she had been tormented by psychological demons, threatening to hurt or kill or commit suicide. She had been in and out of the mental health crisis unit at Marin General Hospital. In one instance, she wound up there after slashing her hands and legs with a razor knife at Northgate Mall in San Rafael. —"Slaying Stirs 911 Probe," Alex Neil, <u>Marin Independent Journal</u>, Nov. 27, 1990, p. A9.

*The "psychological demons" which were tormenting [N.D.] were her powerful unconscious homosexual longings. These eventually focused on the person of Bretnall and, because they had been repudiated by [N.D.'s] ego, led to an orgy of violence rather than to an orgy of homosexuality, which is exactly what transpires in all cases of "running amok." When [N.D.] stated that she was "the devil" and had made love to Bretnall, what she was really saying was that in her paranoid delusion she had become a man and had made love to a woman, the culmination of her deepest unconscious wishes. The tremendous guilt she felt over these "perverse" desires was assuaged somewhat by her self-mutilations and the mutilations she inflicted on the unfortunate Bretnall.*

527     Case A – Patient was a forty-six-year-old divorced man suffering from a psychosis. He had recently broken up with his live-in girlfriend, an event which had triggered his schizophrenic break. He believed he was turning into a woman, and took great pride and pleasure in this fact. During therapy with him it was decided that his male side would be

called 'Mars' and his female side 'Venus.' It was pointed out to him that his present psychotic condition was the result of a very severe conflict between his Mars and his Venus. The patient readily agreed with this explanation.

The thrust of therapy with this patient consisted in the therapist trying to strengthen the patient's Mars while simultaneously allowing his Venus, which had long been deeply repressed, to come out and have her day on stage, so to speak. This she did over a period of several months, while his Mars stood aside and allowed her complete freedom of action and thought.

On one occasion during this time the therapist mentioned to the patient that he had seen a friend of the patient's drive by with a very pretty blond woman by his side. The patient responded that yes, he knew that, because it was actually the patient himself whom the therapist had seen sitting in the passenger seat of the friend's car. When the therapist countered that on the occasion he was speaking of, it had definitely been a blond female he had seen in the car, the patient replied that yes, he understood that, but the blond was really himself. The therapist then acquiesced to the patient in this matter, seeing that it was futile to differ with him about the identity of the pretty female, as the patient so clearly and emphatically identified himself as being this particular woman.

At another point during his therapy, the patient brought the therapist a postcard showing a beautiful, voluptuous female lying naked on a bed, with clouds and some angels overhead. The patient told the therapist that the woman shown on the postcard was really himself, as in his psychotic mind this was how he pictured himself at that moment. His Venus was in full bloom at this time.

Later, as the therapy progressed, the patient's Venus diminished somewhat in power and his Mars began to regain it's rightful place in the patient's psyche.

Towards the very end of his therapy the patient, in one of his sessions, handed over the above-described postcard to the therapist to keep, stating that it no longer represented what the patient looked like. Shortly after this the patient terminated his therapy. (Anonymous case reported to compiler.)

*From the moment this schizophrenic patient was able to accept his passive, feminine, homosexual drives on a conscious level and begin assimilating them into his total concept of himself as a man, he was well on the road to recovery from his severe mental illness.*

528    Case B – Patient was a thirty-seven-year-old married man suffering from extreme anxiety and incipient paranoia.

He reported that one evening, after he had gone to bed, he suddenly began remembering the contents of certain perverse, bisexual phantasies which he had masturbated to many years before, an activity he had discontinued upon realizing how 'unhealthy' it was. He had successfully repressed any memory of these events until this very moment.

Now that he was suddenly confronted again on a conscious level with these long-repressed masturbatory phantasies, he experienced an extraordinary phenomenon. He stated that the very first phantasy he allowed into conscious awareness from its unconscious hiding place caused a transformation in his penis from a state of total flaccidity to full erection and spontaneous orgasmic discharge, all within the space of five seconds or less. When queried about the extremely short time interval between complete penile flaccidity and spontaneous orgasmic discharge, patient answered that the time element may have been even shorter than five seconds, for to him it had seemed like an almost instantaneous happening.

Greatly astonished by what had taken place, patient said he was able to repeat this phenomenon several more times during the same night, naturally with an increasingly longer time lag between conscious awareness of a particular phantasy and the ultimate spontaneous orgasm. Patient further reported that he continued this practice nightly for several months until he had exhausted his store of long-repressed phantasies and until these phantasies had lost their power to stir up any more sexual excitement.

Patient also stated that by the end of this period of phantasy abreaction his anxiety had completely disappeared, along with the incipient paranoia, and that his overall health, both physical and mental, had greatly improved. (Anonymous case reported to compiler.)

*The extreme importance of this case lies in the insight it sheds on the toxic effects of undischarged libido upon the organism. The fact that the patient's penis could be transformed from its flaccid state to full erection and orgasmic discharge in a matter of seconds vividly illustrates the enormity of the force which can be built up by the sexual impulse when it has been denied access to normal orgasmic discharge through the process of repression. Furthermore, it is precisely this undischarged homosexual libido which provides the energy which fuels the myriad symptoms of mental illness, among the most serious of which are delusions and hallucinations. (It was Dr. Maurits Katan who first made this observation in one of his papers dealing with schizophrenia.)*

*In this particular case, it is very clear that the patient's incipient paranoia was directly attributable to the toxic effect of his undischarged homosexual libido, and that if he had been unable to discharge it in the manner in which he did, he soon would have developed a full-fledged case of paranoid schizophrenia, replete with all its classic, malignant features.*

529     She was "terrified of any sexual contact" and dressed in "the
        clothing of a ragtag soldier or a poor monk."  Weakened by
        poor nutrition, plagued by migraines (which were no doubt
        exacerbated by her fasting) and handicapped with abnormally
        small, feeble hands, she naturally decided that strenuous
        manual labor was the only means to grasp social and spiritual
        truth.  Her relentless determination to do men's work led to a
        chain of Buster Keaton-like misdaventures – overturning a
        farmer's plow, sending her fellow soldiers diving for cover
        during rifle practice in Spain and ultimately being sent home
        when, while nearsightedly wandering around the campsite, she
        stepped into a pot of boiling water.  —Laura Miller (review of
        <u>Simone Weil</u> by Francine Du Plessix Gray and Francis Du
        Gray), <u>The New York Times Book Review</u>, August 5, 2001
        (page not noted).

        *Simone Weil, described by reviewer Laura Miller as
        "the French philospher, activist and mystic," died in 1943 in
        an English psychiatric institution, apparently a suicide, after
        years of self-imposed semi-starvation.  She was 43.*

        *As we can see from the main quotation above, Simone
        was afflicted with schizophrenia due to her severe bisexual
        conflict and gender confusion.  She was male in everything but
        body, and she did a very proficient job of destroying that
        hated body by starving it for years and finally killing it
        outright.*

        *Her only salvation would have been for her to accept
        her obviously deeply repressed homosexual nature and then to
        act upon it.  But as Freud once said so pessimistically, in
        schizophrenia the victory lies with repression.  Tragically, that
        was the case with Simone Weil as it is with countless other
        unfortunates.  But schizophrenia is not necessarily always a
        "death sentence," for as Frieda Fromm Reichmann once
        explained , it takes a lot of hearts and minds to cure a
        schizophrenic.  But it can be done.*

*Finally, reviewer Laura Miller says that "The novelist Georges Bataille, who knew and liked Weil, probably put it best when he described her as a 'Don Quixote,' but in Weil's case the enemies titled at were real enough. Only her lance was imaginary." In Freudian terms, that "imaginary lance" was surely her longed-for penis which would have made her the complete man she had so fervently wished to be.*

530     After prolonged silences and occasional desultory remarks which I could not put together, the patient, a woman in her middle twenties, suddenly – and for the first time – started to talk about sexual fantasies she had about being a man, about having a penis, and about becoming like me under these circumstances. At the same time, she started to make gestures as if she were bored, gave evidence of some restlessness, and looked repeatedly at her watch. The overall impact of these manifestations was confusing to me. — Borderline Conditions and Pathological Narcissism, Otto F. Kernberg, M. D., Jason Aronson, Inc., Northvale, New Jersey and London, 1985, p. 197.

*This woman was definitely afflicted with schizophrenia – the "bearded lady" disease – even though her symptoms were not yet florid. Her intense confusion as to which sex she belonged to made her act in ways which conveyed this confusion to her therapist to such a degree that even he began to feel confused, thus giving him a taste of the extreme anxiety she was experiencing.*

531     These were grandiose fantasies, inflated by Nijinsky's sense of self-importance. But they were also connected to his unresolved love-hate relationship with Diaghilev, which preoccupied him a great deal. Diaghilev was more crafty and had greater political skill than he did. Nijinsky thought that Lloyd George resembled Diaghilev; his 'intentions are

terrible.' Clemenceau on the other hand 'seeks the truth.' Paderewski 'is not a pederast' (an example of punning, or what Dr. Greiber called 'clang-associations'). Paramount in Nijinsky's estimation was Woodrow Wilson, President of the United States, for whom he had once danced and with whose pacifism he identified. 'Wilson wants to stop the war but men do not understand him.' —Vaslav Nijinsky, A Leap into Madness, Peter Ostwald, Carol Publishing Group, New York, 1991, p. 189.

*If Nijinsky had remained with his homosexual lover, Diaghilev, instead of attempting to live a heterosexual life with Romola, he would never have succumbed to schizophrenia. His severe mental illness developed as the direct result of the severe bisexual conflict which was engendered by his sudden, impetuous rejection of his previous, long-standing homosexual way of life for what was to him, an alien, heterosexual one. When Nijinsky says that Diaghilev's "intentions are terrible," he is very likely referring to the fact that Diaghilev played the active role in pederasty with Nijinsky, who was the passive partner. He then adds that Paderewski "is not a pederast" – that is, he is not a pederast like Diaghilev was. At a repressed, unconscious level Nijinsky still craved the sexual gratification he had received as the passive partner in his pederastic relationship with Diaghilev, and it was on account of denying this reality that he succumbed to schizophrenia.*

*This brings to mind Freud's dictum that what man represses at his deepest level are his pederastic instincts. This is certainly applicable to Nijinsky's case, for Nijinsky was, and remained throughout his life, basically a homosexual. If he had found the strength to remain true to his own feelings he would have been spared the ravages of his schizophrenic illness.*

532        For example, when on 10 May a male patient invited him to play billiards, Nijinsky accepted, but then began 'to manipulate his cue' in his usual provocative way until 'it dropped on the other man's foot.' An argument broke out, and Nijinsky challenged the patient to a fight. An attendant had to intervene and get Nijinsky to apologize, after which the two men were 'reconciled.' (Ibid., p. 230)

*Even though in schizophrenia the victory always lies with repression, as Freud so aptly stated, nevertheless the homosexuality that is being repressed can still find ways to express itself, as this episode so clearly demonstrates. In essence what Nijinsky is symbolically doing here is masturbating in the other man's presence, an act which could be construed as a veiled invitation to the other man to engage in some sort of homosexual activity with him.*

533        Then there was his ambiguous involvement with Herr Vogel (not his real name), a wealthy, unmarried patient, twelve years Nijinsky's senior, who not only looked like Diaghilev, but even claimed to have been a 'dance-director for 5 years.' Vogel played the violin, well enough so that Ludwig Binswanger, who was an amateur pianist, performed with him occasionally. Vogel also had a reputation for enticing other patients into his bedroom, which was strictly against the rules at Bellevue. (Vogel's diagnosis was 'imbecility and hebephrenia.') At first Nijinsky seemed to be attracted to this man, 'stared' at him a great deal, and tried to elicit his friendship, but when Vogel started to reciprocate, Nijinsky began complaining of 'incomprehensible anxieties, and a vague feeling that he wanted to kill me.' These are paranoid reactions. Nijinsky told the doctors that Vogel 'has been looking at me in a funny way. I know he's a good fellow, and yet I can't get rid of the feeling that he wants to do something to me. I know this is 'sick'. It produces a dreadful feeling

around my heart.' [7] (Dr. Greiber had mentioned the 'paranoid content' of Nijinsky's psychosis in St. Moritz. Paranoid suspicions were also described during Nijinsky's last year of touring with the Ballets Russes.)

Recognizing Nijinsky's susceptibility to paranoid thinking, especially the frightful idea that certain men were out to do him harm, Kurt Binswanger now established a policy of controlling his social contacts, much as Diaghilev had done in the past, in order to minimize encounters that might prove to be too stressful. In mixed company Nijinsky tended to be much less disturbed. (Ibid., p. 230)

*Again we see the unmistakable signs of Nijinsky's very strong homosexual drives, this time focused on the person of "Herr Vogel," who reminded Nijinsky of his former lover, Diaghilev. When Nijinsky says of "Herr Vogel" that he, Nijinsky, "can't get rid of the feeling that he wants to do something to me," the "something" is that which Diaghilev used "to do" to Nijinsky, namely, have anal sex with him. Nijinsky's passive pederastic cravings, which he had abruptly repressed after breaking off his affair with Diaghilev, were still very operative and urgent in his unconscious. The severe bisexual conflict which had arisen as the result of his denying these powerful homosexual feelings had caused him to sink slowly but inexorably into the schizophrenia which now enveloped him, and which, in this instance, led to his paranoid thinking that it was "Herr Vogel" rather than himself who wanted to engage in homosexual behavior. "I know this is 'sick,'" says Nijinsky. The fact he had come to believe homosexual behavior was "sick" is partly what had motivated him to repress these feelings, with disastrous consequences for both his mental and physical health.*

534    Because of the severe agitation, especially at night, it was finally decided to reinstate Fritz Wieland as Nijinsky's

attendant, to sleep in the same room and watch over him all day. But now the dancer no longer regarded Wieland as acceptable. He complained about him bitterly in a paranoid way: 'The attendant strikes terror into me and wants to kill me.' He called Wieland a 'black man' (recalling the Blackamoor who slays Petrushka at the end of Stravinsky's ballet) and screamed, 'I'm being killed here like a wild animal, it's awful to terrorize me like that.' To avert what was recognized to be an incipient panic with homosexual overtones, on 21 July Binswanger assigned a female nurse as Nijinsky's roommate, with Wieland sleeping in an adjoining room. This arrangement resulted in immediate improvement: 'The patient has become somewhat calmer at night, and sleeps quite well most of the time.' (Ibid., p. 245)

*Nijinsky was clearly very attracted homosexually to his attendant, Fritz Wieland, but the repression of his homosexuality remained in place and in its stead arose a paranoid delusion that Wieland wanted to "kill" him. The introduction of a female nurse helped to dampen the severe homosexual conflict caused by Wieland's presence. As stated in the previous quotation, "In mixed company Nijinsky tended to be much less disturbed." Obviously the reason for this was that homosexual temptation was not such an unsettling factor for him in mixed company as it was in same-sex company.*

535     As if to rid himself of this most ghastly fantasy and make himself feel alive again, Nijinsky instigated a whole series of animal imitations. He 'jumped around like a monkey on the floor,' started 'eating like a monkey,' and 'sat on his attendant's lap' in order to be petted and fed. (Ibid., p. 246)

*When Nijinsky "sat on his attendant's lap in order to be petted and fed," he was acting like a woman would when she sits on the lap of a man. This is yet another example of*

*Nijinsky's unconscious alienation from the normal masculine sexual role.*

536          Different from the dancer's first admission to Bellevue was his seeming absence of fear. Instead of the earlier dread that something awful might happen, that he might be put to death or die of a heart attack, this time he deliberately sought danger and assaulted others as well as himself with unbridled fury. Similarly absent this time was any inhibition of homosexuality. Nijinsky tried openly to seduce his male attendant, kissed his hands and feet, and said to him, 'You are my wife.' So insistent was he in trying to remove the attendant's wedding ring that the latter finally had to take his ring off and hide it. Nijinsky also chased one of the male doctors and tried to grab <u>his</u> wedding ring. When the doctor resisted, Nijinsky 'hit him and then wept.' He seemed more confused than ever before. The staff observed him 'talking to himself, taking off his shirt and kneeling in front of his attendant with folded hands, eyes screwed-up, gnashing his teeth, ejaculating loud screams and spitting at the attendant.' While in the bathtub, Nijinsky 'made every possible sort of movement with his body.' suggesting the religious ecstasies of saintly Russian catatonics, or an attempt at orgasm. Occasionally, he pointed to his navel, saying, 'This is a woman or an idea.' He may have been trying to express an attitude in regard to Romola's pregnancy, much as he did in 1913, while expecting their first child, or he may have wanted to give birth himself, perhaps to a new idea. He kept talking nonsense, 'emitting words that did not hang together: planet, detective, airplane, medicine, art.' (Ibid., p. 256)

*This is a very graphic description of a man in the throes of an acute attack of catatonic schizophrenia, precipitated, as it invariably is, by intense conflict over homosexual and heterosexual drives. The catatonic is very uncertain about which sex he or she belongs to, and projects this uncertainty onto others in the immediate environment.*

*In Nijinsky's case, he believes his male attendant is a female: "You are my wife." Furthermore, he wishes to be, or thinks he is, a pregnant female, as when he points to his stomach and says "This is a woman or an idea."*

537        Generally, Nijinsky felt more 'calm' and 'agreeable' when left alone with his male nurse, who helped him get dressed and undressed, took care of his hygienic needs, and occasionally gave him a 'colonic irrigation to aid with digestion.' (Ibid., p. 317)

*The "colonic irrigation" administered to Nijinsky by his male attendant "to aid with digestion" could very well have been a symbolic replacement for the passive anal intercourse he had previously experienced in his relationship with his ex-lover, Diaghilev. If so, these particular ministrations would undoubtedly have made Nijinsky feel more "calm" and "agreeable."*

538        The nurse now working for them was a man Romola suspected of getting sexually involved with Nijinsky. 'I can't prove it absolutely,' she wrote Dr. Müller, 'but one day I came into the room unexpectedly, and found a very peculiar situation.' Twice the nurse had been 'left alone with my husband, and his homosexual appearance became apparent to others as well.' Nijinsky was now 'practicing this habit [masturbation] everyday, after lunch. Then he is relaxed. Couldn't this damage his heart?' [60] (Romola need not have worried: orgasms are a healthier way to release tension than convulsions produced with 'dry shock.') She writes that after she confronted the nurse with her concerns about homosexuality, the man 'quit immediately and then made as much trouble for me as he could,' [61] meaning that he reported

to Dr. Müller his own version of what was going on in the hotel. (Ibid., p. 313)

*Nijinsky's homosexual tendencies had by this time become very obvious to everyone connected with his case.*

*An interesting sidelight here is the remark by author Peter Ostwald that "orgasms are a healthier way to release tension than convulsions produced with 'dry shock.'" Unbeknownst to himself, he has revealed the reason E.C.T. (electro-convulsive-therapy) is beneficial in certain recalcitrant cases of schizophrenia when all other methods of treatment have failed. These "convulsions produced with 'dry shock'" are in actuality artificially produced "orgasms" which serve to release the enormous quantity of repressed homosexual excitement which has built up in the organism due to the fact its <u>natural</u> course of discharge through <u>genital</u> orgasm has been blocked by the repressive ego. In Nijinsky's case, the fact he had begun masturbating openly was a very healthy and hopeful sign, for it meant he was now able to release in a more normal manner the intense sexual excitement engendered by his long-repressed homosexual fantasies and cravings, the frustration of which had driven him insane.*

539         Sexuality seems to have been a huge problem for Nijinsky, matched only by his wife's homophobia, although she overcame that, to a certain degree, by accepting female lovers. Romola lived for another twenty-eight years. She travelled widely, usually with Paul Bohus, visited Russia – where she had an amusing interview with Khrushchev – and Japan, where she fell in love with a transvestite actress who remarkably resembled the young Nijinsky. (Ibid., p. 341)

*By falling in love "with a transvestite actress who remarkably resembled the young Nijinsky," Romola was* *attempting to recapitulate her affair with her husband, for emotionally Nijinsky <u>was</u> a "transvestite actress" – a mixture of both male and female, a "bearded lady," a man who became insane as the result of repressing his highly-developed, passive, feminine, homosexual nature. And Romola, too, was a "transvestite actress," for only a woman of a decidedly masculine, homosexual temperament could have wed a man like Nijinsky. Romola's later career confirms the accuracy of this observation, for after Nijinsky's death she shed all pretense of heterosexuality and embraced a basically homosexual way of life.*

540    Altogether, 22 percent had had contact with the police for bizarre or inappropriate behavior as part of their first episode of schizophrenia, including such events as the strangulation of a pet canary, cutting off the heads of the flowers in the family garden, and a male graduate student walking through a quiet suburb in lady's underpants embracing each exposed garbage can. —<u>Schizophrenia Genesis (The Origins of Madness)</u>, Irving I. Gottesman, W. H. Freeman and Company, New York, 1991, p. 192.

*The male graduate student "in lady's underpants" is exhibiting unmistakable signs of the severe bisexual conflict which has driven him crazy. The garbage cans most likely symbolize male figures to whom he is homosexually attracted.*

541    Neither twin was ever interested in girls.

Both Herbert and Nick held various unskilled jobs as delivery boys until age 22. Herbert then began to behave oddly, staring silently into space, sitting in awkward positions for long periods, neglecting himself, grimacing and laughing to himself; he interpreted passing automobiles as the sound of enemy aircraft.

... On January 8, Herbert was admitted to our hospital and came onto the twin register: 'You feel people are deceiving you. ... I'd be reading people's thoughts when I concentrate ... Some people talk backwards and some people you have to get along on top of their talk. [Later] I'm sure an 'interdiscrete society' could help you. Communist aggression mixed with racial intolerance'... Herbert was committed to long-term care in a mental hospital and was still there after more than 28 years.

Unknown to us at the time, Nick was admitted to a different hospital on January 5 after running across a plowed field with his arms outstretched as if in prayer. The night of his visit to Herbert, he was found crying and the next day seemed lost in thought and was making clicking sounds with his tongue. After New Year's Day, he amazed his adoptive father with unintelligible talk; he felt that he had special powers but that they left him when a cigarette pack was thrown away; he smashed a porcelain dog – 'The devil was there and it was either him or me'; he saw a mass of flames and heard voices singing 'Hark, the Herald Angels Sing.' He was admitted to a mental hospital the next day in a confused and agitated state. Like his twin, he had been virtually continuously in hospital for over 27 years. (Ibid., p. 122)

*Herbert and Nick were both afflicted with paranoid schizophrenia as the result of their repressed homosexual cravings. "Neither twin was ever interested in girls."*

542    Thus, a predisposed young man – wrenched from his psychosocial support network, exposed to the rigors of basic military training, his fragile sexual identity threatened by 'homosexual' horseplay in group showers, and fatigued from sleeplessness – decompensates when forced to make his way through strange terrain during nightime maneuvers. (Ibid., p. 225)

*The author does not make clear whether this is an actual or a hypothetical case, however it is a clinically accurate description of an episode of homosexual panic which develops ("decompensates") into a schizophrenic break with reality. Mention is made of the young man's "fragile sexual identity" which is threatened not only by the "'homosexual' horseplay" in the showers but also by the close, all-male environment which he is subjected to on a 24-hour basis. Any young man already afflicted with severe bisexual conflict would be prone to "decompensate" into a homosexual panic and consequent schizophrenic symptomatology if placed in a similar all-male setting of homosexual temptation.*

543    I stopped crying. My socks were still wet. The gray snow from my snowsuit and boots melted onto the rug. I was scared. Lincoln was in a very happy mood. My nose was stopped up and I felt half feverish, but he was too excited to notice.

He pulled my grandmother's hand-crocheted afghan off the couch and a monstrous, humorous creature was revealed. She wore one of my mother's housedresses. Her body was made of pillows. She had coffee cups for breasts and cardboard mailing tubes for legs. She wore my mother's bowling shoes and carried her patent-leather dress-up bag on her white elbow-length gloved hands. Her arms were golf clubs and her neck was a mop handle. Her head was the mop itself; Lincoln had combed it back and held it in place with my barrettes and rubber bands. Aunt Matilda's eyes were covered by my mother's rhinestone sunglasses. Lincoln had made her nose from an old bronzed baby shoe, and Aunt Matilda's mouth was a red pepper. She lay on the couch looking half dead.

'Say hello,' Lincoln ordered me, 'and curtsy.'

'Hello, Aunt Matilda,' I said. I curtsied. Lincoln's voice changed to a falsetto.

'Hello, you darling little sweet thing you,' said Aunt Matilda. 'I can't believe how you've grown grown grown. What a lovely woman you've become. Are you married yet?'

'I'm only five,' I explained.

'Well, I would have taken you for eight on any day,' said Aunt Matilda.

This pleased me immensely.

'I travelled all the way from Oregon just to see you,' said Aunt Matilda. 'Now tell me all about school.'

I was growing impatient. My feet were freezing and I had to go to the bathroom badly.

'I'm in kindergarten,' I said.

Lincoln's voice broke in. 'Stand still,' he commanded me, 'or you'll give your aunt heart failure.'

I tried to obey.

'What do children do in kindergarten?' cooed Aunt Matilda. 'I'm so very old I can't remember.'

I shrugged. 'We learned to tie our shoes.'

'That's lovely, dear,' said Aunt Matilda. 'Why don't you show me how to tie a bow and I'll give you one of the fabulous presents I brought all the way from Oregon.'  —The Four of Us, The Story of a Family, Elizabeth Swados, Farrar, Strauss and Giroux, New York, 1991, p. 12.

*Lincoln Swados, the author's brother, was diagnosed in his freshman year at college as suffering from "schizophrenia with severe paranoid tendencies." As this passage so clearly indicates, he was already markedly sex-role alienated by the time he was thirteen, the age at which he proudly and excitedly constructed his "Aunt Matilda" dummy and played the role of this imaginary visitor from Oregon before an audience of one – his bewildered younger sister, Elizabeth. By no stretch of the imagination could this activity of Lincoln's be called "normal" sex-role behavior on the part of an adolescent male. What it does illustrate. of course, is that Lincoln was already gripped by such intensely conflicting bisexual drives and gender role confusion that a schizophrenic break with reality was inevitable.*

*Although the author takes poetic license in transcribing the exact wording purportedly used by both she and her brother on this particular occasion, nevertheless it is certain she has realistically captured the markedly effeminate nature and tone of Lincoln's dramatic production.*

544       Sometimes he called using made-up voices and never admitted that it was he. I can remember talking to a Marine sergeant from Texas, a rock-and-roll star from England, and a dying female ex-math teacher from the Midwest. (She wanted to confess about all the terrible things she'd done to her students.) I played by brother's straight man, but I wished at times that the strange conversations were over long before he hung up. I was fifteen or sixteen at the time, and didn't want to admit it, but I preferred talking to my boyfriend about movies, jazz, and his mustang to listening to my brother's disjointed poetry. (Ibid., p. 30)

*In his early twenties Lincoln, by now definitely diagnosed as afflicted with schizophrenia, shows additional evidence of his severe bisexual conflict when he plays both the male and female roles during his strange, "schizophrenic" phone calls to his patient, but still-bewildered sister. Lincoln is a classic example of how the "bearded lady" syndrome forms the etiological core of schizophrenic symptomatology.*

545       This was the time that I was receiving strange collect phone calls from New York. I knew the calls were from my brother, but he disguised his voice and refused to tell me his name. Sometimes he posed as a fictional rock-and-roll star, Bart T. Blue. Bart T. Blue told me he was in love with me and asked me to marry him. I never refused. Other times he was a

woman, Marticia Downsfeather, who was calling on behalf of
the orphans of America. She needed brownies, Fritos, and
cans of Chef Boyardee Ravioli. I sent them to my brother's
address and they were never returned. The night my mother
took ill, the phone rang and I picked it up in the middle of the
first ring, as I'd been instructed. My father was a little hard-of-
hearing and didn't hear the phone until the second or third
ring. This time a low, breathy voice chanted in my ear.

> Don't believe what you hear about the inner ear.
> Don't believe what you hear about the inner ear.

The voice chanted this line for several minutes and
then hung up. I tried to imagine the ear inside the ear. The one
which heard what the brain and heart and veins were saying.
(Ibid., p. 192)

*This quotation provides additional evidence of
Lincoln's severe bisexual conflict and "bearded lady" status.*

546   The owner of the theater, Ellen Stewart, called me into her
office and waved some manuscripts in my face. 'What am I to
do with these?' she asked sympathetically. 'They're your
brother's plays. All they are is balls balls balls, honey. Touchin
them, suckin them, bouncin them. I don't want to hurt
Lincoln's feelings, but does he think he discovered being gay?'
      'Maybe it's new to him,' I said in shock. 'Maybe it'll
pass. He's a good writer.'
      'All I see is balls balls balls,' Ellen sighed. 'What do I
do with him?' (Ibid., p. 37)

*Lincoln's powerful homosexual drives, long repressed
and denied, finally surface in his writings. This is actually a
healthy sign, as the repression and denial of these feelings are
what have driven him insane in the first place. By de-*

*repressing them and allowing them into conscious awareness, his ego, or intellect, now has an opportunity to deal with them rationally and thus hopefully to bring them under some semblance of control, rather than having them drive him insane as before.*

547    I have begun the day with men and women who believe themselves to be Robert E. Lee or God the Father and counseled others who shake with the expectation of torture. — The Dinosaur Man (Tales of Madness and Enchantment from the Back Ward), Susan Baur, Harper Collins Publishers, New York, 1991, p. 2.

*For a woman to believe delusionally that she is Robert E. Lee or God the Father shows unmistakable signs of severe sex-role alienation, and this sex-role alienation, always beginning in early childhood, leads inevitably, following puberty, either to a homosexual way of life or else, if these feelings are denied and repressed, to the development of schizophrenic symptomatology.*

548    What was a small, sharp-eyed man really asking for when he showed me his vicious drawings of women with pointed teeth and barbed-wire jewelry, then let me hold the rag doll he cared for with obvious tenderness. (Ibid., p. 3)

*This schizophrenic male demonstrates an intense hatred and fear of women while simultaneously revealing very strong feminine and maternal instincts of his own. His hostility must stem partly from intense jealousy of the female role, jealousy which is an invariable product of every schizophrenic male's severe bisexual conflict. The "penis envy" which plays such an important pathogenic role in the psyche of every schizophrenic female has its exact counterpart in the "vagina envy" felt by every schizophrenic male.*

549         On his other side, a rather shapeless woman with a scarf around her head and a large handbag had settled onto the step. 'Hello, Leonard,' she said warmly to someone I couldn't see, 'I mean, oh dear, *Bernie*. It's you.'

I moved to get a better view and found that she was holding a powdery compact in her hand and smiling at her own reflection. (Ibid., p. 6)

*This patient looks in the mirror and sees the unconscious masculine image she has of herself in its reflection.*

550         As I disentangled myself from his ideas, he floated back to the far corner of the dayroom and knelt before one of the heavy brown chairs that sat in two straight rows in front of the television set. One of the aides had already told me that Mr. Nouvelle performed unnatural acts on invisible men, but from where I stood I could not tell whether the Nicodemosaurus was bobbing up and down or simply praying. I watched for a moment or two and wondered what was going on. Perhaps if I got to know him ... (Ibid., p. 18)

*Mr. Nouvelle is obviously afflicted with very powerful homosexual cravings of an oral nature, the conscious disavowal of which have driven him insane, or schizophrenic.*

551         Our early meetings were totally confusing. He was a Venetian policeman, the Inspector General, my father, or even me, and in turn I was mother, wife, son, daughter, duck egg, and dinosaur. (Ibid., p. 18)

*Probably the most bewildering aspect of these early meetings between the author and Mr. Nouvelle was the intense confusion he displayed concerning not only his own sexual identity but that of the author's as well.*

552        'I <u>told</u> them I was the son who never sucked dick,' he wailed. 'I promised not to eat anything until my eyes were fixed. I gave the sign' – and here he kissed the ends of his fingers from little finger to thumb and back again – 'but still they cut into my brain and took it out by the pailful. When are they going to <u>fix</u> me and send me home to my wives?' (Ibid., p. 20)

*Again we see evidence of Mr. Nouvelle's extremely powerful oral homosexual cravings. When he asks "When are they going to <u>fix</u> me and send me home to my wives?" it's as if he's asking "When are the doctors going to cure me of my intolerable craving to perform fellatio on other men so that I can then be rid of my homosexuality and become sexually interested in women?"*

553        Mr. Nouvelle was born in a small logging town not far from the Canadian border, the youngest of nine children, and came into the world to replace a daughter born barely a year earlier, who had died of whooping cough. Her name was Claudine, and the family called Maurice by his middle name, Claude. Times were hard for the family in those years. His father was apparently drinking to dull the pain of an old back injury, and his mother, still mourning the death of her baby, was sad and very, very tired. The care of Maurice fell to his four older sisters, and it was they who dressed him in frocks like a girl or a doll and pushed him around in a big wicker baby carriage. (Ibid., p. 22)

       Maurice also began to join in the games of his older brother, such as 'dick flicking' in the woods behind the school, but he was always the youngest and smallest, and something of his early years as a 'girl' led the older boys to taunt him. (Ibid., p. 22)

*Sex-role alienation began for Mr. Nouvelle at a very early age. He was treated by his family as if he were a girl almost from the very beginning of his life. Furthermore, the fact the father was an alcoholic meant he could not have been an adequate masculine role model for his son, while his obviously depressed mother could not have provided him with sufficient maternal nurturance to enable him to build a healthy self-esteem as a beloved son. Thus Mr. Nouvelle's fate was sealed almost from the moment of his birth. He would become either homosexual or schizophrenic, the outcome depending upon his acceptance or denial of his extremely effeminate nature. As we know, he became schizophrenic, a strict religious upbringing undoubtedly supplying him with one of the major motivations for repressing his powerful homosexual strivings, thus dooming him to a lifetime of emotional chaos and pain.*

554    His delusions concerning sex, greatness, and persecution also flowed into his French, and he was soon able to discuss 'being queered' or squeezing zucchini in either language. (Ibid., p. 23)

... Mr. Nouvelle's answer was incomprehensible. However, he repeated 'taking away' several times, and, as was his custom when agitated, he took an imaginary dick from his pocket and began sucking upon it. Clearly this curious man desired to be understood, and just as clearly the giving away of his secrets and rediscovery of his past felt extremely dangerous to him. (Ibid., p. 23)

*Mr. Nouvelle's barely disguised oral homosexual cravings seem to be the driving force behind his schizophrenic symptomatology.*

555    There followed nightly orgies of incredible proportions, the descriptions of which sounded like the rich

interleafing of a pornographic novel and a poultry breeder's manual. Sweet milk ran from the wombs and penises, a son sucked his mother's zucchini, and duck eggs moved throughout the male and female anatomy as easily as one draws a breath. Soon the invisible ladies moaned in ecstasy, as Mr. Nouvelle drove his thirty-eight good dicks into their cantaloupes and streams of green beans poured from the women's fingers and out their ears. (Ibid., p. 25)

*Here we see delusions of a mother who has a penis (zucchini) which is being sucked by her son, eggs which appear in both males and females, and "invisible ladies" moaning in sexual ecstasy as the patient "drives his thirty-eight good dicks" into their "cantaloupes." The meaning of all this is that the patient is trying to convince himself that he is not, contrary to all the evidence, a man who has very urgent, oral homosexual cravings and is extremely confused as to which sex he really belongs to, but rather that he is an intensely virile and potent male who can provide heterosexual satisfaction to numerous women.*

556   I had watched Mr. Nouvelle take the arms of an empty wooden armchair in his hands, kneel before it, and bob silently up and down, and I had seen him play around with a man known as the Extortionist. The two would bump into each other or poke halfheartedly at each other's private parts. Mr. Nouvelle told me that once he gave a patient a dollar to follow him into the basement of Building 2 and there let him reach into his pants. Because he found no 'dick,' but 'only a small zucchini,' he knew he had chosen a man who was really a woman. (Ibid., p. 27)

*Mr. Nouvelle projects his own intense confusion as to which sex he belongs to onto the man in the basement who, because he has "only a small zucchini," is perceived as being a woman rather than a man.*

557        As we approached the pond, a school of fingerlings darted into the shallow, and abruptly, matter-of-factly, Mr. Nouvelle recounted the story of his first hospitalization – how he believed the men at the logging camp thought he was queer, how they had sent messages to him through the cosmic whine of the screeching saws, and how at last he'd been carried off the job with crazy sounds of wheezing and jeering in his ears. Sometime later he had been taken to a hospital, and there he was questioned, medicated, and given shock treatments that 'walk the thoughts right out of your mind.' Finally he was taken home and there met by a family who 'looked at me like an animal.' (Ibid., p. 33)

*This is a classic case of a paranoid schizophrenic break with reality occasioned, as it invariably is, by the outbreak of powerful homosexual cravings which the patient has denied and repressed.*

558        For nearly a week Mr. Nouvelle ignored this news and then with unbearable energy called back all the magic he had ever used to endure thirty-seven years of chaos and loneliness. He went on a hunger strike and lost 15 pounds. He stuffed his jacket pockets with invisible dicks and sucked on them incessantly. He made the sign by kissing his fingers not once but three times, and he increased his number of wives to a thousand and then to a hundred thousand. (Ibid., p. 35)

*The patient's unconscious defense against his overwhelmingly intense oral homosexual cravings is to deny their reality altogether and instead to insist that he is actually so virile and heterosexual that he has literally thousands of wives.*

559   The last two weeks with the Dinosaur Man were terrible. He was upset and delusional, and there were no reprieves. During our last meeting he caught sight of a new patient, a man of about twenty-five. He stared across the hall at him and poured into that stare the same intense question and promise that he'd held in his eyes when he first looked at me, and before me at his six wives, at a hundred nurses, and at all the women in the world.

'Miss Baur,' he asked, still staring at the patient, 'am I obliged to stay with you the whole hour?'

'No, Mr. Nouvelle.'

'I see Tommy Hammond over there with a bag in his hand,' he continued, swaying toward the young man. 'He may be my Dinosaur son, and I think he has something for me.' (Ibid., p. 36)

*Mr. Nouvelle's powerful current of homosexual lust, the denial of which has driven him insane, is graphically described in this quotation wherein he espies Tommy Hammond across the hall and "poured into that stare the same intense question and promise that he'd held in his eyes" when he had first met the author, Susan Baur, all the nurses on the wards, and his multitude of delusional girlfriends and wives. What the author is describing is a look of profound sexual lust, animal-like in its frankness, and in this instance directed towards the true object of Mr. Nouvelle's deepest sexual desires – another man.*

560   As frequently happened on the ward, it was difficult to know which parts of Mr. Brunetti's stories were true, in the usual sense of the word, and which imaginary, but in his case the essentials were well documented. For over fifteen years this slow-moving rather shapeless man had been steadfastly in love with one of the female patients at Mountain Valley. Most of the time her name was Jolinda Muniz, and she was a short,

sturdy-looking woman who wore coveralls. Occasionally, she was John Hines, a bomb builder for a secret government agency, but this, she explained, did not change her feelings for Mr. Brunetti. It merely made her vision so sharp that she saw the world as if through the wings of a fly. (Ibid., p. 63)

... For her part, Jolinda maintained that 'her friend' was 'OK.' Yes, he gave her things, but nothing she couldn't get herself, and yes, she liked to sit with him on the benches because he never got fresh, and no one bothered her when they were together. (Ibid., p. 64)

... 'I designed the bomb, you know,' said Jolinda Muniz belligerently, as I tried to get her to say and think my words. 'I did. I mean really. It's mine.' (Ibid., p. 65)

*Jolinda Muniz' intense bisexual conflict, and consequently her deep-seated sense of confusion as to which sex she really belongs to, becomes very apparent from the material presented in this quotation. She is truly a "bearded lady."*

561            Conversely, I might have assumed that all noisy patients are likely to be as incomprehensible as Paul Whitman, who, sashaying into the testing room with his T-shirt tied into a bolero, dramatically proclaimed himself to be 'Magnolia.'

'A woman's test,' he squealed, snatching one of the recognition sheets off the table before he'd even begun to read or think the words.

'Flower,' he read. 'Yes, I'll take flowers. 'Bread' is good too. But 'soldier'? No, no, no. Soldiers are for boys. And boys,' he suddenly shouted, his voice deep and menacing, 'don't get pregnant!' With that he clasped his hands over his crotch and shimmied out of the meeting room. (Ibid., pp. 66-67)

*Closely following in Jolinda Muniz' footsteps is yet another "bearded lady," Paul Whitman, otherwise known as*

*"Magnolia." This schizophrenic man presents a picture of such total sexual confusion and conflict that any objective observer would undoubtedly be left shaking his or her head in complete bewilderment as to exactly what was being perceived.*

562       'Mary Frances! Mrs. Quinette!' shouted a patient through the glass, pulling his T-shirt higher up his chest and rubbing his belly.

'Mr. Whitman, don't.'

'They found the baby in my stomach, on the X ray.'

'Mr. Whitman,' repeated the nurse, who was also this patient's advocate or case manager, 'don't yell through the glass. Knock on the–'

'They took an X ray and saw the baby with a snake in it. That proves I'm a woman,' and with that the volatile Mr. Whitman disappeared around the corner and into the men's room. (Ibid., p. 110)

*Mr. Whitman is definitely suffering from a severe case of schizophrenia, the "bearded lady" disease.*

563       After lunch, for example, it was common to see eight to ten men, all smoking, sitting around the periphery of the first-floor lounge. Most were silent, many rocked or tapped. Ivana Goldman negotiated a hot deal with invisible business partners, and an absolutely wild-eyed man, whom I'd seen when I first arrived on the back wards, inscribed enormous figures in the air and claimed to be reading Coptic braille. (Ibid., p. 112)

*Ivana Goldman? The unfortunate Mr. Goldman's sex-role alienation must have begun at a very early age, due in part to his own obviously sexually confused parents having bestowed upon him the feminine equivalent of the name*

*"Ivan." It reminds one of the American country western song called "The Boy Named Sue."*

564        'You've had some hard times?' I questioned sympathetically.

'I could write a book,' said Wanda, leaning back in her old velvet chair and dabbing her eyes with the handkerchief she kept tucked in the cuff of her blouse. 'And no one would believe what I've been through .... My mother named me Lester before I was born, you know. She and my father wanted a boy so bad. But there I was, a little mite.' Her voice began to break. 'A little ... innocent ... baby.' (Ibid., p. 131)

*As much as Wanda's parents may have wanted a boy named "Lester," when they were faced with the disappointing fact that their newborn was of the female sex, they at least gave her a suitably feminine name, unlike the parents of the above-mentioned Mr. Ivana Goldman. Perhaps this may explain why, although suffering from severe mental illness due to her bisexual conflict and confusion, Wanda was nevertheless able to remain on an outpatient basis rather than being committed to a mental hospital, the fate which befell the unfortunate Ivana.*

565        When I first asked Mr. Nouvelle for his earliest memory, the Dinosaur Man was at his most elusive.

'I was eighteen months old,' he said dreamily. 'I slept in my parents' room and I saw them making love. I saw her give my father a hand job and I said, 'I can do better than that,' so I gave him a blow job. It's hard the first time you get caught,' he continued, 'but you just agree with them and say, 'Yes, I'm eating my father. He likes it. It's a good thing to do.' Then they let you alone.' (Ibid., p. 190)

*Mr. Nouvelle's intense oral homosexual cravings, the repression of which has driven him insane, appear to have originated in an early childhood fixation on his father. Rather than developing the more normal, or usual, "positive" Oedipal complex, wherein the son is sexually and emotionally attracted to the mother and identifies in a competitive manner with the father as a male, Mr. Nouvelle developed the "negative" Oedipal complex, wherein a son identifies in a competitive manner with the mother as a female and takes the father as the object of his sexual lust and emotional yearnings, later on transferring this lust to all other men. The "negative" Oedipal complex leads inevitably, in both males and females, to either a frank homosexual orientation or, if repressed, to neurosis or psychosis, as exemplified by Mr. Nouvelle's case. (The "negative" Oedipal complex in the female occurs when the daughter takes her mother as her love object and competes in a masculine fashion with the father for her attention, and later on for that of all other women.)*

566        For example, during my time on 9-2-D, Dallas Grey's memories of Dr. Sweetheart were refreshed and reinforced, and with them Mr. Grey's confidence in himself. Although I never figured out what was going on in this man's mind, apparently something happened that helped him to live outside the hospital for the first time in many years, albeit for a limited time. When I think of Mr. Grey (who chose his own pseudonym by asking to be called Stella Dallas or Zane Grey), I think of a carved wooden box, the kind with a false bottom and a secret drawer that Yankee seamen made on long voyages. I asked myself if there were anything I could do to the outside of such a box – and that is all I had access to – that would influence the inside, but Dallas Grey very quietly suggested that I was asking too many questions. (Ibid., p. 195)

*Dallas Grey, otherwise known as Stella Dallas or Zane Grey, very definitely suffers from the "bearded lady" disease – schizophrenia.*

567          His writings conclude with thoughts of his mother, who was killed by her third husband, Williams's abusive stepfather.

His mother, he said, was his best friend.

'We made brownies together and we shared sandwiches we made,' he wrote. 'I walked in her shoes and she wore my hat and we laughed because we needed each other.'

... In saying his letter was on the way, Williams said: 'You can call it the writings of a madman.'  —"Serial Killer Tells Chilling Tale of Why He Stalked Victims," Rebecca Powers, Gannett News Service, The Marin Independent Journal, Marin County, California, June 19, 1992, p. A4.

*Williams, who has raped and killed numerous women, intuitively realizes he is insane – "You can call it the writings of a madman."*

*The American psychiatrist Harry Stack Sullivan once wrote: "From my material, in which negative instances are conspicuously absent, I am forced to the conclusion that schizophrenic illnesses in the male are intimately related as a sequent to unfortunate prolongation of the attachment of the son and the mother."*

*From the brief description given here of Williams's relationship with his mother, it can be seen that they had developed an extremely close, symbiotic bond, to the extent they would sometimes wear each other's clothing – he would walk in her shoes and she would wear his hat. Such activity constitutes a form of transvestism and implies a marked degree of sex-role alienation and confusion in both parties.*

*As a consequence of his symbiotic bond with his mother, Williams would have developed the characteristics of a "mama's boy," that is, of a basically effeminate and passive male who harbors a certain degree of animosity towards females. These characteristics would eventually lead to either an openly homosexual way of life or, if the homosexuality was repressed, to the development of schizophrenic symp-tomatology, as happened in this case.*

568    [Name Deleted], a diagnosed paranoid schizophrenic, is being held at the Montgomery County jail in Rockville, M.D.. Though he hasn't confessed, police say that during questioning he lapsed into voices – an infant, a woman and a man – who said to look for 'them' in New Jersey. Police combed his boyhood neighborhood of Warren, NJ, but found nothing.

    ... In 1989, [N.D.] was arrested for stealing purses from a church while dressed as a woman. He lived in his car in the church parking lot, less than 25 yards from where police found Laura Houghteling's bloody pillowcase, making a living from doing odd jobs. —"A Deadly Brother Act: 2 Vicious Crimes, Identical Horror," Gina Boubion, San Jose Mercury News, reprinted in the Marin Independent Journal, Marin County, California, Sunday ed., December 13, 1992, p. C7.

*The most obvious signs of the severe bisexual conflict which has driven Mr. [N.D.] insane, or schizophrenic, are the incidents where he spoke in a woman's voice and earlier had dressed in female clothing.*

569    There is this condiscending attitude in business that when you get emotionally and mentally raped, well 'you got screwed' and the accepted results is that the victim is now supposed to go to work at 7-11 or become homeless and the rapist is admired and envied as 'a winner.' I have always admired and tried to copy winners, but rape of any kind is deplorable and against the law. Remember the time when the same sneakering, laughing attitude was bestowed upon drunk

drivers, and the victim got no sympathy? Remember the time when the person raped physically did not dare to report it because of the humiliation and rediculue that the legal system put the [victim] thru. ... When you hire a consultant or an attorney you don't hire for the purpose of getting raped and then having all your efforts towards legal recourse totally thwarted by a corrupt legal system of 'esquires.' Esquires in the dark ages romed the countryside to steel from the working people and give to the prince. Do attorney want us to call them esquires because their allegiance is to the monarchy? — "Excerpts from Gunman's Letter," Gianluigi Ferri, <u>San Francisco Chronicle</u>, July 3, 1993, p. A12.

*Gianluigi Ferri, the author of the above proclamation, pushed to the breaking point by his extreme bisexual conflict, went on a murderous rampage in July of 1993 in San Francisco, killing eight people, including himself, and wounding six.*

*The targets of his outer rage were the employees of the law firm whom he, in his paranoid delusion, believed had "raped" him. The fact that the employees he slaughtered were both male and female illustrates the depth of his bisexual confusion and gender alienation.*

*It is obvious from this letter that Ferri unconsciously identifies himself as a female, one who has been "raped" repeatedly by strong males, i.e. the lawyers of the targeted firm. This complaint appears again and again in this rambling, delusional letter. Unconsciously, of course, he would very much like to be a woman being raped by a strong male, his paranoid schizophrenia being nothing more than a defense against such powerful, unconscious homosexual feelings.*

*When he writes that he "always admired and tried to copy winners," what he is saying is that he has attempted to identify with the strong male figures in his life, but in vain.*

*This effort failed because his unconscious identification as a female was so powerful that it overwhelmed his virile, heterosexual side.*

*Here again we have a tragic example of how the "bearded lady" disease can drive a person insane. In this instance Ferri's bisexual conflict resulted in a deadly episode of "running amok," the frequent consequence of such a paranoid-schizophrenic break with reality.*

570        My future wife is Julia Murray. Before I met her, I had heard about Julia. Julia was – can I say this? Julia had lost her mind for a while. O.K.? Like most transgendered people do. We all get confused, we lose our minds, we end up in hospitals. Julia had lost her mind. And when I was moving into Transie House, Julia was just coming home. We became very good friends. —Sylvia [Name Deleted], <u>New York Times Magazine</u>, June 27, 1999.

*In this short exposition by Sylvia [N.D.], herself a "transgendered" person, the root of mental illness is clearly laid bare, i.e., severe bisexual conflict and confusion. "We all get confused, we lose our minds, we end up in hospitals." This is what schizophrenia is all about, and nowhere has its cause been more clearly illustrated than in the above comments by Sylvia.*

571        Mr. Carlile is at pains to reconcile the many actual sexual anomalies in Hemingway's life, among them his mother's having tried to 'pass him off as a girl' for the first four years of his life, as Mr. Carlile puts it, 'keeping him in dresses and long curly hair and bonnets'; his penchant for switching sexual roles with his wives, and the double standard he held in his acceptance of lesbians and his hatred of male homosexuals. —Christopher Lehmann-Haupt (review of

Clancy Carlile's <u>The Paris Pilgrims</u>), "Books of the Times" section of <u>The New York Times</u>, July 7, 1999.

> *Ernest Hemingway was a victim of the "bearded lady" disease, as are, and have been, millions of others. His paranoid schizophrenia led to his death by suicide (the most serious symptom of schizophrenia) in 1961. From the above quotation, it is very easy to see why Mr. Hemingway developed sex-role alienation at a very early age, leading to severe bisexual conflict and confusion and consequently to his slowly developing madness following puberty.*

572        Responding to some of Hemingway's more extreme behavior near the end of 'The Paris Pilgrims,' Robert McAlmon, his friend and publisher, speculates that 'Hemingway might someday realize that the qualities he found so despicable, so unacceptable and hateful in other men, might be the very qualities he was trying to deny in himself.' The character McAlmon continues. 'But if Hemingway was to escape insanity or suicide, those repressed qualities would someday have to come out'… (Ibid.)

> *The "character McAlmon" in Clancy Carlile's <u>The Paris Pilgrims</u> is a most astute psychologist, unerringly fathoming the psycho-dynamics behind Hemingway's extreme mental turmoil. Furthermore, his brilliant analysis applies not only to Hemingway but to all mentally ill persons, in that the only way "to escape insanity or suicide, those repressed qualities would someday have to come out." This de-repression of the "repressed qualities" is the only way to "cure" the bearded lady disease, and can only be achieved through rigorous psycho-analysis or other depth-oriented psychotherapy.*

573       A man who fatally shot two people and wounded six others in 1980 outside a gay bar in Greenwich Village is seeking to be released from the maximum-security mental hospital where he has been held for 14 years.

      The man (name and age deleted) has admitted that he was suffering from paranoid delusions about homosexuals when he opened fire outside the Ramrod Bar. —The New York Times, news report, July 20, 1999.

      *Referring to quotation 572 further above, the analysis applied to the Ernest Hemingway case by "the character McAlmon," wherein McAlmon says that the homosexual qualities Hemingway found so "despicable, so unacceptable and hateful in other men, might be the very qualities he was trying to deny in himself," applies similarly to all such cases which lead to insanity, such as the one referred to in this news report.*

574       But political crises have turned into bouts of religious zeal in China before. The most notable was in the 1850's, when a failed Confucian scholar named Hong Xiuquan claimed to be the younger brother of Jesus and tried to build the Taiping Heavenly Kingdom in southern China. By the time Hong's enterprise was crushed by Government troops, his murderous Taiping Rebellion had cost millions of lives. (Author not noted.)

      *Here is but one of many unfortunate examples of the devastation the Bearded Lady disease has wrought upon mankind since the beginning of so-called "civilized" existence. Hong Xiuquan was obviously suffering from paranoid schizophrenia, caused by his severe bisexual conflict, and his mental illness resulted in "millions of lives" lost.*

575          At Harvard, Ted felt socially isolated by other students. He recalls that 'their speech, manners and dress were so much more 'cultured' than mine.' There was even greater unease in Ted's life; he suffered from what he calls 'acute sexual starvation.' Sexual references run throughout his book, and although he never ties them into a knot, one cannot help wondering if sexual frustration was his main despair. — Steven J. Dubner (in an article on Ted Kaczynski, the Unabomber), Time Magazine, October 18, 1999, p. 47.

*"Sexual frustration" is the "main despair" of all mentally ill persons, including Ted Kaczynski, a diagnosed paranoid schizophrenic. The "sexual starvation" is caused by the acute conflict between the homosexual and heterosexual drives, which basically cancel each other out, leading to a total blockage of sexual satisfaction, or orgasmic release. The toxic affect of all this undischarged libido is what provides the energy to fuel the actual symptoms of mental illness, such as auditory and visual hallucinations, mania and depression, feelings of persecution, etc., all symptoms of the "bearded lady" disease – schizophrenia.*

576          According to a psychiatric report compiled before his trial, Ted, while in graduate school at the University of Michigan, experienced several weeks of intense and persistent sexual excitement involving fantasies of being a female. During that time period, he became convinced that he should undergo sex-change surgery. (Ibid., p. 47)

*Mr. Kaczynski actually went so far as to schedule an appointment with a psychiatrist to discuss his wishes to be transformed into a woman, but cancelled the appointment at the last minute. It is obvious from his own words that Mr. Kaczynski was no longer able to repress his intense homosexual cravings and that they had now gained ascendency in their struggle with his heterosexual drives.*

*It is important to point out that it was not Mr. Kaczynski's sexual feelings per se which caused him to develop paranoid schizophrenia, but the denial, or repression, of these powerful urges. In and of themselves, they would cause no problems at all, but repressed, they literally drove him insane.*

577      I dreamt several times that my former nervous illness had returned; naturally I was as unhappy about this in the dream, as I felt happy on waking that it had only been a dream. Furthermore, one morning while still in bed (whether still half asleep or already awake I cannot remember), I had a feeling which, thinking about it later when fully awake, struck me as highly peculiar. It was the idea that it really must be rather pleasant to be a woman succumbing to intercourse. This idea was so foreign to my whole nature that I may say I would have rejected it with indignation if fully awake; from what I have experienced since I cannot exclude the possibility that some external influences were at work to implant this idea in me. —Memoirs of My Nervous Illness, Daniel Paul Schreber, Ibid., p. 63.

*In the above quotation, we see that the basic cause of Daniel Paul Schreber's mental illness has finally surfaced – namely, his intense bisexual conflict, with sex-role alienation. His rigid and punishing super ego has tried to keep this conflict repressed in the unconscious, but here it has finally broken through into consciousness where his ego will be forced to deal with it. Unfortunately his ego deals with it in the paranoid manner we can see developing here, when he writes that he "cannot exclude the possibility that some external influences were at work to implant this idea in me." In other words, the "paranoid shift" has begun to take place at this moment in his psyche, and he goes on to develop a full-blown case of paranoid schizophrenia as a result of not being able to admit that these sexual feelings are really products of his own desires and wishes, and not those of some "external" forces being thrust upon him.*

*As we have noted before, Sigmund Freud developed his theory of paranoia from this particular case and it is considered by many to be the most important psychiatric case ever studied, which of course it is. As Macalpine and Hunter said in their notes on the Schreber case, "Schreber's name is legion." Mr. Ted Kaczynski (the subject of Quotations 575 and 576, above) is just one of millions of Schreber's "legion," as is every person mentioned in* Schizophrenia: The Bearded Lady Disease, *be they male or female.*

578        Several were naked. Many were only partly dressed. Few had shoes, though the floor was puddled with urine and scattered with piles of men's feces. The men do not have their own clothes and each morning picked through stacks from the laundry. Unfortunately, the clothes were not carefully sorted, and one man ended up with women's black buckled shoes; a second wore a flowered blouse; the third had on a skirt. ... [name deleted], articulate man of 37, explained that he was schizophrenic, had been there three years and wanted desperately to leave. —"The Global Willowbrook," Michael Winerip, The New York Times Magazine, January 12, 2000, Section 6, p. 61.

*The above scene took place in the state mental hospital in Hidalgo, Mexico. Most noteworthy is the fact that three of the mental patients, afflicted with schizophrenia, chose women's clothing. This was not by accident, as the writer seems to infer, but was determined by the patients' basic sex-role alienation and resultant gender confusion, which is always to be found at the core of the schizophrenic illness, in both male and female, if one investigates deeply enough.*

579      Pol Pot was less comfortable and revealing in a larger arena, making few public appearances even when in power, obscuring his identity, changing residences and warning of treachery from every quarter. When he had a stomach ailment he said his cooks were trying to poison him. When the power at his residence failed, he had the maintenance workers killed.

This fear of treachery – by foreign nations or by poisonous 'microbes' within his own organization – motivated much of his behavior, from his secretiveness to the bloody purges that began to consume his revolution beginning in 1977.

Speaking to a party cadre in 1976, he said: 'We search for the microbes within the party without success; they are buried. As our socialist revolution advances, however, seeping into every corner of the party, the army and among the people, we can locate the ugly microbes.' —When the War was Over, Elizabeth Becker, Simon & Schuster, New York, 1986 (in an article by Seth Mydans, journalist and author, The New York Times, date not noted).

*The above description of Pol Pot – the murderous Cambodian Kymer Rouge leader who ruled Cambodia from 1975 to 1979, instituting a reign of terror which resulted in the deaths of approximately one quarter of his country's seven million citizens – is that of a man suffering from a textbook case of paranoid schizophrenia.*

*All the classic symptoms of this disease are present: the fulminating paranoid suspicions, the grandiose ambitions, and the murderous rage and retaliation when the goals set by these ambitions are thought to be threatened or thwarted in any way. Pol Pot is another Daniel Paul Schreber – "Schreber's name is legion" – a person afflicted with a severe case of paranoid psychosis (schizophrenia) caused by his severe unconscious bisexual conflict, the result of deep-seated sex role alienation and confusion. Pol Pot is but one more of the too numerous examples of the terrible tragedy and suffering that can be inflicted upon society by persons who have been driven insane by their "bearded lady" conflict.*

580     Since his childhood, the phrases used to describe him were uninspiring, polite, mediocre, soft spoken, patient, even shy. (Becker, Ibid.)

*This description of Pol Pot as a young man describes a male figure evidencing somewhat effeminate mannerisms.*

581     He was actually elegant, with a pleasing face, not handsome but attractive. His features were delicate and alert and his smile nearly endearing. At most he nodded his head slightly or flicked his dainty wrist for emphasis. (Becker, Ibid.)

*Again we see evidence of effeminate mannerisms in Pol Pot, bringing to mind the same opposite-sex qualities so often displayed by another madman and mass murderer, Adolph Hitler, a fellow paranoid schizophrenic.*

582     The interview, with Nate Thayer for the Far Eastern Economic Review, portrayed a man succumbing to age, bored and preoccupied with his aches and pains, but free of remorse. 'I came to carry out the struggle, not to kill people' he told his questioner. 'Even now, and you can look at me: Am I a savage person?' (Becker, Ibid.)

*This is an amazing and obviously insane statement made by a man who had just recently ordered one of his oldest friends and closest colleagues in the Kymer Rouge, Son Sen, assassinated, along with many of his relatives, including his grandchildren. Why? Because – insanely suspicious – he believed Son Sen was responsible for the Kymer Rouge's and his own loss of power in Cambodia.*

*The Soviet madman, Joseph Stalin, likewise had hundreds of his closest followers murdered because of his paranoid suspicions of them, not to mention millions of his fellow citizens. The "bearded lady" disease has caused the deaths of many millions of innocent people down through the ages, and this is why it is so urgently necessary to bring schizophrenia's actually quite simple genesis and mechanism into common knowledge, so the necessary steps can be taken to negate the disastrous effects of this horrendous scourge on mankind.*

583  It was, you'll recall, in November 1918 at the army hospital in Pasewalk that Hitler experienced some kind of transformative vision or hallucination. It was a life-changing moment of metamorphosis brought on by the news of the German army surrender – a surrender that, he makes clear in his own account of the moment in <u>Mein Kampf</u> and elsewhere, was accompanied by a simultaneous sickening sense that the November surrender was a betrayal, a sellout, a stab in the back. In that moment of utter collapse (personal and national), total despair, and then subsequent visionary (or hallucinatory) summons, Hitler conceived the mission and the myth that would bring him to power fifteen years later. —<u>Explaining Hitler: The Search for the Origins of His Evil</u>, Ron Rosenbaum, Random House, Inc., New York, 1998, p. 54.

*The "metamorphosis" that Hitler actually experienced at Pasewalk was an acute paranoid schizophrenic episode, or so-called psychotic break with reality, from which he never emerged. The madness of murderous hate and suspicion which consumed his life from this time forward was the direct result of this "metamorphosis," or schizophrenic breakdown, and the world paid dearly on account of it.*

584          In <u>Mein Kampf</u> he tells us he decided on his war against the Jews in November 1918, when, at the military hospital in Pasewalk, he learned, in rapid succession, of the naval mutiny at Kiel, the revolution that forced the abdication of the Emperor, and finally the armistice. 'Everything went black before my eyes,' he wrote. In the ensuing 'terrible days and even worse nights,' while he pondered the meaning of these cataclysmic events, 'my own fate become known to me.' It was then that he made his decision: 'There is no making pacts with the Jews; there can only be the hard: either – or. I, for my part, decided to go into politics.' (Ibid., p. 376)

*Hitler's schizophrenic breakdown was no different in form and content from that suffered by any other schizophrenic down through the ages. It was replete with hallucinations, delusions of grandeur and persecution, and overwhelming rage against the persecutor(s) along with vows of revenge. The tragedy in Hitler's case is that due to the historical and political currents of the time, this madman was able to get into a position of power where he could act out his crazed delusions, rather than being restrained in a mental hospital, where most other severely deranged schizophrenics end up.*

*Unfortunately, as we have seen from the history of the Cambodian dictator, Pol Pot (commented on briefly in the preceding quotations), Hitler was far from being the only madman who rose to a position of power in his society from which he could wreak savage destruction upon society. Joseph Stalin, certainly, should be added to this list, among many other lesser tyrants. "A tyrant is paranoid, cunning and ruthless," one observer has said, and these qualities always spring from paranoid schizophrenic illness. In short, all these monsters were afflicted with the "bearded lady" disease, and thus were as much victims of their own illness as the millions they destroyed, and were then themselves destroyed.*

585       The Hitler family doctor during the years when he was growing up in Linz was a Jew, Eduard Bloch. This is a dramatic enough fact in itself, and coupled with the fact that Block attended Hitler's mother, Klara, during her final illness, it has given rise to some particularly energetic flights of conjecture. Klara, to whom her son was devoted, died of breast cancer when he was eighteen: she suffered great pain, made worse by the application of idioform-soaked gauze. It has been suggested that Block bungled the treatment, or that even if he didn't Hitler assumed he had; either way, it is argued, Hitler was left traumatized, with a festering resentment against 'the Jew.' As against this theory, there are two undoubted facts. Hitler expressed warm gratitude to Bloch at the time (and made him a present of one of his watercolors); more telling still, after the Nazi takeover of Austria in 1938, he gave him special permission to leave the country. Needless to say, for those who subscribe to the theory this simply means that Hitler's hatred of Bloch was buried deep in his unconscious – and all the more virulent in consequence. Most of us, however, would probably prefer to reserve judgement. ––Explaining Hitler: The Search for the Origins of His Evil, Ron Rosenbaum, Random House, Inc., New York, 1998 (in "A Nice Pleasant Youth," John Gross, The New York Review of Books, December 17, 1998, pp. 12-17).

*In reading Ron Rosenbaum's next to last sentence in the above quotation, we find the clue to Hitler's madness. All that is required is the substitution of the word "love" for "hatred" and the genesis of Hitler's paranoid schizophrenia becomes clear. The sentence then reads: "...for those who subscribe to the theory this simply means that Hitler's <u>love</u> of*

*Bloch was buried deep in his unconscious – and all the more virulent in consequence."*

*As Sigmund Freud so brilliantly demonstrated in his famous case of Daniel Paul Schreber <u>Psycho-Analytic Notes on an Autobiographical Account of a Case of Paranoia (Dementia Paranoides)</u>, in every case of paranoia the underlying factor is invariably the denial, or repression of, homosexual love for the person who later becomes the persecutor. The formula is: "I love him (or her)." Then comes the denial – "No, I don't love him (or her), I hate him (or her)." And then finally – "No, I don't hate him (or her); he (or she) hates me and persecutes me, therefore I have to defend myself against that person even to the point of killing him (or her)."*

*In Hitler's case, his deep affection and respect for his childhood physician had a strong element of homosexual love in it, which Hitler violently repressed and disavowed, yet which came back to torment him – the return of the repressed. This is what caused his schizophrenic collapse at the age of twenty-eight when he was in the army hospital at Pasewalk suffering from the effects of mustard gas.*

*Unable to assign the persecutory blame directly on Dr. Bloch, following his "recovery" from his psychotic, or schizophrenic break at Pasewalk, this hatred was displaced on <u>all</u> the Jews. He retained enough "reason" in his paranoid mind that consciously he was unable to think of Bloch, himself, as a persecutor, unlike the case of Daniel Paul Schreber, where Schreber's doctor, Professor Daniel Flechsig, did become the main persecutor in his delusional mind. Hitler, after all, was never so out of control that he had to be locked up in a mental asylum, as was Schreber, because he was able to retain somewhat more of his sanity after his schizophrenic break. Hitler remained "sane" enough to consciously know that Bloch meant him no harm, but was paranoid enough from his repressed homosexual feelings toward Bloch to extend his*

*paranoia to all other Jews, against whom he then proceeded
to defend himself by killing off as many as he could. This was
"displacement" in its extreme. Actually, the fact he did not
have Bloch killed proves the existence of his powerful feelings
of love for him, which in his "crazed mind" he was fortunately
unable to turn into feelings of persecution per se. But in this
particular case of paranoid schizophrenia, Bloch's good
fortune became the terrible misfortune of all other Jews.*

586          What struck Binion most forcefully in listening to the
recordings was how often Hitler articulated his hated (sic) of
Jews as hatred of 'the Jew.' 'It's so strange, in the first years
he's inevitably using the singular – 'the Jew.' I just felt there
had to be a Jew. Now, at first I thought maybe it was the guy
who invented poison gas because Hitler was gassed. Then I
saw a Getrud Kurth,' the analyst who'd worked on the OSS
profile of Hitler for FDR. 'Wonderful woman. She had written
an article called 'The Jew and Adolph Hitler.' … saying just as
I did that 'the Jew' was a person, and look, here's this guy [Dr.
Bloch] who treated his mother and [Hitler] didn't know what
was involved in the treatment, but obviously patients always
blame the doctor unconsciously when something goes wrong.
And Hitler sent Bloch loving postcards afterwards with 'yours
gratefully, Adolph,' and he became the protector of Dr. Bloch
after the 1938 Anschluss.'
          The peculiar relationship between Hitler and the
Jewish doctor intrigued Binion. 'I thought, this is something
worth investigating,' he told me.   —Explaining Hitler: The
Search for the Origins of His Evil, Ron Rosenbaum, Random
House, Inc., New York, 1998, p. 242.

*Historian and professor Rudolph Binion is certainly
correct in his assumption that it is "worth investigating" the
relationship between Hitler and Dr. Bloch, since Bloch played
such an important role in the young Hitler's life, both*

*emotionally and physically – the latter through his continuing intimate physical examinations of Hitler as he was growing up. The fact that Hitler's later schizophrenic delusions of persecution and paranoid rage were directed against "the Jew," proves there really was one single Jewish person at the center of his pathological fantasies, just as in Freud's Schreber case, there was one single male figure at the center of Schreber's delusional system – also his physician, Professor Paul Emil Flechsig.*

*Binion and others have concluded that although Hitler expressed exceedingly fond feelings for Bloch, unconsciously he hated him because he was unable to save his beloved mother from the horrors of an agonizing death from breast cancer, and thus later displaced this hatred onto all Jews. The only problem with this explanation is that paranoid schizophrenic symptoms are invariably caused by the repression into the unconscious of very powerful homosexual feelings, in Hitler's case it being his homosexual feelings for his beloved father figure and early "seducer" – Dr. Bloch.*

587         The epigraph opening the article is a quotation from Nazi Party ideologist Gregor Strasser attacking the attempt by parties on the left to abolish the Weimar Constitution's famous paragraph 175, the clause that made homosexual acts serious crimes. 'But,' the article begins, 'every knowledgeable person knows, especially Gregor Strasser, that inside the Hitler party the most flagrant whorishness contemplated by paragraph 175 is widespread.'

'Now,' they continue, 'Hitler is making Roehm [who'd spent several years in semiofficial exile in Bolivia to let previous homosexual scandals die down] his chief commander, [which] is like trusting the cat to guard the cream.' The Munich Post is *not*, it goes to great length to make clear, condemning homosexuality but rather 'the disgusting *hypocrisy* that the Nazi Party demonstrates outward moral indignation while inside its own ranks the most shameless practices ... prevail.' (Ibid., p. 46)

*Ernst Roehm was one of Hitler's closest comrades and a trusted leader in the Nazi Party, despite widespread knowledge of his flagrant homosexuality. Hitler was eventually reluctantly forced to order the assassination of his old friend, partly to appease the German military establishment, whose backing Hitler eagerly sought in his rise to power. Roehm and many other disgraced party stalwarts were arrested and murdered during the so-called "Night of the Long Knives," all on Hitler's direct orders.*

*Hitler's own sexual orientation has often been called into question by historians, psychologists and ordinary observers and students of that era. The fact he never had children and did not marry until the final moments of his life, his effeminate bearing, voice and gestures as well as his exceedingly emotional – almost hysterical – style of speaking, all lend credence to this view. That he deeply repressed his homosexuality, thus causing his paranoid schizophrenic breakdown at the age of twenty-eight, from which he never recovered, fully supports the truth of the above observations.*

*Hitler was another of Schreber's legions, driven insane by his severe bisexual conflict and gender confusion. If only he had been able to acknowledge his homosexuality at an early age and integrate these feelings into his psyche, without repression, the world in all likelihood would have been spared the Holocaust. "No Hitler, no Holocaust," as had been said by some, correctly so. For it obviously took a madman to create the Holocaust, in conjunction with a "favorable" political climate, plus the crucial fact that the person at the pathological core of Hitler's paranoid illness was a Jew, his once dearly beloved – and later violently repudiated – Dr. Eduard Bloch.*

588          'I have never seen a boy so ineffably saddened,' Bloch would say later. Adolph's suffering was intense. And transformative, Binion believes: 'Hitler's experience of his mother's last illness,' Binion concludes, 'looms behind his later tireless diatribes against 'the Jewish cancer,' the 'Jewish poison,' the 'Jewish profiteer.' '

He cites examples from Hitler's rhetoric of the spectral presence of his mother's medical trauma: 'How many diseases have their origin in the Jewish virus! ... [The Jews are] poisonous abscesses eating into the nation, ... an endless stream of poison ... being driven by a mysterious power into the outermost blood vessels' of the body politic.

Binion deals with the obvious objection to this theory – Hitler's profusions of gratefulness to Bloch at the time, the singular protection he extended to Bloch when he absorbed Austria in 1938, the 'undying gratitude' Bloch himself later described as Hitler's attitude toward him – by insisting that 'consciously Hitler bore Bloch no grudges' because he was both traumatized *and* knew himself to be implicated in the 'order to burn out the abscesses ... to the raw flesh' of his mother. (Ibid., pp. 244-245)

*Proof of the fact Hitler's paranoid delusions about the Jewish people can be traced back to Dr. Bloch are his use of the terms "the Jewish cancer" (his unconscious reference to Dr. Bloch and his mother's cancer treatment), the "Jewish poison," the "Jewish virus." Professor Binion is certainly correct on this score, but he has drawn the wrong conclusion from it. It was not Hitler's unconscious <u>hate</u> for Dr. Bloch that drove him insane, but his profound feeling of <u>love</u> for him, tinged with very powerful homosexual feelings. That "endless stream of poison ... being driven by a mysterious power into the outermost blood vessels" of the German nation, is nothing more than Hitler's own repressed homosexual feelings for his beloved Dr. Bloch. The similarity between the Hitler case and*

*Freud's Schreber case is striking, both men becoming insane over their strongly repressed homosexual feelings for their physician. Paul Emil Flechsig and Eduard Bloch were unknowingly the direct cause of the madness which overtook their patients.*

*"There are more things in heaven and earth, Horatio, than are dreamed of in your philosophy."*

589      The fear of his father's imagined castration threat because of the Oedipus complex added to anxiety, as did identification with his mother while she was also perceived as a phallic castrating figure. All these converged in an unconscious acceptance of an image of himself as castrated and also resulted in the feminine passive inclinations which he disavowed so disastrously. (Ibid., p. 145)

*Here the psychoanalyst Norbert Bromberg gives the psychoanalytic interpretation of the reasons for Hitler's strong, passive, feminine inclinations, the complete disavowal of which eventually led to his psychotic break at Pasewalk and his ensuing madness. Hitler's later constant refrain that Germany had been "stabbed in the back" by the Jews and his use of the phrase the "endless stream of poison ... being driven by a mysterious power into the outermost blood vessels" of the German nation point symbolically to repressed, passive homosexual, anal erotic longings, lending credence to Freud's dictum that what man represses at the deepest level are his pederastic instincts. Hitler reportedly enjoyed having chamomile enemas administered to him – evidence of his passive, feminine, anal erotic nature. In the above references, Hitler was really speaking of himself, and not Germany. It was he who had been "stabbed in the back" and the "endless stream of poison" which was "being driven by a mysterious power into the outermost blood vessels" of the German nation represents his own passive homosexual longings and wishes.*

590          At the end of the interview as we were leaving, Bloch
made a point of telling us 'what a nice pleasant youth' Hitler
was. More than fifty years later, Dr. Kurth can't get over this.
'Outside in the street, Langer and I laughed and laughed at that
– bitter laughter,' she told me, shaking her head.
          It is not that she disputes the possibility that Hitler was
'a nice pleasant youth.' That has always been the crux of the
problem for Hitler explainers – how and why a youth who was
remembered by many as pleasant, at least gentle and harmless
seeming, could turn into a blood thirsty mass killer. It was,
rather, she says, Bloch's insistence on clinging to, selectively
emphasizing, in 1943, the nice gentle aspect which provoked
the bitter laughter. (Ibid., pp. 147-148)

          *The reason Hitler changed from being a "pleasant, at
least gentle and harmless seeming" young man into a "blood-
thirsty mass killer" can be blamed squarely upon the paranoid
schizophrenic break he suffered when he was twenty-eight
years old, while being treated in the army hospital at
Pasewalk, in Pomerania. The vast paranoid delusional system
of persecution and consequent rage which overcame him at
this time remained with him for the rest of his life, with dire
consequences for millions of his fellow human beings.*

591          Still, she had no doubt whatever about the truth of
Bloch's answer to the question Langer put to him about
Hitler's genital normality. He examined Hitler as a youth,
Bloch said, and found that, in fact, there was no genital defect
or testicular deficit. 'Langer asked him whether the
examination included the genitals,' she recalls, 'and he said
'absolutely, they were completely normal'.'
          In which case, bitter laughter might indeed be in order
now, considering all the elaborate theorizing psychoanalysts
and others have erected on the shaky foundation that Hitler
was monorchid, all that cogitating about the probing fingers of

his mother Klara, anxiously searching for the missing testicle in the child Hitler, thus disturbing forever his sexuality and paving the way of his murderous political pathology. (Ibid., p 148)

*It was not the "probing fingers of his mother Klara" which resulted in "disturbing forever his sexuality and paving the way for his murderous political pathology," but the "probing fingers" of young Hitler's family physician, the good Dr. Bloch, occurring during his possibly unclothed routine physical examinations of his "nice pleasant" patient. There can be no doubt that Hitler had formed a strong transference to Bloch as a benign father figure (in contrast to his relationship with his own, often violent and punitive, real father), and that he had developed a love for Dr. Bloch which would have been "normal" under the circumstances. The fact this love contained more than the usual amount of homosexual feeling can be attributed directly to his own extremely close ties to his mother and the disturbed relationship with his father, as well as to the extremely intimate physical examinations by Dr. Bloch. In short, Hitler was a "mama's boy," exceedingly vulnerable to these kinds of homosexual feelings for his physician. Unfortunately, these feelings were deeply repressed by Hitler but came back with a vengeance to terrorize him when he was twenty-eight – "the return of the repressed" – and were the direct cause of his schizophrenic collapse at Pasewalk, as they are in all cases of schizophrenia.*

*It has been said that "Schreber's name is legion," referring to Daniel Paul Schreber, in the famous case wherein Freud developed his brilliant theory of paranoid schizophrenia. Hitler is just another one of the multitude of Schreber's legions, but unfortunately in his case, due to being born in the wrong place at the wrong time, his ensuing madness had terrible repercussions for the world at large.*

592         Question 27: Where was the press conference held at which Nixon said, 'I am not a crook.'? Why did Nixon afterwards slap a bystander?

Answer: The press conference was held at Walt Disney World. On leaving the site, Nixon approached a man and boy standing outside the auditorium and asked the man if he was the boy's mother or his grandmother. When the man replied that he was neither, Nixon slapped the man's face, said 'Of course you're not,' and walked off. —"Watergate: The Quiz," W.S. Moorhead, The Washington Post National Weekly Edition, August 14-20, 1989, p. 12.

*It is well known that many persons close to Richard Nixon during the time he was caught up in the Watergate scandal and in the days immediately preceding his resignation from office were acutely worried about his mental stability. It was reported he walked the halls of the White House late at night conversing with the portraits of former presidents and was exhibiting many other symptoms of being in the midst of a schizophrenic breakdown. More specifically, he was suffering from paranoid schizophrenia, the "bearded lady" disease, as his encounter, quoted above, with the man and his son outside Disney World clearly demonstrates.*

*In asking the man if he was a woman, Nixon was projecting on to him his own unconscious bisexual conflict and confusion as to which sex he himself belonged to. The question itself and the following slap to the bewildered man's face was obviously the act of a "madman," which Nixon was at the time. His paranoia had been commented upon by many observers during his career and, as is invariably the case, it had its roots in unconscious bisexual conflict and gender confusion.*

593         The devil being hunted in three new books is Andrei Chikatilo, who killed some 50 women, boys and girls in

Russia in the 1970's and 80's. He stabbed them, cut off or cut out their genitals, sometimes eviscerated them, and reached sexual climax in the course of these acts. —Julian Symons (book review, title and author not noted) <u>The New York Times Book Review</u>, March 14, 1993, p. 6.

*Mr. Chikatilo is obviously insane, afflicted with schizophrenia, the "bearded lady" disease.*

594     Andrei Chikatilo was a colorless figure, a vulnerable backward child who had later done his time in the army, then worked in physical education, taught Russian language and literature in a vocational school and eventually became a supply clerk in a huge industrial complex. In all these occupations he was inefficient, unsuccessful. He was married with two children, but, as his wife said, sexually inadequate, capable of ejaculation but not erection. He obtained true satisfaction only by stabbing, biting, evisceration, occasional cannibalism. (Ibid., p. 6)

*Mr. Chikatilo's severe bisexual conflict and gender confusion kept him from performing in a normal heterosexual manner with his wife.*

595     To a certain extent he was the invisible man, the average Soviet citizen, a Communist Party member who listened to the radio, watched television, believed what he was told. He was an apparently faithful husband, a good father and grandfather, affectionate to his grandchildren. Many of his victims were picked up at Rostov railway or bus stations. (Ibid., p. 6)

*Beneath the façade of this "average Soviet citizen" lurked a raving maniac, a man driven mad by his repressed bisexual cravings and his frustrated desire to be a woman.*

596        At his trial the prisoner, who was placed in an iron cage in the Rostov courthouse, behaved at times like a madman. He suggested the judge would like to have sex with him, said he was a woman about to give birth, dropped his trousers to reveal his genitals, asked for a Ukranian lawyer. It is likely that he was hoping to persuade psychiatrists that he was insane. (Ibid., p. 7)

*Any psychiatrist who would not believe that this murderous man was insane would have to be insane himself! In the insightful words of Daniel Paul Schreber, Freud's famous paranoid schizophrenic, "I would like to meet the man who, faced with the choice of either being a demented human being in male habitus, or a spirited woman, would not prefer the latter." If Andrei Chikatilo had been able, like Schreber, to consciously accept his urges to be a female and play the passive feminine role in sexual intercourse with another male, he would have been spared his terrible paranoid schizophrenic insanity, and his murderous psychotic spree undoubtedly would never have taken place. Schreber, as Sigmund Freud pointed out in his famous study of the case, regained partial sanity after he was finally able, after many years of the most severe psychosis, to consciously accept his passive feminine homosexual urges, although still not accepting full responsibility for these ego-dystonic feelings. Instead, he attributed them to God's plan for him to establish a new species of human beings on the earth.*

597        OCEANSIDE – The profile emerging of the Wisconsin drifter jailed in connection with the weekend slashing death of a 9-year old Northern California boy is one of a clean-cut, but troubled man.

[Name Deleted], 20, faces an arraignment today on charges he killed Matthew Cecchi of Oroville while in a public restroom at Oceanside harbor as the boy's aunt waited for him outside the door. Police said [N.D.] confessed to the killing when he was arrested Monday in Hollywood for stabbing and trying to rob a woman on her way to work.

As word reached {N.D.'s] hometown of St. Coix Falls, just outside Minneapolis, that he was suspected in the murder, friends and neighbors expressed concern and disbelief. Andy Jepson attended Unity High School in Balsam Lake, Wisconsin, with [N.D.] and said his friend was interested in alternative religions and occasionally came to school dressed in women's clothing.

'That's just the way he was,' said Jepson, a senior. 'He acted different.'   —Associated Press, Marin Independent Journal, Marin County, California (date not noted).

*[Name Deleted] was afflicted with paranoid schizophrenia, the "bearded lady" disease, as can be seen from his friend's comment that he occasionally came to school dressed in women's clothing and "He acted different." The reason he acted "different" was because he was already in the grip of schizophrenia. In the two years before the horrendous murder reported above, [N.D.] had spent time aimlessly touring the country by Greyhound bus, during which period his mental illness grew more and more intense until finally, he stated, he was hearing voices (auditory hallucinations) instructing him to kill someone. This is yet another tragic example of how severe bisexual conflict and gender confusion leads to paranoid schizophrenia, with its often horrifying and tragic consequences.*

598         After the suicide of his wife, Nadezdha, in 1932, Stalin led a bizarre and lonely life, up most of the night with his collection of frightened Politburo colleagues. He forced them to sit through repeated movies and long drunken dinners, and even to dance with one another while he watched.  —Steven

Erlanger, The New York Times, 1995 (month and day not noted), p. 44.

*There was obviously a very strong homosexual element in these all-male parties which Stalin orchestrated between himself and his "frightened Politburo colleagues." Actually, "terrified" would probably be a better word to describe the feelings of his captive audience whose members never knew from one minute to the next when his raging paranoia would fixate on one or another of them, with usually fatal consequences.*

*Over a period of time, Stalin would become unconsciously enamored homosexually with a member of this inner circle. The "paranoid shift" would then become operative, i.e., "I love him – no, I don't love him; I hate him – no, I don't hate him; he hates me and is trying to destroy me, so I have to kill him first." And of course this is what Stalin did, many, many times. His fulminating paranoid schizophrenia resulted not only in the destruction of many of his closest colleagues, but also of millions of other innocent human beings, caught up in his pathological delusions of persecution and megalomania, all products of his "bearded lady" disease.*

599          Members of the dictator's entourage were always at risk. On Stalin's orders, the wife of Mikhail Kalinin was arrested and tortured while her husband continued to serve as the country's titular president. The wives of foreign minister, Vyacheslav Molotov, and of Stalin's personal secretary, Alexander Poskrebyshev, were also imprisoned. —Patricia Blake, Time Magazine, June 26, 1989, p. 83.

*Not only were Stalin's men friends always in deadly peril due to his paranoid schizophrenia, fueled by his repressed homosexuality, but also were the wives of these men. Why? The only answer can be – simple jealousy. Stalin was jealous that the men he loved had wives that they loved. If he could get rid of the wives, then it would lessen the competition. These particular "boyfriends" were married and loved their wives, when he wanted them to love only him, as he loved them. These feelings were, of course, deeply repressed and were an integral part of his paranoid schizophrenia.*

600    After World War II the Soviet government undertook a propaganda campaign to entice Russian emigres in the West to return home. Thousands accepted the offer of Soviet citizenship and the chance to help rebuild their devastated motherland. In return for their devotion, most were summarily executed or imprisoned, victims of either Stalin's paranoia – he thought they must be imperialist spies – or of a state that reserved some of its greatest cruelties for those who trusted and believed in it. —A.O. Scott, "Film Review," The New York Times, April 7, 2000.

*This is just one of many examples of the terrible destruction wreaked upon innocent people by Stalin's paranoid schizophrenic delusions. He was a man driven mad by the bearded lady disease, and the world suffered greatly for it, just as it has done with Hitler, Mao, Pol Pot, and countless other madmen down through the ages, and unfortunately most likely will in the future as well.*

601    The cultural revolution was started for precisely that reason. The aging Mao saw plunging knives in every shadow. Old comrades, who had long ago become terrified sycophants, were still seen as threats. The smallest criticisms that had been made against Mao years before were still brooded over and became in his paranoid mind clear signs of simmering rebellion. That is why he decided, in 1966, to incite millions of frustrated teenagers to pounce on their teachers, fathers,

mothers, and finally even the top party leaders, apart from Mao himself, a handful of useful courtiers, and the coterie of extremists around Jiang Quing, Mao's detested wife.

In May, 1966, the <u>People's Party</u> announced that Mao was 'the source of our life' and whoever dared to oppose him 'shall be hunted down and obliterated.' A frenzied murder spree in every Chinese city was followed by extensive purges inside the party, orchestrated, as always, by the expert in these matters, Kang Sheng.[11]  —"Divine Killer," Ian Buruma (a review of <u>Mao: A Life</u> by Philip Short, and <u>Mao Zedung</u> by Jonathan Spence), <u>New York Review of Books</u>, February 24, 2000, p. 24.

*Here is but one more example of how a world leader, afflicted with paranoid schizophrenia – the "bearded lady" disease – inflicted untold death and suffering on millions of his own people. The comparison between Mao and Stalin is remarkable, especially the fact that Mao's "old comrades" had become "terrified sycophants," and that many were destroyed due to his paranoid suspiciousness, as had been the case with Stalin's own inner circle.*

602    Mao's China, then, like Hitler's Reich, was to be a <u>Gesamtkunstwerk</u> of one man's crazed imagination. In 1959, a year after he made this statement, Mao embarked on his Great Leap Forward, one of the most fatal schemes (in sheer numbers, <u>the</u> most fatal) cooked up in the twentieth century. The idea that China, by having everyone melt down pots and pans in their courtyards and conduct bizarre agricultural experiments cribbed from Stalin's ideological scientists, would catch up with Britain in a few years was pure fantasy. But up to 30 million people died as a result. (Ibid., p. 23)

*Mao's Great Leap Forward was a direct product of his grandiose and megalomaniac delusions engendered by his paranoid schizophrenia. They were totally divorced from reality and consequently caused enormous human and material damage when put into practice.*

603 Spence puts all this lunacy down to Mao's wholesale divorce from reality. No one could or would tell him the truth about anything anymore. (Ibid., p. 24)

*"Lunacy" is just another word for paranoid schizophrenia. Lunacy, madness, insanity, craziness all add up to the same thing – and Mao was a classic case of a man afflicted with the "bearded lady" disease, otherwise known as paranoid schizophrenia.*

604 Hitler and Mao both suffered from 'neurasthenia,' an affliction that is no longer fashionable but was apparently so prevalent in Mao's entourage that his doctor called it the 'Communist disease.' The main symptoms are insomnia, headaches, dizzy spells, and impotence. Mao's potency, so his doctor informed us, was much affected by his political fortunes. Things went well when Mao felt on top of things, but any threat, real or imagined, to his absolute grip on power and the chairman wilted, no matter how many girls shared his bed. Such psychosomatic problems are perhaps the price people pay for living in a state of permanent anxiety of being knifed in the back, either by courtiers or, in the case of the courtiers, by the tyrant himself. (Ibid., p. 20)

*Mao's "impotence" was caused by his severe bisexual conflict, the root of his paranoia, as is invariably the case.*

605 More interesting is the question of what drives certain people, sometimes, it seems, quite unremarkable people, to become the killers of millions. Is it just a peculiar set of circumstances? Is it an axiomatic matter of absolute power

always leading to moral anesthesia? Or were such people as Mao, Himmler, Pol Pot, Hitler, and Stalin not in fact mediocre at all, but evil geniuses who grabbed the chance to do their worst? (Ibid., p. 20)

*The above-mentioned persons were not "evil geniuses." They were all individuals afflicted with paranoid schizophrenia, and their "evil" deeds were the direct product of their madness.*

606     For in the end, or perhaps from the very beginning, there was but one overriding concern, in aid of which all policies, principles, and artistic visions were twisted and turned, and that was Mao's own power, his need for total control, his pathological fear of impotence. (Ibid., p. 24)

*Mao's "pathological fear of impotence" was exactly that – his pathological fear of the powerful homosexual impulses he had deeply repressed, and which had consequently driven him mad, due to the toxic affect of the accompanying undischarged libido.*

607     An admirer when he first joined 'Group One' (the code name for Mao's personal staff), Li grew progressively more disillusioned, not just with Mao but with the party and the regime. In part, he was repelled by Mao's personal conduct, particularly his penchant for sex with an endless succession of young women, sometimes two or three at a time. Wang Dongxing, Mao's chief of security, speculated to Li that Mao's compulsive sexual adventures reflected a fear of death. But Li was also dismayed by Mao's politics and policies.
        Imagining enemies everywhere, Mao vindictively persecuted many of his most loyal followers. His grandiose schemes for revolutionizing China led to economic, social and moral disaster.  —The Private Life of Chairman Mao, Dr. Li

Zhisui, edited by Anne F. Thurston, translated by Tai Hung, Random House, New York, 1994 (as reviewed by Arnold R. Isaacs in <u>San Francisco Book Review</u>, date and page not noted.)

*Mao's "compulsive sexual adventures" reflected not "a fear of death," but a fear of his own unconscious homosexual cravings. In Psychoanalytic terms, Mao suffered from the "Don Juan syndrome," – a.k.a. satyriasis – which invariably is a defense against repressed, unconscious homosexual wishes. (The same holds true for nymphomania in females.)*

*The close tie between Mao's compulsive sexuality and his paranoid schizophrenia is self-evident. The reviewer, Arnold R. Isaacs, writes that "Imagining enemies everywhere, Mao vindictively persecuted many of his most loyal followers." As history shows, Stalin's and Pol Pot's own paranoid schizophrenia caused them to treat their own "loyal followers" in exactly the same murderous fashion.*

*Furthermore, Isaacs writes that Mao's "grandiose schemes for revolutionizing China led to economic, social and moral disaster." Again, the similarities in actions and results between Mao, Stalin, and Pol Pot are glaringly evident. Schizophrenia, the "bearded lady disease," has caused untold disaster to the world, and will continue to do so until its cause, severe bisexual conflict and confusion in the individual, is recognized for what it is and treated accordingly.*

608   For myself, I wish now that in covering China, South Africa under apartheid, the Soviet Union and wars in Afghanistan and the former Yugoslavia, among other places – scars, all, on the conscience of the 20th century – I had made further allowance for, or understood better, the role of wounded psyches in producing the Maos, Stalins, Vorsters, Najibullahs, Karadzics and Arkans I wrote about along the way. —John F. Burns (review of <u>Mao: A Life</u> by Phillip Short, and <u>Mao</u>

Zedong by Jonathan Spence), <u>The New York Times Book Review</u>, February 6, 2000, p. 6.

*It is greatly hoped that <u>Schizophrenia: The Bearded Lady Disease</u> will provide the reader with the insight and ability to "understand better" the "wounded psyches" of the 20<sup>th</sup> and 21<sup>st</sup> Centuries (and of all centuries) which have had such a devastating impact on the world around them. That, simply, is the purpose of this compendium - to shed light on exactly what caused these psyches, and millions of others like them, to be so grievously wounded, with such horrendous results.*

609     It was a memorable scene in downtown Fairfax Saturday. Mark, a macho cowboy type from West Marin, sat at the Parkade enjoying his morning cup of coffee. A colorfully dressed man with multiple tattoos, a shaved head and three rings in one of his eyebrows approached and asked for help.
'Excuse me,' the man politely started. 'I have done so many bad things in my life that I'm afraid my karma is going to catch up to me and I'll die a violent death in the near future.'
Mark took a big swig of coffee and then asked in a deep voice, 'Is that all?'
'No. Lately, I have been having female tendencies, especially in the way I like to dress. I think that you may have the answer,' the man pleaded.
Mark looked thoughtful for a moment and turned to the man. 'Yes, I do have the answer,' he said. 'I think you should cross-dress for a week – and then blow yourself away.'     —
"Code of the Zen West," Alex Horvath, the <u>Pacific Sun</u>, Marin County, California, Sept. 14-20, 1994.

*The "colorfully dressed man" who approached Mark in the coffee shop is obviously suffering from schizophrenia, caused by his severe bisexual conflict and gender confusion.*

*And the fact he stated he was afraid he would "die a violent death in the near future" points very strongly to suicidal ideation, which is always the outcome most to be feared in schizophrenia.*

*This unfortunate schizophrenic male appears homosexually drawn to Mark, whom he says "may have the answer." What he really seems to be implying is that if Mark would love him as he would a woman, then all his homosexual desires could be gratified and he would find happiness and regain his mental equilibrium.*

*Unfortunately, Mark's rather unenlightened advice to "blow yourself away" only reinforces the man's strong suicidal bent. (It would be interesting to know the final outcome stemming from this brief and rather tragic encounter.)*

610     He later re-enacted Slavik's final terror for his ex-roommate Gale Croxell.

'He came over to my house before the cops got him and said he'd killed these chicks, and at first I couldn't believe it,' Croxell remembered. 'So he lay down on the ground to show me how he did Linda Slavik, and in a woman's high voice, said, 'Don't do it, don't do it.' And then he said, 'Once you've killed, you can always kill again.'   —Kevin Fagan (in an article on Darrell Rich), <u>San Francisco Chronicle</u>, March 13, 2000.

*Darrell Rich was executed at San Quentin prison on March 15, 2000, for the rape and murder of Linda Slavik and several other young women. The fact he would lay on the floor and imitate Linda Slavik's voice in describing how she pleaded with him before he murdered her shows a strong unconscious female identification on his part, demonstrating, as always, the severe bisexual conflict and confusion at the root of his schizophrenic illness.*

611    As a boy Rich's parents 'fought constantly and he had few friends,' his lawyers argued in the trial. They divorced when he was 15 and he stayed with his 'domineering' mother, who ran an in-home day care center.

'His academic performance deteriorated … he was suspended for fighting, and was sometimes truant,' the court transcripts read. At age 17, he became so depressed 'he went hunting and shot himself in the chest in what was possibly an attempted suicide.' By age 19 he was doing time in the California Youth Authority for attacking someone with a tire iron after drinking. (Ibid.)

*The so-called "domineering mother" and an absent or else passive, ineffectual father form the classic psycho-analytic parental model which can produce either homosexual or schizophrenic children, the homosexual and schizophrenic being the opposite sides of the same coin, so to speak.*

*The fact Mr. Rich shot himself in the chest at 17, in what was obviously a suicide attempt, bespeaks the malignant depression which assails all schizophrenics and which leads so often to their self destruction. And by boasting of his murderous deeds to his friends, Mr. Rich was in reality committing suicide, knowing in all probability he would be denounced to the authorities, arrested, convicted, sentenced to death and executed.*

612    Then in 1977 his wife left him and moved out of the state after he hit her several times, investigators said. A year later, at the age of 23, Rich began his summer of raping and killing.

'Sure, he was a hard-ass, a real fighter if you messed with his bike or got him mad, but in a million years I would never have thought he would do what he did to those women,' said Gale Croxell, who worked with Rich and roomed with him until shortly before his arrest. 'He played on our company softball team. He liked to go drinking and riding his bike, like most other guys around here. He didn't stand out.' (Ibid.)

*Mr. Rich's unconscious bisexual conflict became increasingly severe as time went on, until it caused him to have a psychotic – or schizophrenic – break with reality, leading directly to his murderous rampage. In other words, he "ran amok," and running amok in any culture is invariably the direct result of severe bisexual conflict and confusion in the individual which, finally becoming unbearable, triggers a psychotic rage with all its attendant destruction, either suicidal or homicidal.*

613　Rich's attorneys argued he suffered from 'explosive disorder and major depression.' And they noted that after his arrest, he said in bewilderment that 'he didn't understand how he could have done what he did.' Prosecutors and investigators countered that the mental defense was overblown. He was just a normal country boy who went inexplicably sour, they said.

'I've been a detective 30 years, and I knew Darrell from the time he was a little boy, but I never saw anything as horrible as the things he did,' said Shasta County Sheriff's Lt. Bradd McDannold, who helped track down the killer. 'If I had an answer to why he went so bad, I'd be a very wealthy individual.'

'Some things you just can't explain.' He said sadly. (Ibid.)

*The explanation for Mr. [N.D's] horrible crimes lies in his ever deepening schizophrenic illness, which finally "exploded" into homicidal rage, as is the case with all individuals who set out on murderous rampages, or run amok, and always to the great detriment of their fellow citizens.*

614     Bossier City, La. – Six youngsters aged 10 to 14 found a man
        hanging from a tree near a park yesterday, gagged, handcuffed
        and wearing women's clothes. Police said his death was
        accidental and sexual in nature. —<u>Marin Independent Journal</u>,
        Marin County, California, July 11, 2000, p. A5.

        *The "bearded lady" disease claims yet another tragic
        victim. Although the death may possibly have been "accidental
        and sexual in nature," nevertheless the victim must have been
        in a suicidal frame of mind to end up as he did.*

615     'That was the physical transformation. The emotional
        transformation was feeling what it feels like to go out in your
        everyday life as a transgendered person. Some people thought
        I was a boy. But there were also people who didn't know what
        gender I was. And if that was the case, they didn't want to
        have anything to do with me. It was a very lonely and sad and
        hopeless feeling. I hope I was able to communicate that.'
                While making the movie, Swank lost touch with her
        female side. When filming ended, 'I was floating between
        genders. I wasn't quite a boy, and I wasn't quite a girl. It was
        actually a scary place to be because I was out of touch with
        me, like I was in some way channeling Brandon. I didn't know
        if I was ever going to be able to find myself again.' —"Hilary
        Swank Playing Oscars by Ear," Ruthie Stein (staff writer), <u>San
        Francisco Chronicle</u>, March 19, 2000.

        *Hilary Swank conveys in this interview many of the
        emotions the schizophrenic person feels – that is, not knowing
        to which sex he or she really belongs. The major difference
        here is that Ms. Swank's feelings of sexual confusion are
        conscious ones, whereas in the schizophrenic they are always
        unconscious. The person afflicted with schizophrenia is
        unaware that the reason he or she experiences "lonely and sad
        and hopeless" feelings is due to these unconscious*

*"transgendered" emotions which make other more "normal" persons wary of them, thus contributing to their sense of isolation and loneliness. The end result of these feelings can be the development of severe depression, ending in suicide.*

*"When filming ended, 'I wasn't quite a boy and I wasn't quite a girl. It was actually a scary place to be because I was out of touch with me, like I was in some way channeling Brandon. I didn't know if I was ever going to be able to find myself again.'"*

*Ms. Swank thus sums up perfectly the predicament schizophrenic persons find themselves in – namely, not knowing at an unconscious level whether they are male or female. Only intensive psychoanalytically oriented psychotherapy can help them rediscover and decide on their emotionally true, conscious standing in the world as either male or female. This is the only path that can lead to their ultimate recovery from severe mental illness.*

616     At 17, he joined the marines to get away from his mother, but he was unable ever to shake the sense of perpetual grievance with which she had imbued him, or his anger at a world that stubbornly refused to grant him the recognition she had taught him should be his.

    Not surprisingly, the military did not suit him. Cold, sarcastic, withdrawn, he was taunted as 'Ozzie Rabbit' and 'Mrs. Oswald' by his fellow marines, and was court-martialed and found guilty twice, first for shooting himself in the arm with a .22 pistol he was unauthorized to carry and again for pouring a drink over the head of a sergeant who had dared assign him to K.P. duty. He subsequently suffered an apparent breakdown, weeping and firing shots into the night while on guard duty. After that he was called 'bugs.' —Case Closed - Lee Harvey Oswald and the Assassination of John F. Kennedy, Gerald Posner, Doubleday, New York, 1994 (The

New York Times Book Review, date of review and name of
reviewer not noted).

> *We can see from the above quotation that Lee Harvey*
> *Oswald, the assassin of President John F. Kennedy, was*
> *afflicted with schizophrenia at an early age, which, of course,*
> *is always the case, even though the more severe symptoms of*
> *the disease might not appear until later in life. (This is the*
> *reason the original name for the disease was "dementia*
> *praecox" – or precocious dementia – until it was changed to*
> *"schizophrenia" by Dr. Eugen Bleuler, a contemporary of*
> *Sigmund Freud's who was much influenced by Freud's*
> *discoveries.) In Oswald's case, the more severe symptoms of*
> *the "bearded lady" disease appeared early in his late teens –*
> *as was shown by his psychotic actions in the Marine Corps as*
> *quoted above.*
>
>     *It is most interesting that his fellow Marines intuited*
> *Oswald's already severe bisexual conflict and confusion by*
> *referring to him as "Mrs. Oswald" and "Ozzie Rabbit," the*
> *latter obviously not a name one would apply to a masculine,*
> *gung-ho Marine type. It was immediately clear to his fellow*
> *Marines that Oswald was an effeminate "mama's boy," and*
> *later that he was "bugs," or crazy.*

617   But, as his newly opened K.G.B. files make clear, the Soviets
turned out to be no more admiring of him than his fellow
Americans had been. He had to slash his wrists to keep from
being expelled from the country once his tourist visa ran out.
Two Soviet psychiatrists independently declared him 'mentally
unstable,' according to Yuri Nosenko, a K.G.B. defector, and
he was finally granted asylum only because the Soviets feared
that if he succeeded in his next try at suicide, they might be
blamed for murdering an American tourist. (Ibid.)

*Obviously the Soviets thought Oswald was so seriously mentally ill that he was a definite risk for suicide, and suicide has been called – and rightly so – the most serious symptom of schizophrenia.*

618 He proclaimed himself head of a local chapter of the Fair Play for Cuba Committee but failed to attract a single member. And he talked of hijacking a jet and forcing it to take him and his family to Cuba, which he had now persuaded himself was the only place he could find a revolutionary role worthy of his talents; while in the grip of this last vision, he took to bounding around his home in his underwear, herding imaginary fellow passengers until his frightened wife began whispering to their daughter, 'Our papa is out of his mind.' (Ibid.)

*Oswald was certainly "out of his mind" by this time, being firmly in the grip of paranoid schizophrenic delusions of grandeur, or of what the author, Gerald Posner, calls his "vision."*

619 In September 1963, Oswald turned up in Mexico City, seeking a visa to enter Cuba and bringing with him a fat dossier to impress the authorities: in it, he claimed to be a skilled translator, specialist in 'Street Agitation,' 'Radio Specker and Lecturer,' 'organizer,' ideologist, soldier and potential spy. Once the Cubans saw it, he assured his wife, he would be welcomed eagerly to Havana. 'You laugh now,' he told her, 'but in 20 years when I am prime minister, we'll see how you laugh then.'

The Cubans and Russians did not laugh; Oswald's visit was too unnerving for that: he wept, shouted, pulled a revolver that he said he carried because the F.B.I. was out to kill him. His application was denied, nonetheless. (Ibid.)

*From the above description of Oswald's activities, it is glaringly obvious he was suffering from delusions of grandeur and delusions of persecution, all common symptoms of paranoid schizophrenia. In short, "Mrs. Oswald," or "Ozzie Rabbit," was now a raving maniac and had been for some time – a time-bomb waiting to explode, as explode it did when he assassinated President Kennedy along with the first police officer who tried to arrest him afterwards.*

*And Marina, Oswald's wife, only aggravated his madness further by taunting him about his inadequate marital sexual performance, while concurrently expressing admiration for President Kennedy and stating that the President reminded her of a former boyfriend in Russia.*

*Thus the mounting pressure from his severe bisexual conflict and confusion finally reached the breaking point, and he "ran amok," killing the person he was most obsessed by. Invariably there is a powerful element of unconscious homosexual attraction in these paranoid obsessions. Homosexual attraction which is denied and turned into delusions of persecution by the paranoid person produces the classic "paranoid shift": first the denial – "I love him – no, I don't love him, I hate him:" then the paranoid shift – "no, I don't hate him, he hates me and is persecuting me, therefore I have to kill him to protect myself."*

*Lee Harvey Oswald suffered from schizophrenia, the "bearded lady" disease, and history will long remember the tragic consequences.*

620   In [PASSPORT TO ASSASSINATION: The Never-Before Told Story of Lee Harvey Oswald by the KGB Colonel Who Knew Him; Birch Lane/Carol Publishing,] Oleg M. Nechiporenko, a retired officer in the foreign intelligence division of the K.G.B. who was one of the three Soviet officials who interviewed Oswald in Mexico City, confirms Mr. Posner's version of his bizarre visit: 'We decided we could

not take Oswald seriously. His nervousness ... his rambling and even nonsensical speech at times, his avoidance of answering specific questions and the shifts from strong agitation to depression, gave us reason to believe that his mental state was unstable or that, at the very least, he suffered from a serious nervous disorder. —The New York Times Book Review (review of Passport to Assassination: The Never-Before Told Story of Lee Harvey Oswald by the KGB Colonel Who Knew Him, by Oleg M. Nechiporenko, Birch Lane/Carol Publishing, 1993) (name of reviewer and date of review not noted).

*It must now be obvious to even the most casual observer that Lee Harvey Oswald was a madman, a person suffering from paranoid schizophrenia, an illness which had wrapped him in its suffocating folds from a very early age – specifically, from puberty onwards.*

*As stated previously, the original name for schizophrenia – dementia praecox, or precocious dementia, was assigned this devastating illness primarily because it had been observed to strike its victims in their early teens, or concurrent with the first stirrings and manifestations of puberty. You would think that an immediate etiological connection would have been made between these two phenomena, i.e., the development of schizophrenia alongside the development of puberty, and the conclusion drawn that schizophrenia must somehow be connected to a person's sexual feelings and strivings. But unfortunately no such uniform connection was made then, nor ever, as a matter of fact, until the writings of Dr. Edward J. Kempf appeared in America in the early 1930's and 1940's. Of course Sigmund Freud was the first significant voice to blame the "neuroses" on the repression of unconscious sexual "perversions," but Dr. Kempf was the first to expand these findings to encompass <u>all</u> mental illness – the psychoses as well as neuroses.*

*Lee Harvey Oswald was driven insane because he had repressed his strongly passive, feminine, homosexual nature – his "Mrs. Oswald" side, as named by his fellow Marines in boot camp.*

*As Daniel Paul Schreber, the famous psychotic, once wrote: "I would like to meet the man who, faced with the choice of either being a demented human being in male habitus, or a spirited woman, would not prefer the latter." Rather than consciously accepting the "spirited woman" part of himself, Oswald unconsciously chose to keep it repressed, thus leading to his "dementia."*

*It should be noted here once again that Schreber's "formula" applies also to women – that is, if a woman represses her "spirited man" side, she, too, becomes "demented."*

621    He asked that "the person who will wash my body near the genitals must wear gloves on his hand so he won't touch my genitals."

Mr. Atta, said to be painfully shy around women throughout his life, asked that women play no role at his funeral. "I don't want any woman to go to my grave at all during my funeral or any occasion thereafter," he wrote. "I don't want a pregnant woman or a person who is not clean to come and say goodbye to me because I don't approve of it." —"Will Suggests Suspect Had Long Planned to Die for Beliefs," Philip Shenon and David Johnson, The New York Times, October 4, 2001 (page not noted).

*Mohammed Atta, the suicidal terrorist who flew a plane into the North Tower of the World Trade Center, here clearly demonstrates his powerful repressed homosexual tendencies, demonstrated first by his intense, stated dislike of, and disgust for, womankind in general, and then by his extreme over-reaction to having another man touch his genitals, even after he was dead.*

*There cannot be the slightest doubt that Atta suffered from paranoid schizophrenia, the bearded lady disease, caused by his intense bisexual conflict and gender confusion. He was noticeably effeminate as a child and it is said that he used to sit on his mother's lap until he entered the University of Cairo. His father was constantly berating his mother for making a "girl" out of him. When he finally left the family and went to Hamburg, he formed a very close bond with a group of like-minded men. He finally began dating a girl, his first ever "romantic" experience with the opposite sex. When this romance ended, Atta became "distraught," according to his father, and it was at this time that the extraordinary change in his nature took place. From a shy, timid, diffident young man, he suddenly metamorphosed into an aggressive, "holy" warrior, bent on a suicidal mission.*

*It was at this juncture that he had his schizophrenic break with reality which set him on his course toward death and almost unimaginable destruction. In the words of Harold Searles, the insightful psycho-analyst, "Not infrequently the schizophrenic illness is precipitated in a setting of rejection in a love affair."*

*It is ironic that Atta was at one time bearded but was clean-shaven when he perished in his suicidal flight into the World Trade Center. He was a classic victim of schizophrenia, the bearded lady disease, as were the thousands of his victims who also suffered and died because of it. It has often been said that suicide is the most serious symptom in schizophrenia, and it certainly was in this incredibly tragic case.*

622　But Lewis's sufferings were not heroic; they were human and they wore him down. By the end of his time as governor, he was ordering inhumane policies against the Indians that his wiser subordinates ignored. He was drinking and taking opium. In his last days, he headed down the Natchez Trace, telling his servant that Clark was on the Trace, too. "He heard me comeing on," Clark later wrote. "He was certain ... that I had heard of his situation and would come to his releaf."

On a lonely ridge in Tennessee, Lewis remarked to his hostess at the inn, "Madame, this is a very pleasant evening," and later that night he put a pistol to his head. —"Undaunted Craziness," Brian Hall, The New York Times, January 21, 2003 (page not noted).

*Meriwether Lewis was suffering from paranoid schizophrenia – the bearded lady disease – when he killed himself that "very pleasant evening" at the Inn on the Natchez Trace. He was hallucinating that his beloved friend and fellow explorer, William Clark, was coming to save him, or "comeing on" to his "releaf," as Clark later wrote. The great tragedy of this case is that Clark could have saved Lewis, but only by declaring as great a love for Lewis as Lewis had for him. In short, Lewis was in love with Clark and had been for some time, but it was an unrequited love, Clark being predominantly heterosexual whereas Lewis was predominantly homosexual, albeit at a deeply repressed level. It was the repression of and consequent frustration of his great love for Clark that drove him into his final schizophrenic breakdown and resulting suicide.*

*Lewis had shown signs of mental illness from his boyhood on. A story was told that when he was a boy in Virginia he would go out at night hunting in the middle of winter in his bare feet, leaving a bloody track behind him from the cuts he received from the snow and ice. As Brian Hall, the author of The New Times article, "Undaunted Craziness," tells us, President Thomas Jefferson himself observed that Lewis had "undaunted courage" but then added that "while he lived with me in Washington I observed at times sensible depressions of the mind."*

*Lewis was so anxious to have Clark accompany him on his journey west that he told him he would make sure he would be named a co-captain of the expedition.*

*Instead of the promised captaincy, President Jefferson commissioned him a second lieutenant, a bitter blow to Clark, since Lewis had previously served under Clark in the Army before receiving his appointment as Jefferson's personal secretary. When Lewis wrote to Clark to invite him on the expedition, he told him that "I should be extremely happy in your company." This is a very telling statement as it provides a glimpse into the very deep feelings of affection and love that Lewis had for Clark.*

*Lewis exhibited increasing signs of mental illness during the four years it took for the Corps of Discovery to accomplish its mission. As author Brian Hall states, Lewis demonstrated "a recklessness bordering on flirtation with death." This sort of recklessness is always a sign of the deep, suicidal depression that is inevitably an integral part of the schizophrenic illness. Lewis would walk out into grizzly bear country by himself whereas his men went in groups; he led his men on unnecessarily dangerous trips through the rapids in their canoes; split his party into four groups and led his own into territory dominated by hostile Indians. He was displaying a recklessness and heedlessness to danger that was becoming increasingly pathological as the trip progressed. As Brian Hall tells us, "He seems emotionally exhausted. He threatens to burn down an entire village when a saddle and horse robe go missing." These are the actions of a man slowly losing control of his emotions and sinking deeper and deeper into his schizophrenic illness.*

*After his return from his epic journey, Lewis was wined and dined by an admiring group of his contemporaries, but he seemed to take no great pleasure in the attention bestowed upon him. Brian Hall remarks that Lewis "would write to friends about courting some beauty, but then act to* *ensure that nothing came of it. On the eve of Clark's marriage, Lewis wrote to an old friend, another lifelong bachelor, about 'that <u>void in our hearts</u> ... I never felt less like a hero than at the present moment ... but on this I am determined, <u>to get a wife</u>.'"*

*Of course he never did "get a wife," due to his severe bisexual conflict and ensuing final schizophrenic breakdown, during which he hallucinated that his dear friend Clark was, in Clark's words again, "comeing on" to save him from his suicidal depression. Lewis died of a "broken heart" in the true romantic sense, in that he knew at an unconscious, and perhaps by then even conscious, level, that his great love for Clark could never be reciprocated.*

*"I should be extremely happy in your company" would never be realized again.*

623    Phil Morowski, an acquaintance, said that when McVeigh returned from the Gulf War, he complained that the Army had implanted a computer chip in his buttocks apparently to keep track of him.    —Lee Hancock and David Jackson, <u>Dallas Morning News</u>, (reprinted in the <u>Marin Independent Journal</u>, Marin County, California, April 23, 1995, p. 1).

*The fact that Mr. McVeigh believed the Army had implanted a computer chip in his buttocks to monitor his whereabouts points immediately to the certainty he was suffering from paranoid schizophrenia, the "bearded lady" disease. This is a classic symptom of this condition – namely, the psychotic belief that an unfriendly entity has implanted some kind of a device in or on the body to control or monitor the schizophrenic person's actions. The fact that in Mr. McVeigh's case the implantation took place "in his buttocks" strongly points to unconscious, passive, anal erotic cravings.*

624      William McVeigh portrayed his son as a bright person who, as a boy, could never quite succeed either in school or at sports. As an adult, his father said, Timothy McVeigh bounced from job to job because he could not stand pressure, could not take orders, and could not handle the responsibilities of day-to-day work. —"McVeigh's Letters Show Deep Anger," Jo Thomas, The New York Times (date and page not noted).

*The above portrayal of his son by his father is a portrayal which matches almost exactly that of all young schizophrenic persons, male or female.*

625      Previously undisclosed letters by Timothy J. McVeigh to his younger sister before the bombing of the federal building in Oklahoma City reveal him as deeply frustrated and at one point suicidal over his inability to confide the extent of his anti-government activities to his family.

     Mr. McVeigh's letters, along with conversations at his father's house in upstate New York, revealed so much anger and alienation that when the bomb exploded on April 19, 1995, eventually killing 168 people, members of his family suspected him almost immediately, they later told the Federal Bureau of Investigation. (Ibid.)

*The fact Mr. McVeigh was "suicidal" obviously points to a deeply disturbed individual, one made so by his paranoid schizophrenic delusions of persecution and grandiosity, triggered, as always, by the total sexual frustration caused by his bisexual conflict.*

626      At one point, he wrote, he had gone to the house of their grandfather, who has since died, and considered killing himself there.

'I have an urgent need for someone in the family to understand me,' Mr. McVeigh told his sister. 'I will tell you, and only you.' (Ibid.)

*Mr. McVeigh's "urgent need" to have someone "understand me" was really an urgent need for him to understand himself, to understand that he had been driven psychotic by his repressed bisexual conflict and confusion, the invariable ingredients in schizophrenia, the "bearded lady" disease, with which he was so tragically afflicted – tragic not only for himself but also for the 168 other innocent persons also destroyed by his malignant illness.*

627     But Jennifer McVeigh thought the breaking point came earlier, in 1991, at Fort Bragg, N.C., where he was an unsuccessful candidate for the Special Forces. Army records show that Mr. McVeigh dropped out of the program after saying he could not meet the physical demands. (Ibid.)

*His failure with the Special Forces points up continuing failure in his life that his father mentioned earlier in comments about his son – namely, that as a boy he was unable to find success in either sports or school and that later he could not hold a steady job due to his inability to stand the pressure connected with the normal masculine responsibilities of life. In short, he was not "man enough" to fit in with other "manly" men. (It reminds one of Lee Harvey Oswald's similar inability to fit in with his Marine Corps comrades, and their taunting him with epithets such as "Mrs. Oswald" and "Ozzie Rabbit." At some unconscious level, McVeigh must have been aware of this fact, and such insight could easily have caused him to reach a "breaking point" in his schizophrenia and set into slow motion the process of his "running amok," ending with the final tragedy of the Oklahoma City bombing.*

628    Joe Solino Jimero was publicly beheaded in Saudi Arabia for stabbing and beating surgeon Rashid Abu Jabal to death after the doctor reattached his penis.

Authorities said Jimero had cut off his penis because he wanted to become a woman. —The Pacific Sun, Marin County, California (date and page not noted).

*Occasionally schizophrenic males such as Mr. Jimero will amputate their own genitalia when the pressure from their bisexual conflict becomes too much to bear, consequently causing them to become floridly psychotic as their long repressed feminine strivings overwhelm their ego.*

629    A 73-year old Milwaukee woman claimed she became sexually attracted to other women and started having spontaneous orgasms after an electric bingo scoreboard fell on her head. The woman asked for $90,000 from the church where the bingo game took place, but the judge threw out her case because she refused to undergo court-ordered psychological examination. (News story, publication not noted.)

*This woman had obviously been repressing her intense homosexual feelings for a long time, perhaps her entire life, until the point was finally reached where it was no longer possible for her to deny them, at which time her body took over and discharged involuntarily the dammed up libido. The shock of the bingo board falling on her must have weakened her physical and psychological defenses sufficiently so that these powerful repressed feelings were finally able to break through and discharge themselves naturally through orgasmic release. This case demonstrates the enormous toxic potential of these unconscious, repressed homosexual feelings and shows how the only "cure" for their toxicity is by means of orgasmic release, or discharge.*

*This case is somewhat similar to the case of Daniel Paul Schreber, the schizophrenic German judge, whose name was made famous by Freud's study and interpretation of his paranoia. Schreber, in his memoirs, attributed his mental breakdown to one night wherein he experienced six or seven involuntary orgasmic discharges, or what are commonly referred to as "wet dreams." Freud speculated in his case study of Schreber that these orgasms were connected with homosexual fantasies which Schreber had been repressing, and which had finally become so intense due to their denial that they, as in the case of the woman in the above quotation, took over the bodily apparatus and discharged themselves, thus reducing the enormous anxiety and tension under which these two persons were laboring. The "bingo woman" was consciously able to accept her homosexual feelings as her own, to a certain extent, but Schreber was completely unable to and consequently developed a very severe case of paranoid schizophrenia.*

*The toxic effect of undischarged libido is the "smoking gun" in all mental illness, and the only real "cure" is to arrange somehow for this undischarged libido to be discharged as nature intended it to be, that is, through genital orgasm. But since most people would rather "die than admit to" their homosexual feelings, bringing about this curative release of repressed homosexual excitement through orgasm is the most difficult problem in the psychotherapy of all emotionally disturbed persons.*

*Actually, rather than refer to the mentally ill as "emotionally" disturbed, a far better and more accurate term would be to call them "toxically" disturbed, the toxicity being the result of repressed, undischarged homosexual libido. When Freud wrote that in all psycho-analyses one of the primary tasks facing the analysand is for him or her to return to the earlier, now repressed, "perverse" masturbatory fantasies and discharge them genitally once again, he was in effect saying that to get well in the analysis, the patient must revisit these old fantasies and work through them, both physically and emotionally, before it would be possible to move on into mature adulthood and heterosexuality, which in reality are one and the same thing.*

630    Being born a woman is my awful tragedy. From the moment I was conceived I was doomed to sprout breasts and ovaries rather than penis and scrotum, to have my whole circle of action, thought and feeling rigidly circumscribed.    —The Unabridged Journals of Sylvia Plath, 1950-1962, (transcribed from the original manuscript at Smith College, edited by Karen V. Kukil) Anchor Books, New York (from book review, publication not noted).

*These are the words of the poet, Sylvia Plath, a schizophrenic woman who committed suicide at the age of 30, after many years of mental illness. She is expressing in the above quotation the feelings of all mentally ill women, the major difference being that in her case these feelings appear to be recognized at a conscious level, whereas, generally, they are deeply repressed and denied. (Anyone doubting Sigmund Freud's formulation of "penis envy" in certain women needs look no further than the above quotation for proof of its accuracy and validity.)*

*Conversely, in the unconscious psyche of the schizophrenic, or mentally ill male, could be found the following reconfiguration of Sylvia Plath's words: "Being born a man is my awful tragedy. From the moment I was conceived I was doomed to sprout penis and scrotum rather than breasts and ovaries, to have my whole circle of action, thought and feeling rigidly circumscribed." While these opposite-sex thoughts predominate in the repressed unconscious of the mentally ill person, they are present in the conscious awareness of the overtly homosexual person. For the homosexual often states that he or she has the brain of one sex but the body of the other, i.e., a male mind in a female body for the lesbian, and a female mind in a male body for the homosexual man.*

631   In a smarmy matriarchy of togetherness it is hard to get a sanction to hate one's mother; so how do I express my hate for my mother? In my deepest emotions I think of her as an enemy: somebody who 'killed' my father, my first male ally in the world. She is a murderess of maleness ... what a luxury it would be to kill her, to strangle her skinny veined throat ... But I was too nice for murder. (Ibid.)

*It is easy to see why Sylvia Plath had such a difficult time identifying herself as a woman when her first and most important female role model was such a hated figure, a "murderess of maleness" as she so venomously describes her mother.   However, Ms. Plath had unconsciously identified with her mother to a certain extent, as can be seen in her description of herself in her poem "Lady Lazarus":*

*"Herr God, Herr Lucifer,*
*Beware*
*Beware.*
*Out of the ash*
*I rise with my red hair*
*And I eat men like air."*

*A woman who "eats men like air" could likewise be called a "murderess of maleness." Thus Ms. Plath has partly become the one person she hates most in the world – her own mother.*
*Note should also be made here of the fact that "Lady Lazarus" is a "bearded lady" reference – Lazarus being a male in mythology. In reality, Ms. Plath unconsciously*

*realizes that she, like her mother, is a "bearded lady," half man, half woman. It is this deep gender confusion and resulting bisexual conflict which was the direct cause of her lifelong schizophrenia and eventual death by suicide.*

632    Bodfish, 56, kept a diary for 22 years and wrote frequently that she hated her body, according to police. In excerpts released yesterday, she described it as a 'stupid piece of s_ _ _ that should be beaten to death.'

She also wrote of the 'Bl. D.C.,' which investigators believe is the 'Blue Demon Conscience' that she refers to as a person and says should be beaten. Police say it was possibly an alter ego constructed by Bodfish or part of her troubled psyche. —"Diary Leads to Theories in Orinda Mom's Death," Charlie Goodyear (Chronicle staff writer) San Francisco Chronicle, March 31, 2000.

*Margaret Bodfish was a transvestite who lived as a man. When she was beaten to death, suspicion fell on her son, who committed suicide the following day. Thus her wish that her female body, which she described as a "stupid piece of s_ _ _ that should be beaten to death" was fulfilled. She had undergone removal of both breasts. Bodfish was obviously suffering from schizophrenia due to her severe bisexual conflict and sex-role alienation. She was a true "bearded lady."*

*In her diary, she wrote that "When Bl. D.C. mouths go off, go silent. Don't speak to her or about her. Don't speak. Walk over to the nearest good solid object. Pick it up. Come back. Hit her up the side of the head. Total silence. No comment after, either. Silence." [Reported by Gary Klein (staff reporter), Marin Independent Journal, March 31, 2000, p. A11.]*

*Thus it can be seen that Margaret Bodfish, like the poet, Sylvia Plath, had developed schizophrenia as the direct result of her hatred of being born a female and of her overpowering wish to be a male and assume the male role in life. This wish, if followed to its logical conclusion, would lead to loving other women both sexually and emotionally. This final consummation of their deepest and most intense desires seems to have been avoided and frustrated by both women, consequently leading directly to their mental illness, the "toxic effect" of undischarged homosexual libido invariably being the precipitating factor.*

633          [Name omitted] – who, according to police and prosecutors, is known locally as 'The Man Hater' – was arraigned yesterday on a charge of assault with a deadly weapon with a hate-crimes enhancement... [Name omitted], 38, an unemployed houseboat resident, was arrested Wednesday after an incident in the Sausalito waterfront. Sausalito Officer Mike Embley said the alleged victim was going to the public boat ramp to get his boat when [name omitted], shouting obscenities and accusing the man of raping her, poked him in the stomach with a six-foot oar and then clubbed him six times with it.

Embley said [name omitted] is known to police for shouting at male strangers and accusing them of sexually assaulting her. Authorities said she was already on probation for a misdemeanor conviction for assaulting a delivery man for the United Parcel Service.

'She has a habit of walking up and down the street yelling at men,' Embley said.   —"Gender-Based Attack Blamed on 'Man Hater'," Gary Klein (staff reporter) <u>Marin Independent Journal</u>, Marin County, California, November 10, 2000.

*This obviously paranoid schizophrenic woman, who in earlier times would have been safely locked away in a mental hospital, is here displaying her propensity for being a "a murderess of maleness" in a very clear manner, in contrast to the more subtle manifestations of such feelings attributed by Sylvia Plath to her mother, Aurelia, and then demonstrated by Ms. Plath herself in her poem "Lady Lazarus."*

634    "Of course they are much younger like the sort of person I've mentioned.... . I feel often as if I were similar to the girls that love the Beatles so wildly since they seem so attractive and amusing to me." ... "Nash was always forming intense friendships with men that had a romantic quality," Donald Newman observed in 1996... "He was very adolescent, always with the boys,"... Newman recalled: "He tried fiddling around with me. I was driving my car and he came onto me." D.J. and Nash were cruising around in Newman's white Thunderbird when Nash kissed him on the mouth. D.J. just laughed it off. —A Beautiful Mind, Sylvia Nasar, Simon & Schuster, New York, 1998, p. 169.

*Any male (or female) who harbors such powerful opposite-sex emotional feelings as those chronicled here – emotional feelings which are invariably accompanied by the corresponding opposite-sex sexual feelings – would be in serious jeopardy of developing schizophrenia were he (or she) to attempt to deny or repress these feelings in order to live an ostensibly "normal" heterosexual life. In this particular instance, of course, that is exactly what happened and a schizophrenic illness soon manifested itself.*

635    In five short years, between the ages of twenty-four and twenty-nine, Nash became emotionally involved with at least three other men. He acquired and then abandoned a secret mistress who bore his child. And he courted – or rather was courted by – a woman who became his wife. (Ibid., p. 167)

> *The severe bisexual conflict and confusion outlined here will inevitably lead to schizophrenia when the complex is denied and repressed into the unconscious as the result of being unresolvable on the conscious level. Once in the unconscious it inevitably forms the pathogenic core of the ensuing shcizophrenic illness.*

636        Cohen said: "His psychoanalysts theorized that his illness was brought on by latent homosexuality."[4] These rumored opinions may well have been held by Nash's doctors. Freud's now-discredited theory linking schizophrenia to repressed homosexuality had such currency at McLean that for many years any male with a diagnosis of schizophrenia who arrived at the hospital in an agitated state was said to be suffering from 'homosexual panic.'[43] (Ibid., p. 259)

> *It is exceedingly ironic that the author of <u>A Beautiful Mind</u> refers to "Freud's now-discredited theory linking schizophrenia to repressed homosexuality" when, in fact, her book can be considered a classic case history proving beyond any reasonable doubt the correctness of that "now-discredited" theory. Furthermore, the author makes no mention of how Freud's theory has been "discredited" or by whom. It is akin to referring to Darwin's theory of evolution as his "now-discredited" theory, again without going into any particulars as to why or by whom it has been discredited.*

637        But several studies have since shown that basic military training during peacetime can precipitate schizophrenia in men with a hitherto unsuspected vulnerability to the illness.[15] Although study subjects were all carefully screened for mental illnesses, hospitalization rates for schizophrenia turned out to be abnormally high, especially for draftees. (Ibid., p. 126)

*For men with a powerful latent homosexual orientation, suddenly being thrown together with a group of other men on a very intimate basis, can, and often does, trigger a classic "homosexual panic" leading to schizophrenic symptomatology. Furthermore, being draftees, these men are usually rather unwilling subjects of this forced male bonding and intimacy.*

638        Having already called Julius Nyerere, the president of Tanzania, a coward, an old woman and a prostitute, he announced that he loved Mr. Nyerere and "would have married him if he had been a woman." He said he expected Queen Elizabeth to send him "her 25-year old knickers" in celebration of the silver anniversary of her coronation.

In other comments he offered to become king of Scotland and lead his Celtic subjects to independence from Britain. —Michael T. Kaufman, Obituaries, <u>The New York Times</u>, August 17, 2003, p. 22.

*Idi Amin, the maniacal, homicidal ruler of Uganda for eight years during the 1970's, who is reliably reported to have been responsible for the demise of at least 300,000 of his fellow citizens, obviously was afflicted with paranoid schizophrenia, the bearded lady disease. This is confirmed by the history of his life and by some very revealing information contained in the above quotation, especially in the first few lines where Mr. Amin discussed his feelings about Julius Nyerere, the president of Tanzania. When he calls Mr. Nyerere a "coward, an old woman and a prostitute," he is in reality projecting onto Mr. Nyerere his own deeply repressed, unconscious image of himself. He then confesses his love for Mr. Nyerere, stating he "would have married him if he had been a woman." Again, the true psychological meaning of this utterance is that he, Idi Amin, wishes that he himself were a woman and that Mr. Nyerere would marry him. In any case, the homosexual overtones in this remark are very clear.   The projection of a person's own repressed, unconscious wishes and feelings onto others is an invariable phenomenon in paranoid schizophrenia.*

*Further proof of Amin's schizophrenia are his statements that he wished, or expected, that Queen Elizabeth would send him her "25-year old knickers," and that he wished to become King of Scotland.  It is interesting to note that Amin wished to have in his personal possession a piece of clothing worn by a female who just happened to be a queen, making that item of clothing the ultimate in femaleness, or at least most likely to be considered so in his disordered mind.*

*In conclusion, Amin here demonstrates the invariable bisexual conflict and gender confusion which forms the core of schizophrenia.  His name is one more to be added to that long list of schizophrenic leaders who, due to their bearded lady disease, have wreaked untold horror and tragedy upon the innocent citizens of their countries.*

*(Note:  Allegations that Amin suffered from untreated syphilis have never been proved.  Furthermore, the symptoms of organic general paresis caused by tertiary syphilis are easily distinguishable from the symptoms of paranoid schizophrenia and Idi Amin displayed all the classic symptoms of this latter disease, including delusions of grandeur, persecution, manic-depression, and hysteria, to catalogue just a few of its most common manifestations.)*

639        This list didn't include the important questions, like how did he discover gravity or why did he suffer a mental breakdown at the pinnacle of his career?

Did Isaac Newton ever have sex, the voyeuristic modern wants to know?   He never married, never kept company with a woman and apparently never had a lover. Though he never recorded details of his private life, his notes do occasionally reveal his feelings about sexuality, and they are morbid – suffused with horror and disgust, sometimes of a religious nature.

Once he wrote John Locke that he wished him dead, "being of opinion that you endeavoured to embroil me with woemen." —[James Gleick, Think Tank, <u>The New York Times</u>, August 16, 2003, and author of "Isaac Newton," Pantheon.]

*Sir Isaac Newton experienced a mental collapse due to his severe bisexual conflict. Because of his intense dislike of women, his erotic affections must necessarily have been concentrated on men. This state of affairs would obviously have led him into overt homosexuality if he had granted them free, conscious reign. The fact he did not, and instead repressed them, instead led inevitably to his schizophrenic psychosis, or his "mental breakdown at the pinnacle of his career." It should be noted here that any man expressing such an extreme loathing of women as Newton evidenced is invariably motivated by a very powerful unconscious envy of the female state of being, a state which would most nearly meet his deepest emotional, physical, and sexual needs if unrepressed.*

*Thus Newton, for all his brilliance and genius, like so many others of lesser intellect, became a helpless victim of the bearded lady disease. Again quoting Daniel Paul Schreber, the famous schizophrenic patient and memoirist, "I would like to meet the man who, faced with the choice of either being a demented human being in male habitus, or a spirited woman, would not prefer the latter."*

And, finally, one of Sigmund Freud's favorite quotations:

"There are more things in heaven and earth, Horatio,
Than are dreamt of in your philosophy."
Wm. Shakespeare's <u>Hamlet</u>, Act 1, Scene 5, Line 166

# Afterword

It is time to bring this compilation of quotations and comments to a conclusion as the process itself could go on ad infinitum. For in every case of mental illness, if one digs deeply enough, the factors of bisexual conflict and confusion in the causation of the condition become readily apparent. This is a fixed law of nature, no more – no less. It is hoped that anyone taking the time to read completely through this work will agree with this assessment. If not, then it would appear that no amount of proof would be sufficient to convince the skeptic.

The one quotation in *Schizophrenia: The Bearded Lady Disease* which best summarizes what mental illness is all about is contained in the statement made by the person many consider – and correctly so – to be the most famous psychiatric patient to date, namely, the German judge, Daniel Paul Schreber, author of *Memoirs of My Nervous Illness*, published in 1911. As Sigmund Freud said of him: "The wonderful Schreber ... ought to have been made a professor of psychiatry and director of a mental hospital." Interestingly, Freud never included the following quotation from Schreber in his own case study of Schreber's madness.: "I would like to meet the man who," wrote Schreber, "faced with the choice of either being a demented human being in male habitus, or a spirited woman, would not prefer the latter."

What Schreber is explaining here is that the only way an insane man can regain his sanity is to accept his female side, as he himself had partly done while hospitalized for his paranoid schizophrenia. And although he didn't further expound on this deep truth, or law of nature, the exact same criterion applies equally to women, namely, that for an insane woman to regain her sanity, she must first accept her masculine strivings. That these opposite-sex strivings always carry a powerful affect of homosexuality with them is what makes them so terrifying to most people and is the reason they are so violently repressed and denied, thereby leading to mental illness. This is the basic lesson to be learned from Schreber's experience of madness and the lesson the compiler of these 639 quotations has tried to emphasize and demonstrate in this study. Hopefully it has not been in vain.

# Bibliography

Anonymous: *Quotations 239, 240, 574*

Anonymous Case Reported to Compiler: *Quotations 527-528 (inclusive)*

Arieti, S., M. D., *Interpretation of Schizophrenia.* New York: Basic Books, Inc., 2<sup>nd</sup> ed. 1974. *Quotations 133-146 (inclusive)*

Atcheson, R., *The Bearded Lady, Going On The Commune Trip And Beyond.* New York: The John Day Company, 1971. *Quotations 376-378 (inclusive)*

[Author not noted], "Businessman Spots a Murder Suspect," *Associated Press, San Francisco Chronicle,* 9 November 1978. *Quotation 486*

[Author not noted], "Dancer's Suicide by Rattlesnake," *Associated Press, San Francisco Chronicle,* 19 December 1974. *Quotation 487*

[Author not noted], "Doctor Tells of [Name Deleted] Pain," *San Francisco Chronicle* [date and page not noted]. *Quotation 485*

[Author not noted], "Samurai Woman Sane Enough to be Tried," *San Francisco Chronicle* [date and page not noted]. *Quotation 483*

[Author and title of article not noted], *Associated Press, Marin Independent Journal,* Marin County, California [date not noted]. *Quotation 597*

[Author and title of article not noted], *Marin Independent Journal*, Marin County, California, 11 July 2000. *Quotation 614*

[Author and title of article not noted], *The New York Times*, 20 July 1999. *Quotation 573*

[Author and title of article not noted], *The Pacific Sun*, Mill Valley, California [date not noted]. *Quotation 628*

Avery, P., "Killer on LSD 'Heard the Lord'," *San Francisco Chronicle* [date and page not noted]. *Quotation 482*

Barnes, M., and Berke, J., *Mary Barnes (Two Accounts of a Journey Through Madness)*. New York: Harcourt Brace Jovanovich, Inc., 1971. *Quotations 321-331 (inclusive)*

Bateson, G. (ed), *Perceval's Narrative (A Patient's Account of His Psychosis) 1830-1832*. Stanford: Stanford University Press, 1961. *Quotation 244*

Baur, S., *The Dinosaur Man (Tales of Madness and Enchantment from the Back Ward)*. New York: Harper Collins Publishers, 1991. *Quotations 547-566 (inclusive)*

Bazin, N. T., *Virginia Woolf and the Androgynous Vision*. New Brunswick, New Jersey: Rutgers University Press, 1973. *Quotations 429-438 (inclusive)*

Becker, E., *When the War was Over*. New York: Simon & Schuster, 1986 [in an article by Seth Mydans, *The New York Times*, date not noted]. *Quotations 579-582 (inclusive)*

Bell, Q., *Virginia Woolf, a Biography*. New York: Harcourt Brace Jovanovich, Inc., 1972. *Quotations 414-428 (inclusive)*

Bieber, I., et al., *Homosexuality, A Psychoanalytical Study of Male Homosexuals*. New York: Vintage Books (Random House), 1962. *Quotations 477-481 (inclusive), 505*

Binswanger, L., "The Case of Ellen West (An Anthropological-Clinical Study)," *Existence,* May, R., Angel, E., and Ellenberger, H. F. (eds.). New York: Simon & Schuster, 1958. *Quotations 248, 249*

Bishop, E. [as told to James Merrill]. *Quotation 98*

Bizjak, T., "A Son's Tragic Slide," *San Francisco Chronicle*, 15 March 1989. *Quotation 492*

Blake, P. [title of article not noted]. *Time Magazine*, 26 June 1989. *Quotation 599*

Bleuler, E., *Dementia Praecox or the Group of Schizophrenias*. New York: International Universities Press, 1950. *Quotations 5, 6, 57, 208-238 (inclusive), 454-456 (inclusive), 508*

Boisen, A.T., *The Exploration of The Inner World: A Study of Mental Disorder and Religious Experience*. Philadelphia: University of Pennsylvania Press, 1936. *Quotation 308*

Boubion, G., "A Deadly Brother Act: 2 Vicious Crimes, Identical Horror," *San Jose Mercury News,* [reprinted in *Marin Independent Journal,* Marin County, California, 13 December 1992]. *Quotation 568*

Bowers, M., "The Onset of Psychosis – A Diary Account," *Psychiatry*, Vol. 28, 1965. *Quotation 253*

Brody, E. B., *Psychotherapy With Schizophrenics,* Redlich, F.C. (ed.). New York: International Universities Press, Inc., 1952. *Quotations 14, 15*

Brown, J. C., *Immodest Acts (The Life of a Lesbian Nun in Renaissance Italy).* New York and Oxford, England: Oxford University Press, 1986. *Quotation 305*

Buckle, R., *Nijinsky.* New York: Simon & Schuster, 1971. *Quotations 302, 303*

Burnham, D. L., Gladstone, A.I., and Gibson, R.W., *Schizophrenia and the Need-Fear Dilemma.* New York: International Universities Press, Inc., 1969. *Quotations 125-132 (inclusive)*

Burns, J. F. [a review of *Mao: A Life* by Philip Short, and *Mao Zedong* by Jonathan Spence], *The New York Times Book Review,* 6 February 2000. *Quotation 608*

Buruma, I., "Divine Killer" [a review of *Mao: A Life* by Philip Short, and *Mao Zedong* by Jonathan Spence], *New York Review of Books,* 24 February 2000. *Quotations 601-606 (inclusive)*

Bychowski, G., *Homosexuality and Psychosis in Perversions, Psychodynamics and Therapy,* Lorand, S., M. D. (ed.). New York: Random House, 1956. *Quotations 265, 266*

Caplan, G. (ed.), *American Handbook of Psychiatry.* New York: Basic Books, Inc. Vol. II, 2$^{nd}$ ed., 1974. *Quotations 461-466 (inclusive)*

Cheek, F. E., "A Serendipitous Finding: Sex Roles and Schizophrenia," *Journal of Abnormal and Social Psychology,* Vol. 69, No. 4, 1964. *Quotation 250*

Chesler, P., Ph.D., *Women and Madness*. Garden City, New York: Doubleday & Company, Inc., 1972. *Quotations 347-351 (inclusive)*

Cotter, H., "Visions of Childhood Showing Purity and Evil," *The New York Times,* 19 April 2002. *Quotation 520*

Custance, J., *Wisdom, Madness and Folly (The Philosophy of a Lunatic)*. New York: Pellegrini & Cudahy, 1952. *Quotations 245, 506*

Des Lauriers, A. M., Ph.D., *The Experience of Reality in Childhood Schizophrenia*. New York: International Universities Press, Inc., 1962. *Quotations 297-299 (inclusive)*

Dubner, S. J. [in an article on Ted Kaczynski, the Unabomber], *Time Magazine*, 18 October 1999. *Quotations 575, 576*

Du Plessix Gray, F., and Du Gray, F., *Simone Weil*. New York: Viking Press, 2001 [as reviewed by Laura Miller, *The New York Times Book Review,* 5 August, 2001]. *Quotation 529*

English, O. S., M. D., Hampe, W. W., Jr., M. D., Bacon, C., M. D., and Settlage, C. F., M. D., *Direct Analysis and Schizo-phrenia,(Clinical Observations and Evaluations)*. New York and London: Grune & Stratton, 1961. *Quotations 306-307 (inclusive)*

Erlanger, S. [title of article not noted], *The New York Times* [day and month not noted], 1995. *Quotation 598*

Fagan, K. [title of article not noted], *San Francisco Chronicle*, 13 March 2000. *Quotations 610-613 (inclusive)*

Farmer, F., *Will There Really Be a Morning?* New York: G. P. Putnam's Sons, 1972. *Quotations 439-441 (inclusive)*

Fenichel, O., M.D., *The Psycho-Analytic Theory of Neurosis*. New York: W. W. Norton & Company, Inc., 1945. *Quotations 69-71 (inclusive)*

Ferri, G., "Excerpts from Gunman's Letter," *San Francisco Chronicle*, 3 July 1993. *Quotation 569*

Forbath, P., *The River Congo*. New York: E.P. Dutton, 1979. *Quotation 161*

Ford, C. S., Ph.D., and Beach, F. A., Ph.D., *Patterns of Sexual Behavior*. Harper & Brothers, Publishers, and Paul B. Hoeber, Inc. Medical Books, 1951. *Quotations 467-474 (inclusive)*

Frame, J., *Faces in the Water*. New York: George Braziller, 2$^{nd}$ ed., 1962. *Quotations 352-359 (inclusive)*

Freeman, T., Cameron, J.L., and McGhie, A., preface by Freud, Anna, *Chronic Schizophrenia*. New York: International Universities Press, 1958. *Quotations 13, 17-27 (inclusive)*

Freud, S., *The Origins of Psychoanalysis (Letters to Wilhelm Fliess, Drafts and Notes: 1887-1902)*. New York: Basic Books, Inc., 1954. *Quotations 260-261 (inclusive)*

Freud, S., "Psycho-Analytic Notes on an Autobiographical Account of a Case of Paranoia (Dementia Paranoides) (1911)," *The Standard Edition of The Complete Psychological Works of Sigmund Freud*, Vol. XII. London: The Hogarth Press and the Institute of Psycho-Analysis, 1958. *Quotations 61, 494*

Freud, S. [Quotation from *The Standard Edition of The Complete Psychological Works of Sigmund Freud*, Vol VII. London: The Hogarth Press and the Institute of Psycho-Analysis, 1953]. *Quotation 513*

Fromm-Reichmann, F., M. D., *Principles of Intensive Psychotherapy.* Chicago: The University of Chicago Press, 1950. *Quotations 72-76 (inclusive)*

Garcia, D., "Woman Painfully Recalls Family's Brutal Murder," *San Francisco Chronicle*, 20 October 1990. *Quotation 524*

Goethe. *Quotation 491*

Goodyear, C., "Diary Leads to Theories in Orinda Mom's Death," *San Francisco Chronicle*, 31 March 2000. *Quotation 632*

Gottesman, I.I., *Schizophrenia Genesis (The Origins of Madness).* New York: W. H. Freeman and Company, 1991. *Quotations 540-542 (inclusive)*

Grant, V. W., Ph.D., *This is Mental Illness (How it Feels and What it Means).* Boston: Beacon Press, 1966. *Quotations 251-252 (inclusive)*

Green, H., *I Never Promised You A Rose Garden.* New York: New American Library, Inc. (Holt, Rinehart and Winston, Inc.), 1964. *Quotations 442-453 (inclusive)*

Green, R., M. D., *Sexual Identity Conflict in Children and Adults.* New York: Basic Books, Inc., 1974. *Quotation 168*

Guntrip, H., *Schizoid Phenomena, Object-Relations, and the Self.* New York: International Universities Press, Inc., 1969. *Quotations 122-124 (inclusive)*

Halbfinger, D. M., "Our Towns," *The New York Times,* 24 March 2002. *Quotation 518*

Hall, B., "Undaunted Craziness," *The New York Times,* 21 January 2003. *Quotation 622*

Hancock, L., and Jackson, D. [title of article not noted], *Dallas Morning News,* reprinted in *Marin Independent Journal,* Marin County, California, 23 April 1995. *Quotation 623*

Harris, J., "Strange Bedfellows," *The Smithsonian Magazine,* December 2001. *Quotation 519*

Hill, L. B., M. D., *Psychotherapeutic Intervention in Schizophrenia.* Chicago: The University of Chicago Press, 1955. *Quotations 62–67 (inclusive), 459-460 (inclusive), 475, 514*

Horvath, A. [title of article not noted], *Pacific Sun,* Mill Valley, California, 14-20 September 1994. *Quotation 609*

Jefferson, L., *These are My Sisters, a Journal From the Inside of Insanity.* Garden City, New York: Anchor Press/Doubleday, 1974. *Quotations 360-369 (inclusive)*

Jung, C. G., M. D., *The Psychology of Dementia Praecox.* New York and Washington, D.C.: Nervous and Mental Disease Publishing Company, 1936. *Quotations 155-157 (inclusive)*

Kaplan, B. (ed.), *The Inner Word of Mental Illness (A Series of First-Person Accounts of What It Was Like).* New York, Evanston, Illinois and London: Harper and Row, 1964. *Quotations 169-178 (inclusive)*

Katan, M., M. D., "The Importance of the Non-Psychotic Part of the Personality in Schizophrenia," *International Journal of Psycho-Analysis,* No. 35, 1954. *Quotations 498-504 (inclusive)*

Kaufman, M. T., Obituaries, *The New York Times*, August 17, 2003, *Quotation: 638*

Kempf, E .J., M. D., "Bisexual Factors in Curable Schizophrenia" (Presented at the Annual Meeting of the American Psychiatric Association, May 18, 1948), *Journal of Abnormal and Social Psychology, Vol. 44(3), 1949. Quotation 1*

Kempf, E. J., M. D., *Psychopathology*. St. Louis, Missouri: C.V. Mosby Co., 1920. *Quotations 179-207 (inclusive), 262, 497, 507*

Kernberg, O. F., M. D., *Borderline Conditions and Pathological Narcissism*. Northvale, New Jersey and London: Jason Aronson, Inc., 2nd ed., 1985. *Quotation 530*

Klein, G., "Gender-Based Attack Blamed on 'Man Hater'," *Marin Independent Journal*, Marin County, California, 10 November 2000. *Quotation 633*

Kukil, K. V., *The Unabridged Journals of Sylvia Plath, 1950-1962*, transcribed from the original manuscript at Smith College, New York: Anchor Books [from book review, publication not noted]. *Quotations 630-631 (inclusive)*

Kvarnes, R. G., M. D., and Parloff, G.H. (eds.), *A Harry Stack Sullivan Case Seminar, Treatment of a Young Male Schizophrenic*. New York: W. W. Norton & Company, Inc., 1976. *Quotations 287-290 (inclusive)*

Laing, R. D., *The Divided Self*. Baltimore, Maryland: Penguin Books, 1965. *Quotations 241-243 (inclusive)*

Lehmann-Haupt, C. [a review of *The Paris Pilgrims* by Clancy Carlile], "Books of the Times" section, *The New York Times*, July 7, 1999. *Quotations 571-572 (inclusive)*

Lewis, N. D. C., M. D., *Research in Dementia Praecox*. Northern Masonic Jurisdiction of the Scottish Rite, 1936. *Quotations 150-154 (inclusive)*

Lidz, R. W., M. D., and Lidz, T., M. D., "Homosexual Tendencies in Mothers of Schizophrenic Women," *The Journal of Nervous and Mental Diseases*, Vol. 149, No. 2. Williams and Wilkins Co., 1969. *Quotation 264*

Lidz, T., M. D., Fleck, S., M. D., and Cornelison, A. R., M.S.S., *Schizophrenia and the Family*. New York: International Universities Press, Inc., 1965. *Quotations 162-167 (inclusive)*

Lidz, T., and Fleck, S., "Schizophrenia, Human Integration, and the Role of the Family," *The Etiology of Schizophrenia*, Don D. Jackson, M. D. (ed.). Basic Books, Inc., New York, 1960. *Quotations 148-149 (inclusive)*

Maine, H., *If A Man Be Mad*. Garden City, New York: Doubleday & Company, Inc., 1947. *Quotations 332-333 (inclusive)*

May, R., *Love and Will*. New York: Dell Publishing Co., Inc. [W. W. Norton & Company, Inc.], 1969. *Quotation 68*

McClelland, D. C., and Watt, N. F., "Sex-Role Alienation in Schizophrenia," *Journal of Abnormal Psychology*, Vol. 73, No. 3, 1968. *Quotations 267-280 (inclusive)*

Mendel, W. M., *Schizophrenia (The Experience and Its Treatment)*. San Francisco, California, Washington, D.C. and London: Jossey-Bass Publishers, 1976. *Quotations 158-160 (inclusive)*

Menninger, K. A., M. D., *Man Against Himself.* New York: Harcourt, Brace & World, Inc., 1938. *Quotations 77-82 (inclusive), 521-522 (inclusive)*

Milford, N., *Zelda.* New York, Evanston, Illinois and London: Harper & Row, 1970. *Quotations 334-346 (inclusive)*

Miller, M., *On Being Different.* New York: Random House, 1971. *Quotation 246*

Milton, J., *Paradise Lost*, Book One. *Quotation 97*

Moorhead, W. S., "Watergate: The Quiz," *The Washington Post National Weekly Edition*, 14-20 August 1989. *Quotation 592*

Nasar, S., *A Beautiful Mind.* New York: Simon & Schuster, 1998. New York. *Quotations 634-637 (inclusive)*

Nechiporekno, O. M., *Passport to Assassination: The Never Before Told Story of Lee Oswald by the KGB Colonel Who Knew Him.* Birch Lane/Carol Publishing, 1993 [in *The New York Times Book Review,* name of reviewer and date of review not noted]. *Quotation 620*

Neil, A., "Slaying Stirs 911 Probe," *Marin Independent Journal*, Marin County, California, 27 November 1990. *Quotation 526*

Nijinsky, R. (ed.), *The Diary of Vaslav Nijinsky.* Berkeley and Los Angeles, California; London: University of California Press, 1971. *Quotation 304*

Nijinsky, R., *Nijinsky.* New York: Pocket Books, 1972. *Quotations 300-301 (inclusive)*

Opler, M. K., "Schizophrenia and Culture" [publication not noted], August 1957. *Quotation 523*

Ostwald, P., *Schumann, the Inner Voices of a Musical Genius.* Boston: Northeastern University Press, 1985. *Quotations 406-413 (inclusive)*

Ostwald, P., *Vaslav Nijinsky, A Leap into Madness.* New York: Carol Publishing Group. *Quotations 531-539 (inclusive)*

Pernoud, R., *Joan of Arc, by Herself and Her Witnesses.* New York: Stein and Day Publishers, 1969. *Quotations 387-404 (inclusive), 476*

Perry, H. S., *Psychiatrist of America, The Life of Harry Stack Sullivan.* Cambridge, Massachusetts, and London: The Belknap Press of Harvard University Press, 1982. *Quotation 375*

Podvoll, E. M., M. D., *The Seduction of Madness.* New York: Harper Collins (Publishers), 1990. *Quotation 525*

Porter, R., *A Social History of Madness.* New York: E.P. Dutton, 1989. *Quotations 509-512 (inclusive)*

Posner, G., *Case Closed-Lee Harvey Oswald and the Assassination of John F. Kennedy.* New York: Doubleday, 1994 [in *The New York Times Book Review*, name of reviewer and date of review not noted]. *Quotations 616-619 (inclusive)*

Powers, R., "Serial Killer Tells Chilling Tale of Why He Stalked Victims," *Gannett News Service, The Marin Independent Journal*, Marin County, California, 19 June 1992. *Quotation 567*

Rosen, J. N., M. D., *Direct Analysis (Selected Papers)*. New York: Grune & Stratton, 1953. *Quotations 106-114 (inclusive)*

Rosenbaum, R., *Explaining Hitler: The Search for the Origins of His Evil*. New York: Random House, Inc., 1998. *Quotations 583-591 (inclusive)*

Rosenfeld, H. A., *Psychotic States (A Psycho-Analytical Approach)*. New York: International Universities Press, 1966. *Quotations 118-121 (inclusive)*

Rubin, T. I., M. D., *Lisa and David*. New York: Ballantine Books, 1962. *Quotations 2, 58*

Rubin, T. I., M. D., *Platzo and the Mexican Pony Rider*. New York: Ballantine Books, 1965. *Quotation 247*

Scheflen, A. E., M. D., *A Psychotherapy of Schizophrenia: Direct Analysis*. Springfield, Illinois: Charles C. Thomas Publishers, 1961. *Quotations 115-117 (inclusive)*

Schreber, D. P., *Memoirs of My Nervous Illness*, translated by Ida Macalpine and Richard A. Hunter. London: Wm. Dawson & Sons, Ltd., 1955. *Quotations 3-4, 7-12, 59-60 (inclusive), 405, 577*

Scott, A. O., [film review], *The New York Times*, 7 April 2000. *Quotation 600*

Searles, H. F., M. D., *Collected Papers on Schizophrenia and Related Subjects.* New York: International Universities Press, 1965. *Quotations 28-56 (inclusive)*

Searles, H. F., M. D., *The Non-Human Environment (In Normal Development and in Schizophrenia).* New York: International Universities Press, Inc., 1960. *Quotations 83-96 (inclusive)*

Sechehaye, M., *Autobiography of a Schizophrenic Girl; with Analytical Interpretation.* New York: New American Library, Grune and Stratton, Inc., 1951. *Quotations 379-383 (inclusive)*

Segal, H., "Some Aspects of the Analysis of a Schizophrenic," *International Journal of Psycho-Analysis*, Vol. 31, 1950. *Quotation 263*

Shenon, P., and Johnson, D., "Will Suggests Suspect Had Long Planned to Die for Beliefs," *The New York Times,* 4 October 2001. *Quotation 621*

Showalter, E., *The Female Malady (Women, Madness and English Culture, 1830-1980).* New York: Pantheon Books, 1985. *Quotations 315-320 (inclusive)*

Simon, B., M. D., *Mind and Madness in Ancient Greece.* Ithaca, New York, and London: Cornell University Press, 1978. *Quotations 254-257 (inclusive)*

Spolar, C., "No Home and Not Much Hope," *The Washington Post National Weekly Edition*, 27 March -2 April 1989. *Quotation 493*

Stanton, A. H., M. D., and Schwartz, M. S., Ph. D., *The Mental Hospital (A Study of Institutional Participation in Psychiatric Illness and Treatment).* New York: Basic Books, Inc., 1954. *Quotations 258-259 (inclusive)*

Stein, R., "Hilary Swank Playing Oscars by Ear," *San Francisco Chronicle*, 19 March 2000. *Quotation 615*

Stefan, G., *In Search of Sanity, The Journal of a Schizophrenic.* New Hyde Park, New York: University Books, Inc., 1965. *Quotations 370-374 (inclusive)*

Stoller, R. J., M. D., *Sex and Gender.* New York: Jason Aronson, 2nd ed., 1974. *Quotations 292-296 (inclusive)*

Stoller, R. J., M. D., *Splitting (A Case of Female Masculinity).* New York: Dell Publishing Co., Inc., 1973. *Quotations 99-105 (inclusive)*

Sullivan, H. S., M. D., *Clinical Studies in Psychiatry*, New York: W. W. Norton & Company, Inc., 1956. *Quotation 291*

Sullivan, H. S., M. D., *Personal Psychopathology (Early Formulations).* New York: W. W. Norton & Company, Inc., 1972. *Quotations 285-286, 495-496 (inclusive)*

Sullivan, H. S., M. D., *Schizophrenia as a Human Process.* New York: W. W. Norton & Company, Inc., 1962. *Quotations 281-284 (inclusive)*

Swados, E., *The Four Of Us, The Story of a Family.* New York: Farrar, Strauss and Giroux, 1991. *Quotations 543-546 (inclusive)*

Sylvia [Name Deleted], *The New York Times Magazine*, June 27, 1999. *Quotation 570*

Symons, J. [book review, title and author not noted], *The New York Times Book Review*, 14 March 1993.  *Quotations 593-596 (inclusive)*

Thomas, J., "McVeigh's Letters Show Deep Anger," *The New York Times* [date not noted]. *Quotations 624-627 (inclusive)*

Turner, Jeanne. *Quotation 240*

Thomas, J., *"McVeigh's Letters Show Deep Anger," The New York Times* [date not noted]. *Quotation s 624-627 (inclusive)*

Van Dusen, W., *The Presence of Spirits In Madness*. New York: The Swedenborg Foundation, Inc., 4th ed., 1983. *Quotations 515-517 (inclusive)*

Walker, B., *Sex and the Supernatural*. New York, Evanston, Illinois, San Francisco and London: Harper & Row, Publishers, 1970. *Quotations 488-490 (inclusive)*

Ward, M. J., *The Snake Pit*. New York: The New American Library, 1946. *Quotations 309-314 (inclusive)*

Winder, C. L., "Some Psychological Studies of Schizophrenics," *The Etiology of Schizophrenia,* Don D. Jackson, M. D. (ed.).  New York: Basic Books, Inc., 1960. *Quotation 147*

Winerip, M., "The Global Willowbrook," *The New York Times Magazine*, Section 6, 12 January 2000. *Quotation 578*

Wolfe, E., *Aftershock (The Story Of A Psychotic Episode)*. New York: G.P. Putnam's Sons, 1969. *Quotations 457-458 (inclusive)*

Woolf, V. [publication not noted]. *Quotation 386*

Woolf, V., *Orlando*. New York: New American Library, 1928; New American Library of World Literature, Inc., 1960. *Quotations 384-385 (inclusive)*

Zhisui, Dr. L., *The Private Life of Chairman Mao*, Thurston, A.F. (ed.); translated by Tai Hung-chao. New York: Random House, 1994 [as reviewed by Arnold R. Isaacs, *San Francisco Book Review*, date not noted]. *Quotation 607*

# Index of Case Names
## (page references)

* Presented at the Annual Meeting of the American Psychiatric Association, May 18, 1948.

# SHORT ARTICLES AND NOTES

## Bisexual Factors in Curable Schizophrenia *

By Edward J. Kemp
Wading River, Long Island, New York

Kraepelin, over fifty years ago, gave psychiatry, after a long series of remarkable studies of many psychoses, his famous differentiation of dementia praecox as an incurable, progressively deteriorating, nervous and mental disease, and manic depressive psychosis as a repetitious, cyclical, autogenous recoverable reaction. Thereafter psychiatry, generally, adopted this concept, particularly for its useful simplification of many legal, administrative, and custodial problems.

Over thirty years ago Freud, Bleuler, and Jung, then the leaders of psychoanalytic methods, reinforced the Kraepelinian theory by arriving at the conviction, from a small number of ineffectually treated cases, that dementia praecox, now renamed schizophrenia, was based on some unknown, constitutional cerebral or other pathology and was incurable by psychoanalytic methods. Unfortunately for thousands of patients, this conviction has continued to influence most psychoanalysts and other psychiatrists to neglect the psychopathology of schizophrenia, although Meyer, White, and Jelliffe had at this time demonstrated the prejudicial unsoundness and injustice of the belief from the evidence of a number of autogenous social recoveries made under intelligent nursing.

In 1912, after reading Freud's *Studies in Hysteria* and White's *Mental Mechanisms* and some papers by Meyer and Jelliffe on the affective disorders in dementia praecox, I ventured at the Indianapolis State Hospital to try, on some selected cases on my wards, the psychoanalytic technique Freud was then using. Among them were two women who had been diagnosed dementia praecox by Dr. Max Bahr, then clinical psychiatrist at the hospital. These diagnoses would today I am sure be accepted as correct.

The psychotherapy began with the intentional cultivation of a positive *sympathetic rapport*, later called *transference*, with each patient in order to get her to confide in me the secrets of her troubles with herself. I was able to induce each one to tell me what she knew about herself. Each patient had worked herself into an automatically repetitious convergence of mind on preoccupations with past social ridicule, frustrations, and inferiorities covering shame, guilt and struggle with unspeakable autoerotic cravings, producing an attitude of indifference to present and future social relations. In each instance the repetitious pressure of the erotic cycle was regarded with obsessive dread, anxiety, and inferiority, followed by pleasurable infatuations and indulgence, ending in remorse, shame, and anxiety, often to the degree of hopeless despair and impulses to suicide. Each one had special kinds of sexual infatuation, and thought and fought with them in highly individualized ways although with similar stupefying preoccupations, restlessness, sleeplessness, and incapacity to work, learn, or eat normally. As usual, the treatment soon came to an impasse beyond which the patient could not make progress and talked in confused, repetitious circles with superficial distractions and painful discouragement at not being able to think of anything else.

I then decided to adopt, contra to Freud, the innovation of persuasively, aggressively, insistently working on each patient with direct and leading questions in order to break through the self-repressive fear of me and of themselves and what they might remember and say and do impulsively. In each instance, within a few hours, decisive autoerotic fantasies, memories, and emotions were released and rapidly increased to a passionate flood with its autonomic tides converged upon me. Their reactions to my sympathetic, controlled interest varied from narcissistic disappointment, anger, and self doubt and negative reversions to coming back for more analytic help.

Case A was a young wife with compulsive jealousy, autoerotic inferiorities, paranoid thinking, socially specifically conditioned hysterical jerking spells that involved all of her body, and conditioned vomiting, visual constriction, and hemianesthesia. She recovered in a psychologically interesting series of well-differentiated steps as she recalled the accumulative repressed memories and emotional reactions to a series of painfully humiliating experiences with her foster-mother, mother-in-law, and husband.

Case B, a once fairly efficient young woman stenographer, had an extremely severe, symbolically and physically self-cleansing compulsive mysophobia with suicidal desperation which had continued

415

for a year without relaxation. Her preoccupations had completely incapacitated her for doing any kind of work. She recovered after recalling her repressions and assimilating them through talking out in fragments the meaning to her of her autoerotic infatuations for genital, anal, and fecal fantasies with masturbation, centered upon her father. She had been progressively cultivating a semi-seclusive, shut-in, weakening social attitude, and became precipitated into a panic when she suddenly realized during an erotic episode that her secrets were suspected by her sister.

Both cases were fully reported to Dr. Adolph Meyer in 1913 and led to my becoming a member of his staff. Both cases were later published in my *Psychopathology* in 1920 with a large series of other cases of dementia praecox, including every type (9). Case A was also published in the Journal of *Abnormal Psychology* in 1917 (6). [For other publications on this psychopathology, see Kempf (4, 5, 7, 8, 10, 11).] Many of these cases had been treated with sufficient success at the Phipps Psychiatric Clinic through 1914 and Saint Elizabeths Hospital up to 1919 for them to be discharged as social recoveries *with insigh*t into how the pathological thinking had been progressively cultivated. The degree of insight and social adaptability distinguished them from the ordinary form of autogenous social recovery without insight.

The great importance of the quality of a person's insight as an indication of his sociability was developed for psychiatry by Adolph Meyer over forty years ago. It is as fundamental for psychiatry and general psychology as Freud's re-discovery of the ancient knowledge of hypnotic, good, and evil suggestion (see Frazer, 3) as repressed unconscious activity. By insight is meant the understanding of the emotional and other attitudinal interactions in oneself and other people. Recognition of the importance of developing insight or understanding for everyday life has been traced by Breasted (2) back through the ancient Greeks and Hebrews to the Egyptians as far as 3000 B.C., and seems to have developed with the beginning of the consistent culture of conscience and equilateral fraternalism to replace primitive unilateral opportunism.

The two Indianapolis cases of schizophrenia were, it now seems from the history of recorded cases, the first to have been successfully treated in America or Europe by the Freudian psycho-analytic method. Some of the Phipps and Saint Elizabeths patients reacted with decisive changes toward recovery with only one or two hours of active analytic-suggestive psycho-

416

therapy. Since 1920 this series of more or less successfully treated cases has been extended in private practice under improved methods of analysis of the *ego-attitude* towards its physiological cravings under the culture of its familial and other social requirements.

From 1915 to 1925 I had to accept many intolerant criticisms from leading Freudian psychoanalysts for daring to modify Freud's passive technique and his theory of the dynamic processes involved in the neuroses and psychoses. Freud, as late as the end of World War I, had continued to assume the existence of a "censor" in the mind in order to explain the evidence of uncompromising conflicts and self-repressions. Although he had made the important scientific discovery that repressed, unconsciously emotivated thoughts continue to act in part as determinants of conscious thinking and behavior, he was unable to work out a theory of the psychophysiological processes that was satisfactory to himself, as the series of later experimental changes in his theory showed. When he divided the personality into the *id*, *ego*, and *superego* he had only renamed the ancient Hebraic triangular concept of *body, mind*, and *spirit*. His differentiation of all reactions into *life* and *death* and *love* and *hate* instincts was unsatisfactory. It neglected the endless pressure of development of body, ego-attitude and mind attended by fear of failure, as basic emotivations in all struggles for survival, maturation and reproduction.

Numerous controversial discussions had made evident the need for working out a consistent explanation of human and other animal behavior that specifically interrelated physiopsychological and psychophysiological circular sequences of reaction. These must include the integrative actions of the two neuromuscular systems, conditioning of reflexes, endocrine and autonomic emotivation, bisexual differentiation, and the social culture of the ego-attitude. Since 1912 I have devoted most of my studies in this direction, as some of you know.

Freud had continued, as late as 1923, in seeing the repressed factors as the chief cause of the neuroses although it had been shown in my *Autonomic Functions and the Personality* (1918) and *Psychopathology* (1920) that, while the character of the physical and mental symptoms is determined by the repressed functions maintaining themselves repetitiously in conditioned, pathological, postural autonomic and somatic, neuromuscular, circular reflex tensions, the intensity of the conflict is caused principally by the intolerant, self-controlling, repressive work of the ego-attitude. Anxiety is then not a so-called "free floating" nervousness, but the variable compulsion to act in oppositely conditioned ways at the same time, producing indecision under auto-nomic-affective pressure with conflicting reciprocal inhibition in autonomic and somatic organs. The fearful distress and weakness of the resulting tremors in these organs is relieved by obsessive, compulsive tensions driving to wishful thinking that distorts the values of the ego and its social environment.

Because resistance in orthodox psychoanalytic circles to innovations in treating the psychoses and in explaining their physiopsychology and psycho-physiology continued with purblind obstinacy and deprived thousands of young men and women of the possibility of relief I was advised by some leading psychologists and psychiatrists to talk with Freud personally about our respective theories, methods, and results. G. Stanley Hall arranged the interview, which extended over two days in the Austrian Tirol.

Freud had been for a number of years developing the technique of sitting behind the patient, who would be required to lie on a couch and give way to expressing free associations of thought regardless of their nature or emotivation. While this procedure, although seriously time-consuming, was often highly successful with intelligent people who could hold themselves interested in the causes of their symptoms, he generally failed to get free, releasing associations from schizophrenics who, because of intense narcissism, would not endure the recall of painful injuries to it.

My method was to sit face to face and eye to eye with the patient across a small empty table in order to hold the patient's attention on his analysis. I was able to demonstrate to Freud from several case histories how, with considerable foreknowledge of the personal and family history and the psychobiological pressure of growth and bisexual differentiation with or against the ego's attitude, one can make direct and leading questions with the certainty that releasing specific repressions helps to reintegrate the personality and reduce the resistance to recurrent emotivations and thoughts. Freud finally concluded that a more directed and active technique was justified in the psychoses and encouraged me to continue my work. I think he was also influenced in this direction by Ferenczi, who was then developing more aggressive psychoanalytic methods. By 1930 Brill, who was Freud's authorized representative in America and who had previously been one of the severest critics of the psycho-analytic treatment of the psychoses, published several papers demonstrating the successful use of more aggressive psychoanalytic methods with non-hospitalized schizophrenics. Contributions on the successful treatment of schizophrenia have now been made by many psychiatrists, which cannot be listed here. Today, shorter, more aggressive and improved methods are being developed by many psycho-somaticists as well as psycho-analysts after thirty years of obsessive rejections. It is a pleasure to see that Alexander and French (1) have also become converts to trying more practical and individualized methods.

Every human, like the lower primates and other mammals, is a plastic, bisexual mechanism in which every cell, organ, and the organism as a whole and all of its behavior are bisexually differentiated in more or less male and female ratios by chromosomal, gonadal, and socially conditioning factors. Therefore, social and other environmental successes and failures have more or less masculinizing or feminizing reactive effects upon the social-sexual attitude. Every person's ontogeny recapitulates its phylogeny and begins with herm-aphroditic, self-loving, poly-orificial (oral, anal, and genital) autoeroticism. It passes through phases of autoerotic development up to late adolescence, attended with more or less homosexual infatuation and experimentation, and eventually matures by conversion of affection towards heterosexualism and reproduction.

Naturally the chromosomal, gonadal, and social determinants may work more or less in alliance or opposition with one another. The physician, therefore, should work them out as far as possible in each case. The family history often indicates hereditary, chromosomal, sexual pathology, whereas the development of secondary bisexual characters reveals the ratio of male and female gonadal determination. The personality shows the effects of family and other social appeals, approvals and rewards, and dis-approvals, threats and punish-ments, upon the bisexual differentiation of its attitude through childhood and adolescence and even in adulthood. When all three factors are bisexually abnormal the achievement of heterosexuality and mental integrity under social condemnation is obviously impossible. Pathological gonadal ratios can often be corrected by administering fitting ratios of endocrines. Pathological social conditioning in chromasomal and gonadal normals can very often be readjusted to potent hetero-sexuality if the social pressure has not been too seductive or intolerant too early in childhood and the person has not become too infatuated with perverted pleasures. Persons having as much as a high school education seem to be able to learn how to make emotional readjustments to normal and gain insight more readily than persons of lower mental levels.

Wherever we find a person who is in an emotionally driven psychopathological attitude we also find that one or more persons in his family or business from whom he cannot escape is egotistically obsessed to force or seduce that person into states of introverted, frustrated, affective confusion and mental indecision, even to the extent of destruction of his personal integrity. The interpersonal conflict tends to repeat itself to the egoistic pleasure of the dominant person and suffering of the defeated person. As a result the latter, more than the former, becomes progressively, endlessly preoccupied with mulling over what was said and done to him in order to make things come out right with egoistic satisfaction to himself. Such vicious circles of thinking and feeling tend to grow accumulatively and become increasingly autoerotic and regressive. They are the opposite of heterosexual and even homosexual exchanges in constructive directions.

More than thirty years of intensive investigation of these problems permits me to make the general statement that in man every case of emotional neurosis or psychosis is the result of more or less conflict and confusion involving bisexual differentiation. In other animals also conflicting excitations producing indecision and anxiety involve sexual functioning pathologically. Dementing schizophrenia is essentially a regression to the cloacal level of hermaphrodism. I am quite sure that it would be easy to demonstrate these factors in any case and often within an hour of investigation.

The usual objection made to these statements is that since all men and women have been more or less autoerotic in youth and have not developed serious neuroses or psychoses, autoeroticism cannot be an important factor. My reply is that it is not so much the autoerotic fixation as the cultivation of the ego's attitude toward it that produces the destructive conflict. The objection to this view has been that most schizophrenics under commitment in hospitals are freely erotic and unrestrained. My reply is that this condition develops as the ego becomes disorganized and confused by the endless autoerotic pressure, and as the ego becomes reintegrated it resumes the old self-repressive, sensitive attitude without insight. In other words, an attitude of any normal ego that is fitted for doing accurately any responsible kind of work is at that time sexually repressive because the erotic attitude is not fit for doing such work. The normal person can change from a working to an erotic attitude or vice versa in adaptation to the immediate social situation, whereas the pathologically erotic person cannot do this as the result of many unsolved, pathological, interpersonal interferences during the development of his bisexual differentiation.

The psychotherapy of neuroses and psychoses is practically differentiated into two important steps, as experience has shown. The first step is best begun with the impressive sympathetic advantages of the first interview. Without taking a routine case history or making notes at the time, well-directed analytic-suggestive questioning is begun with the precise purpose of inducing the patient into adopting a less fearful, more relaxed attitude toward his sexual cravings, whatever they are and no matter how strong and repetitious they are, and talking about them freely. The patient has generally convinced himself that he is the only one of his kind as a result of the superior moral pretensions of his elders having been especially aimed at him. As he realizes that his attitude toward his sexual cravings and methods of trying to manage them, and not the cravings as such, have produced his illness, he improves decisively and his capacity for working and thinking becomes adequate for the needs of everyday life.

The second step is more involved and requires the inductive analytic conversion of the conditioned erotic and other emotional cravings to heterosexuality whenever possible. The former step is usually well started in an hour or two of confidential, sympathetic, understanding talk with the patient if the physician is not preoccupied with thinking in terms of neurology and toxicology. Psychological miracles often follow as the sexual fight becomes reduced. I am sure that literally thousands of autoerotic young men and women and children in our institutions and outside, who must otherwise remain incurable psychopaths, will be helped to readjust to a healthy personal integrity when psychiatrists adopt this method. The analytic readjustment to heterosexuality requires more time but generally it can be carried on outside of the hospital in private practice. It requires the recall and reliving of every decisive episode that tended to produce a repetitious emotional displacement until a normal readjustment follows without striving.

I have seen a number of patients that have been treated by insulin, metrazol, and electric shock and some who have been treated by frontal lobotomy or lobectomy who have improved sufficiently to be discharged as social recoveries. These cases have, however, little or no insight and retain, in milder form, their neurotic distortions. Hence most of them are doomed to eventual regression when they must live under the old conditions that formerly excited their repressions. On the other hand, patients who have acquired insight and released their repressed, conditioned emotivations and assimilated them by changing to more tolerant and practical and less conscientious but not conscienceless attitudes generally remain stable through most stresses. The effective results of electric or chemical shock therapy or cerebral surgical shock therapy seem largely due to breaking up the intense fixation of attentive integration on fighting repressively against the conditioned emotivations involved in autoeroticism and homosexuality. Thereby the mind becomes able to resume interest in new everyday realities by producing a here-and-now, socially more carefree, happy-go-lucky, animal attitude. I think, however, that it is utterly unjustifiable to perform a surgical operation on the brain for this purpose without first sincerely attempting analytically to re-educate the patient on how to manage his sexual cravings without fighting against himself.

\*\*\*\*\*\*\*\*\*\*\*\*\*\*

Dr. Edward J. Kempf was a Life Fellow of the American Psychiatric Association and of the Association for Research in Nervous and Mental Disease; a member of the American Medical Association, the American Psychopathological Association, the American Association for the Advancement of Science, the New York Academy of Sciences, and the American Psychological Association. He was the author of over 30 papers and books, including his famous <u>Psychopathology</u>, published in 1920, and <u>The Origin and Evolution of Bisexual Differentiation</u>, published in 1947.

Dr. Kempf graduated from medical school at Case Western Reserve University in Cleveland, Ohio, in 1910; interned at the state mental hospital in Cleveland from 1910-11 and at the state mental hospital in Indianapolis, Indiana, from 1911-13. He performed his residency at Phipps Psychiatric Clinic, Johns Hopkins University Hospital, Baltimore, Maryland, from 1913-14. From 1914 to 1920 he was a clinical psychiatrist at St. Elisabeth's Hospital in Washington, D.C.

## REFERENCES

1. Alexander, F., & French, T.M. *Psychoanalytic Therapy*. New York: Ronald Press, 1946.
2. Breasted, J.H. *The Dawn of Conscience*. New York: Scribner's, 1934.

3. Frazer, J.G. *The Golden Bough*. New York: Macmillan, 1922.

4. Kempf, E.J. The Integrative Functions of the Nervous System Applied to Some Reactions in Human Behavior and Their Attending Psychic Functions. *Psychoan. Rev.*, 1915, 2, 151-165.

5. Kempf, E.J. Some Studies in the Psychopathology of Acute Dissociation of the Peronality. *Psychoan. Rev.*, 1915, 2, 361-389.

6. Kempf, E.J. A Study of the Anaesthesia, Convulsions, Vomiting, Visual Constriction, Erythema and Itching of Mrs. V.G. *J. Abn. Psychol.*, 1917, April-May.

7. Kempf, E.J. *The Autonomic Junctions and the Personality*. Washington: Nervous and Mental Disease Publishing Co., 1918.

8. Kempf, E.J. The Psychoanalytic Treatment of Dementia Praecox. Report of a Case. *Psychoanal. Rev.*, 1919, 6, 15-58.

9. Kempf, E.J. *Psychopathology*. St. Louis: Mosby, 1920.

10. Kempf, E.J. Affective-Respiratory Factors in Catatonia. *Med. J. & Rec.*, 1930, 131, 181.

11. Kempf, E.J. Fundamental Factors in the Psychopathology and Psychotherapy of Malignant Disorganization Neuroses. *Med. Rev.*, 1937, 146, 341.

Printed in the United States
143480LV00003B/1/P

9 781410 703453